High Anxiety

Habent sua fata libelli

High Anxiety

Masculinity in crisis in early modern france

edited by
Kathleen P. Long

Library of Congress Cataloging-in-Publication Data

High anxiety : masculinity in crisis in early modern France /
edited by Kathleen P. Long.
p. cm. — (Sixteenth century essays & studies ; v. 59)
Includes bibliographical references and index.
ISBN 0-943549-91-4 (alk. paper) — ISBN 0-943549-92-2 pbk.
: alk. paper)
1. French literature—16th century—History and criticism. 2.
Masculinity in literature. 3. Masculinity—France. I. Long, Kathleen P., 1957–. II. Series.

PQ239 .H54 2001
840.9'353—dc21

2001035159

Cover illustration: "De Secretia natura" from M. Maier, *Atalanta fugiens, hoc est, emblemata
nova de secretis naturae chymica* (Oppenheim: Hieronymus Galler for Johann Theodorus de
Bry, 1618).
Text is set in Bembo and DTC Optimum. Display type is DTC Optimum.
Cover and title page by Teresa Wheeler, Truman State University designer.
Printed in U.S.A. by Thomson-Shore, Dexter, Michigan

The paper in this publication meets or exceeds the minimum requirements of the American
National Standard for Permanence of Paper for Printed Library materials Z39.48 (1984).

Contents

Acknowledgments

would like to thank Catharine Randall, whose advice and work on early versions of this collection were crucial for advancing the project. I am grateful to the contributors themselves, who demonstrated incredible patience and understanding as the project went through various phases. I thank Ray Mentzer for taking this project on, and to the readers who provided valuable advice. Most of all, however, I would like to thank Paula Presley and her team at Truman State University Press, who performed the herculean labors of making this collection look and sound its best; their work has been truly impressive.

A number of people inspired this collection; the contributors themselves, of course, but also my colleagues. Mitchell Greenberg, whose work appears in this collection, has been an intellectual inspiration. Nelly Furman encouraged me to ask questions about gender and its relation to epistemology long before such pursuits were in vogue; may she long continue to be in the avant garde of intellectual pursuits. Lawrence Kritzman's work on gender and sexuality also had a significant influence on my own. Finally, I would like to thank the students who heard versions of my own work, and discussed this collection with me: Duane Rudolph, Shannon Clute, Nicolas Barras, Justin Portnoy, and Patricia Gravatt.

Kathleen P. Long, Editor

Introduction

The past decade has seen explosive growth in the number of "critical inquiries" pertaining to gender, sexuality, and the body.[1] These explorations reach as far back as the early modern period.[2] Until quite recently, these issues were viewed predominantly from the perspective of feminism and queer theory, and the body itself theorized as transgressive or "other" than masculine. Ironically, this insistence on the feminine body in opposition to a little-defined masculine norm seems to retain the binary categories which have driven discussions of gender difference since the early modern period, categories of spiritual/physical, high/low, masculine/feminine, which one would assume postmodern criticism was poised to unravel. Recent studies have indeed raised the possibility of defining this abstraction known as masculinity, and of its problematic hold on culture;[3] some of the most intriguing work in this field is being done in relation to the early modern period, such as the work of both Mark Breitenberg and Lynn Enterline.[4] Nonetheless, the representation of masculinity in early modern French culture has received little attention to date.

Much of the work on the relationship between gender and identity formation in early modern Europe has viewed the Continent through predominantly English lenses, as if cultural specificities had no relevance to the understanding of particular cultural manifestations. This perspective effaces the issue of the very particular contexts in which gender identity (designated as *sexe* in early modern French, and thus conflated to some degree with essential biology) is problematized. The rigid hierarchies of church and state, which overlay a more fluid society and culture, privilege the masculine at the dawn of the early modern period. From Aristotle on, the male is defined as the ideal, the perfected state of humankind, but the vehement insistence on this assumption, echoed by the often violent misogyny of the *querelle des femmes,* reveals an anxiety about the status of masculinity that becomes particularly evident in the late Middle Ages and the Renaissance. For a variety of reasons, most obviously the social disorder ensuing from the Wars of Religion, this anxiety seems to become quite acute in France subsequent to the Calvinist reformation, and does not abate even in the seventeenth century, perhaps from fear of a return to the upheavals of the preceding century. Rather, it becomes the grounding for an examination of the nature of political power, as Mitchell Greenberg's article in this collection demonstrates.

Recent criticism links the rise of the modern subject and of a certain notion of individualism to the seventeenth century; this link is exposed clearly in the works of Dalia Judovitz and Greenberg.[5] But, even if the modern individual was largely formed in the classical era, the crucible of this formation was the Renaissance, a period in which clear-cut distinctions of gender were already being questioned and the relationship between an individual and his public role was already fraught with tension. One need only think of the catechisms the Catholic Church in France imposed upon suspected Protestants in order to test their religious beliefs, or the *dragonnades*—the billeting of soldiers with Protestant families, with the intent that these soldiers would force Protestants to convert to Catholicism. Certainly many individuals hid their private beliefs from public view, but the Wars of Religion and the almost continuous persecution they fostered from the mid-sixteenth century on created a context in which public and semipublic examinations of conscience were held on a fairly regular basis, forcing a significant minority to choose between playing a public role of acquiescence or enduring often severe punishment or death.[6] Although some studies gesture towards this area of inquiry, the effect of the Reformation and Counter-Reformation on the constitution of the notion of the individual largely remains to be explored.[7] Stephen Murphy's and Catharine Randall's essays in this collection raise at least one aspect of this issue; perhaps other studies will follow.

In the domain of philosophy, recent revisionist views of the body look back beyond Hegelian dialectic and the binary system it might seem to confirm, to Spinoza as the avatar of monism.[8] There seems to be a hesitation, however, to reach back past the seventeenth century, to explore the effects of medieval and Renaissance philosophies on the development of modern notions of the gendered self. For example, the renaissance of Pyrrhonian skepticism at the midpoint of the sixteenth century links a sustained critique of dogmatism to a demonstration of cultural relativity. In particular, Sextus Empiricus's discussion of ethics (the Tenth Mode of suspension of judgment in the *Outlines of Pyrrhonism*) expresses a concern with the position of the philosopher relative to social norms.[9] This concern is founded on a belief in the unstable nature of sign systems, an argument that informs most of the second book of the *Outlines*, and often finds its voice in examples of differing sexual norms: "We oppose habit to habit in this way: … while the Persian thinks it seemly to wear a brightly dyed dress reaching to the feet, we think it unseemly" (1.14.148). "And we oppose habit to the other things, as for instance to law when we say that amongst the Persians it is the habit to indulge in intercourse with males, but amongst the Romans it is forbidden by law to do so" (1.14.152). "And habit is opposed to dogmatic conception when…Aristippus considers the wearing of feminine attire a matter of indifference, though we consider it a disgraceful thing" (1.14.155). In France, at least initially, the Counter-Reformation church adopts fideistic skepticism as a means to impose its authority, using the argument that our senses and our reason deceive us, and thus no individual can know anything for certain.[10] As a consequence, the individual must accede to church doctrine as well as to the predominant social and cultural norms. This accession to predominant modes is, in part, the argument Sextus Empiricus makes in his *Outlines of Pyrrhonism* to explain how the skeptic can function in the world and in society (1.8.16–17, 13). But even as Sextus seems to accept such social norms, he problematizes them, and never more thoroughly than in his discussions of masculine and feminine dress and of sexual behavior (1.14.148–155). In imposing the skeptical suspension of judgment on these questions, Sextus creates an epistemological space in which alternative sexualities and ambiguous gender efface the normative binary systems. This conjunction of epistemological uncertainty, fluid gender roles, and social instability, or relativity, is echoed in numerous works produced in and around the court of Henri III of France (1574–89), from the poetry of Philippe Desportes, through popular pamphlets, to alchemical and medical treatises.[11]

The Catholic Church in France, in using fideistic skepticism to justify some of its doctrines, seems at first to grant permission for such a reconsideration of Pyrrhonian thought. The ensuing revival of this philosophy reaches beyond matters of church doctrine to inform critiques of French society and of the court in particular.[12] These critiques, from the *Isle des Hermaphrodites* (and subsequent utopian and antiutopian literature such as the *Terre australe connue* by Gabriel de Foigny) to the *Parnasse Satyrique,* intertwine their criticism of social structures, particularly power structures, with issues of gender and sexuality.[13] Their revised views of the place of individual identity in society are linked closely to the portrayal of problematized gender roles.[14]

Notions of masculinity in particular seem destabilized by this intellectual climate as well as by the accession of women to power (Catherine de Médicis and Elizabeth I of England are the two most obvious examples). It should not surprise us that masculinity is the focus of this so-called crisis; after all, since the dawn of the *querelle des femmes,* femininity has been embattled in France.[15] In sixteenth-century France and elsewhere, woman is defined most frequently in relation to man (in what Sextus calls circular reasoning); thus, any crisis in the definition of the feminine would suggest a concomitant questioning of the masculine, which is indeed what our contributors discovered in numerous works of the period.[16]

Nor are these fluid or unstable notions of gender easily cast aside at the advent of absolutism. Evidence suggests that these ideas remain present well into the seventeenth century, carried through by the remnants of skepticism found in the early *libertin* movement and maintained at the court by the revival of carnivalesque forms, for example, the *farces* as adapted by Molière, and by remarkable individuals, such as the transvestite abbé de Choisy.[17] This questioning of gender roles reaches even into what is supposedly the most normative of structures: marriage, as depicted in fairy tales for example. In spite of—or because of—the rise of absolutism, the issue of gender roles seems to reach closer to the heart of political structures in the seventeenth century, reflecting a reality of economic and political upheaval that is disguised by the rhetoric of political order, hegemony, and containment, as Greenberg's article on Louis XIV and Molière demonstrates. Thus, early modern skepticism presages our postmodern notions of the factitious nature of gender roles. Our notions of the relationships between gender and power rise from the representations of monarchy and of the family that were fostered under the reign of Louis XIV.[18]

The evolution of an early modern crisis in masculinity can be traced from a profound questioning of gender roles that is delineated in the works of numerous women authors of the early sixteenth century. Louise Labé's construction of a space for the feminine subject, particularly in her famous letter to Clémence de Bourges, is an example of this revisionism, and thus we propose to begin this anthology on masculinity with Cathy Yandell's essay on feminine transgressions. Combining a philological approach with the perspectives of postmodern feminisms and using the vehemently derogatory reactions to Labé's works and life by her contemporaries and later critics as a starting point, Yandell traces the creation of a poetics of transgression in Labé's *Œuvres.* This transgression is signaled by Labé's use of various synonyms for this word itself, and characterized by a bypassing of rhetorical tropes and poetic forms generally associated with masculine institutions, such as confession in the church or the *"concours des blasons"* organized by Clément Marot. These transgressions also re-create the woman as the subject of literary production rather than the object of exchange or the site of reproduction.

This shift in roles for Labé is echoed by the so-called transgressions of other women—that is, the surpassing of their socially defined roles and status to accede to domains usually claimed by masculine figures. Louise de Savoie, Marguerite de Navarre, and Catherine de Médicis serve as examples of feminine appropriation of political power, often seen as a violation of what we now know to be the recently minted Salic law; this appropriation is then interpreted by many male authors as threatening to the social order, even emasculating.

With these examples of transgressive femininity in mind, we turn to the responses of male authors who seem to perceive these problematic role-reversals as a menace. Stephen Murphy's "Cybele, Catherine, and Ronsard's Witnesses" uses a sociohistorical approach, along with detailed rhetorical analysis, to trace the vehement fear evoked by the accession of Catherine de Médicis even to unofficial power. In political pamphlets of the time, this loss of masculine control is portrayed as a castration, and the castration in turn is associated with a loss of voice—particularly in Protestant polemics, which refer with some frequency to the Latin word *testes,* which means both testicles and witnesses. Ronsard renders this view more complex, as he associates masculine lack (metaphorical castration) with poetic production in a move that presages both Freud's notion of castration anxiety and the Derridean construct of the supplement as rhetorical covering of a lack.

This reversal of loss or lack, as an attempt to reassert masculine control and at least the aura of superiority, is viewed from a rhetorical perspective by Jeffery Persels's "Masculine Rhetoric and the French *Blason anatomique.*" The essay explores the devices used by authors of *blasons* to mimic appropriation of the female body in order to revalidate masculinity. Just as Marot's "beau tetin" remains imperfect without male intercession, so the female body remains fragmentary and abject without the inspired ordering imposed by the male poet. This seemingly self-aggrandizing move, together with the exaggerated depictions of masculinity in Rabelais's *blason* of Gargantua's codpiece, hints at overcompensation for some lack. Ironically, the technique of appropriation delineated by the *blason* suggests that masculine corporeality is inexpressible unless inscribed in a representation of the female body.

Combining feminist- and queer-theory perspectives on male bonding with early modern scientific accounts of gender, Kirk Read observes this paradoxical movement of overcompensation taken to an extreme in "Mother's Milk from Father's Breast: Maternity without Women in Male French Renaissance Lyric." The perceived threat to masculine identity also frees the male poet to create and to nurture in feminine guise, and elicits a less controlled, but perhaps more inspired, approach to poetic production. At the same time, this appropriation of the maternal function re-creates the feminine as the ground upon which men relate to each other, much like the female body in the *concours des blasons*, thereby effacing the threat of a truly independent feminine force.

This appropriation, and thus effacement, of the feminine frees writers like Montaigne to write "androgynously," as Tom Conley contends in "Montaigne *moqueur:* 'Virgile' and Its Geographies of Gender." Conley uses the lens of his own graphic analysis, the *Political Writings* of Jean-François Lyotard, and Lyndal Roper's revision of Thomas Laqueur's *Making Sex* to reconcile Montaigne's presentation of gender with current theories of the body that insist on a representation mediated by a variety of "social imaginaries." As Conley contends, "'Sur des Vers de Virgile'...constitutes a welter of interrogations about how a subject is born into gender, and how he or she mediates it through the imaginary dedifferentiation experienced in writing." Montaigne's writing, in this case, transgresses and surpasses the binary codes of male and female, and inhabits a zone that, it could be contended, is transgendered. This space is articulated by what Conley calls "a poetics of mockery," thus echoing Judith Butler's notions of performativity and parody, as explored in *Gender Trouble.* The creation and manipulation of space and structure in "Virgile" at once enfolds the author and language in and excludes them from that which is feminine.

This attempt to control the feminine through appropriation and effacement continues even today in the critical reception of Rabelais, as Amy Staples contends in "Primal Scenes/Primal Screens: The Homosocial Economy of Dirty Jokes." The insistence of many modern critics upon justifying Rabelais's misogyny rather than taking some critical distance from it speaks volumes about the continuing threat that women present to the construction and preservation of certain codified norms of masculinity. The response to this perceived threat is exclusion of women as readers by means of jokes at their expense and of readings that they cannot possibly share. By scrutinizing post-Freudian discussions of wit or humor through the lens of recent feminist works on free speech and censorship, Staples demonstrates that the modern or postmodern bears the burden of the legacy of early modern notions and crises of the masculine subject.

My essay, "Jacques Duval on Hermaphrodites," explores the relationship between the origins of modern clinical medicine, based largely on internal examinations instead of textbook images, and the evolution of medicine towards a male-dominated science and away from the world of midwives. Jacques Duval, while proposing some revolutionary advances in the practice of medicine, also declares quite enthusiastically the superiority of both male physiology and male doctors; this conjunction can be traced clearly to the struggle, as Duval himself puts it, for control of medicine between midwives and surgeons on the one hand, and the more educated doctors on the other. Yet even as Duval privileges masculinity, he calls it into question with his evaluation of the case of Marin le Marcis, in which physiology renders doubtful the distinctions between the sexes. Nonetheless, masculinity prevails by means of early modern clinical medicine, as the "true sex" of Marin is discovered through an internal examination.

The complex and problematic nature of early modern masculinity is perhaps most evident in depictions of the institution of marriage, which Lewis Seifert analyzes from a sociopsychoanalytic perspective in "Pig or Prince? Murat, D'Aulnoy, and the Limits of Civilized Masculinity." In d'Aulnoy's "Le Prince Marcassin," Murat's "Le Roi Porc," and Perrault's "La Barbe bleue," threats and/or acts of violence are the natural complement to the hero/husband's monstrous appearance. Yet, it is not so much violence as its resolution and justification that preoccupy these narratives. D'Aulnoy, Murat, and Perrault accomplish this by rewriting the common folkloric structure wherein wives must assume the guilt for their husbands' aggression. In so doing, however, these writers displace the narrative's attention from the monstrous husband onto his "civilized" antithesis, albeit in quite different ways. Taken as a whole, these three fairy tales attest to a return of the violence repressed through the civilizing process, which is itself a malaise at the heart of the increasingly masculinized public sphere of late-seventeenth-century France.

As Seifert suggests, and Greenberg confirms in his analysis of "Molière's Body Politic," attempts to conceptualize the male body—and therefore by extension the body politic—as contained and more orderly than the grotesque female body are undermined by representations of the paternal body as leaky or lacking. Greenberg uses the screen of Freudian and Kleinian accounts of early infantile sexual development, particularly their discussions of the anal stage, to analyze Molière's critiques of the social structure of the family, and, by extension, of the state. Harpagon's very desire to maintain control of his money in *L'Avare* leads to displacements that put his paternal authority, his masculinity, and his wealth in jeopardy. Argan's bodily obsessions in *Le Malade imaginaire* similarly destabilize the microcosmic body politic that is his family. Thus, the obsessive desire for containment and order produces the opposite effect, a carnivalesque world turned upside down. This view of familial and social hierarchy as inherently unstable reflects the realities of a culture in the midst of "epochal changes...in epistemology, in economies, in theology and philosophy, in the arts."

Greenberg's essay suggests the fragility of a body politic constructed on the assumption of masculine perfection. In Virginia Marino's "A Curious Study in 'Parallel Lives': Louis XIV and the Abbé de Choisy," the subversive potential of this problematized masculinity is taken to the very heart of power in seventeenth-century France. Current research theorizing the significance of actual and literary manifestations of transvestism derives principally from Robert Stoller's psychological model of the "phallic woman." Briefly, this view sees the male transvestite as fetishistic, enjoying, while cross-dressed, the anticipation of the ultimate revelation of his actual manhood. Staging an internal battle of the sexes, he takes pleasure in the knowledge and enactment of his vanquishing capacity, for his trompe-l'oeil self-creation proves that he can be a better woman than the biological female if he so chooses. Alternate theories explore the symbolic value of such concepts as the phallus, thus inviting a revision of the basic binary categories of sexual identity. A reconsideration of the case of the seventeenth-century historian François Timoléon de Choisy offers the site for a conjunction of these avenues of inquiry and even more radical possibilities. First, acknowledging the fluidity of both gender and behavior makes possible critical attempts to escape the confines of familiar binarisms. Second, uncovering how sartorial practices constitute power plays allows us to rethink these strategies in terms of the political and psychological defiance they entail. Choisy's political life and the textual strategies he deploys in his historical narratives provide a provocative example of shattered binarisms and the reclaiming of a political voice by the traditionally disempowered.

The implications of destabilized gender for both religious and political authority are delineated in Catharine Randall's "Masculinity, Monarchy, and Metaphysics: A Crisis of Authority in Early Modern France." Here, Randall distinguishes very different fears on the part of Protestants and Catholics, and argues that the portrayal of deviant sexuality by Protestants signals a critique of abusive authority, whereas for Catholics this deviance was threatening to proper authority and social order. The anxiety that hovers over masculine identity in this period is enmeshed in a complex network of anxieties concerning the distribution of power and the status of political, theological, and epistemological authority. Similarly, Protestant, and later Jansenist, works seem to focus on exaggerated distinction as a sign of degenerate humanity: the truly spiritual being should rise above gender distinctions. In the context of Jansenism, the issues of gender and authority become even more complex, carrying further the theorizations of and concerns surrounding the relationship between masculinity and power as well as the effect of difference, whether gender/sexual or religious, as a problematizing force in this context.

These essays, then, trace an evolution from a vehement misogynist reaction to feminine transgressions of stereotypical roles delineated by classical philosophers and played out in much religious doctrine to women's accession to power or voice. This evolution passes through an effacement of the feminine other by means of appropriation, to considerations of the factitious nature of that social construct known as masculinity. The profound effect of this questioning of the masculine norm, begun in the sixteenth century, and played out in the course of the seventeenth century, can be seen in the transformations of social and political institutions, such as marriage, the monarchy, the marketplace, and the church, up to and well past the Revolution.

It is of no small significance that the anxiety observed by the authors of these studies can be read at various levels of the text and through a wide range of methodologies. At the detailed level of philological or graphic analysis, at the level of rhetorical tropes and structures, from a psychoanalytic or sociohistorical vantage point, the institution of masculinity is perceived as vulnerable, easily assailed by this wide range of intellectual scrutinies. These essays, then, reveal an awareness on the part of early modern authors of the fragility of this institution as well as a desire to reinvent masculinity as a more open, accommodating, and flexible means of defining one's identity.

Notes

1 For example, Judith Butler, *Bodies that Matter: On the Discursive Limits of Sex* (London: Routledge, 1993); Elizabeth Grosz, *Volatile Bodies: Toward a Corporeal Feminism* (Bloomington: Indiana University Press, 1994); Moira Gatens, *Imaginary Bodies: Ethics, Power, and Corporeality* (London: Routledge, 1996); Juliet Flower MacCannell and Laura Zakarin, eds., *Thinking Bodies* (Stanford: Stanford University Press, 1994), to name but a few.

2 Jonathan Goldberg, *Sodometries: Renaissance Texts, Modern Sexualities* (Stanford: Stanford University Press, 1992); Jean Brink, Alison Coudert, and Maryanne Horowitz, *Playing with Gender: A Renaissance Pursuit* (Urbana: University of Illinois Press, 1991); Jean Brink, ed., *Privileging Gender in Early Modern England* (Kirksville, Mo.: Sixteenth Century Journal Publishers, 1993); Lawrence D. Kritzman, *The Rhetoric of Sexuality and the Literature of the French Renaissance* (Cambridge: Cambridge University Press, 1991); Françoise Jaouën and Benjamin Semple, eds., *Corps Mystique, Corps Sacré: Textual Transfigurations of the Body from the Middle Ages to the Seventeenth Century,* Yale French Studies, no. 86 (New Haven: Yale University Press, 1994); Julia Epstein and Kristina Straub, eds., *Body Guards: The Cultural Politics of Gender Ambiguity* (London: Routledge, 1991); Veronica Kelly and Dorothea E. Von Mücke, eds., *Body and Text in the Eighteenth Century* (Stanford: Stanford University Press, 1994); Thomas Laqueur, *Making Sex: Body and Gender from the Greeks to Freud* (Cambridge: Harvard University Press, 1990); Caroline Walker Bynum, *Fragmentation and Redemption: Essays on Gender and the Human Body in Medieval Religion* (New York: Zone Books, 1991); Marie-Hélène Huet, *Monstrous Imagination* (Cambridge: Harvard University Press, 1993).

3 Among them, Peter F. Murphy, ed., *Fictions of Masculinity: Crossing Cultures, Crossing Sexualities* (New York: New York University Press, 1994); David Rosen, *The Changing Fictions of Masculinity* (Urbana: University of Illinois Press, 1993); Andrew Perchuk and Helaine Posner, eds., *The Masculine Masquerade: Masculinity and Representation* (Cambridge: MIT Press, 1995).

4 Mark Breitenberg, *Anxious Masculinity in Early Modern England* (Cambridge: Cambridge University Press, 1996); Lynn Enterline, *The Tears of Narcissus: Melancholia and Masculinity in Early Modern Writing* (Stanford: Stanford University Press, 1995); one thinks also of Juliana Schiesari, *The Gendering of Melancholia: Feminism, Psychoanalysis, and the Symbolics of Loss in Renaissance Literature* (Ithaca: Cornell University Press, 1992), in relation to this latter work.

5 Dalia Judovitz, *Subjectivity and Representation in Descartes: The Origins of Modernity* (Cambridge: Cambridge University Press, 1988); Mitchell Greenberg, *Subjectivity and Subjugation in Seventeenth-Century Drama and Prose: The Family Romance of French Classicism* (Cambridge: Cambridge University Press, 1992).

6 Any who doubt the extensive and extended nature of this persecution need only consult the "Archive Antoine Court" at the Municipal and University Library in Geneva, a vast collection of documents relating to the persecution of Protestants in France from the sixteenth through the eighteenth centuries.

7 In particular, Natalie Zemon Davis, *The Return of Martin Guerre* (Cambridge: Harvard University Press, 1983), which touches all too briefly on this issue; for a study of accounts of martyrdom, see Catharine Randall Coats, *(Em)bodying the Word: Textual Resurrections in the Martyrological Narratives of Foxe, Crespin, de Bèze, and d'Aubigné* (New York: Peter Lang, 1992); most recently, Nancy Roelker, *One King, One Faith: The Parlement of Paris and the Religious Reformation of the Sixteenth Century* (Berkeley: University of California Press, 1996), has touched on this issue.

8 See Moira Gatens, "Spinoza, Law, and Responsibility," in *Imaginary Bodies,* 108–24; also Gilles Deleuze, *Spinoza: Practical Philosophy,* trans. Robert Hurley (San Francisco: City Lights Books, 1988); idem, *Expressionism in Philosophy: Spinoza,* trans. Martin Joughin (Cambridge, Mass: Zone Books, MIT Press, 1992).

9 The Tenth Mode of suspension of judgment in Sextus Empiricus, *Outlines of Pyrrhonism,* Loeb Classical Library (Cambridge: Harvard University Press, 1969).

10 See Richard Popkin, "The Influence of the New Pyrrhonism," in *The History of Scepticism from Erasmus to Spinoza* (Berkeley: University of California Press, 1979), 66–86.

11   The most striking example in poetry is the elegy on the transvestite Achilles, "Pour Monseigneur le Duc d'Anjou," written when Charles was still alive, and thus clearly directed at Henri; see Victor Graham, ed., *Cartels et masquarades: Epitaphes* (Geneva: Droz, 1960), 30–31. Regarding popular pamphlets, one thinks in particular of the *Histoires prodigieuses* of Pierre Boaistuau (1561–), continued by Claude Tesserant, *Quatorze histoires prodigieuses* (Paris, 1567). See also the "Histoire d'un homme avec des cheveux de femme," which is a sustained critique of Nero and Heliogabalus, and the "Histoire de deux enfans Hermaphrodites…," both of which equate ambiguity of gender with social disorder. For alchemical treatises, see Clovis Hesteau de Nuysement,*Visions hermétiques,* ed. Sylvain Matton (1620; reprint Paris: Bibliotheca Hermetica, 1974). For medical treatises, see Ambroise Paré, *Des Monstres et prodiges,* ed. Jean Céard (Geneva: Droz, 1971), 24–30, which was originally published in 1573 and contains complex accounts of hermaphroditism and gender transformations, evoking an anxiety about the social disorder that such instabilities might entail.

12   For an assessment of one skeptical critique of the court of Henri III of France, see Kathleen Long, "Hermaphrodites Newly Discovered: The Cultural Monsters of Sixteenth-Century France," in *Monster Theory: Reading Culture,* ed. Jeffrey Cohen (Minneapolis: University of Minnesota Press, 1996).

13   The *Isle des Hermaphrodites* has appeared in its first new edition since the early eighteenth century; see Claude-Gilbert Dubois, ed., *Isle des Hermaphrodites* (Geneva: Droz, 1996). For Gabriel de Foigny's work, see *Terre australe connue,* ed. Pierre Ronzeaud (Paris: Champion, 1990). For a collection of satirical political poems often attributed to Théophile de Viau and published in 1622, see *Parnasse Satyrique* (Paris: Duquesne, 1861). The best-known poem is probably the opening sonnet: "Phylis tout est foutu, je meurs de la vérole," which ends with the lines, "Mon Dieu, je me repens d'avoir si mal vescu: / Et si vostre courroux à ce coup ne me tue, / Je fais voeu désormais de ne foutre qu'en cu." The collection also contains a number of invectives against courtiers and dialogues between them, in which French law is discussed in an irreverent fashion; see "Pour un Courtisan" and "Quatrains contre des Courtisanes." There are also a number of parodies of litanies and prayers; for example, the "Quatrains: Délivre moy Seigneur."

14   A useful if brief article on *L'isle des Hermaphrodites* is Donald Stone, "The Sexual Outlaw in France, 1605," *Journal of the History of Sexuality* 2 (1992): 597–608, which traces the formulation in the novel of a different notion of individual identity and worth from that predominant in the sixteenth century.

15   For a history of the *querelle,* see Joan Kelly, "Early Feminist Theory and the 'Querelle des Femmes,'" in *Women, History, and Theory* (Chicago: University of Chicago Press, 1984), 65–109.

16   Laqueur, *Making Sex,* "New Science, One Flesh," 63–113.

17   See Popkin, *Scepticism,* "The 'Libertins Erudits,'" 87–109.

18   For an assessment of later manifestations of this relationship, see Lynn Hunt, *The Family Romance of the French Revolution* (Berkeley: University of California Press, 1992).

Louise Labé's Transgressions

Cathy Yandell

The derogatory epithets directed at Louise Labé[1] during her lifetime and since are included in virtually every edition of her work and repeated in numerous commentaries, bibliographies, biographies, and anthologies, from Calvin's over-wrought "plebeia meretrix" [vulgar courtesan][2] to Claude de Ruby's "ceste impudique Loyse l'Abbé, que chacun sçait avoir fait profession de courtisanne publique jusques à sa mort" [this immodest Louise Labé, whom everyone knew to be a prostitute until her death].[3] A woman writing love poetry in early modern Europe often received such criticism because, as Ann Rosalind Jones observes, "she was entering into public discourse, exposing the beauty of her language, akin to her body, to the masculine gaze."[4] Yet the critical obsession with Louise Labé's sexual conduct continues well beyond her immediate literary heirs: the first question that Gérard Guillot addresses in his 1962 biography of Labé is "fut-elle ou non une courtisane?" [was she or was she not a prostitute?], and he then recounts the story of a contemporary high school in Lyon that refused to be christened with her tainted name.[5] As recently as 1981, Paul Ardouin described Pernette du Guillet as "très éloignée de Louise Labé par la pureté de ses moeurs" [very distant from Louise Labé in the purity of her morals].[6] Louise Labé's reputation for engaging in controversial behavior thus remains firmly established even in late-twentieth-century critical discourse.

Criticisms of Louise Labé most frequently target—implicitly or explicitly—her sexual behavior; but even among early modern critics, these statements are often embedded within complimentary language about her intellectual capacities and her poetic genius. In 1584, for example, Pierre de Saint-Julien described her work, "oeuvre qui sent trop mieux l'erudite gaillardise de l'esprit de Maurice Scève, que d'une simple Courtisane" [work that is much more redolent of the erudite ribaldry of Scève's spirit, than of a simple courtesan].[7] Of all poets, Colletet later writes, Louise Labé is the most worthy of comparison to Sappho, "tant par la délicatesse de son Esprit que par l'irrégularité de sa conduite" [as much by the refinement of her spirit as by the irregularity of her conduct].[8] Similarly, L'Abbé Iraihl cites "la beauté du génie, [le] talent de faire des vers enjoués, délicats, et faciles et…le déreglement de [sa] conduite" [the beauty of her genius, her talent for crafting playful, delicate, and smooth verses, and…the unruliness of her behavior].[9]

Déréglement, irrégularité, impudicité, transgression—these terms dominate the negative critiques of Louise Labé's conduct. What is the relationship between Louise Labé's allegedly audacious, transgressive behavior and the nature of her literary production? What rules—the *règle* of *dérèglement* and *irrégularité*—does she break? And perhaps most important, what is the function of these transgressions? Where do they lead? As a point of departure for responding to these questions, I propose to examine three of Louise Labé's rhetorical strategies, each of which illustrates one of the concepts enclosed within the term *transgression*.[10] I will further posit the relationship of these transgressive rhetorical strategies to the topos of production implicit in Labé's work. *Transgression* (from *trans-gredi,* to go beyond) etymologically signifies surpassing, going beyond boundaries. It also denotes the violation of a law or the breaking of a rule. A third, more specific meaning incorporates the notion of sin, or an offense against God. Through an examination of the different senses of *transgression* revealed in the topos of the distaff, the lyrical portrait, and the conceit of *erreurs,* I hope to shed light on some of the inner workings of Labé's poetic corpus.

In what is arguably Louise Labé's most celebrated line, the poet exhorts young women to rise above their spindles and to pursue the practices of study and writing:

> Je ne puis faire autre chose que prier les vertueuses Dames d'eslever un peu leurs esprits par-dessus leurs quenoilles et fuseaus, et s'employer à faire entendre au monde que si nous ne sommes faites pour comander, si ne devons nous estre desdaignees pour compagnes tant es afaires domestiques que publiques, de ceus qui gouvernent et se font obeïr.[11] (pp. 41-42)

> [I can only beseech virtuous women to raise their minds above their distaffs and spindles and to make the world understand that even if we are not made to command, we should not be disdained as participants in private or public affairs by those who govern and ensure that others obey them.]

Not only does writing appropriately take women into the public arena, Labé argues later in this preface, but it also brings glory, honor, and pleasure. In other activities (such as spinning), she notes:

> ...quand on en ha pris tant que lon veut, on ne se peut vanter d'autre chose, que d'avoir passé le tems. Mais celle de l'estude laisse un contentement de soy, qui nous demeure plus longuement.[12] (p. 42)

> [...when you have done (those activities) as long as you wish, you can say only that you have passed the time. But study leaves you in a state of contentment, which is longer lasting.]

Thus Louise Labé begins her collected works by positing the dominion of the distaff as anathema to women's critical vocation of writing. The dramatic implications of Louise Labé's call to action can be appreciated fully only within the context of the distaff's multiple manifestations—linguistic, social, and literary.

Serving as the quintessential emblem of women's social place, the "quenouille" denotes the female line in a succession as early as the sixteenth century. It metonymically represents women or "old wives," as in the collection of axioms entitled *Les Evangilles des quenouilles,* published in the late fifteenth century. "Quenouille" also appears in idiomatic expressions denoting women's potential power: "tenir de la quenouille," according to Cotgrave, means "to hold...his wife to be his Maister." The proverb "A la quenouille le fol s'agenouille" is echoed by its sixteenth-century English counterpart, "fooles kneele to distaves, weake men unto women."[13] In iconographical representations, the distaff serves to denote the exclusively female domain as well: when a man is pictured with a distaff, he becomes burlesque and ridiculous.[14]

The distaff has received considerable critical attention of late, particularly as scholarly inquiry has established the parallel between misogyny and privatization on the one hand, and nascent feminism and resistance to domesticity on the other.[15] In a recent article on the iconography of spinning, Frances Biscoglio outlines the two traditions from which the image of the spinning woman emerges. In primitive myth and classical antiquity, the spinning woman represents the creator, life-giver, intermediary, and source of wisdom, as in the spinning Parcae, who control human destiny. In the Judeo-Christian tradition, however, the spinner embodies the ideal woman, the *mulier economica* of Proverbs 31, a model of virtue who is charitable, industrious, and obedient.[16] The distaff of Louise Labé's preface figures very firmly within this second context. In ironic contrast to the term "quenouille," implying female authority in the expressions cited above, the distaff in sixteenth-century French discourse fulfills the social function of keeping its mistress as far away from power as possible. Erasmus, for example, recommends spinning silk, weaving tapestries, or playing a musical instrument as respectable activities to occupy a noblewoman.[17] Other humanist conduct manuals prescribe spinning as a safeguard against idleness because, as Juan Luis Vives warns in *l'Institution de la femme chrestienne* [Education of a Christian woman], "s'elle pense seule, elle pense mal" [if she thinks alone, she thinks evil].[18] Seen within the context of widespread public anxiety about the potentially pernicious use of free time by women, the distaff serves in these texts as an instrument of regulation and confinement.

In 1559, four years after Louise Labé's works appeared, Pierre de Ronsard published in his *Second livre des meslanges* a poem entitled "La quenoille," in which the poet underscores the distaff's vital function: it keeps his lady occupied. Marie stands in worthy company as Ronsard's poet establishes an equivalency between her and Pallas Athena, goddess of wisdom, patron of the arts, peace, and war. Athena had as companion and friend a distaff, who will henceforth be called Marie. A brief examination of the poem reveals the purposes to which, in the eyes of the poet, Marie's distaff should be put: it will occupy the lady as she pines for the poet in his absence. Here the distaff offered by the poet—"cher present que je porte à ma chere Marie" [dear present that I offer to my dear Marie]—constitutes a rather demagogical gift to Marie:

A fin de soulager l'ennuy qu'elle a de moy [To relieve her pining over me
....

Quenoille je te meine où je suis arresté: Distaff, I am taking you where I am held
                                              captive;

Je voudrois racheter par toy la liberté.[19]   Through you, I would like to regain my
                                              freedom.]

          (p. 1.236–37, lines 10.122–23)

The "pointe" (or conceit) ending the poem magnifies the domestic object's grandeur in language worthy of a mock encomium: the distaff, offered by a "loyal amy," surpasses in its glory both scepters and crowns. Thus in this text the distaff serves to
underscore Marie's place (and, synecdochically, women's place) as she engages in shel-
tered, sanctioned activity while the poet breaks away.

In Ronsard's *Sonnets pour Hélène,* the domain of the distaff serves to remind Hélène
of her subordinate status as she wastes away for having refused the poet's verdant love
years before. She is described as crouching by the fireplace, "devidant et filant /
...regrettant mon amour et vostre fier desdain" [winding and spinning ... regretting my
love and your proud disdain].[20] In both cases the distaff represents a form of banishment
for the female addressee: in the first example as a means of granting the poet's own freedom from Marie, and in the second as a punishment for Hélène's heartless rejection.

The contradiction between contemporaneous moralists' and poets' enthusiastic
championing of the distaff on the one hand, and on the other, Louise Labé's pointed
reference to rising above it in order to write, reveals the extent of the woman poet's
transgression. The poet's simple exhortation to put spinning aside, when seen as explicitly calling into question socially sanctioned women's work and thus women's place,
takes on a revolutionary quality. This is not to say, of course, that Louise Labé is the
only sixteenth-century woman to interrogate the icon of the distaff: Hélisenne de
Crenne assails it and Catherine des Roches, in her later poem "A ma quenouille," paradoxically glorifies it. In Catherine's poem, the exalted distaff serves as a subterfuge for
her writing.[21] But Louise Labé's injunction to rise above the distaff declares a clear
hierarchy between writing (discouraged for women, but desirable) and traditionally
female work (encouraged, but undesirable), and thus constitutes the most devastating
critique of all. In her bold preface not only does Labé open herself to charges of arro-
gance, but she also transgresses (goes beyond boundaries) by challenging the most cherished icon of female subjugation in early modern Europe.

Labé's lyrical portraiture illustrates the poet's *transgression* in the second sense of the
term—that of disobeying rules—by deviating significantly from established poetic
practice in her use of the *blason.* During a literary moment immediately following the
considerable success of the *blason* (particularly the *Blasons anatomiques du corps feminin*)
and during the apogee of the Petrarchan praises of body parts such as Du Bellay's "Ces
cheveux d'or, ce front de marbre" [This golden hair, this marble forehead], Baïf's "O
beaux yeux azurins, ô regards de douceur!" [O beautiful azure eyes, O sweet looks!],
and Tyard's "De tes cheveux si blondement dorez" [Of your hair so lightly golden], it is
not surprising that Louise Labé should include such a poem in her Italianate sonnet

sequence.[22] Labé's second sonnet, "O beaux yeux bruns, ô regars destournez" [O beautiful brown eyes, O averted gazes] (p. 123), a predecessor or a response to Olivier de Magny's sonnet by the same title, has been analyzed extensively, particularly in reference to the ambiguous blurring of subject and object in the first two quatrains, which are identical in the two poems. Nicolas Ruwet and Françoise Charpentier, among others, examine different aspects of what François Rigolot calls "un brouillage voulu" [an intended scrambling] in these two poems.[23] Ann Rosalind Jones concludes that "the parallel established between the sonnets of Labé and Magny effaces sexual and textual difference."[24] While linguistic blurring is indeed undeniable in the two sonnets, the final lines underscore nonetheless both textual and conceptual divergence, revealing Louise Labé's significant departure from the *blason* tradition. A brief examination of the tercets, specifically in relation to Petrarch's "O passi sparsi," which serves as an obvious model for Magny and a probable model for Labé, elucidates the discernible difference between two poets from Lyon. Labé's version of the tercets is as follows:

O ris, ô front, cheveus, bras, mains, et doits:	[O laughter, O forehead, hair, arms, hands, and fingers,
O lut pleintif, viole, archet, et vois:	O plaintive lute, viol, bow, and voice,
Tant de flambeaus pour ardre une femmelle!	So many torches to inflame a woman!
De toy me plein, que tant de feus portant,	I begrudge you, because although you bear so many flames
En tant d'endrois d'iceus mon coeur tatant,	That touch my heart in so many ways,
N'en est sur toy volé quelque estincelle.	Not even a spark has fallen upon you.]

(p. 122)

Compare Magny's version of the final lines:

O pas espars, ô trop ardente flame	[O scattered steps, O too ardent flame
O douce erreur, ô pensers de mon ame,	O sweet wandering, O thoughts of my soul
Qui ça, qui là, me tournez nuict et jour,	Who torment me night and day,
O vous mes yeux, non plus yeux mais fonteines,	O you, my eyes, no longer eyes but fountains,
O dieux, ô cieux et personnes humaines,	O gods, O heavens and humans,
Soyez pour dieu tesmoins de mon amour.[25]	Serve as witnesses of my love to god.]

And finally, compare the tercets of Petrarch's "O passi sparsi":

o bel viso, ove Amor inseme pose	[O lovely face where Love has put
gli sproni e'l fren ond' el mi punge et volve	both the spurs and the rein with which he rakes and turns me
come a lui piace, e calcitrar non vale;	as he pleases, and no kicking avails;
o anime gentili et amorose,	O noble loving souls,
s'alcuna à 'l mondo, et voi, nude ombre et polve:	if there are any in the world, and you, naked shades and dust:
deh, ristate a veder quale è 'l mio male! [26]	ah, stay to see what my suffering is!]

Whereas Labé continues the enumeration of the lover's characteristics in lines 9 and 10 ("O ris, ô front, cheveux, bras…") and resolves them in line 11 ("Tant de flambeaux pour ardre une femmelle!"), Magny slips immediately into a faithful translation of scattered parts from the first three strophes of the Petrarchan sonnet ("O pas espars," "O passi sarsi," "ô trop ardente flame," "ô fero ardore," and so on). While in the final tercet Labé launches a "pointe" back to the addressee, Magny concludes instead with an apostrophe centered upon the poet's own sentiments. Indeed, the last two tercets of Magny's sonnet and Petrarch's entire sonnet (with the exception of "o bel viso" in line 9) are solipsistically focused on the poet himself: all of the characteristics and sentiments evoked are those of the poet.[27] While Magny returns to the Petrarchan focus on the lover's inner turmoil in his conclusion, Labé syntactically combines lover and beloved in the last tercet. Thus in expressing her desire that the addressee's love be ignited as well, Louise Labé rejects the solipsistic tendency of both Petrarch's and Magny's *blasons,* proposing here, as elsewhere, reciprocity as a model.[28]

This example of difference in Labé's verse within the blazoning tradition in Petrarch and Magny should not be construed as isolated. The three *blason*-like poems alluded to earlier by Tyard, Baïf, and Du Bellay all end with the poet's own desire in relation to the living composite of female body parts just described. Tyard concludes, for example: "Tant de ses traitz sur moy qu'il se fascha / De plus m'occire, et moy de plus mourir" [So many arrows had he aimed at me that he was distressed not to be able to kill me any longer, and I was distressed for no longer being able to die].[29] Similarly, in the *Blasons anatomiques du corps feminin,* the body part being eulogized often arouses a specific sentiment or desire in the poet, with which he concludes the poem. The final lines of Albert Legrand's "L'oreille," for example, read:

Oreille donc qui tout entend,	[Ear who hears all, then,
Pour me rendre bien fort content,	To make me extremely happy
Escoute moy quand je voudray,	Listen to me when I desire it,
Et croy tout ce que te diray.[30]	And believe everything I tell you.]

Scève's "Blason de la larme," also, not surprisingly, ends with a ponderous Petrarchan apostrophe to the tear:

Mais bien descends à gros bruyantz ruis-seaulx,	[But fall in great loud streams
Et tellement excite ton pouvoir,	And arouse your power
Que par pitié tu puisses esmouvoir	So that you can move by compassion
Celle qui n'a commiseration	The one who does not take pity
De ma tant grande et longue passion.[31]	Upon my great and enduring passion.]

In these verses Scève solicits the tear's help in securing the love of his lady, but once again the impetus of the poem (and the concluding syntactical emphasis) is unmistakably the poet's own passion. Robert Cottrell has shown that Scève's focus in the *blasons* shifts from object to subject as the poet places his own maleness, his own "generative power" in front of the lady's image.[32] While initially in this *blason* the pronoun "celle" to denote the lady suggests her unified subjectivity, it is immediately eclipsed by the immensity of the poet's desire.

All of these blazoning poets insist—sometimes obsessively—on particularized attributes of the woman's body, which fail to coalesce into a unified subject within the poem. The Petrarchan poet transforms the totality of the woman's body into scattered, fetishistic parts. As Nancy Vickers has noted, though the "I" of the *Rime sparse* is itself fragmented, "the intolerable absence [of Laura's body] creates a reason to speak, and permits a poetic 'corpus,'" thus unifying the speaker's self.[33] In all of the poems considered above, the speakers' sentiments dominate, yet only Louise Labé's sonnet assigns a unified form to the beloved, reassembling his fragmented parts in the pronoun "toy," which represents the addressee in his entirety. Furthermore, the juxtaposition of this embodied "toy" with the implied "je" in "de toy me plein" in the final tercet produces a linguistic equality between speaker and addressee that is systematically absent from other *blasons*. In light of these examples, then, it is evident that by according a unified subjectivity to both speaker and addressee in the poem, Louise Labé's only *blason* sonnet transgresses the well-established conventions of the genre.

Labé's more explicit critique of the mentality underlying the *blasons* is evident in other sonnets as well. As François Lecercle argues in *La chimère de Zeuxis,* if poets unceasingly enumerate the same physical traits, those traits must fulfill some function other than realistic and descriptive.[34] Thus the image of the body becomes no longer descriptive but instead prescriptive, according to preestablished rhetorical models. In "Sonnet 23," Louise Labé declares her opposition to the methods of the *blasonneur* from the perspective of the *blasonnée*. She questions the sincerity of the *blasonneur's* lauding the quintessential body parts which allegedly cause his suffering:

Las! que me sert, que si parfaitement	[Alas! What good does it do me
Louas jadis et ma tresse doree,	That long ago you praised my golden braid,

Et de mes yeus la beauté comparee   And the beauty of my eyes compared
A deus Soleils, dont Amour finement   To two suns, from which Cupid
Tira les trets causez de ton tourment?...   Deftly shot his arrows, source of your tor-
    ment?]

(p. 134)

Labé's speaker further challenges the motives behind the blazoning poet's praise:

Donques c'estoit le but de ta malice   [So the goal of your malice
De m'asservir sous ombre de service?   Was to subjugate me under the guise of
    service?]

(p. 134)

Thus the addressee, now turned speaker, speaks out against the potential abuses of the *blasonneur's* rhetorical formulae. What does she proffer in their stead? Once again, Labé's response is one of reciprocity:

Mais je m'assur', quelque part que tu sois,   [But I am assured that wherever you are,
Qu'autant que moy tu soufres de martire.   Your suffering and pain are as great as
    mine.]

(p. 134)

What goes around, comes around, and the speaker is convinced in her concluding verses that the addressee will eventually suffer equal pain, in no uncertain terms: "autant que moi." Here the construction of an equivalency between lovers illustrates Labé's overcoming of what Deborah Lesko Baker terms "the ontological disorientation of the Petrarchan lover."[35] Baker argues that Louise Labé transforms the position of woman in Renaissance discourse from an object to a subject of erotic and artistic desire. Baker's thesis is particularly germane to this sonnet, wherein the poet explicitly calls into question the woman's status as *blasonnée*. The speaker begins the sonnet as the psychological, specular, and grammatical object ("que me sert," "m'asservir," "ma tresse dorée") and concludes it explicitly positing her own subjectivity ("je m'assur"). Rather than turn the tables and reduce her addressee to the status of an objectified *blasonné*, however, the poet accords him both affective and grammatical equality ("autant que moy tu soufres de martire").

Louise Labé suggests in "Sonnet 21" that the techniques used in *blason*-making are problematic not only for the addressee but also for the speaker. In what might be termed a formal "anti-*blason*" from the writer's perspective, Labé's poet avows the difficulty she encounters in attempting to craft an idealized description of the ideal male lover:

Quelle grandeur rend l'homme venerable? [What height makes man worthy of ado-
    ration?

Quelle grosseur? quel poil? quelle cou- leur?	What size? What hair? What color?
Qui est des yeus le plus emmieleur?	Who has the sweetest eyes?
Qui fait plus tot une playe incurable?…	Who is the first to inflict an incurable wound?]

(pp. 132-33, sonnet 21)

Dudley Wilson, in his reading of this poem, argues that the conventions governing the male and female anatomies are different and thus "le vocabulaire anatomique de la poétesse possède un certain nombre de lacunes par rapport à celui du poète" [the anatomical vocabulary of the female poet is deficient compared to that of the male poet].[36] Certainly Labé's poet acknowledges in this sonnet the open-ended possibilities for describing a male lover. But the tercets reveal a much more pointed message. In response to the questions of the quatrain, Louise's poet responds:

Je ne voudrois le dire assurément,	[I do not wish to say for certain,
Ayant Amour forcé mon jugement:	Since Love has coerced my judgment,
Mais je say bien et de tant je m'assure,	But I know and am convinced
Que tout le beau que lon pourroit choisir,	That all the beauty one could choose
Et que tout l'art qui ayde la Nature,	And all the art that assists nature
Ne me sauroient acroitre mon desir.	Would be incapable of increasing my desire.]

(p. 133)

The central question in these verses seems to have little to do with insufficient vocabulary for the physical description of male models. The poet clearly states instead, "Je ne *voudrois* le dire assurément." Why does the poet resist crafting a flattering portrait of her lover? She responds to this question in the remaining verses of the sonnet: because the putative list of desirable characteristics is irrelevant to the poet's desire. Labé's poet emphatically rejects the creation of an idealized model (male or female), not only because she asserts that beauty is in the eye of the beholder (thus introducing a psychological dimension into the discourse of specularity), but also because she insists that stylized rhetorical ploys, "tout l'art qui ayde la Nature," would be incapable of intensifying her desire.

An articulation of the poet's desire also figures prominently in the third sense of *transgression*, violating divine law, which is evoked in Louise Labé's treatment of the amorous tropes of confession and repentance. The conceit of *erreurs* is significant not because Louise Labé employs it, but rather because she seems studiously to avoid it. On several occasions she grazes the motif, but in every case she subverts it, adapting it to her own very different ends. The conceit of *erreurs,* often figuring at the beginning of a collection of love lyrics, expresses for the most part the contrived repentance of the poet. Petrarch's allusion to his *giovenile errore* in the first sonnet of *Rime sparse* serves as a prototype for this tradition: "et del mio vaneggiar vergogna è'l frutto"[37] [and of my raving, shame is the fruit]. Similarly, Pontus de Tyard, in the last line of his first sonnet, proclaims himself "Prest d'endurer honteuse penitence / Pour les erreurs de ma jeunesse vaine"[38] [Ready to endure shameful penitence / For the wanderings (errors) of my vain youth], and Scève, too, includes the notion of *erreurs* in the liminary huitain of the *Délie*. These disclaimer poems incorporate considerable ambiguity, however, given that they denote the will to repudiate manifestations of youthful, lusty thoughts while simultaneously preceding poems that record and thereby re-create those same thoughts. Yet within the poems themselves, the conceit stands unadultered: the poet repents.

Given Louise Labé's clear affinity for Italian love poets and their French imitators, the reader might reasonably expect to encounter the topos of *errore* early in her collection.[39] Indeed, embedded in Louise Labé's first elegy are several verses that promise to state the poet's *erreurs:*

Et maintenant me suis encor contreinte	[And now I am constrained again
De rafreschir d'une nouvelle pleinte	To revive with a new lamentation
Mes maus passez. Dames, qui les lirez,	The griefs of my past. You ladies who will read of them,
De mes regrets avec moy soupirez....	Sigh with me about my regrets.]

(p. 108)

But several lines later the poet clarifies her position that an apology is out of the question, since it is Cupid who "inflames" women. Women who fall prey to love's wounds should never be blamed, since the noblest souls are the most susceptible:

N'estimez point que lon doive blamer	[Do not imagine that those whom Cupid has inflamed
Celles qu'a fait Cupidon inflamer.	Should be blamed...
... les plus nobles esprits	... The noblest spirits
En sont plus fort et plus soudain espris....	Are taken the most strongly and suddenly.]

(p. 108)

I do not mean to imply, of course, that Labé's poet does not plead for the understanding and approbation of her critical cohorts, the "dames lyonnaises." On the contrary, winning the approval of her readers constitutes a central question in both the elegies and the sonnets. But rather than admit to wrongdoing, Labé justifies and explains her behavior. Instead of "confessing" in the Petrarchan mode, the poet constructs a legal strategy in her own defense, circumventing the topoi of confession and repentance. Another case in point is the beginning of elegy 3:

Quand vous lirez, ô Dames Lionnoises,	[When you read, O ladies of Lyon,

Ces miens escrits pleins d'amoureuses noises,	These writings filled with amorous rumbling,
Quand mes regrets, ennuis, despits et larmes	When my regrets, my sorrows, my angers and tears
M'orrez chanter en pitoyables carmes,	You will hear me sing in pitiful verses,
Ne veuillez pas condamner ma simplesse,	Do not condemn my simplicity,
Et jeune erreur de ma fole jeunesse,	And the young wandering (error) of my foolish youth
Si c'est erreur...	If it is error...]

(p. 115)

Once again all signs point to a confession with the inclusion of the familiar words "jeune erreur." But the poet immediately subverts her own declaration: *si c'est erreur.* By whose definition are amorous exploits classified as *"erreurs"?* Only by the reader's, it would appear, and the poet sets out to secure the reader's allegiance: "mais qui dessous les Cieus / Se peut vanter de n'estre vicieus?" [but who under the heavens / Can boast of having no imperfections?]. She then proceeds to demonstrate what truly constitutes vice: "Mentir, tromper, et abuser autrui" [Lying, cheating, and abusing others] (p. 116). But if despite the poet's reasoning to the contrary, the reader should continue to categorize sexual desire as a vice, she offers yet another justification:

Mais si en moy rien y ha d'imparfait,	[But if there is anything imperfect in me,
Qu'on blame Amour: c'est lui seul qui l'a fait.	Let love be blamed: it is he alone who did it.]

(p. 116)

The *si* of "si c'est erreur" and "si en moy rien y ha d'imparfait" are reminiscent of the numerous ambiguous *si* of "Sonnet 24": "si j'ay aymé," "si j'ay senti mile torches ardentes," "si en pleurant, j'ay mon tems consumé," "si j'ay failli" [if I have loved, if I have felt a thousand burning torches, if I have spent my time weeping, if I have failed]. The hypothetical *si* underscores that all experience can only be fully known and grounded in the individual body. In all these cases, the poet implies that although the reader might construe it otherwise, no one is immune from the vicissitudes of love; thus she explicitly deflects charges of malfeasance: "Et gardez vous d'estre plus malheureuses" [And avoid being more miserable yourselves] (p. 135). The poet's justification of her passion appears airtight: first, Eros is to blame, and second, love's pangs are both insuperable and universal. Despite the plaintive tone of both the elegy and the sonnet, the poet's syllogistic declarations eschew the notion of *"erreurs"* and culminate in the triumph of her desire.

A related rhetorical manifestation of the *"erreurs"* conceit is the use of the poetic devise *repentir* or retraction (from the Latin *retractare,* to draw back). The retraction, frequently used by Petrarch as well as his Italian and French imitators, is ubiquitous in sixteenth-century verse. Once again, the significance of this device in Louise Labé's poetry is not its presence, but its absence, particularly in the case of Labé's and Magny's sonnets that begin identically, "O beaux yeux bruns, ô regars destournez" [O beautiful brown eyes, O averted gazes]. Both Petrarch and Magny include a prominent retraction in their sonnets—"oi occhi miei (occhi non già, ma fonti)" [O my eyes, not eyes but fountains] and "O vous mes yeux, non plus yeux mais fonteines" [no longer eyes but fountains]—that Labé excludes. This omission could perhaps be attributed to mere coincidence, were it not for the absence of retraction in the whole of Louise Labé's work.[40] Her rhetorical approach, in fact, seems to be quite the opposite: in her famous *basium* poem, there are certainly no retractions, and the explicit repetition underscores the audacity of her invitation:

Baise m'encor, rebaise moy et baise:	[Kiss me, kiss me again and again,
Donne m'en un de tes plus savoureux,	Give me one of your most delicious ones,
Donne m'en un de tes plus amoureux....	Give me one of your most amorous ones....]

(p. 131)

Thus stylistically as well as psychologically, Louise Labé's poet neither admits to specific *"erreurs"* nor repents. She explains, implores, repeats, justifies, fantasizes, and cajoles, but she does not repent. Her *transgression* is therefore magnified: while on the surface Labé's speaker appears to be begging the "dames lyonnoises" for forgiveness, upon closer examination of the rhetoric, we see that she resists this formulation in favor of firmly standing her ground. While the topos of repentance had already been secularized by Petrarch and his imitators, Louise Labé goes further still by excising it from her amorous vocabulary. In so doing, she posits an independence from the doctrine of atonement that, were it transposed into the realm of Catholic orthodoxy, would border on sacrilege.

Louise Labé has thus transgressed by going beyond boundaries, violating literary laws, and bypassing the tropes of confession and repentance. To return to my opening question: What do these rhetorical infractions reveal about Louise Labé's larger literary and social designs? In his *Interpretation and Overinterpretation,* Umberto Eco proposes criteria for determining what he calls the *intentio operis,* or the intention of the text (as distinguished from the intention of the author or that of the reader). Foremost among these criteria is the plausibility of a given semantic isotopy.[41] It seems to me that at least one semantic isotopy governing the three rhetorical strategies I have just discussed is that of production. And in all cases, production has as its catalyst *détournement*—resistance or refusal. In exhorting women to renounce spinning cloth in favor of spinning words, Louise Labé defies the ubiquitous emblem of the distaff. As the woman poet repudiates the established masculine model of fragmented lyrical portraiture, and its implicit ideology, she produces in its stead a new model—of verse and of relation—based on mutuality or reciprocity. And in transgressing the structures of confession and repentance by refusing to classify her desires as *erreurs,* she privileges in her text the expression of female erotic imagination.

One obvious response to the question of where these transgressions lead is that through literary infractions Louise Labé, like other writing women in early modern Europe, turned to production as a chosen substitute for being that which is produced (by their families as carriers of class values) or that which reproduces.[42] But beyond that, it is significant that Louise Labé's creative productions resulting from the rhetorical strategies I have addressed all find their origins in what might be called negative space: the defiance of the distaff, the absence inherent in the fetishistic description of body parts, and even more paradoxically, refusal as the agent of production (as in the case of not admitting to transgressions).[43] Certainly I would not claim that Louise Labé in particular or women writers in general have a monopoly on literary transgression. The Petrarchan poets cited earlier, for example, transgress previous convention in a number of ways. Yet the fact remains that sixteenth-century charges of transgression were levied not against the Petrarchan poets but against Louise Labé. Was it the blatant sensuality expressed in verses by a woman poet that readers found threatening? Or were the more subtle and more subversive transgressions—productions of a new order out of a negative space—more threatening still? However we adjudicate these questions, it is clear that all of Louise Labé's transgressions continue to attract readers' attention, whether our interest be rhetorical, historical, political, or prurient. These transgressions also challenge us to rethink if not the *raison d'être,* then certainly the *raison d'écrire* of women writers in early modern France.

Notes

1. Some of the ideas exposed here are also included in the chapter on Louise Labé in Cathy Yandell, *Carpe Corpus: Time and Gender in Early Modern France* (Newark: University of Delaware Press; London: Associated University Presses, 2000), 85–127. While there is not enough overlap to necessitate permission from the publisher to reprint, I am grateful to Associated University Presses for their cooperation.

2. Jean Calvin, *Gratulatio ad venerabilim presbyterium dominum Galorielum de Saconay, praecentorem ecclesiae lugdunesis* (Pamphlet against Gabriel de Saconay, precentor of the church of Lyons), 1560, cited in Louise Labé, *Œuvres complètes*, ed. François Rigolot (Paris: Gallimard, 1986), 242. Page numbers are referenced in the text. All subsequent quotations of Labé's work will be from this edition. For an interesting analysis of the reasons Louise Labé would not have been attracted to the Huguenot movement, see Natalie Zemon Davis, *Society and Culture in Early Modern France* (Stanford: Stanford University Press, 1975), 82–86.

3. Claude de Rubys, *Les Privileges, franchises et immunitez octroyées par les Rois treschretiens, aux consuls, eschevins, monens, et habitans de la ville de Lyon, et à leur posterité* (Lyon: Gryphe, 1573), cited in Louise Labé, *Œuvres complètes*, 243. On the translation of "courtisan" as "prostitute," see Henri Estienne, *Apologie pour Hérodote* (Paris, 1566) who defines the term as "le moins déshonneste synonyme de putain" [the least unseemly synonym of whore], cited by Edmond Huguet, *Dictionnaire de la langue française du seizième siècle* (Paris: Champion, 1925), 2:609. Not all contemporaneous critics agreed with this assessment of Louise Labé, of course. For example, François Billon, *Fort expugnable de l'honneur du sexe feminin* (Paris: Ian d'Allyer, 1555), launches a counterattack: "Pour myeux amplifier l'Histoire antique de laquelle Cleopatra, ilz s'efforcent souventeffois [*sic*] de l'accoupler a une moderne, par l'exemple...la belle Cordiere de Lyon, en ses safres déduytz: sans qu'ilz ayent l'entendement de considerer que s'il y a chose en sa vie qui puisse estre taxée, les Hommes premierement en sont cause, comme Autheurs de tous maux en toutes Creatures: ny sans pouvoir compenser en elle, les graces et gentilles perfections qui y sont" [To explain ancient history such as Cleopatra, they often try to compare her to a modern woman, for example... "the beautiful rope-maker's wife" (Labé), with her lascivious entertainments. They fail to consider that if anything in her life can be reproached, men are primarily the cause of it, as authors of all evil. And they fail to admit the graces and fine perfections found in her] (15r).

4. Ann Rosalind Jones, *The Currency of Eros: Women's Love Lyric in Europe, 1540-1620* (Bloomington: Indiana University Press, 1990), 28.

5. Gérard Guillot, *Louise Labé: Sa vie et ses œuvres* (Paris: Pierre Seghers, 1962), 51.

6. Paul Ardoin, *Maurice Scève, Pernette du Guillet, Louise Labé: L'amour à Lyon au temps de la Renaissance* (Paris: Nizet, 1981), 90.

7. Pierre de Saint-Julien, *Gemelles ou Pareilles, Recueillies de divers auteurs* (Lyon, 1584), cited in Louise Labé, *Œuvres complètes*, 243.

8. Guillaume Colletet, *Vie des poètes françois*. Bibliothèque Nationale Manuscript, nouvelles acquisitions françaises, 3073. Cited also in Louise Labé, *Œuvres*, ed. Blanchmain (Paris: Librairie des bibliophiles, 1875), viii. Colletet notes that Louise Labé "savait tout et même beaucoup plus qu'elle n'eut dû savoir"[She knew everything and even much more than she should have known] (257r).

9. L'Abbé Irailh, *Querelles littéraires, ou, mémoires pour servir à l'histoire de révolutions de le république des lettres depuis Homère jusqu' à hos jours* (Geneva: Slatkine, 1967). Cited by Fernand Zamaron, *Louise Labé: Dame de franchise* (Paris: Nizet, 1968), 76.

10. One kind of literary transgression, Louise Labé's departure from the Petrarchan lyric model, has usefully been studied by a number of critics, including Jones, *Currency of Eros*, Deborah Lesko Baker, *The Subject of Desire: Petrarchan Poetics and the Female Voice in Louise Labé* (West Lafayette, Ind.: Purdue University Press, 1996), and Gillian Jondorf, "Petrarchan Variations in Pernette du Guillet and Louise Labé," *Modern Language Review* 7.1 (1976): 766–78. I am indebted to all of them in my readings of Louise Labé.

11. For further readings of this preface, see François Rigolot, "La Préface à la Renaissance: Un discours sexué?" in *Cahiers de l'Association internationale des études françaises* 42 (1990): 121–36, and

Baker, *Subject of Desire*, 11–40. Paula Sommers, "Louise Labé: The Body in the Text," in *Renaissance Women Writers: French Texts/American Contexts*, ed. Anne R. Larsen and Colette H. Winn (Detroit: Wayne State University Press, 1994), 88–90, analyzes the extent to which the speaker assumes her own body in the prefatory letter.

12. On the related question of women writers' concept of time as it relates to the process of writing, see Cathy Yandell, "Carpe Diem, Poetic Immortality, and the Gendered Ideology of Time," in *Renaissance Women Writers*, 115–29.

13. See *A Dictionarie of the French and English Tongues*, ed. Randall Cotgrave (1632–).

14. Frances M. Biscoglio, "Unspun Heroes: Iconography of the Spinning Woman in the Middle Ages," *Journal of Medieval and Renaissance Studies* 25 (1995): 164. On the gendering of tasks, see also Merry Wiesner-Hanks, "'A Learned Task and Given to Men Alone': The Gendering of Tasks in Early Modern German Cities," *The Journal of Medieval and Renaissance Studies* 25 (1995): 95, who shows that in Reformation ideology, when women performed an activity such as sewing clothes, it was defined as domestic work; when men performed the same activity, also in their own homes, it was considered production.

15. See Juliana Schiesari, "The Face of Domestication: Physiognomy, Gender Politics, and Humanism's Others," in *Women, "Race," and Writing in the Early Modern Period*, ed. Margo Hendricks and Patricia Parker (London: Routledge, 1994), 55–56; Joan Kelly, *Women, History, and Theory* (Chicago: University of Chicago Press, 1984), 65–109; Constance Jordan, *Renaissance Feminism: Literary Texts and Political Models* (Ithaca: Cornell University Press, 1990), 100–105; *Rewriting the Renaissance: The Discourses of Sexual Difference in Early Modern Europe*, ed. Margaret W. Ferguson, Maureen Quilligan, and Nancy Vickers (Chicago: University of Chicago Press, 1986), xv–xxxi.

16. Biscoglio, "Unspun Heroes," 165.

17. "C'est pourquoi ceux-là font fort bien, qui ne voulant pas faire apprendre un métier à leurs filles, à cause de leurs grandes richesses ou de la dignité de leur rang et de leur fortune, leur apprennent l'art de travailler en tapisserie, ou de filer de la soïe, ou de joüer de quelque instrument, afin qu'elles aïent dequoi éviter l'oisiveté" [This is why they who do not wish their daughters to learn a trade, because of their great riches or the dignity of their status and fortune, do so well to teach them the art of tapestry or spinning silk or playing some instrument, so that (the daughters) will have something to do to keep idleness at bay]. See Erasmus, *Le mariage chretien*, 106–7.

18. Juan Luis Vives, *Institution de la femme Chrestienne tant en son enfance, què mariege et viduité, aussi de l'Office du mery. Le tout, composé en latin par Loys Vives, et nouvellement traduict en lengue françoyse*, trans. Pierre de Changy (Lyon: Chez S. Sabon, pour a. Constantin, n.d.).

19. Compare vv. 36–39 of Theocritus, "The Distaff," in *Poems*, trans. Anna Rist (Chapel Hill: University of North Carolina Press, 1978), 201, for a possible model for Ronsard's poem, where the spindle serves the male poet's purposes in a different way: "Theugenis shall have the name / of the best bespindled wife, / to remind her all her life / of her poetry-loving friend."

20. Pierre de Ronsard, *Œuvres complètes*, ed. Jean Céard, Daniel Ménager, and Michel Simonin (Paris: Gallimard, 1993–94), 1:401; idem, *Œuvres complètes*, ed. Paul Laumonier (Paris: Société des Textes Français Modernes, 1914–75), 17:265.

21. Hélisenne de Crenne, *Œuvres* (1560) (Geneva: Slatkine, 1977), O4v. On various readings of Catherine's "A ma quenouille," see Tilde Sankovitch, *French Women Writers and the Book: Myths of Access and Desire* (Syracuse: Syracuse University Press, 1988), 53, who reads the poem as an exposition of the poet's polarization: "Torn between the pen and the spindle, between the female muse and the male-originated conventionality, both of which represent, torturingly, herself and not-herself, Catherine seems here mutilated and alienated, whether she opts for one or the other"; in contrast, Ann Rosalind Jones, "Surprising Fame: Renaissance Gender Ideology and Women's Lyric," *The Poetics of Gender*, ed. Nancy K. Miller (New York: Columbia University Press, 1985), 85, sees the distaff as transforming the household emblem into a "shelter against insult and infamy," and in idem, *The Currency of Eros*, 61, it resolves "an apparently irreconcilable ideological opposition." Constance Jordan, *Renaissance Feminism: Literary Texts and Political Models* (Ithaca: Cornell University Press, 1990), 183, reads the spindle as a "sign promising the realization of a poetic vision of heroic dimensions." Anne Larsen and Colette Winn, from different perspectives,

read the poem as a salutory fusion of the two poles of Catherine's existence: see Anne R. Larsen, "The French Humanist Scholars: Les Dames des Roches," in *Women Writers of the Renaissance and Reformation,* ed. Wilson, 239, and Colette Winn, "Mère/fille/femme/muse: Maternité et créativité dans les œuvres des Dames des Roches," *Travaux de Littérature* 4 (1991): 55–68. It seems to me that while Catherine does indeed make the case for a kind of "mixed life" in this sonnet and elsewhere, the scales in her work are weighted heavily in favor of bold, humanist endeavors over safe and sanctioned domestic roles. Rather than echo Helisenne de Crenne's assailing of the distaff (O4v) or prefigure Marie de Gournay's sweeping repudiation of it, Catherine more subtly but deftly adapts the distaff to her own political purposes; see Marie de Gournay, *"Égalité des hommes et des femmes* (1622)," in *La fille d'alliance de Montaigne,* ed. Mario Schiff (Geneva: Slatkine, 1978), 61. Whether done consciously or not, the effect of Catherine's distaff is one of subversion under the guise of reconciliation.

22. Joachim Du Bellay, *L'Olive,* ed. E. Caldarini (Geneva: Droz, 1974), 119; Antoine de Baïf, *Amours de Francine,* ed. M. Auget-Chiquet (Paris: Hachette, 1908), 2:102; and Pontus de Tyard, *Les Erreurs amoureuses,* ed. John McClelland (Geneva: Droz, 1967), 134–35.

23. See Nicolas Ruwet, *Langage, musique, poésie* (Paris: Seuil, 1972), 193ff.; Françoise Charpentier, "L'ordre et triomphe du corps," in Françoise Charpentier, ed., *Œuvres poétiques de Louise Labé précédées des Rymes de Pernette du Guillet, avec un choix de Blasons du corps féminin* (Paris: Gallimard, 1983), 12–16; Louise Labé, *Œuvres,* ed. Rigolot, 23. Compare also Rigolot's reading of Labé's sonnet as an ironic response to Magny's: François Rigolot, *Louise Labé Lyonnaise ou la Renaissance au féminin* (Paris: Honoré Champion, 1997), 88–95.

24. See Jones, *Currency of Eros,* 165.

25. Olivier de Magny, *Les Souspirs,* ed. David Wilkin (Geneva: Droz, 1978), 65–66; also reprinted in Rigolot, ed., *Labé,* 228.

26. *Petrarch's Lyric Poems,* ed. Robert M. Durling (Cambridge, Mass.: Harvard University Press, 1976), 306; the translation is by Durling.

27. For a transposition of this question into the late twentieth century, see Luce Irigaray, *Ethique de la différence sexuelle* (Paris: Les Editions de Minuit, 1984), 128–29, whose linguistic study suggests that males tend to speak more self-referentially, even when it is a question of loving another person.

28. For further analysis of Labé's use of the *blason,* see François Rigolot, *Louise Labé Lyonnaise ou la Renaissance au féminin,* 100–106, and Jones, *Currency of Eros,* 161–72.

29. Tyard, *Les Erreurs amoureuses,* 135.

30. *Blasons anatomiques du corps feminin* in *Blasons, poésies anciennes recueillies et mises en ordre,* ed. D. H. Méon (Paris: Guillemot, 1809), 16.

31. *Blasons,* ed. Méon, 13.

32. Robert Cottrell, "Scève's *Blasons* and the Logic of the Gaze," *Esprit Créateur* 28 (summer 1988): 76. See also Lawrence D. Kritzman, *The Rhetoric of Sexuality and the Literature of the French Renaissance* (Cambridge: Cambridge University Press, 1991), 105, who argues that in the *blasons,* discrete bodily attributes metaphorically elicit hunger or thirst. He notes further that in this genre the female body is conceptualized as being elsewhere (111).

33. Nancy Vickers, "Diana Described: Scattered Woman and Scattered Rhyme," in *Writing and Sexual Difference,* ed. Elizabeth Abel (Chicago: University of Chicago Press, 1982), 106–7. Compare Elizabeth Cropper, "The Beauty of Woman: Problems in the Rhetoric of Renaissance Portraiture," in *Rewriting the Renaissance,* 175–190, for her related thesis claiming that the woman herself is necessarily absent from the *paragone* of Renaissance portraiture and poetry.

34. François Lecercle, *La chimère de Zeuxis: Portrait poétique et portrait peint en France et en Italie à la Renaissance* (Tubingen: Gunter Narr Verlag, 1987), 3.

35. Baker, *Subject of Desire,* 161.

36. Dudley B. Wilson, *Descriptive Poetry in France from Blason to Baroque* (New York: Barnes & Noble, 1967), 28–29.

37. Petrarch, *Rime sparse,* 37.

38. Tyard, *Les Erreurs amoureues,* 96.

39. Labé wrote the first sonnet of her collection in Italian; the influence of Petrarch on her work is unmistakable.

40. While a negative construction begins Labé's Italian sonnet ("Non havria Ulysse o qualunqu'altro mai," 121), it technically does not constitute a retraction.

41. Isotopy was defined by A. J. Greimas as "a complex of manifold semantic categories making possible the uniform reading of a [text]"; see A. J. Greimas, *Du sens* (Paris: Seuil, 1979), 88, translated and cited by Umberto Eco, *Interpretation and Overinterpretation*, ed. Stefan Collini (Cambridge: Cambridge University Press, 1992), 62.

42. For an insightful presentation of this question, see Jones, *Currency of Eros*, 12 seq.

43. By "negative space" I do not mean "beyond the structure of significance itself," as Peter Stallybrass and Allon White define it in *Politics of Transgression* (Ithaca: Cornell University Press, 1986), 18, but rather in the sense of antimatter in particle physics. Much as the interaction of matter and antimatter calls forth energy (according to the laws of conservation of mass energy), so Louise Labé's destruction of canonical images and rhetorical strategies actuates the possibility of creation.

Masculine Rhetoric and the French *Blason anatomique*

Jeffery Persels

T he sixteenth-century *vogue* of the French anatomical *blason* illustrates a conspicuously masculine use of figurative language.[1] It amounts to a distinctly male
rhetoric based, paradoxically, not on representation of the male body and its
specific gender attributes, but on the encomiastic dismemberment of the female body.
The exclusively male *blasonneurs* consciously subvert what they objectify as characteristically feminine into praise of the omnipotence of masculine creation and into self-referential and self-congratulatory verse. Such privileging of a masculinist trope is,
moreover, far from exclusive to the *blason*. Not only does it renew the classical evaluation of rhetoric according to a scale of virile qualities—one has only to consult Cicero,
Tacitus, or Quintilian—but it also participates in what I argue is early modern humanism's manifest desire to link itself to the vitality of the masculine, as Rabelais's prose, for
example, demonstrates.[2]

Implicated in the 1534 Affaire des Placards, the poet Clément Marot fled France
for the temporarily Lutheran-sympathizing haven of the court of Ferrara. Under the
cultivated influence of Duchess Renée de France and her circle—which included
Madame de Soubise and her daughter, to whom Marot addressed other verse—he
composed in 1535 an epigram now commonly referred to as "Le beau tétin" [The
beautiful breast]. This particularly skillful distillation of native medieval French and
Renaissance Italian anatomical love lyric traditions must have met with some success
as a contest of sorts was organized, the fruits of which were allegedly dispatched to
Marot and the duchess at Ferrara. Maurice Scève's "Le sourcil" [The eyebrow] was
crowned *blason* laureate, and the first of many editions of the poems was printed as
early as 1536.[3]

Over the next fifteen years or so, the collection was augmented through several
reeditions, to the point where all the body parts considered worthy of poetic elucida-
tion, prurient or otherwise, found singular, if not double or even triple, rendition. The
mode suffered, according to some (including Marot himself), from the often maladroit
pornography of its lesser practitioners and from the advent of the pendant *contreblason*.[4]
This genre of counter or mock encomium, which delights in vituperating the original
object of desire, was initially and playfully launched by Marot himself in what has
become known as "Le laid tétin" [The ugly breast], and was most assiduously cultivated
by the heavy-handed Christian moralizer Charles de la Hueterie.[5]

The genre is, in fact, a troubling avatar of the love lyric, particularly if one takes offense at its salacious aspects, as La Hueterie did and as, for very different reasons, the editor Françoise Charpentier seems to do in the preface to her anthology of *blasons ana-tomiques* (offered as a "dossier" in *Œuvres poétiques de Louise Labé,* still the most accessible if incomplete modern edition of the poems). While praising the initial charm of Marot's "Beautiful Breast," she does not hesitate to lament the creation of the "regrettable 'Ugly Breast'" and what she calls the "realistic" *blason* in general. She qualifies much of the work of the *blasonneurs* as "raw," "satirical," "brutal," "crude," and "violent."[6] Such verse seems indeed to represent a violent discursive dismemberment of the female body, what Nancy Vickers has called "the poetics of fragmentation," into parts the sum of which can never hope to equal a whole.[7] Woman is metonymically subsumed in the erotic play centered on one body part at a time. The *blason* thus becomes emblematic of the literally trenchant and so reductive power of a male gaze; its buoyant and irreverent feast of the disjointed body reflects the integrity of the masculine by its very refraction of the feminine.

In marking the salient distinctions between the *blason anatomique* and its medieval predecessors, Alison Saunders cites the increasing self-assurance of the poetic voice, what Lawrence Kritzman has described as the "virtuoso of a corporeal rhetoric."[8] The physical description of parceled female bodies, according to Saunders, "serves simply as a prelude to what is for the *blasonneur* the more important aspect—the effect of this beauty on his own subjectivity and sensibility." Robert Cottrell has explored the logic of that ultimately self-sufficient male gaze in Maurice Scève's five *blasons.* He maps the trajectory of Scève's description from the ostensible cult of the lady-object to actual worship of his own poetic creation, of "what he has produced, his own thing, 'ceste despouille mienne,' the record of his maleness, of his generative power, which he has placed in front of the lady's image where it can be admired and praised by all who care to 'look,' who care to read."[9] All these readings suggest that authorial focus shifts ultimately from object to subject, that the *blason* is less about praise of the other's beauty and more about the poet's own artistic and aesthetic virtuosity.

Moreover, the nature of these encomia, so conspicuously illustrative of masculine desire, encourages the development of a poetic style peculiar to the representation of that desire, a style which reflects the intentional virility of much sixteenth-century French humanist writing. As I discuss elsewhere, there is a case to be made for this identification, one which argues for a contemporary context in which the phenomenon of the *blason's* masculinist trope may be most effectively read. Aside from the joyous phallic triumph of the *Gargantua* excerpt, which I treat below, Rabelais's earlier *Pantagruel* makes a highly nuanced effort to tie up the success of evangelical humanism's political and spiritual agenda with Panurge's own *aiguillettes* (points used to attach a codpiece to upper stocks). That is, pantagruelism displaces scholasticism and related outmoded "isms" precisely because, through its eponymous prophet and his disciples, it is identified with virile health and virile display. It is not mere coincidence that related proselytizer Marguerite de Navarre focuses precisely on and censures this identification of masculinity with reason in her arguably misandrous tale cycle, *L'Heptaméron*. The bluster of masculinity is discredited by the female tellers as destructive, unethical, irrational, and most importantly, contrary to the precepts of Pauline Christianity.[10]

The following interpretations of three specific examples are designed to highlight that identification, that style, that bluster. I examine first the most celebrated and paradigmatic *blason*, Marot's "Beautiful Breast"; second, what I consider to be a key, contextualizing antecedent to that poem, the overt hymn to masculine potency that is François Rabelais's 1534 description of Gargantua's codpiece; and finally, Rémy Belleau's later, less well known rhetorical act of male bonding with Pléiade leader Pierre de Ronsard, "La cerise" [The cherry] of the 1550s. First, Marot's "Beautiful Breast":

(1) Tetin refect, plus blanc, qu'un œuf,	(1) [Plump breast, whiter than egg,
(2) Tetin de satin blanc tout neuf,	(2) Breast of newest white satin,
(3) Tetin, qui fays honte à la Rose,	(3) Breast who shames the rose,
(4) Tetin plus beau, que nulle chose,	(4) Breast more beautiful than anything.
(5) Tetin dur, non pas tetin voyre,	(5) Firm breast, not of flesh surely,
(6) Mais petite boule d'Ivoyre,	(6) But rather a little ball of ivory,
(7) Au milieu duquel est assise	(7) In the middle of which sits
(8) Une Fraize, ou une Cerise,	(8) A strawberry, or a cherry,
(9) Que nul ne voit, ne touche aussi,	(9) That none sees nor touches either,
(10) Mais je gage, qu'il est ainsi:	(10) But I wager that this is so.
(11) Tetin doncq au petit bout rouge,	(11) Breast with the little red tip,
(12) Tetin, qui jamais ne se bouge	(12) Breast who never stirs,
(13) Soit pour venir, soit pour aller,	(13) Neither to come nor to go,
(14) Soit pour courir, soit pour baller:	(14) Neither to run nor to dance.
(15) Tetin gauche, Tetin mignon,	(15) Left breast, darling breast,
(16) Tousjours loing de son compaignon,	(16) Breast ever far from its twin,
(17) Tetin, qui porte tesmoignage	(17) Breast who gives a hint
(18) Du demeurant du personnage,	(18) Of the rest of the body,
(19) Quand on te voit, il vient à maints	(19) When we see you,
(20) Une envie dedans les mains	(20) Many of us have hands
(21) De te taster, de te tenir:	(21) That itch to touch you, to hold you,
(22) Mais il se fault bien contenir	(22) But we must hold ourselves back
(23) D'en approcher, bon gré ma vie,	(23) From approaching you, upon my life!
(24) Car il viendroit une autre envie.	(24) For another itch would come of it.
(25) O Tetin ne grand, ne petit,	(25) O Breast neither large nor small,
(26) Tetin meur, Tetin d'appetit,	(26) Ripe breast, appetizing breast,
(27) Tetin, qui nuict, et jour criez	(27) Breast who night and day cries out:
(28) Mariez moy tost, mariez,	(28) Marry me soon, marry me!

(29) Tetin, qui t'enfles, et repoulses	(29) Breast who swells and pushes back
(30) Ton gorgerin de deux bons poulses,	(30) Your gorget a good two inches,
(31) A bon droict heureux on dira	(31) Rightly will he be called happy
(32) Celluy, qui de laict t'emplira,	(32) Who with milk will fill you,
(33) Faisant d'ung Tetin de pucelle,	(33) Making of the maiden's breast
(34) Tetin de femme entiere, et belle.[11]	(34) A woman's breast, whole and beautiful.]

Providing the model for the subsequent tournament—and tournament with its medieval resonance is an appropriate metaphor, an exclusive contest entr'hommes for poetic dominance—Marot's "Beautiful Breast," for all its seeming licentiousness, is first and foremost a rhetorical exercise in controlling male desire. Through skillful syntactical sleight of hand, he manages both to bare that breast which "Nature customarily hides"[12] and then to cloak it in a mantle of orthodox probity. A master of the discursive striptease, Marot takes the assumed male reader to the brink of sexual fulfillment only to pull back and redeem his frustrated desire by rechanneling it into the sanctioned outlet of legitimate paternity.

To do this, he subverts inherited structures of the satirical encomium, which, as both Saunders and Annette Tomarken go to some lengths to demonstrate, was primarily descriptive. The blason marotique is not the ungainly, clumsily pictorial depiction of female beauty in the fashion of its medieval French precursors and of such lesser, contemporary blasonneurs as Marot's arch-rival François Sagon (whose "Pied" or "Foot" is irretrievably pedestrian). Rather, the blason marotique is a plastic, narrative device for giving a detailed account of the mechanics of masculine desire and poesis.

The poem initially turns on the commonplaces of poetic metaphor and analogy. Predominant are affinities to naturally occurring substances, precious and ordinary: eggshell, white satin, roses, and ivory for the breast proper; strawberries and cherries for the nipples, calling ultimately on all five senses to flesh out the object. The optical, tactile, olfactory, and gustatory comparisons (not to mention the aural pleasure of the rhyme) intensify our physical sensitivity to the allurements of the breast, across which the octosyllabic verse brushes teasingly. The poetic distance of mere description, of such abstract objectification, is narrowed however when the first-person pronoun, here announcing the switch to narrative, trespasses on the chastity of the breast: "Que nul ne voit, ne touche aussi / Mais je gage qu'il est ainsi" (lines 9–10). Soon thereafter, the actual gaze, evoked by the earlier comparisons, is indulged in the demonstration of the breast's youthful tautness. Sated, it gives way to the desire to feel, to touch, to caress, and the brilliantly allusive yet stumbling alliteration—"De te taster, de te tenir" (line 21)—inexorably leads the poet to the very brink of the tacitly understood consummation, "Car il viendroit une autre envie" (line 24).

At this crucial moment Marot draws back, apostrophizing with a manifestly reluctant cry of barely controlled excitement—"O Tetin ne grand, ne petit" (line 25)—and hastens to legitimize the expression of his very illegitimate desire. He immediately invokes, and for the first time, the mature breast (*tetin meur*), making it cry out for marriage.[13] Rampant male desire is, in effect, to be denied, subjugated, and sublimated to the demands of the only sanctioned form of sexual expression, productive conjugal intercourse, what Saunders notes is a "curiously domestic and even moral conclusion"—one which distinguishes it sharply from its possible Italian models.[14] Happy is the man, not who succumbs to the purely sexual allure of the maiden's breast, but whose desire ends in literal physiological fulfillment: conception. The metamorphosis from seductive virgin breast to woman's breast bursting with milk redefines the initial concept of beauty. Purely erotic beauty is redeemed. The male gaze rights itself and stands back in wonder at the fruit of its own labors, both the fertile, impregnated woman metonymically displayed in the cornucopian breast, and the trajectory of male desire that is the *blason* proper.

The male has in essence appropriated the breast for his own, he has filled it, made it beautiful; its beauty is corrected, complete only through his fertilizing intercession. The breast, as Kritzman similarly concludes, "becomes an object of narcissistic beauty that paradoxically endows the male figure with the power to impregnate the woman and transform her into an ideal maternal object."[15] The beautiful breast becomes the poem and vice versa, and in so doing the poem surpasses in importance the ostensible object of the encomium. The reader or the listener, like Marot, delights not in the beautiful breast but in the virtuosity of its representation. Even more importantly, Marot lays express claim to that representation: his rhetorical strategy both narrates and enacts for us explicitly this procreative arrogation, the Scévian "despouille mienne" explicated by Cottrell.[16]

The *blason,* as I have said and as Marot's "Beautiful Breast" illustrates, is less a rhetorical celebration of womanhood, of the feminine, than it is of male potency and male poesis. And this celebration was not limited to the love lyric or even to verse in general but extended even to such work of seriocomic earnestness as François Rabelais's evangelical humanist chronicles. As if expressly to foreshadow the mode by providing a most flagrant example of such masculine appropriation, Rabelais took care to include a curiously detailed description of the infant giant's *braguette* [codpiece] in the 1534 *Gargantua*. It amounts to a remarkable prose *blason de la braguette,* and like the later *couillon* or "little testicle" poems of the 1546 *Tiers livre* (chapters 26 and 28), links Rabelais to the popularity both of the mock encomium tradition and humanist exploitation of the masculine trope:

Pour la braguette: feurent levées seize aulnes un quartier d'icelluy mesmes drap, et feut la forme d'icelle comme d'un arc boutant, bien estachée joyeusement à deux belles boucles d'or, que prenoient deux crochetz d'esmail, en un chascun desquelz estoit enchassée une grosse esmeraugde de la grosseur d'une pomme d'orange. Car (ainsi que dict Orpheus *libro de lapidibus,* et Pline *libro ultimo*) elle a vertu erective et confortative du membre naturel. L'exiture de la braguette estoit à la longueur d'une canne, deschicquetée comme les chausses, avecques le damas bleu flottant comme davant. Mais, voyans la belle brodure de canetille, et les plaisans entrelatz d'orfeverie, garniz de fins diamens, fins rubiz, fines turquoyses, fines esmeraugdes et unions Persicques, vous l'eussiez comparée à une belle corne d'abondance, telle que voyez es antiquailles, et telle que donna Rhea es deux nymphes Adrastea et Ida, nourrices de Jupiter. Tousjours gualante, succulente, resudante, tousjours verdoyante, tousjours fleurissante, tousjours fructifiante, plene d'humeurs, plene de fleurs, plene de fruictz, plene de toutes delices. Je advoue dieu s'il ne la faisoit bon veoir. Mais je vous en exposeray bien dadvantaige au livre que j'ay faict *De la dignité des braguettes.* D'un cas vous advertis, que si elle estoit bien longue et bien ample, si estoit elle bien guarnie au dedans et bien avitaillée, en rien ne ressemblant les hypocriticques braguettes d'un tas de muguetz, qui ne sont plenes que de vent, au grand interest du sexe feminin.[17]

[From the codpiece was taken up sixteen-and-a-quarter ells of the same cloth (of his upper stocks—that is, white muslin). And the form of it was like a flying buttress, most merrily fastened with two beautiful gold buckles, caught up by two enamel hooks, in each of which was set a big emerald the size of an orange. For—as Orpheus says, in his book *On Stones,* and Pliny, in his last book—it has the virtue of erecting and comforting the natural member. The outlet of the codpiece was of a cane's length, slashed like the hose, with the beautiful blue damask floating as before. But if you saw the lovely gold embroidery and the attractive pleating with precious stones, garnished with fine diamonds, fine rubies, fine turquoises, fine emeralds, and great Persian pearls, you would have compared it to a lovely cornucopia, such as you see in the antique shops, and such as Rhea gave to the two young nymphs Adrastea and Ida, wet nurses of Jupiter—always gallant, succulent, always verdant, always flourishing, always fructifying, full of humors, full of fruits, full of delights. I acknowledge God if it was not good to see it! But I will expound much more about it in the book I have done *On the Dignity of Codpieces.* But I will tell you one thing, that if it was very long and very full, so was it well furnished inside and well victualed, and wholly unlike the hypocritical codpieces of a bunch of fops, which are full only of wind, to the great disadvantage of the feminine sex.][18]

Rabelais here, as elsewhere in his chronicles, focuses the richness of his rhetoric on indulgent praise of the male member and its attributes, invariably represented metonymically by the "magnificent codpiece" of sixteenth-century fashion, which, in this unique and therefore determining instance, proves not to be hyperbolic. The child giant's genitals merit the lengthiest and costliest sartorial attention of Gargantua's livery, and are thus set off as the quintessential sign and promise of manhood, a thesis supported by the subsequent possessive bickering of his nannies:

—Elle est à moy, disoit l'une.

—C'est la mienne, disoit l'aultre.

—Moy, (disoit l'aultre) n'y auray je rien? Par ma foy je la couperay doncques.

   —Ha couper, (disoit l'aultre) vous luy feriez mal ma dame, coupez vous la chose aux enfans, il seroyt monsieur sans queue.[19]

["It's mine," one would say.

"No, mine," would say another.

"And I," another would say, "shan't I get anything? My word, then I'll cut it off."

"Huh, cut it off!" said another. "You'd hurt him, Madam; do you go cutting their things off children? He'd be Sir No-tail."][20]

In this joyously and literally phallocentric celebration, Gargantua seems a last offshoot of the swollen-membered race of the Rabelaisian golden age, the extinction of which women mourn at the beginning of *Pantagruel:* "Et d'iceulx est perdue la race, ainsi comme disent les femmes, car elles lamentent continuellement qu'*il n'en est plus de ces gros* etc."[21] And as such, his infancy bears trappings of the divine.

Leo Steinberg's controversial rehabilitation of medieval and Renaissance depictions of Christ's sexuality suggests an interesting frame of reference for this rare, if not unique, rendering of sixteenth-century infant eroticism.[22] Mary and/or Anne inspecting the Christ child's genitals or pointing them out to verifying Magi, confirm that the divine child is indeed "complete in all the parts of a man," irrefutable proof of the Incarnation. Rabelais's prose *blason* of the ornate reliquary designed to house Gargantua's sex confirms the child-prince's wholeness, his incarnation (a confirmation strengthened by the burlesque "annunciation" of his birth out of Gargamelle's left ear). He, by virtue of the one part, the penis, is complete in all the parts of a man.

Rabelais supposes further that the reader would make automatic comparison between this masculine sign sine qua non and the mythical horn of plenty. The complete analogy transfers the entire stock of the cornucopia's fertile qualities to the codpiece. The association between sexual potency and textual allusion, an association persuasively argued and explicated by Terence Cave, provides the comic elevation and crescendo of the description.[23] It builds accordingly on a scaffold of classical authority, expensive adornment, divine comparison—the horn of plenty awarded to the nurse-maids of Gargantua's implied divine predecessor—and finally deific attributes, in the verbal frothing over the fertile qualities of the horn, now conflated with the original subject. The codpiece indeed appears as a sort of emblem or motto-bearing device, one with which the reader is already familiar from Panurge's earlier celebratory *braguette*.[24]

Finally, our narrator refers us to the authoritative book-length study he has composed on this very topic, *On the Dignity of Codpieces,* the only book, aside from the present chronicles, for which Rabelais's narrator takes credit. The book comically takes its place in the Rabelaisian corpus, both "body" and "writings," alongside the institution of the Christian humanist prince that, it has been argued, is the purpose of both *Pantagruel* and *Gargantua*.[25] Just as Montaigne will assert of his penis a half-century later—"Chacune de mes pieces me faict esgalement moy que toute autre. Et nulle autre ne me faict plus proprement homme que cette cy"—Gargantua's magnificent codpiece and its equally magnificent contents (for so the narrator testifies: "so was it well furnished inside and well victualed") both symbolize and define the greatness of the prince they adorn.[26] Far from suggesting any damaging disproportion between codpiece and penis, between masculine sign and signified manhood (as one might well fear in the case of Panurge, Rabelais's other, lesser champion of the fashion), the *blason* of Gargantua's princely *braguette* illustrates a desire to associate the Rabelaisian agenda, incarnated in the body of its triumphant giant-prince, with the fullness and plenitude of perfected virility. Fallen everyman and comic apostle Panurge aspires to this fullness and plenitude but fails, inevitably, to attain it. The future king of Utopia quite literally embodies a utopian ideal of virile repleteness. He carries within his "well-furnished" and "well-victualed" codpiece the rhetorically attested procreative promise of his idealized rule, of the evangelical humanist reform—a promise to be fulfilled at the close of the dynasty's chronicles. If Panurge, by way of contrast, embodies (with a comic wink from Rabelais) the masculine crisis provoked by the reality of man's distance from this ideal, such a contrast only serves to underscore the pervasiveness of the desire to associate the ideal with the virile in humanist discourse.

The fertility of Marot's beautiful breast, due solely to its sanctioned conjunction with the male's completing, fulfilling power, is thus preceded by the cornucopian codpiece, which is complete unto itself. Sheathed in such man-made enhancements, the *blasonneurs,* Rabelais especially, write against women, not to produce the traditionally misogynistic diatribe characteristic of the *querelle des femmes,* but to emphasize in a highly rhetorical manner—that of defining, defending, and admittedly stretching the measure of the masculine—the value and import of their identity and their endeavors. Such rhetorical emphasis matches their ideal of manhood, reflected in the peculiarly overstated virile fashion silhouette of the sixteenth century. Marot's "Beautiful Breast" participates then in a rhetorical tradition that Rabelaisian prose style did much to define. To very different ends—the light love lyric versus ideological portraiture—they make pointed use of contemporary masculine signifiers.[27]

These two ends are joined, to a degree worth elucidating, in a later poem by Pléiade poet Rémy Belleau, who, influenced by the *blasonneurs* of twenty years previous, renders explicit in his "La cerise" [The cherry] a consciously masculine appropriation and validation of rhetoric and poetics, whether Marotic or Rabelaisian, in what amounts to a gendered ideology of love poetry. Addressed with patent modesty to that "favorite of Apollo," Pierre de Ronsard, the epistle runs to more than 240 verses. It belongs to a series of poems Belleau called his "petites inventions" [little inventions], originally published as *Petites hymnes de son invention* [Little hymns of his own invention] together with his 1556 translation of Anacreon's odes. In "The cherry," Belleau defines invention as a golden age gift of the gods "pour adoucir nos passions" (line 18), meaning both "to mitigate our sufferings" and "to sweeten our desires"—a deft double entendre he exploits throughout the poem, for the cherry is made to perform both functions.[28]

Belleau mythologizes from the start the subject of his hymn. After ostensibly establishing his friend as a greater poet of flowers and fountains, he accepts the humble cherry as his poetic lot, with the thinly veiled ambition to make it—that is, the eponymous cherry and its hymn—worthy of Ronsard's superior attention. The poetic undertaking is consciously designated as an effort to privilege the poetic process in the context of rivalry, one poet vying with the other. The cherry is already commandeered to this end, and is of course immediately associated with female anatomy: "son beau teint, / Dont celuy de m'amye est teint" [its beautiful hue, / Which tints my love's complexion] (lines 9–10). The cherry is eventually conflated with the nipple, a convention already exploited in Marot's "Beautiful Breast," as we have seen.[29]

In the hallowed topos of an Ovidian golden age, replete with wine, grain, Athena's olive, and Apollo's laurel, Belleau introduces the cherry, discovered and cultivated by none other than "le Dieu Jardinier" [the gardener God], one of Priapus's more common epithets.[30]

(65) Print la Cerise, et tout divin	(65) [He took the Cherry and, god that he was,
(66) La planta dedans son jardin	(66) Planted it in his garden,
(67) Et l'enta comme la seconde	(67) And grafted it then and there,
(68) Pour l'entretien de ce bas monde.[31]	(68) For the sustenance of this lowly world.]

That which is soon to become conflated with the nipple and then metonymically read as woman is a creation of the phallic god of male potency, a significant origin for both the fruit and the *blason* it inspires, firmly planted in the domain of things male.

The cherry meets with instant popularity, particularly among the female goddesses: the muses are especially fond of this new fruit, and Juno herself leaves off nectar for it. Their pillage of an "invention" destined for mere mortals reaches such a point that Priapus finds it necessary to shut the garden gate against these divine poachers. The source for this poem's immediate inspiration, the cherry, ingested by the classical goddesses of that inspiration, depicted as so many insatiable bacchantes, becomes inextricably associated with them. It is incarnated through them—as in the "twin" nipple to which Belleau will soon refer—and, conveyed to the male poet through women, both threatens and beckons with the traditionally dangerous temptations of the female sex.

The next phase of the hymn strikingly recalls Marot's "Beautiful Breast," not only in the first-person narrative and the weightless octosyllabic verse, but also in the analogy between his love of the cherry and the maiden's love of her breast, and it develops further the association between woman and cherry:

(157) Que j'ayme autant,…	(157) [Which I love as much,
………	………
(159) Que la rose ayme le matin	(159) as the rose loves the morning

(160) Et la pucelle son tetin.[32]   (160) And the maiden her breast.]

Belleau descriptively praises this preeminent fruit among fruits—calling upon muses, nymphs, fruit, and cherry vendors, to aid in his mock-epic song—and caresses the cherry with all the sensual, anaphoric rhetoric and rhythm of Marot's *blason:*

(125) Ainsi ce doux fruit prend naissance,   (125) [And thus this sweet fruit springs to
                                                       life,

(126) Prend sa rondeur, prend sa crois-   (126) Grows round, grows big,
        sance,

(127) Prend le beau vermeillon qui teint   (127) Turns the beautiful vermilion which
                                                       dyes

(128) La couleur palle de son teint.[33]   (128) The paleness of its complexion.]

Like Marot also, Belleau shifts skillfully between high poetic encomium and playful love banter:

(149) Les autres fruits en leur semence   (149) [The other fruits retain in their seed
(150) Retiennent une mesme essence,   (150) The same essence,
(151) Mesme jus, et mesme couleur,   (151) Same juice, and same color,
(152) Mesme bourgeon, et mesme fleur: (152) Same bud, and same flower:
(153) Mais la Cerise verdelette,   (153) But the youthful Cherry,
(154) Palle, vermeille, rondelette,   (154) Pale, vermilion, plump

          ....

(161) Est en liqueur plus differente   (161) Is in liqueur more variable
(162) Que la marine en sa tourmente,   (162) Than the sea in its torment,
(163) En son teint plus que l'arc en ciel,   (163) More colorful than the rainbow,
(164) En douceur plus que le roux miel.[34] (164) Sweeter than honey.]

The cherry is a panacea for all maladies, from sexual frustration to stomachache: "Donnant au sain contement / Et au malade allegement" [Giving contentment to the breast / And relief to the ill].[35] The delicately detailed portrait of the cherry, which serves to distinguish it as preeminent among fruits, functions rhetorically much as Marot's portrait of the breast. By thus setting the humble cherry apart and above, Belleau distinguishes the hymn in its praise that he is composing and which bears its name. Unlike other fruits, or poems, which share the "same" creative process—and here the repetitive use of "mesme" is telling—this fruit, or poem, is different, and has cornucopian cure-all qualities, to which Belleau skillfully returns at the close in what amounts to an *envoi* to Ronsard.

Belleau first switches, however, to a more personal register, fantasizing a scene which, in highly erotic terms, stages the drama of poetic inspiration. He evokes a desired encounter with his lady, who plucks with her lips from a branch lovingly bent down to her—the goddess Juno or perhaps a muse incarnate—by the poet.

(191) Puis apres de la mesme main	(191) [Then afterwards, with the same hand
(192) Doucement descouvrir son sein	(192) Softly uncover her bosom
(193) Pour baiser la sienne jumelle	(193) In order to kiss the twin
(194) De sa ronde et blanche mamelle.[36]	(194) Of her round and white breast.]

The poet passes from this love's nibble of the real fruit to its "twin," his own kiss on her gently exposed nipple. "[L]a baisottant, / la caressant, la mignottant" [nuzzling, / caressing, fondling the nipple], he draws back, in Marotic imitation, from the compelling seduction of the breast: "Cachez vostre beau sain, mignonne, / Cachez, cachez las!" [Hide your beautiful breast, my sweet, / hide it, hide it, alas!].[37] He then effects an astonishing metamorphosis in the most syntactically tortured passage of the hymn, as if to mimic the frustration and physiological suffering of a self-imposed abstinence.

(198) …[I]l m'étonne,	(198) […(I)t startles me,
(199) Ja me faisant mort devenir	(199) Well near killing me
(200) Par l'outrage d'un souvenir	(200) With the outrage of a memory
(201) Que j'ay de ce marbre qui tremble,	(201) That I have of this trembling marble,
(202) De ceste Cerise, qui semble	(202) Of this cherry, which seems
(203) Rougir sur un mont jumelet	(203) To blush on twinned peak,
(204) Fait de deux demi-rons de lait,	(204) Made of two half-moons of milk;
(205) Par qui ma liberté ravie	(205) On account of which my ravished liberty
(206) Dedaigne maintenant la vie,	(206) Now disdains this life,
(207) Par qui je cesse de sonner	(207) On account of which I cease to sing
(208) Celle que je te veux donner,	(208) Of the one I want to give you,
(209) Mon Ronsard, or que redevable	(209) My Ronsard, now however beholden I am
(210) Je te sois, si suis-je excusable	(210) To you, yet am I excused
(211) Par une extreme affection	(211) By a troubled state of mind
(212) D'avoir changé de passion.[38]	(212) From having changed passion.]

This cherry, the nipple of his lady, robs him of his freedom by, the reader may assume, his enslavement through sexual desire, and threatens his life through extreme passion, which ironically the cherry was "invented" to "sweeten" and "mitigate," as the poet expressly defined for us early on. This cherry, perhaps most importantly for the poet, distracts him from his original purpose, that of offering a cherry, that is, the eponymous hymn he is composing, to his friend Ronsard. Belleau bids his lady friend hide her breast so that his sexual desire might not interfere with pure poesis. Female beauty moves from inspiration leading to poetic furor to incitement to a merely carnal furor—an obstacle to poetic creation. Just as the phallic gardener god Priapus had to bar the gate against a marauding Juno and the muses, so Belleau, the aroused poet, must bar the gate against them—against the goddesses, cherries, nipples, and women. His poem—the corrected cherry, destined for a fellow male poet—channels the desire it has aroused into the creative process, appropriating it, taking it away from the muses and from women. Having written himself into a sexual frenzy, he risks being distracted by his own pornographic musing but ultimately is not. The caution against the dangers of poetic and carnal furor that this hymn seems designed to illustrate requires a different denouement. Control can and must ultimately remain the creator's alone, and that control is exercised in and through the poem itself, which, as its name has ever told us, is the cherry. And so the cherry metamorphosizes from fruit to nipple to the text itself, and the conflation of all three is presented to Ronsard for editing.

The conceit of the remaining verses plays off of this conflation. Belleau, while having just demonstrated mastery of his desire, of poesis, yet begs excuse for his "rude et longue chanson" [rough and lengthy song], unworthy of Ronsard's preeminence, and for exposing his weakness of flesh. The cherry/nipple/poem is not yet ripe, and Belleau begs Ronsard to bring it to maturity by the application of his higher poesis:

(222) S'il te plaist, par la confiture	(222) [Please, with the confection
(223) De ton saint miel Hymettien,	(223) Of your holy Hymettian honey
(224) Et du crystal Pegasien	(224) And of the Pegasian crystal
(225) Qui sort de ta bouche sacree,	(225) That flows from your sacred mouth,
(226) Tu la rendras toute sucree,	(226) Make it oh so sweet,
(227) A fin que par toy meurissant	(227) So that ripened by you
(228) On ne la trouve pourrissant.[39]	(228) It will be found rotten by no one.]

Should Ronsard fulfill his request, Belleau states that he need not fear for his cherry/nipple/hymn the ravages of nature: hail, insects, birds, both literal and figurative. He closes his hymn with an analogy between his cherry and those restorative cherries which Ronsard's beloved sends often to Ronsard:

(240) Pour ton estomach devoyé	(240) [For your stomach,
(241) D'estre courbé dessus le livre,	(241) Ruined from being bent over books,
(242) Pour la faire à jamais revivre.[40]	(242) So that you'll make her immortal.]

The cherries and nipples of Ronsard's lady heal the illness that comes from the bookish endeavor of singing her praises, of giving her everlasting life through verse.

Belleau's "Cherry" thus employs many of the rhetorical strategies of Marot's "Beautiful Breast"—strategies that are inherent in the evolution of that fashion.

Woman, here as in the *blason* tradition, metonymically subsumed in the cherry/nipple/ hymn, is set forth as a purely male creation, a mere pretext for a persuasive exchange on poetics from man to man. This is particularly evident in this case since Belleau composes his hymn as an avowed *communiqué entr'hommes*—not unlike the *concours des blasons*—that is, between himself and Ronsard (and Marot), about what it is they do as male poets.

Like Marot's beautiful breast, the cherry in all its connotations stems from male potency and poesis. Within the context of Belleau's myth, the cherry is nurtured by the phallic god of gardens, Priapus; it is his "invention," his "gift" to a suffering mankind, just as Athena's was the olive tree, and Apollo's the laurel. Analogous to Priapus's offering the fruit to humankind, the male poet (Belleau) initially bends down the cherry branch to his inspirational lady/muse. Subsequently and more importantly, he proffers the cherry branch he himself has transformed from fruit to nipple to encomium to Ronsard, another male poet. Like Belleau, Ronsard is himself engaged in a poetic undertaking: creating lyric poems destined ostensibly to lend immortality to his own inspirational lady/muse, whose curative function is to act as figurative midwife to his delivery, to bring him cherries (read nipples as well) as restoratives in the midst of his debilitating poetic furor. Like Marot, Belleau exploits the very stuff their poems are made of—praise of women's beauty and love—to write to Ronsard about what it is they do as male poets and how they do it: they turn feminine beauty into verse and by so doing appropriate it, create it, and transform it into masculine beauty, which they then share with one another, as so many trophies of their triumph over desire. We find ourselves back in the conclusion of Marot's "Beautiful Breast," where the maiden's breast, or the poem, is completed only through male intercession, that is, the fertilization that ultimately leads to the milk-swollen breast, to the fulfilled and fulfilling verse creation, the value of which is both expressed and enhanced by the use of masculine rhetorical figures.

Whether the subject is the female body or male genitalia, the French Renaissance *blason* is a self-referential exercise in masculine braggadocio: men versify on the virtues, inherent or appropriated, of being male. The *blason* is also an exploitation of those virtues to give value to the poetical or rhetorical endeavor: it is good because it is masculine. There was nothing particularly new about this exploitation, but the *blasonneurs,* as these key examples demonstrate and perhaps more than other writers of the French Renaissance, seemed to take particular delight in exposing the mechanics of this association in their works. What is both object and impetus of both their desires and creations they intentionally edge out in favor of the privileged masculine self.

Notes

1. An earlier version of this chapter was presented at the Sixteenth Century Studies Conference (Saint Louis, Mo., 1993). I am grateful to Professor Mary McKinley for her invaluable encouragement and advice regarding its original and final forms.
2. On this argument and for specific classical references, see Jeffery C. Persels, "Bragueta Humanística, or Humanism's Codpiece," *Sixteenth Century Journal* 28 (1997): 79–99.
3. There were seven editions of the *blasons anatomiques* between 1536 and 1572, whether appended to the French translation of Leone Battista Alberti's *Hecatomphile*, or after 1543, published independently, along with the *contreblasons*. On the various editions in an exhaustive descriptive history of the genre, see Alison Saunders, *The Sixteenth-Century Blason Poétique* (Berne: Peter Lang, 1981), and Annette Tomarken, *The Smile of Truth: The French Satirical Eulogy and Its Antecedents* (Princeton: Princeton University Press, 1990). On Marot's sojourn in Ferrara and the celebrated poetic *concours* over which he and Duchess Renée allegedly presided, see specifically C. A. Mayer, *Clément Marot* (Paris: Nizet, 1972), 301–9, and Saunders, *Blason Poétique*, 88–91, 113–39. Little is historically verifiable concerning this contest. It is reasonably conjectured that the *blason* vogue caught on rapidly: the majority of the known poems "were in fact written and printed within a year of Marot's *Beau tetin*," by at least sixteen poets, as named in the first separate edition of 1543 (Saunders, *Blason Poétique*, 116–17).

    Critical attention to the *blason* has grown since the early 1980s. Saunders, *Blason Poétique*, and Tomarken, *Smile of Truth* (only a part of which deals with the *blason*) remain, to my knowledge, the most in-depth studies, and both treat mainly the historical development of the form. See also Alison Saunders, "'La Beauté que femme doibt avoir': La vision du corps dans les blasons anatomiques," published along with other papers germane to the topic, especially those by S. M. Newton Obe and G.-A. Pérouse, in *Le corps à la Renaissance: Actes du XXXe Colloque de Tours, 1987* (Paris: Aux Amateurs de Livres, 1990); Nancy J. Vickers, "The Body Re-Membered: Petrarchan Lyric and the Strategies of Description" in *Mimesis: From Mirror to Method, Augustine to Descartes*, ed. John D. Lyons and Stephen G. Nichols (Hanover, N.H.: University Press of New England, 1982), 100–109; Cathy Yandell, "*A la recherche du corps perdu*: A Capstone of the Renaissance *Blasons anatomiques*," *Romance Notes* 26 (1985): 135–42; Robert Cottrell, "Scève's *Blasons* and the Logic of the Gaze," *L'Esprit créateur* 28 (1988): 68–77; and Lawrence Kritzman, *The Rhetoric of Sexuality and the Literature of the French Renaissance* (Cambridge: Cambridge University Press, 1991), 97–111.
4. Clément Marot, *Œuvres poétiques*, ed. Gérard Defaux, 2 vols. (Paris: Classiques Garnier, 1994), 1:339, lines 75–82, for his later disclamation, "A ceulx, qui après l'epigramme du beau tetin en feirent d'autres":

    (75) Mais, je vous prie, que chascun Blason-   (75) [But I beg you, let each Blasonneur
         neur

    (76) Veuille garder en ses Escripts honneur: (76) Keep his writings honorable.

    (77) Arriere motz, qui sonnent sallement,   (77) Away with base-sounding words!

    (78) Parlons aussi des membres seulement,   (78) Let us speak only of those parts

    (79) Que l'on peult voir sans honte descou-   (79) That one may see without shame uncov-
         vers,   ered,

    (80) Et des honteux ne soillons point noz Vers: (80) And not sully our verses with the shameful
                                                             ones.

    (81) Car quel besoing est il mettre en lumiere   (81) For what need is there to bring to light

    (82) Ce, qu'est Nature à cacher coustumiere?   (82) That which nature customarily hides?]

    All references to Marot's poetry will be to this edition. All translations from the French are my own, unless otherwise indicated, and make no claim beyond the utilitarian.

5. Marot's bitter enemy Charles de la Hueterie, secretary to the duke of Vendôme, sought (along with the equally orthodox François Sagon) to replace Marot as *valet du roi* during the latter's exile in Ferrara and was duly taken to task for it in the "Frippelippes" epistle: "L'aultre ung Huet de sotte grâce,

/ Lequel voulut voler la place / De l'absent." Marot, *Œuvres poétiques*, 141, lines 47–49 [The other was a Huet (pun on *Hueterie:* "cry" or "howl") of foolish grace who wanted to take the place of the absent one (Marot).] Critics such as Pierre Jourda tend to dismiss his relatively copious *blason* contribution: "[Il] n'écrivit pas moins de dix-sept pièces, plus sales et bêtes les unes que les autres"; *Marot* (Paris: Hatier, 1956), 30 [He wrote no fewer than seventeen poems, each one as dirty and stupid as the other]. La Hueterie's *contreblasons* merit, however, more attention as more highly principled antidotes to the perceived moral poison of the *blason* proper. La Hueterie fought fire with fire. His reaction to seeing his censuring efforts blithely collated with the *blasons* in subsequent editions can only be conjectured.

6. Françoise Charpentier, ed., *Œuvres poétiques de Louise Labé précédées des Rymes de Pernette du Guillet, avec un choix de Blasons du corps féminin* (Paris: Gallimard, 1983): "A l'autre extrême, on voit apparaître le contrepoint d'un discours cru, satirique, à l'occasion, brutal assurément jusqu'au grossier, où le corps de l'autre (féminin toujours) opère une rentrée en force, d'une violence parfois à peine supportable" (13); "Le charmant *Beau Tétin* de Marot en marque la frontière, qu'il franchira (on peut le regretter) avec un assez fâcheux contreblason du *Laid Tétin*. Au-dessous, nous sommes dans le domaine du blason réaliste" (15).

7. Vickers, "Body Re-Membered," 100.

8. Saunders, *Blason Poétique*, 67; Kritzman, *Rhetoric of Sexuality*, 97.

9. Cottrell, "Scève's *Blasons*," 76.

10. See Jeffery Persels, "'Qui sommes tous cassez du harnoys,' or, the *Heptaméron* and Uses of the Male Body" in *Heroic Virtue, Comic Infidelity: Reassessing Marguerite de Navarre's* Heptaméron, ed. Dora E. Polachek (Amherst, Mass.: Hestia Press, 1993), 90–102.

11. Marot, *Œuvres poétiques*, 2:241–42.

12. See n. 4 above.

13. In a suggestively analogous situation, François Rabelais's Panurge interprets the chimes of the bells as mimetic of speech, as does Marot, and in the same vein: "Marie toy, marie toy: marie, marie. Si tu te marie, marie, marie, tres bien t'en trouveras, veras, veras. Marie, marie"; François Rabelais, *Œuvres complètes*, ed. Mireille Huchon (Paris: Gallimard, n.d.), 436. The context of Panurge's interpretation lends interesting support to my reading of Marot's *blason*: he finds in the sound of the bells reassurance that he will dominate his wife, his house, and especially his marriage bed.

14. Saunders, *Blason Poétique*, 96.

15. Kritzman, *Rhetoric of Sexuality*, 101.

16. Cottrell, "Scève's *Blasons*," 76.

17. Rabelais, *Œuvres complètes*, 25–26.

18. *The Complete Works of François Rabelais*, trans. Donald M. Frame (Berkeley: University of California Press, 1991), 22–23.

19. Rabelais, *Œuvres complètes*, 35.

20. *Complete Works of François Rabelais*, 31.

21. Rabelais, *Œuvres complètes*, 218. "And of these the race is lost, as the women say, for they continually lament that 'There are no more big ones like that, etc.'"; *The Complete Works of François Rabelais*, 138.

22. Leo Steinberg, *The Sexuality of Christ in Renaissance Art and in Modern Oblivion* (New York: Pantheon, 1983), 15–16, cites the tradition from Saint Augustine on down: "Ecce qui est vir perfectus, caput et corpus, *quod constat omnibus membris* quae suo tempore complebuntur...."; *De civitate Dei*, trans. William M. Green (Cambridge, Mass.: Harvard University Press, 1957), 22:18, emphasis added [Here is described the perfect man—the head and the body *which consists of all the members* whose number will be made up at the proper time]. Caroline Walker Bynum, "The Body of Christ in the Later Middle Ages: A Reply to Leo Steinberg," *Renaissance Quarterly* 39 (1986): 399–439, has, however, taken issue with much of Steinberg's thesis.

23. See especially the chapter devoted to Rabelais by Terence Cave, *The Cornucopian Text: Problems of Writing in the French Renaissance* (Oxford: Clarendon Press, 1979), 183–222. Cave opens his discussion of Rabelais and the paradoxical notion of *copia* with the image of Gargantua's codpiece. Cave reads the profusion of grammatically feminine epithets for the codpiece as evidence of

"ambivalence of genders" or "androgyny" (185). I think the epithets reinforce the masculine rhetorical strategy of appropriating traditionally female reproductive figures, what Cave calls "an aggressively male fiction," just as does Marot's *blason* (186). In both instances, as Cave concedes of *Gargantua* and the early Rabelais, the image is "predominantly affirmative" (204).

24. For a related reading of the sexual implications of the infant Gargantua's real, neoplatonically inspired device, see Jerome Schwartz, "Scatology and Eschatology in Gargantua's Androgyne Device," *Etudes rabelaisiennes* 14 (1977): 265–75.

25. On this interpretation of Rabelais's agenda see especially Edwin Duval, *The Design of Rabelais's Pantagruel* (New Haven: Yale University Press, 1991).

26. Michel de Montaigne, *Essais,* ed. Albert Thibaudet and Maurice Rat (Paris: Garnier, 1962), 866. "Each one of my parts makes me myself as much as every other one. And no other makes me more properly a man than this one"; *The Complete Essays of Montaigne,* trans. Donald M. Frame (Stanford: Stanford University Press, 1965), 677.

27. See n. 10 references. Marguerite de Navarre, as a related example, filters much of her indictment of masculine notions of honor in the *Heptaméron* through the very markedly gender-specific discourse of her male storytellers. With the exception of Dagoucin, their signifier of choice, wielded with as much conviction as Gargantua's codpiece, is the heavy armor of their aristocratic, warrior estate, which both makes them and breaks them in the service of their ladies, and for which, so they argue, they are not receiving the appreciation they deserve.

28. All French citations of Belleau's poem are taken from Rémy Belleau, *Œuvres poétiques,* ed. Ch. Marty-Laveaux (Geneva: Slatkine Reprints, 1965), 71–78.

29. In her suggestive reading of "La cerise," Camilla J. Nilles hastens to put distance between it and the then "degenerated" *blason* tradition, linking it instead to the Italian convention of the bernesque *capitoli,* calling to our attention that a goodly portion of it is, in expected Pléiade fashion, something of an "ennobled" adaptation of Giovanni Mauro's obscene verse dedicated to the *fava* [bean]. This connection and her reading of it are persuasive, but Belleau's hymn nonetheless echoes Marot's earlier *blason* and is most definitely and consciously erotic and not "devoid of sexual innuendo," as Nilles suggests of some parts. Logically building on the imitated source, Nilles seeks the same phallic metaphor in the cherry that Mauro establishes in the bean and concludes suggestively that Belleau's adaptation, in its seeming shift from phallus to nipple, is "diffuse" and "elusive," not to say confused, in its sensuality and "erotic significance." This, I argue, is part of a larger poetic strategy: the appropriation of the feminine by masculine rhetoric. See Camilla J. Nilles, "Imitation and Sublimation in Rémy Belleau's 'La cerise,'" *Symposium* (1987): 67–80.

Béroalde de Verville's later, enigmatic *Moyen de parvenir,* Hélène Moreau and André Tournon facsimile, eds. (ca. 1616; reprinted Aix-en-Provence: Université de Provence, 1984), 14–17, contains a related association between cherries and female anatomy. In "Ceremonie," though in this instance the season's first cherries—spread upon white sheets and then gathered up by the miller's nude daughter, all for the voyeuristic delectation of the seigneur's assembled male guests—are explicitly linked to the girl's genitalia, which she desperately seeks to hide from sight while bending to pick up the fruit. I thank Catharine Randall for directing me to this passage.

30. Rabelais, *Œuvres complètes,* 436, 628, for example, makes this association on more than one occasion.

31. "La cerise," lines 65–68.

32. "La cerise," lines 157, 159–60.

33. "La cerise," lines 125–28.

34. "La cerise," lines 149–54, 161–64.

35. "La cerise," lines 179–80. "Giving contentment to the healthy and comfort to the sick." In this quality the cherry recalls an attribute of the female sexual organs as praised by the earlier *blasonneurs.* In the anonymous "Blason du con," for example, they constitute an analogous:

(19)	Source d'amour, fonteine de doulceur:	(19)	[Spring of love, fountain of sweetness,
(20)	Petit ruisseau appaisant toute ardeur,	(20)	Little stream that cools all heat,
(21)	Mal et langueur	(21)	Eases all ill and languor.]

See Clément Marot et al., *Sensuivent les Blasons anatomiques du corps femenin, ensemble les contreblasons de nouveau composez, et additionez avec les figures* (Paris: Langelier, 1543).

36 "La cerise," lines 191–94.
37. "La cerise," lines 197–98.
38. "La cerise," lines 198–212.
39. "La cerise," lines 222–28.
40. "La cerise," lines 240–42.

Primal Scenes/
Primal Screens
The Homosocial Economy of Dirty Jokes

Amy Staples

> *The men save up this kind of entertainment, which originally presupposed the presence of a woman who was feeling ashamed, till they are "alone together."*
>
> *We can only laugh when a joke has come to our help.*
>
> —Sigmund Freud, *Jokes and Their Relation to the Unconscious*

n his article "Freedom of Interpretation: Bakhtin and the Challenge of Feminist Criticism," Wayne Booth ponders the question: "What might it mean to say, as many have said before me, that Rabelais's great works, *Gargantua* and *Pantagruel,* are flawed by their sexism—or in the earlier language, their antifeminism?"[1] In light of this question, this chapter studies the readings of male critics regarding the function and treatment of women in Rabelais's texts, and more specifically, in the much-studied scene of the Parisian lady in *Pantagruel.*[2] Particularly interesting are Wayne Booth's readings of the scene, though other critics are important to show what I consider to be a systematic blindness concerning questions of misogyny and gender on the part of Rabelais's male readers. Freud's essay on the tendentious joke is used for a possible explanation of the position of the male critics; Carla Freccero and Jane Gallop, in their readings of Booth and Freud respectively, provide both the ammunition for a counterargument to the male critics and the inspiration for a possible venture into the boys' playground.

Natalie Zemon Davis, Joan Kelly, and Constance Jordan, among others, have written at length about the *querelle des femmes* and the place of women in both medieval and Renaissance society, and their work has shown that there were indeed positive depictions of women during Rabelais's time. Davis, for example, states in her chapter entitled "Women on Top" that "in hierarchical and conflictful societies that loved to reflect on the world-turned-upside-down, the topos of the woman-on-top was one of the most enjoyed. Indeed, sexual inversion—that is, switches in sex roles—was a widespread form of cultural play in literature, in art, and in festivity." She later adds, in summary of her argument, "The woman-on-top flourished, then, in preindustrial Europe and during the period of transition to industrial society." Both Kelly and Jordan show the *querelle des femmes* within its historical context and give numerous examples of the authors and the arguments, with all their ambiguities and contradictions, from both sides of the polemic. François Rigolot writes that "the debate between 'feminist' and 'antifeminist' forces, known as the *querelle des femmes*, concerned woman's physiological and theological inferiority, and Rabelais' symbolic representations of gender identity and sexual difference appear firmly grounded in that tradition, no matter how unacceptable its terms may be to modern sensibility."[3] If it is true that the *querelle des femmes* forced writers from medieval times up through the seventeenth century to take a position, Rabelais took his; but why?

Though there are certainly moments when Rabelais supports the opinions of thinkers such as Aristotle and Galen on the biological inferiority of women, that is, that females are defective, underdeveloped, imperfect males, I am more interested in his position concerning what we now term gender, as opposed to sex, that is, the social and cultural construct versus the biological one.[4] On this front, Rabelais tends to neglect women quite systematically. For example, all the women in his works remain unnamed except Gargamelle (mother of Gargantua) and Badebec (mother of Pantagruel), who are disposed of quite quickly in the stories. While Rabelais might be what I call an equal opportunity offender—that is, he manages to offend just about everyone—the scenes which are most degrading to women are not based on the women's social class or position, as many male critics claim, but on the very fact that the subjects are women. Rabelais obsesses about many things, but why the vehemence in the scene of the Parisian lady? Why the maliciousness and destructiveness of his enterprise? Why does one see throughout, as Freccero puts it, "the fear that always agitates the environs of the feminine in Rabelais' text"?[5] It is more troubling to many women that scenes like that of the Parisian lady are meant to be offensive: how are we to deal with this?

Booth, Rabelais's most feminist modern male reader, states outright: "I am suggesting, then, that Rabelais's work is unjust to women not simply in the superficial ways that the traditions have claimed but... in its fundamental imaginative act." Booth begins with one of Rabelais's greatest admirers, Mikhail Bakhtin, and when it comes time for him to speak of Bakhtin's approach to "the woman question" in regard to Rabelais, he appears stunned to find that Bakhtin has no place for "the influence of sexual differences" in his schema of who might be reading Rabelais's, and Booth's own, texts.[6]

Booth states that "the fact that Rabelais is far from unique is the very reason why a feminist critique is important," but he seems to think most readers who discuss Rabelais's so-called antifeminism get bogged down in the details. If anything, where he seeks to reduce their criticism to "an easy and useless case," he instead underlines the numerous instances of sexism in the texts: "An easy and useless case for the charge of sexism could be made—and indeed it has often been made—simply by listing the immense number of moments in which women are degraded, mocked, humiliated, or explicitly pronounced as inferior to men." In contrast, Booth's basis for judging Rabelais goes like this: "A surprising amount of worthless attack and defense has been conducted as if the problem is to determine what Rabelais says about women.... But surely what we shall want to grapple with is not words or propositions in isolation but the total 'act of discourse' that the author commits. Rabelais cannot be blamed for an act of injustice unless we have some reason to believe that his work as a whole ... is vulnerable to the charge." Booth wants to see whether Rabelais's work as a coherent whole is open to the charge of antifeminism. He is initially rather categorical in his assessment: "There is really no passage that counters the general address to males and implied exclusion of female readers. It is not only that there are no significant female characters; it is that even the passages most favorable to women are spoken by and to men who are the sole arbiters of the question."[7] Booth says, then, that in both his "total act of discourse" and in detail, Rabelais reveals himself to be fundamentally antifeminist.

Despite Booth's statements that Rabelais's work is unjust to female characters in superficial and fundamental ways, and that Rabelais does not take into consideration female readers, he prefers not to speak ill of Rabelais. Indeed, he reveals as much about himself as about his chosen authors when he finds himself unable to give up his overall view on Rabelais and Bakhtin, which is that "a man of great genius wrote a book offering a rich imaginative experience to men of sensitive and liberal spirit, and a male critic of great genius wrote a defense of that great book, addressed to other men." In light of his finding both men to be "of great genius," Booth terms feminist criticism of Rabelais as "pick[ing] at a possible flaw in a great imaginative author."[8]

Booth's failed attempt at feminist criticism is imbued with his love of Rabelais and Bakhtin. He usually groups Rabelais and Bakhtin together as two of a kind when he makes general statements about their relation to female readers. For example, he allows that "the truth is that nowhere in Rabelais does one find any hint of an effort to imagine any woman's point of view or to incorporate women into a dialogue. And nowhere in Bakhtin does one discover any suggestion that he sees the importance of this kind of monologue, not even when he discusses Rabelais' attitude toward women." Later Booth writes, "Just as the voices of women are flatly excluded from Bakhtin's work—sex is not even included among the sources of the 'languages we are made of'—they never enter, even by remote implication, the work of Rabelais."[9] And for all his glorification of Bakhtin, Booth recognizes that Bakhtin has no place for "the influence of sexual differences" in his schema of who might be reading Rabelais's, or Booth's own, texts.

We might congratulate Booth for attempting to take on a feminist reading of Rabelais, something many male colleagues systematically refuse to do. Most male critics avoid the gender issue in one way or another; Gérard Defaux, Edwin Duval, and Jerome Schwartz say the fate of the Parisian lady is a class/social issue, or they speak of an attack on the language of love; another approach is to speak of the scene's religious symbolism and/or biblical intertextuality, as Rigolot argues in "Rabelais, Misogyny, and Christian Charity."[10] In other examples, the haute dame de Paris scene is read, and then dismissed, as simply Panurge being Panurge, which is to say, the scene is merely an example of "boys will be boys."

Some critics ignore the issue completely: Bakhtin, as Booth recognizes, has no place for "the influence of sexual difference" among all the possible elements that make up "what I call 'I.'" Others fail to mention that when he speaks of the chapters on what he terms "the Sausage People," he ignores the fact that the Andouilles of the *Quart Livre* are specified as women.[11] It would appear that women simply do not exist for Bakhtin. But one could also mention Raymond La Charité, who has given himself the project of showing Rabelais's coherence and who manages to write at length about the episode of the old woman, the lion, and the fox without discussing the position of the old woman: he spends most of his time on Pantagruel as lion and Panurge as fox; the "hag" is mentioned only in passing.[12] It is not a question of modernity, either: Bakhtin may have an excuse for completely excluding women from his work, since *Rabelais and His World,* published in 1965, was written in 1940. A number of critics continue to skirt the issue of the status of women in Rabelais's works, even when this issue is relevant to their chosen objects of inquiry.

In general terms, Edwin Duval sees Panurge as "a thief and a prankster whose victims are almost without exception the rich, the proud, and the powerful, and the guardians of the old order." Concerning the episode with Panurge and the haute dame de Paris, he claims that Panurge is humiliating the woman because of her social position, a position that would make her one of "the rich, the proud, and the powerful, and the guardians of the old order"—but because she is a woman, Duval can hardly argue that she is either powerful or a guardian of the old order. He states: "All of Panurge's pranks involve the debasement of assumed grandeur. This is most obvious in his treatment of rich nobility. Panurge's favorite targets are ladies whose fine clothing sets them apart as socially superior." Panurge would thus be in some ways a spokesman for the author Rabelais, himself vaunted by mostly male critics for "turning the world upside down." Duval maintains that "the purpose behind all Panurge's pranks is to turn the social order upside down by elevating the poor and wretched and by humbling the rich and powerful.... This systematic inversion of high and low stations—and particularly the debasement of the exalted—is fundamental to Panurge's role."[13] Unfortunately, in Duval's—and yes, assuredly in Rabelais's—system, there is no recognition that women, too, were of what Duval terms here a "low station," or that women might be seen as being socially, economically, politically, and so forth (as he will later put it) "the last in this world who are scorned by their superiors."

For according to Duval this is strictly a class issue, and has nothing to do with the haute dame de Paris's being a woman. The Parisian lady, he says, is simply an example of a rich noble who must be knocked down, preferably literally, from her pedestal: "[Panurge's] obscenity, vulgar jokes, dirty tricks, all serve the single end of deflating the pretensions of the first of this world, humiliating those who have exalted themselves above their brothers, and promoting the last in this world who are scorned by their superiors as vulgar. The humiliation inflicted by Panurge on the elegantly dressed 'haulte dame de Paris' is, here again, emblematic."[14]

Duval even goes so far as to declare that "[Panurge] never harms these victims physically," which probably would come as a surprise to someone in the situation of the haute dame de Paris. Apparently being sprinkled with a powder made of the genitals of a bitch in heat, and being chased and pissed upon by 600,014 male dogs does not constitute physical harm in his eyes. But at least he recognizes the obscenity of the scene; La Charité, on the other hand, refers to it as "an unequaled scene of spicy irreverence and sexual display."[15]

Schwartz more or less echoes Duval, though he does allow that "Panurge is plainly offensive, especially to women, and his practical jokes can be fatal to his victims." But for Schwartz, as for Duval, this is a social issue, and has nothing to do with gender. According to Schwartz, Panurge is also attacking the Parisian lady's language, which of course cannot be separated from the social attack he is making: "Clearly, Panurge's aggressive attempt to seduce the 'grande dame' is an attack on the conventions of Neoplatonic and Petrarchan amatory discourse that subverts the social order by dissolving all respect for hierarchy, feminine honour, and marriage, and that reduces the sexual function to his own physical need."[16]

Contrary to Duval and Schwartz, Booth's take on the episode, recounting the humiliation and degradation of the haute dame de Paris, is based on Bakhtin and his conceptualization of laughter: "Bakhtin recognizes that any full defense of Rabelais must deal with the quality of the laughter sought in such moments." Booth would appear to endorse wholeheartedly Bakhtin's view that this laughter is a "great progressive force," and that such scenes are "used to produce a regenerative, an affirmative, a healing—finally a politically progressive—laughter."[17] Here Booth reads the scene and the laughter it produces in exceedingly positive terms, and is, at the moment, content to leave it at that.

Despite this healing, progressive, Bakhtinian laughter, all is not right with Booth. It does take a while, but many pages into his article, it becomes apparent what has really been troubling Booth all along: "Finally, the answer will not do, just because—and here is the scandal indeed—I find that my pleasure in some parts of this text has now been somewhat diminished by my critical act.... The fact is that reading now, try as I may to 'suspend my disbelief,' reading now I don't laugh at this book quite as hard or quite as often as I used to."[18] In a very explicit way, Booth holds feminists responsible for his now reading the text differently: "I draw back and start thinking rather than laughing, taking a different kind of pleasure with a somewhat diminished text. And neither Rabelais nor Bakhtin can be given the credit for vexing me out of laughter and into thought: it is feminist criticism that has done it." The good old days of being "transported with delighted laughter" upon reading about Panurge's revenge on the Parisian lady are over. Readers must now think about what they are reading, and why they are laughing, and Booth finds this to be a "scandal."[19]

The real "scandal" for Booth is that now his two heroes are somehow tainted, and again, grim feminist criticism is to blame. Booth seems quite devastated by the whole affair. In what is perhaps the most revealing passage of his article, he declares: "For someone like myself, having changed my views, however slightly, about the greatness of a classic, the effect is something like that of losing a brother, or a part of my past, or a part of myself." He continues by insisting on his "regret at the loss," and in another version of the same article, Booth terms it "this painful fact of personal loss."[20] Being forced to think about his laughter and being forced to listen to feminist criticism takes Booth's pleasure away; he is faced with a personal loss, and a critical one, indeed.

In a 1992 symposium paper on Booth's reading of the haute dame de Paris scene, Freccero noted that in his article "Freedom of Interpretation," Booth "simultaneously validates and undercuts the feminist challenge he has presented."[21] I would add that he does this not only thematically, not only in all the many contradictions in his article, but that he also shows a great deal of conflict, reticence, and reluctance in regard to feminist criticism and even concerning his own so-called feminist project. He does this, for example, when he speaks of his own efforts at feminism by using terms such as "belatedly," "finally," "reluctantly," "my first and belated effort at feminist criticism." He advances the concept of feminist criticism as an "alien voice" to him, to which he is "forced to listen." To cite but one of the many examples of this, Booth states that his article is based on "my somewhat surprised surrender to voices previously alien to me: the 'Mikhail Bakhtin' who speaks to me, muffled by my ignorance of Russian, and the 'feminist criticism' that in its vigor and diversity and challenge to canonic views has—belatedly, belatedly—forced me to begin listening."[22]

Freccero notes in the Panurge episode a passage from obscenity to the dirty joke. Panurge tries to seduce the Parisian lady, and when she resists, he goes from being aggressive to being hostile and cruel, and eventually, sadistic. The juxtaposition of this scene and Freud's essay on the tendentious joke is quite striking. Freud makes the distinction between the "hostile joke (serving the purpose of aggressiveness, satire or defence)" and the "obscene joke (serving the purpose of exposure)."[23] Here is a rather lengthy passage from the essay, to be read next to the progression of Panurge's "seduction" scene:

> We know what is meant by "smut": the intentional bringing into prominence of sexual facts and relations by speech.... It is a further relevant fact that smut is directed to a particular person, by whom one is sexually excited, and who, on hearing it, is expected to become aware of the speaker's excitement and as a result to become sexually excited in turn.... Smut is thus originally directed towards women and may be equated with attempts at seduction. If a man in a company of men enjoys telling or listening to smut, the original situation, which owing to social inhibitions cannot be realized, is at the same time imagined. A person who laughs at smut that he hears is laughing as though he were the spectator of an act of sexual aggression.[24]

This description fits Panurge and his démarche extremely well. In his attempt to seduce the Parisian lady, Panurge begins directly by telling her "ce seroit bien fort utile à toute la républicque, délectable à vous, honneste à vostre lignée et à moy nécessaire que feussiez couverte de ma race" [it would be most useful for the entire republic, pleasurable for you, honorable for your descendants, and necessary to me that I beget upon you]. He proceeds by "monstrant sa longue braguette" [showing her his long codpiece].[25] These scenes reveal the rather infantile nature of his seduction attempts, always following the same pattern: he tries to woo her with his words, she resists, and he proceeds by showing her his named *"longue braguette."*

Unfortunately for Panurge and any necessity he may feel, the Parisian lady refuses him at every turn. Her continued refusal in these scenes, spread over two days, will, of course, lead to her ultimate humiliation and degradation at his hands. Freud provides the technical explanation:

> If the woman's readiness emerges quickly the obscene speech has a short life; it yields at once to a sexual action. It is otherwise if quick readiness on the woman's part is not to be counted on, and if in the place of it defensive reactions appear. In that case, the sexually exciting speech becomes an aim in itself in the shape of smut. Since the sexual aggressiveness is held up in its advance towards the act, it pauses at the evocation of the excitement and derives pleasure from signs of it in the woman. In doing so, the aggressiveness is no doubt altering its character as well, just as any libidinal impulse will if it is met by an obstacle. It becomes positively hostile and cruel, and it thus summons to its help against the obstacle the sadistic components of the sexual instinct.[26]

At the end of chapter 21, after numerous refusals on the part of the Parisian lady, Panurge finally resorts to his less-than-idle threat: "Vous ne voulez doncques aultrement me laisser un peu faire? Bren pour vous! Il ne vous appartient tant de bien ny de honneur; mais, par Dieu, je vous feray chevaucher aux chiens." [You do not want me to do a little something? Shit for you! You are not worthy of such a great favor or honor, but by God, I will have you ridden by dogs]. He promptly carries out his threat when, that very evening, he searches for and finds a female dog in heat ("une lycisque orgoose"), fattens it up overnight, kills it the next day, and grinds up its genitals, sprinkling the powder made from them on the haute dame while she is in town at church. Its effect is immediate: "Tous les chiens qui estoient en l'église acoururent à ceste dame, pour l'odeur des drogues que il avoit espandu sur elle. Petitz et grands, gros et menuz, tous y venoyent, tirans le membre, et la sentens, et pissans partout sur elle. C'estoyt la plus grande villanie du monde [All the dogs that were in the church ran to this lady, because of the odor of the medicines that he had spread on her. Small and large, fat and thin, all came there, pulling on their member, sniffing and pissing all over her. It was the most villainous thing in the world]. Panurge then retires to observe "le déduyt" (the text refers to this scene as "le déduyt," "le mystère," or "ce spectacle"). The other women present during this scene try to save the Parisian lady: Rabelais's text mentions that the dogs were pissing all over the Parisian woman, "en sorte que toutes les femmes de là autour avoyent beaucoup affaire à la saulver. Et Panurge de rire" [so that all of the women from all around had much work to save her. And Panurge to laugh].[27] The women are not mentioned again.

The most essential component of this type of so-called humor, according to Freud, is that a third person participate: "The woman's inflexibility is therefore the first condition for the development of smut, although, to be sure, it seems merely to imply a postponement and does not indicate that further efforts will be in vain. The ideal case of a resistance of this kind on the woman's part occurs if another man is present at the same time—a third person—for in that case an immediate surrender by the woman is as good as out of the question. This third person acquires the greatest importance in the development of the smut; to begin with, however, the presence of the woman is not to be overlooked."[28] As noted above, Freud's use of the term "inflexibility" puts the woman in a less than positive light here, seeming to imply that her not yielding is both feigned and temporary. In addition, are we to assume that what Freud calls the "ideal" case of resistance on the part of the woman is "ideal" for men? Freud later states:

> Generally speaking, a tendentious joke calls for three people: in addition to the one who makes the joke, there must be a second who is taken as the object of the hostile or sexual aggressiveness, and a third in whom the joke's aim of producing pleasure is fulfilled.... The course of events may be thus described. When the first person finds his libidinal impulse inhibited by the woman, he develops a hostile trend against that second person and calls on the originally interfering third person as his ally. Through the first person's smutty speech the woman is exposed before the third, who, as listener, has now been bribed by the effortless satisfaction of his own libido.[29]

And so Panurge calls in Pantagruel:

> Et arrivé au logis, dist à Pantagruel: "Maistre, je vous prye, venez voeir tous les chiens du pays qui sont assemblés à l'entour d'une dame, la plus belle de ceste ville, et la veullent jocqueter." A quoy voluntiers consentit Pantagruel, et veit le mystère, lequel il trouva fort beau et nouveau.[30]

> [And, having arrived at his lodgings, he said to Pantagruel: "Master, I pray you, come and see all the dogs in the country who have gathered around a lady, the most beautiful of this city, and they want to fool around with her." To which Pantagruel consented happily, and he saw the mystery, which he found very beautiful and novel.]

Notice that Panurge does not mention his own involvement in the affair (though Pantagruel surely knows Panurge is the main protagonist in this mystery): the Parisian lady who has made the unfortunate mistake of refusing Panurge is described by him in a seemingly innocent way and admittedly, in quite positive terms, as "une dame, la plus belle de ceste ville." Sarah Kofman explains that "le faiseur de mot déverse sur [son ennemi] verbalement son agressivité et jouit par ce procédé de sa défaite. La présence du tiers renforce sa jouissance car il confirme par son rire sa victoire tandis que le tiers triomphe lui-même par procuration"[31] [The word-maker pours upon his enemy, verbally, his aggression and enjoys his defeat by this means. The presence of a third party reinforces his pleasure, because he confirms this victory by his laugh, even as this third man is triumphing by proxy].

This Pantagruel/Panurge "couple" is open to some surmising. As Schwartz notes, "Pantagruel, before he knows anything of Panurge, is, as it were, magnetically attracted to him. It is as if Pantagruel were destined to befriend this man and no other; this man so different from himself in every way is to become his inseparable companion throughout the long odyssey of Rabelais's novels." When they finally do meet, "Pantagruel is immediately and deeply drawn toward Panurge."[32] All the vocabulary here points to the pair's bond of love (love at first sight, perhaps? or love before sight?): the themes of magnetic attraction, of being deeply drawn to each other, of being inseparable companions, and so forth. The title of chapter 9 has already announced that it will speak of "Comment Pantagruel trouva Panurge, lequel il ayma toute sa vie" [How Pantagruel found Panurge, whom he loved all of his life], and while the first thirteen chapters of the book concern Pantagruel himself, the remainder of *Pantagruel* might more precisely be titled *Panurge,* since it is for the most part the adventures of Panurge (many of which include Pantagruel). It should come as no surprise that it is after the haute-dame-de-Paris/male-bonding scene that Panurge is characterized as Pantagruel's constant companion.

Where he could not dominate her physically into yielding to him, Panurge, through language and for the benefit of his fellow male, dominates the woman with his joke, with his words. Kofman speaks of this substitution of words for the act, of "la possibilité pour [des tendances agressives refoulées] de se décharger autrement que par des voies de fait, par un équivalent, un substitut de l'acte, par le langage" [the possibility of (repressed aggressive tendencies) to discharge themselves in other ways than in action, by an equivalent, a substitute for the act, by language].[33]

Freud remarks of sexual aggressiveness, "By making our enemy small, inferior, despicable or comic, we achieve in a roundabout way the enjoyment of overcoming him—to which the third person, who has made no efforts, bears witness by his laughter."[34] For Panurge's scene to succeed, it requires "a male third term"; for the scene to be viewed as humorous, it needs Pantagruel, it needs the involvement of the male narrator Alcofribas—and by extension it needs Booth.

Freccero zeroes in on Booth's story of reading aloud Rabelais to his "young wife as she did the ironing." By his own admission, Booth is rather perplexed at why, even though she "could easily tell that [he] expected her to be as fully transported as [he] was," his wife does not laugh quite as heartily as he does.[35] If it is clear how Pantagruel, Booth, or the male reader traditionally has reacted to reading such scenes, how can the Parisian lady, Booth's wife, or the female reader respond? Freccero notes the few options for Booth's wife, or any female reader: "The female reader, newly espoused as she must feel to the venerable society of critics, finds herself once again in a position of complicity against her sex, laughing along with the joke, or becoming, herself, an object of revenge, like Panurge's lady, paying dearly for her lack of humor and her willingness to resist."[36] Thus, the only options for the female reader are either to laugh against women, that is, become "one of the boys," or be made an object of revenge, which is to say, to be placed in the role of the woman upon whom the original vengeful joke has been played.

Freccero responds to Booth's article, which she terms "a modern version of the 'querelle de Rabelais' on the question of feminism," by posing an all-important question about the choice Booth himself has made.[37] She asks,

> Why does Booth choose the episode of Panurge and the Parisian noblewoman to address the question of feminist criticism, humor, and the pleasure of the text? Could it be because it constitutes a primal scene of sorts, a scene of masculine confrontation with alterity and its attempt to incorporate that alterity through seduction or erasure? Could it be because, as Jane Gallop has argued, it is precisely the woman who does not leave the room who interrupts the homosocial economy (academy?) of dirty jokes told among men?[38]

Why, then, does the male reader laugh at scenes like that of the Parisian lady, and why, ultimately, does Booth's "young wife" not find the situation so amusing?[39] Freccero points out that whereas the narration leads the reader, an implied male, to see the events from the male Panurge's point of view in the dialogue, the Parisian lady consistently says no, consistently refuses Panurge. Freccero notes elsewhere:

> "The text enlists the complicity of the reader.... The narrative acts to guide the (male) reader's interpretation of the episode through a presumed identification with Panurge, whose point of view the (male) narrator Alcofribas consistently takes by insisting upon the Lady's hypocrisy. Furthermore, Pantagruel is called in, as the figure for the reader, to witness the spectacle and approve."[40]

Freccero then asks the question that is probably an obvious one to female readers of Rabelais, but which seems not to have occurred to male readers: "But what if such an identification does not take place? What if that alien, woman, finds herself reading this text and witnessing, as Nancy Miller imagines Mrs. Booth to be doing, 'a scene of male bonding (a man and his best friends) which excludes her'?"[41] Moreover, it is not simply a question of nonidentification: there is a real violence here. About the scene of the 600,014 male dogs' chasing after and pissing on the Parisian woman, Freccero notes that Panurge has the dogs rape the woman, being unable to do it himself:

> Panurge's revenge upon the "haute dame de Paris" testifies to the triumph of her resistance, for he desists from verbal seduction, resorting to an "argumentum ad baculum" that reveals his fundamental impotence. Rather than raping her himself, he acts according to the substitutive logic at work in previous chapters, replacing himself with the dogs in the final act of coming on top of her or covering her over.[42]

As Freccero puts it, "according to the logic of the joke, the Lady does get what she really wants, only from unexpected admirers";[43] Booth's comment on the same scene, which he relegates to a footnote, declares, "The laughter it invites is surely informed with the feeling: that's exactly what those resistant bitches deserve."[44] Here again, all women who refuse to yield as well as all women who fail to laugh, Booth's wife included, could be construed as "those resistant bitches," and are potential targets for the same fate suffered by the bitch in heat. In this chapter, he does not physically dismember or kill the woman, but kills a dog in her stead. As Freccero surmises about Booth's wife, "Perhaps she sensed the danger of her situation. Freud remarks that, 'The person who laughs at smut he hears is laughing as though he were the spectator of an act of sexual aggression,' and one might wonder whether she (or any woman) could manage more than an uneasy chuckle."[45]

Just as the Parisian lady disappears from Rabelais's story, so does Booth's wife disappear from his narrative; as quickly as she appeared in the text, she is gone: not seduced, but erased; or should I say not seduced and, therefore, erased? This is where Booth accuses feminist criticism of taking away the pleasure of his text. Freccero remarks that "feminist criticism is the intrusion of the denunciatory virago into the pleasurable scene of reading between a man and his book, his master, his father. And three, in this case, is a crowd." At this point in his article, Booth's wife presumably goes back to her ironing, and Booth turns back to the two masters, two fathers he had never really left—Rabelais and Bakhtin. In this way, Freccero explains, "a difficult menage à trois resolves itself into male bonding when, at last, the woman leaves the room," and Booth thus plays out his oedipal scene.[46] As Jane Gallop observes: "The woman is lost, but the man is consoled.... [T]he other sex has been irretrievably lost. But no matter, it was worth it to gain a sameness, to find an identification...."[47]

Freccero cites Gallop on the negative Oedipus haunting the scene: "Besides the familiar Oedipus, every boy also has the desire to murder his mother and marry his father."[48] Booth's return to his masters, his "return to the same," as Freccero calls it, would posit him in the rather unfortunate and, for him, threatening position of a woman, and he is none too happy about it. Gallop explains why the heterosexual male critic who is forced to imagine himself in the position of the woman feels so threatened: "Identification with the father equals patriarchal power; desire for the father equals castration, humiliation"; Booth's own words admit as much: "The effect is something like that of losing...a part of myself...this painful fact of personal loss."[49]

Freccero notes that "Booth, like Panurge, fails in his attempt and experiences that failure as a lack of virility."[50] At the same time, she remarks that Booth somehow manages to feel vindicated by the end of his article. He does this by performing a circular movement in his text: the only way for him to extricate himself from his dilemma is to go back whence he started, to the question of freedom. Booth's only way out of his predicament (the "two violations," the "two distortions": stating that Rabelais's work is flawed by sexism and spending time on "the ideological fault, not on the greatness, thus doing a disservice to Rabelais") is to return "to listen to the two masters themselves," the masters who will either "survive gloriously" (Rabelais) or "respond triumphantly" (Bakhtin).[51]

Booth is not simply blinded by his two masters; he also identifies completely with them (though not always in a very flattering way): "I myself uncritically accepted, until well past middle age, something like the perspective [Rabelais] offers."[52] Booth even sees himself as their equal: "I am convinced... that Rabelais himself would have welcomed my effort at intruding a new voice into his chorus.... It would be absurd to blame [Rabelais and Bakhtin] for faults that I would almost certainly have exhibited, living in their time and place."[53] The filial succession is clear: Rabelais-Bakhtin-Booth. What is more, there is a passage where Booth imagines Bakhtin speaking. Booth begins with the words, "I hear him saying" and then pretends, for more than half a page, to be Bakhtin "respond[ing] triumphantly."[54] Thus, as Freccero has shown, "Booth enacts a double gesture of canon maintenance; not only does he redeem Rabelais for the great works of Western literature, but he strengthens a paradigm of masculine reading."[55]

François Rigolot's recent reading of the haute dame de Paris episode (which he terms "the most gratuitous and loathsome of Panurge's pranks") makes passing reference to Freccero's work, but only as a stepping-stone to his conclusion that "although the episode has been the object of some probing scrutiny, little attention has been paid to the biblical intertext."[56] Rigolot sees a parallel between the three consecutive seduction attempts on the part of Panurge and the three temptations of Christ in Christ's encounter with the devil. Panurge is thus attacking the Parisian lady in what Rigolot calls a replay of Genesis, and is, secondarily, making an attack on her language: "[Panurge's] offensive seduction attempt may be seen as a replay of Genesis as well as an attack on the conventional language of love in civilized society."[57] Rigolot also notes Pantagruel's active participation in the episode:

> Far from distancing himself from Panurge's dirty tricks, Pantagruel shows unequivocal approval of what he considers creative genius. When Panurge gleefully entreats Pantagruel to watch the humiliation of the Parisian lady, Pantagruel gladly accepts the invitation and acknowledges the enjoyment of the show.... To Pantagruel, the lady's degradation is simply a good show, a fine and original mystère.[58]

Rigolot is right to underline Pantagruel's role in the scene, and the contradiction it affords with Pantagruel's role as a messiah figure. In citing the work of Edwin Duval and Gérard Defaux, Rigolot allows that "if, as some modern critics claim, the Christian law of caritas is the central issue of Rabelais' epic, then the eponymous hero has obviously forgotten his mission. As a Good Samaritan, he should rush to the lady's rescue. Instead, fascinated by, and offensively acquiescent in, Panurge's antisocial instincts, Pantagruel sides with the devil and forsakes an innocent victim." Rigolot's own religious reading of the scene seems to concur with Duval's and Defaux's assessment of Pantagruel as messiah; he later declares that "not even Pantagruel, whose identity as a type of messiah is promoted by the mock-epic fiction, shows the slightest pity for [the Parisian lady]. He simply abandons her to the dogs." Rigolot also makes note of the role of the narrator of *Pantagruel,* whom most critics (Freccero being the notable exception) tend to ignore—this narrator who very definitely takes sides in the story: "As blind as his hero, Alcofribas gleefully stresses the comic aspect of the climactic dog scene, with total disregard for the lady's tragic distress."[59]

In following the logic of what he calls the biblical intertext, Rigolot makes of Panurge a satanic figure. It should be noted that even within Rabelais's work, Panurge is given devil-like qualities (by Alcofribas, Panurge, and others), and that many critics refer to him as a figure of the devil. Rigolot is led to make his most original claim in making the Parisian lady a Christlike figure:

> Panurge is not, however, the triumphant Satan of Genesis…but the Satan of the Gospel, thrice defeated by the word of God. If this comparison is true, then his victim, the Parisian lady, should be seen as a Christlike figure. This interpretation runs counter to the traditional view that the "haughty dame" somehow deserves the degradation Panurge inflicts on her.[60]

Rigolot then goes even further in stating: "In Rabelais' rewriting of the *ecce homo* scene (John 19:5) the Parisian lady takes the place of the humiliated Christ: she becomes the woman of sorrows in what is perhaps the most unexpected example of imitatio Christi in the literature of the period." Rigolot later modifies his views slightly and is careful to say that Panurge is not entirely the devil, and the Parisian lady is not entirely Christlike. He does this, though, by elevating Panurge and lowering the Parisian lady. Rigolot holds that although Panurge is in many ways patterned after Satan, his "verbal virtuosity lends redeeming power to his 'diableries,'" and that "Panurge may be similar to Satan in some ways, but he is essentially worthy of Pantagruel's love." The attitude of the Parisian lady, on the other hand, "involves a degree of complicity, which fits perfectly with the male-coded misogyny of the story (the so-called realism) but contradicts her portrayal as an innocent victim and Christlike figure." Rigolot is forced to concede that "although patterned after Christ, [the Parisian lady] departs radically from her holy model."[61]

Rigolot's argument is not entirely convincing; the parallels he draws between some of the biblical texts he cites and what he claims to be the similar passages from Rabelais are a bit forced. If, in fact, the Parisian lady is Christlike, why is she not resurrected or redeemed, either in this scene or somewhere else in the story? While the Parisian lady is most certainly a victim of Panurge's cruelty, she is not a willing victim as Christ was; she did not voluntarily put herself in this position. And I doubt Rigolot would claim that she is portrayed as a savior of any kind—there is no indication of this in the text. Nonetheless, Rigolot's article is interesting in a number of ways, one of which is his outright rejection of the question of gender in regard to the scene with the Parisian lady. We need to examine Rigolot's recent interpretation with a rather remarkable passage from his article, precisely where one might most expect gender to come into question.

The passage is near the end of the article, where Rigolot summarizes his reading of the haute dame de Paris scene, and it concerns Booth: "At any rate, it is no longer possible to read Panurge's 'sexual harassment' scene as Wayne Booth and his wife once did, when they were 'transported with delighted laughter' by it. Like the Booths at a later stage, one is forced to 'draw back and start thinking rather than laughing.'"[62] What is amazing here is that Rigolot has grouped Booth and his young, ironing, unnamed wife together in their reaction to the scene. Rigolot apparently has either overlooked or perhaps did not understand the crux of Booth's article (and in Freccero's readings of his article): Booth's wife did not react as he did; this fact underlies Booth's perplexity on the subject. In his recounting of the Booth scene involving a sexual difference of readings, Rigolot seems quite unable to conceive that a female reader might react differently than the male reader, in this instance Booth himself.

Why are male critics so eager to defend Rabelais and sing his praises? What are their investments in the continued valorization of his writings? Why is the discourse in Rabelais studies coveted and run by such an overwhelming male group of critics? One needs only to glance at the bibliographies and acknowledgments of the many books on Rabelais to see what a boys' club it is. With a few notable exceptions, such as Hope Glidden and Alice Berry, the bibliographies are overwhelmingly male, even those published after Freccero's work. There is little difference between Booth's genuflections before Rabelais and Bakhtin, before the masters/fathers, and all the time the other male critics spend (in their acknowledgments and in their books themselves) patting one another on the backs and thanking their male colleagues for the important work they have done. Why are female critics or readers so threatening to the male critics that these men either completely ignore the female critics or completely reject them, exclude them, erase them out of existence? Sarah Kofman allows that

> Au couple hétérosexuel primitif s'est substitué un couple "homosexuel"; le tiers masculin…finit par jouer un rôle de premier plan…le retournement de l'homme contre la femme a comme conséquence son détournement du sexe féminin: comme si, à son tour effarouché par celle qui résiste farouchement à ses charmes, pris de panique, il préférait, désormais misogyne, s'en tenir à des liens plus virils, et ne s'intéresser plus aux femmes que pour s'en moquer.[63]

> The homosexual couple replaces the primitive heterosexual couple; the masculine third party, in the end, plays a principal role…the turning of man against woman has as a consequence his turning against the entire female sex; as if, made fierce in his turn by her who fiercely resists his charms, panicking, he prefers, thenceforth misogynist, to cling to more virile relations, and not to take any further interest in women except to mock them.

Eve Sedgwick's work on what she terms "male homosocial desire" is of particular interest here: perhaps Rabelais's male readers enjoy the homosociality of the scene of the haute dame de Paris—with its Panurge-Pantagruel couple bonding at the expense of women—more than they would like to admit. As Freccero declares, "In these chapters the woman's defiled body…becomes the pretext for male bonding, the ground upon which their friendship is cemented."[64] Male critics seem to be quite drawn to these chapters where, as Freccero notes, "the stage is set for the defacement and eventual elimination of woman from the plot of the story."[65] Perhaps they want to be a part of the scene with the Parisian Lady, perhaps they want to play the role of Pantagruel, who gets called in to both witness and approve of the spectacle of it all. In this context, women can only be an obstacle to the mens' pleasure: they put an end to it by their very presence. Here again, Freud's work may help enlighten the situation:

> And here at last we can understand what it is that jokes achieve in the service of their purpose. They make possible the satisfaction of an instinct (whether lustful or hostile) in the face of an obstacle that stands in its way. They circumvent this obstacle and in that way draw pleasure from a source which the obstacle had made inaccessible. The obstacle in the way is in reality nothing other than the woman's incapacity to tolerate undisguised sexuality, an incapacity correspondingly increased with a rise in the educational and social level. The woman who is thought of as having been present in the initial situation is afterwards retained as though she were still present, or in her absence her influence still has an intimidating effect on the men.[66]

Thinking about why male critics are so keen on valorizing Rabelais, thinking about their own particular investments, both as individuals and as a group, brings me back to Booth. He recounts in a later version of his article on Rabelais and feminism how he was not only "transported with laughter" regarding Panurge's revenge on the Parisian lady, but also "rushed to tell [his] (male) friends about it."[67] Is it merely a coincidence that Booth "rushed to tell [his] (male) friends about it"?

In pondering the question of whether one should call Rabelais on his "antifeminism," Booth twice cites *Penthouse* magazine as an example of what is really offensive; that is, he attacks the pornography he sees in *Penthouse* instead of the pornography of Rabelais. He then feels compelled to transcribe, at length, a gang rape story from *Penthouse* in which a woman is raped by five men while her husband watches but ignores her. When she wakes up the next afternoon, her husband, named Vic, brings her coffee. In recounting the story, the unnamed woman says, "I nearly screamed with joy as [my husband] said, 'I guess you're a real woman after all.'"[68]

A man watches as five other men rape his wife; he is able to intervene but chooses not to, although he does watch; he then congratulates her for being a "real woman after all." Lest it appear that we have strayed from the discussion about Rabelais, we might ask about this man who watches but does not come to help the woman. Is he not of the same mold as Pantagruel, who, in François Rigolot's words, "should rush to the lady's rescue. Instead, fascinated by, and offensively acquiescent in, Panurge's antisocial instincts, Pantagruel sides with the devil and forsakes an innocent victim.... Not even Pantagruel...shows the slightest pity for her. He simply abandons her to the dogs."[69]

Most male readers of Rabelais tend to ignore women completely; for example, by denying the issues of misogyny and gender in both Rabelais's work and in their own. In this way, they can work on the scene of the Parisian lady but refuse even to contemplate the possibility that her being a woman has something to do with Panurge's degrading treatment of her. And if they rarely admit that Rabelais might be misogynist or antifeminist, they still feel compelled to refute the argument in some way, often by saying that misogyny or antifeminism is just a tiny part of Rabelais, or that female readers should simply have a better sense of humor about it. They do make one concession: women do not have to be transported with delighted laughter, but they do have to laugh, all the same. Booth's attempt is more insidious, because it works under the guise of feminist criticism, though I hope to have shown that his final result is anything but feminist. Despite his best efforts, his very real reluctance to allow female critics into Rabelais studies is keenly evident. In his critical gesture, Booth reenacts (as do the male critics we have seen here, in one way or another) the very scene of the Parisian lady. The women must be done away with so that those in power, male critics, can return to their delighted laughter. If they are unable to seduce the woman, at least they will have entertained the men. And while their inseparable companions and colleagues, who are deeply drawn to both Rabelais and to one another, will certainly thank them for this "effortless satisfaction of [their] own libidos," the female critics who interrupt that laughter should beware, for these boys do not want to lose their collective masculine cultural and social power, their authority to read and to judge for everyone, and they certainly do not want their power in the academic world to be threatened, either. If, as Ann Rosalind Jones remarks on François Rigolot's recent reading of the scene of the *haute dame de Paris*, "Rigolot suggests that present-day feminist readings of Panurge's love trick are a source of gender trouble in recent Rabelais studies," let us hope for more and more "gender trouble in Rabelais studies."[70]

Notes

1. Wayne Booth, "Freedom of Interpretation: Bakhtin and the Challenge of Feminist Criticism," *Critical Inquiry* 9 (1982): 45–76.
2. François Rabelais, *Pantagruel,* in *Œuvres complètes* (Paris: Gallimard, 1955), chap. 21, p. 260, "Comment Panurge feut amoureux d'une haulte dame de Paris," and "Comment Panurge feist un tour à la dame Parisianne qui ne fut poinct à son adventage," chap. 22, p. 264.
3. Natalie Zemon Davis, *Society and Culture in Early Modern France* (Stanford: Stanford University Press, 1975), 129, 150. Joan Kelly, "Early Feminist Theory and the *Querelle des Femmes*" in *Women, History, and Theory: The Essays of Joan Kelly* (Chicago: University of Chicago Press, 1984); Constance Jordan, "Terms of the Debate" in *Renaissance Feminism: Literary Texts and Political Models* (Ithaca: Cornell University Press, 1990). François Rigolot, "Rabelais, Misogyny, and Christian Charity: Biblical Intertextuality and the Renaissance Crisis of Exemplarity," *PMLA* 109 (1994): 225.
4. Thomas Laqueur, *Making Sex: Body and Gender from the Greeks to Freud* (Cambridge: Harvard University Press, 1990), discusses at length the issue of biological inferiority; see particularly "Destiny Is Anatomy," 25–62, and "New Science, One Flesh," 63–113. Much debate has surrounded Laqueur's presentation of early modern attitudes towards sexual difference.
5. Carla Freccero, *Father Figures: Genealogy and Narrative Structure in Rabelais* (Ithaca: Cornell University Press), 31.
6. Booth, "Freedom of Interpretation," 54, 66; Mikhail Bakhtin, *Rabelais and His World* (Cambridge: MIT Press, 1965).
7. Booth, "Freedom of Interpretation," 57, 64, 68.
8. Booth, "Freedom of Interpretation," 56, 63.
9. Booth, "Freedom of Interpretation," 65–66; Wayne Booth, "Rabelais and the Challenge of Feminist Criticism," in *The Company We Keep: An Ethics of Fiction* (Berkeley: University of California Press, 1988), 414.
10. See Gérard Defaux, *Le Curieux, le glorieux et la sagesse du monde dans la première moitié du XVIe siècle* (Lexington, Ky.: French Forum Publishers, 1982), and idem, *Pantagruel et les sophistes: Contribution à l'histoire de l'humanisme chrétien au XVIe siècle* (The Hague: Nijhoff, 1973); see also Edwin Duval, *The Design of Rabelais' Pantagruel* (New Haven: Yale University Press, 1991), and Jerome Schwartz, *Irony and Ideology in Rabelais: Structures of Subversion* (Cambridge: Cambridge University Press, 1990). See also Rigolot, "Rabelais, Misogyny, and Christian Charity," 225.
11. Booth, "Freedom of Interpretation," 54–55.
12. Raymond de La Charité, *Recreation, Reflection, and Re-Creation: Perspectives on Rabelais' Pantagruel* (Lexington, Ky.: French Forum Publishers, 1980), chaps. 5 and 15.
13. See Edwin Duval, *Design of Rabelais' Pantagruel,* 74–75.
14. Edwin Duval, *Design of Rabelais' Pantagruel,* 140.
15. Edwin Duval, *Design of Rabelais' Pantagruel,* 74; La Charité, *Recreation, Reflection, and Re-Creation,* 49.
16. Schwartz, *Irony and Ideology,* 38–39.
17. Booth, "Freedom of Interpretation," 61–62.
18. Booth, "Freedom of Interpretation," 68.
19. Booth, "Freedom of Interpretation," 68.
20. Booth, "Freedom of Interpretation," 73; idem, "Rabelais and the Challenge," 412.
21. Carla Freccero, "Feminism, Rabelais, and the Hill/Thomas Hearings: Return to a Scene of Reading" (paper presented by invitation of the Department of Romance Studies at Cornell University, 1 November 1992), 4.
22. Booth, "Freedom of Interpretation," 47.
23. Sigmund Freud, *Jokes and Their Relation to the Unconscious,* tr. James Strachey, The Standard Edition of the Complete Works of Sigmund Freud, vol. 8 (London: Hogarth Press and the Institute of Psycho-analysis, 1966), 97.
24. Freud, *Jokes,* 97.
25. François Rabelais, *Pantagruel,* in *Œuvres complètes* (Paris: Gallimard, 1955), 260.

26. Freud, *Jokes,* 99.
27. Rabelais, *Œuvres complètes,* (1955), 264–66.
28. Freud, *Jokes,* 99.
29. Freud, *Jokes,* 100.
30. Rabelais, *Œuvres complètes,* (1955), 266.
31. Sarah Kofman, *Pourquoi rit-on? Freud et le mot d'esprit* (Paris: Galilée, 1986), 164.
32. Schwartz, *Irony and Ideology,* 27–28.
33. Kofman, *Pourquoi rit-on?* 161.
34. Freud, *Jokes,* 103.
35. Booth, "Freedom of Interpretation," 68.
36. Carla Freccero, "Damning Haughty Dames: Panurge and the Haulte Dame de Paris," *Journal of Medieval and Renaissance Studies* 15 (1985): 57–58.
37. Freccero, "Damning Haughty Dames," 58.
38. Freccero, "Feminism, Rabelais, and the Hill/Thomas Hearings," 4–5.
39. Does Booth's wife have a name? Does the Parisian lady? Or does this lack of name simply reflect Rabelais's, Bakhtin's, and Booth's view that this could be any (and thus, every) woman?
40. Freccero, "Damning Haughty Dames," 62.
41. Freccero, "Damning Haughty Dames," 62.
42. Freccero, "Damning Haughty Dames," 65.
43. Freccero, "Damning Haughty Dames," 61.
44. Booth, "Freedom of Interpretation," 61.
45. Freccero, "Feminism, Rabelais, and the Hill/Thomas Hearings," 8.
46. Freccero, "Feminism, Rabelais, and the Hill/Thomas Hearings," 9–11.
47. Jane Gallop, *Thinking through the Body* (New York: Columbia University Press, 1988), 34.
48. Gallop, *Thinking through the Body,* 37.
49. Gallop, *Thinking through the Body,* 38; Booth, "Rabelais and the Challenge," 412.
50. Carla Freccero, "The 'Instance' of the Letter: Woman in the Text of Rabelais," in *Rabelais' Incomparable Book: Essays on His Art,* ed. Raymond de la Charité (Lexington, Ky.: French Forum Publishers, 1986), 45–55; here, 46.
51. Booth, "Freedom of Interpretation," 69–70.
52. Booth, "Rabelais and the Challenge," 409.
53. Booth, "Freedom of Interpretation," 70–71.
54. Booth, "Freedom of Interpretation," 70.
55. Freccero, "Damning Haughty Dames," 58.
56. Rigolot, "Rabelais, Misogyny, and Christian Charity," 226.
57. Rigolot, "Rabelais, Misogyny, and Christian Charity," 227.
58. Rigolot, "Rabelais, Misogyny, and Christian Charity," 230.
59. Rigolot, "Rabelais, Misogyny, and Christian Charity," 230, 232.
60. Rigolot, "Rabelais, Misogyny, and Christian Charity," 230.
61. Rigolot, "Rabelais, Misogyny, and Christian Charity," 231, 233–34.
62. Rigolot, "Rabelais, Misogyny, and Christian Charity," 234.
63. Kofman, *Pourquoi rit-on?* 176–77.
64. Freccero, *Father Figures,* 35.
65. Freccero, "The 'Instance' of the Letter," 47.
66. Freud, *Jokes,* 100–101.
67. Booth, "Rabelais and the Challenge," 410.
68. Booth, "Rabelais and the Challenge," 391.
69. Rigolot, "Rabelais, Misogyny, and Christian Charity," 230, 232.
70. Ann Rosalind Jones, "Introduction: Cluster on Early Modern Women," *PMLA* 109 (March 1994): 187–89; here, 188.

Catherine, Cybele, and Ronsard's Witnesses

Stephen Murphy

My point of departure and return is "Le Pin," a curious poem which first appears in *Le Septiesme livre des Poëmes* of 1569. Its narrative core is a retelling of the story of Attis and Cybele; in particular, the moment when the maddened Attis castrates himself, followed by his lament for his situation, and then his metamorphosis into a pine tree. The bloody catastrophe provides an occasion for the poet's commentary. As he first reports the self-emasculation, the disapproving poet exclaims:

(45) Ta raison fut en fureur convertie,
(46) Qui te coupas ta meilleure partie:
(47) O bon Atys! aveuglé de malheur,
(48) Tu te coupas le membre le meilleur,
(49) Tes deux tesmoings, gros de glere foeconde,
(50) Sans qui seroit un desert ce grand Monde:
(51) Ce n'est ton doigt, ton oreille, ou ta main,
(52) Mais les autheurs de tout le genre humain.[1]

(45) [Your reason was turned into madness,
(46) Dear Attis, who cut off your best part!
(47) Blinded by misfortune,
(48) You cut off your best member,
(49) Your two *tesmoings*, Full of fertile glair,
(50) Without which this whole world Would be a desert;
(51) Not your finger, your ear, or your hand,
(52) But the authors of all the human race.]

This condemnation is expressed with the voice of a familiar Ronsard, the putative naturalist who reveres universal fecundity and is scandalized by its negation. However, the story's conclusion (the transformation of Attis into a pine tree by the goddess Cybele) introduces another interpretation of the central event. This is an allegorical interpretation, which takes Attis as the seeker of philosophical wisdom and Cybele as Philosophy (137–38)[2]:

(145) Tu n'as coupé (ce n'est que Poësie)
(146) Tes deux tesmoings: mais de ta fantaisie
(147) Tu arrachas folles affections,

(145) [You did not cut off (that's only Poetry)
(146) Your two *tesmoings*; rather, you tore away from your
(147) Imagination those mad inclinations,

■ 55

(148) Mondains plaisirs, humaines pas- (148) Worldly pleasures and human passions,   sions

(149) Qui te troubloient, pour heureuse- (149) Which troubled you, in order to live
ment vivre,   happily

(150) Et contempler ta Cybele & la (150) And contemplate your Cybele and
suyvre.   follow her.]

How are we to take these contradictory apostrophes to Attis? True, the rhetorical turn of *correctio* or epanorthosis is common enough in Ronsard's poetry.[3] We could also say simply that the original condemnation concerns the immediate sense of the story, while the later commendation applies to the moral allegory Ronsard draws from it.[4] A long mythographic tradition attempts just such a revisionist reading of the Attis myth, including notably the emperor Julian's apologia for Cybele, Lucretius, and Saint Augustine.[5] But particular attention to one word may reveal in Ronsard's story of Attis and Cybele a wider-ranging importance and a more radical contradiction.

That word occurs in both the passages already cited (as well as v. 40), namely, *tesmoings*. Is it, as the editor, Paul Laumonier, declares, merely "un synonyme discret de testicules"?[6] Of course, such a gloss provides a starting point; what may appear obscure upon a first reading becomes clear when we realize that Ronsard is treating *tesmoings* as if it had the same ambiguity as Latin *testes*. The twin meanings of witness and testicles provided a pun to Latin writers at least since Plautus.[7] The pun persists in Romance languages, including compounds. We find *testimoni* with this double sense in sixteenth-century Italian texts: in at least one Roman pasquinade, and in *novelle* by Bandello and Firenzuola.[8] In French, Ronsard is not the first to use *tesmoings* in this way. It shows up in Des Périer's *Nouvelles Recreations* (1558), and most instructively, in Baïf's comedy *Le Brave* (1567).[9] The latter was a version of Plautus's *Miles Gloriosus,* near the end of which the double meaning of *testes* lends itself to a legal pun: "si posthac prehendero ego te hic, carebis testibus" [If I ever catch you here again, you will be lacking your testicles/witnesses][10] Through the use of *témoins,* Baïf's version maintains Plautus's pun:

Si jamais ceans te retreuve, [If I ever find you in here again,
J'auray les témoins pour la preuve"[11] I'll have the *témoins* to prove it]

An awareness of the potential for double meaning in this word enables us to see an extra dimension in other, apparently innocent, passages. For example, in revision to his "Response aux injures" from 1567 on, Ronsard writes to his Protestant adversary: "Tes escris sont tesmoins que tu m'as desrobé"[12] [Your writings are *tesmoins* which you have stolen from me]. So that the question in interpreting "Le Pin" becomes: How can we understand both testicles and witness in the poem?

Tesmoings works in a way similar to what Michael Riffaterre calls "hypogram-generating dual signs.... Finding himself unable to understand the word as given in the text and as determined by grammatical function, the reader is forced to look elsewhere for a second, albeit simultaneous, interpretation, and to read a pun into the word."[13] The reader of "Le Pin" is likely to be brought up short by the inappropriateness to this context of *tesmoings* in its normal, ocular, or legal sense. "Ungrammaticality is...maximal, since the text has to extrapolate beyond a single language in order to find a homonym."[14] In earlier French uses of the pun, some indicator points towards Latin for the requisite ambiguity—whether that indicator be the Italian *novella* tradition, with its more Latinate vocabulary, or Plautus's text behind Baïf's play. In Ronsard's case, context encourages that extrapolation to Latin; namely, the setting of classical myth and, in particular, the intertext explicitly provided by Catullus's *carmen* 63.[15] The effect resembles that of a new coinage; or as Boileau puts it in his condemnation of Ronsard, "en français parlant grec et latin."[16]

Thus far, the pun possesses an intertextual status. But another contemporary occurrence complicates the matter by its dependence on the historical situation. In June 1575 the Parisian chronicler and collector of texts Pierre de l'Estoile noted that Queen Mother Catherine de Médicis had fallen ill, apparently after eating too many "crestes et rognons de coq" [cock's combs and testicles], of which she was quite fond.[17] L'Estoile dutifully recorded a series of four Latin epigrams which subsequently circulated in Paris. For the following month he offered a larger number of poems in French and Latin, several of which develop political metaphors from the Queen Mother's gluttony. Here are two from June and one from July which may serve as examples:

(1)

Foemina miraris, Salica cur lege refixa,	[You marvel how a woman, After annulling the Salic law,
Audax imperio Gallica colla premat.	Boldly presses Gallic necks to her authority.
Evirat, heu! Gallos, cristas testesque revellens:	Alas! she unmans cocks (*Galli*), tearing off their crests and testicles;
Imperium in Gallos inde virago tenet.	A virago holds sway over the French (*Galli*).]

(2)

Semper testiculos Gallorum prodiga coenat	[An unbridled woman dines on the testicles of cocks (*Galli*)
Foemina, et hunc avide quum vorat illa cibum,	And, as she devours this food,
Compressis dicit labris: "Sic Gallica castro	She smacks her lips and says, "Thus I castrate Gallic courage,
Pector[a], sic Gallos eviro, sic subigo!"[18]	Thus I unman the French (*Galli*), thus I subdue them!"]

(3)

Quid mirum Gallos instructos grandibus olim	[What wonder if the French (*Galli*), formerly equipped with great *testes*,
Testibus, Eunuchos nunc evasisse vietos!	Now turn out to be shrivelled eunuchs?
Foemina magna Deum Mater, peregrina, profusa,	A mighty woman, Mother of the gods, an extravagant foreigner,
Altera nunc Cybele, magnas invecta per urbes,	Another Cybele, borne loftily through mighty cities on horseback,
Sublimisque in equis, Gallos, gentem omnipotentem	Compels the French (*Galli*), formerly an all-powerful people,
Olim, castratos hodie atque virilibus orbos	Now castrated and deprived of their virile member,
Membris, esse sibi famulos, mollesque ministros	To be her servants and flabby priests, weak of mind and member.
Atque Sacerdotes, sine mente et mentula inertes,	
Cogit. Sic Galli, servato nomine, sed re	Thus the French (*Galli*), maintaining the name but lacking the thing,
Amissâ, Cybelen Gallii, Eunuchique sequuntur.[19]	Follow Cybele as emasculated priests (*Galli*) and eunuchs.]

As the first two texts show, the author or authors use *testes* interchangeably with *testiculi*, in the fairly straightforward sense of "testicles." There may be more here than meets the eye, however, as elsewhere L'Estoile shows awareness of the possibilities for punning on both *testes* and *témoins*.[20] Admittedly, the poet spends more metaphoric energy on the ambiguity of *Galli*, at once "cocks" and "Frenchmen." In this way Catherine's voracity provides a lesson concerning both nationalism and gender; she becomes a virago violating the Salic law and thereby unmanning good Frenchmen. But between June and July someone discovered a more interesting pun, based on the triple sense of Galli: not only cocks (that is, the gastronomic occasion) and Frenchmen (the political lesson), but also the emasculated priests of the goddess Cybele. By means of this pun on Galli, Catherine's sins take on gastronomical, political, and mythological dimensions. A satiric use of mythology becomes a vehicle for the political attack. The French males' shameful subjection is specified as the procession of Cybele and her priests, made famous by Lucretius and Virgil.[21]

Moreover, L'Estoile's texts are not only playing off classical pretexts; in numerous public festivities of these years, the identification of Catherine with a triumphant imperial Cybele was standard iconography. For example, in their "Tour de France" of 1564 through 1566, Catherine and Charles IX found the royal entry to Bayonne adorned with a tableau representing the Queen Mother surrounded by her children. The anonymous verses attached identify the latter as "les fruicts de Sibelle feconde."[22] Verses in both Latin and French by Jean Passerat for the entry to Troyes echo the same terms.[23] An even more precise precedent is supplied by the official gift bestowed by the city of Paris on Charles IX upon his official entry there in 1571. This gift was also a centerpiece of the public ceremony itself. It comprised, on a pedestal, a triumphal chariot drawn by the figures of two lions; in the chariot, "Cibelle mere des Dieux, representant la Roine mere du Roy," surrounded by her divine children Neptune, Pluto, and Juno (representing respectively the dukes of Anjou and Alençon, and Marguerite). Twin columns supported the figure of Jupiter, representing the king.[24] If there were any doubt that the 1571 spectacle staged a *mise-en-scène* of the Virgilian passage, it is laid to rest by the appropriate verses from the *Aeneid,* inscribed on the pedestal beneath the chariot.[25] The account of the 1571 royal entries, published by Simon Bouquet the following year, contains not only a detailed description of the divine chariot, but other reiterations of the central mythological identification.[26] In this light, we are bound to be interested by the fact that Ronsard himself collaborated on all aspects of the ceremony.[27]

In addition to those nearly contemporary, public portrayals of the Queen Mother as Cybele, there is a literary fact to consider. As any reader of Ronsard knows, he too liked to identify Catherine with Cybele. In the 1555 ode "A la Royne Mere" which became the second in the *Third Book of Odes,* he calls her "une autre Mere Cybelle."[28] Similarly, this identificatioon appears in the eclogue "Daphnis et Thyrsis" of 1564, and in the "Bergerie" and "Les Nues, ou Nouvelles," both of 1565, all major poems which establish some of the standard pastoral/mythological identifications of the French court in the 1560s and later.[29] The motivation for equating Catherine with Cybele in these poems, as elsewhere, is evidently the regal fertility which belatedly bestowed upon France an abundant royal family. Baïf calls her the "Mère de la France," or Magna Mater.[30] "Plus que Rhea nostre Royne est feconde / De beaux enfans" [Our queen is more fertile in beautiful children than Rhea], declares Ronsard in 1559, making the common identification of Rhea with Cybele as mother of the gods.[31] In such passages the poet operates in the Virgilian tradition of a revered imperial Cybele, famously imitated by Du Bellay in the sixth sonnet of the *Antiquitez de Rome.*[32] Such a tradition also includes Cybele's role in the *Franciade* as a tutelary deity for the epic's hero Francus (as Athena is for Odysseus or Venus for Aeneas), actively promoting the foundation of the French royal dynasty.[33] At the center of Ronsardian mythology, as it harmonizes with official iconography, Magna Mater reigns. Her fertility bestows the races of gods and of kings, and so provides a foundation for Ronsard's poetry.

In contrast to that "high" Cybele, there also exists a tradition of a "low," satirical Cybele, which Ronsard also continues. This latter tradition emphasizes the goddess's age, which makes inappropriate her passion for young Attis, as well as the grotesque procession of her castrati/priests carrying on the custom established by Attis. This picture develops in the antipagan polemics of early Christian writers such as Arnobius, Firmicus Maternus, and Prudentius.[34] One of Ronsard's *Folastries* as well as his "Palinodie à Denise," his "Dithyrambes," and a sonnet of the *Nouvelle continuation des Amours* all represent, in various combinations, the goddess as "une vieille ridée" and the grotesque procession of "les escouillés de Cybele."[35] When the poet himself enters the picture, he makes an explicit effort to dissociate himself from the worship of Cybele, emphasizing that "entre Atys et moy il y a difference."[36] On the one hand, the declaration of that difference belongs to the lover/poet's obligatory phallic swagger. But in addition, the distinction of poet and Attis as mutually exclusive, as well as the grotesqueness and sterility associated with the goddess, make Cybele a figure inimical to poetry.

It is not my intention to survey the figure of Cybele in the works of Ronsard,[37] but I would like to suggest that the existence of a "high" and a "low" Cybele does not mean we can simply separate some occurrences as one and some as the other form of the figure. Rather, both Cybeles are always present in varying doses. The imperial Mother, surrounded by the triumphant evidence of her fertility, is shadowed by the satirical hag leading her sterile crew. After all, a similar ambivalence characterizes ancient attitudes towards the goddess, an Earth mother wielding power over both life and death.[38] And Ronsard's version of that ambivalence is what makes the identification Catherine/Cybele a questionable homage. To put it in terms of intertexts: Ronsard cannot pretend that the queen, the Queen Mother, is only the Virgilian Cybele; she cannot hide the traces of the Catullan Cybele, provoker of superstition, madness, and self-mutilation.

Catherine's iconographical doubleness, matching the doubleness of Cybele, is reflected onomastically in the striking use of the name Catin. There are two Catins for Ronsard: one is the old slut of the third *Folastrie*, who resembles one of the wrinkled "escouillés de Cybele," and illustrates the more recent development of the name in French as a derogatory common noun.[39] The other Catin, as we find her named in a characteristically pastoral manner in the eclogue "Daphnis et Thyrsis," represents Catherine de Médicis. That is, Daphnis and Thyrsis are transparently Charles IX and the future Henri III, singing the praises of their mother Catin: "Douce elle m'a nourry, comme autrefois Cybelle / Sur les mons Idéans nourrissoit ses enfans"[40] [Kindly she nursed me, just as Cybele used to nurse her children on the hills of Ida].

Of course, Catherine de Médicis as represented by contemporary testimony does strike us as an ambiguous figure, reducible to neither the panegyrics nor the invectives. She appears as a somewhat mannish widow insistently dressed in black, and so of uncertain gender; Etienne Jodelle declares, by way of praising her, "nous avons en une Royne un Roy" [in a queen we have a king].[41] During the long minority of Charles IX she was the closest thing to a monarch in France, and the well-known effeminacy of Henri III only put into higher relief Catherine's contrary image. She was also notorious for her doubleness in politics: it was uncertain, at any given moment, whether she was pursuing her middle course by favoring, or appearing to favor, the Catholic extremists or the Protestants.

But that last word returns to the question of witness in the central ideological conflict of the age. The Protestants owe their very name to the act of witnessing. We might tentatively distinguish three varieties of that act that characterize Calvinism. First, *témoin* and *témoignage* are theologically weighted terms running throughout Calvin's works. In the *Institutions*, for example, he crucially defines sacrament as a "tesmoignage de la grace de Dieu" [a manifestation of the grace of God].[42] The Reformers notoriously insist upon the sovereignty of that testament which is scripture. In the Bible and in sacraments, God is the one who testifies—that is, signifies his will.

Second, those who die for their faith act as witnesses. For Calvin, to suffer martyrdom is "rendre tesmoignage à la verité de Dieu au besoing" [to bear witness to God's truth when necessary].[43] In Crespin and Goulart's *Histoire des Martyrs,* Protestant martyrs are persistently called *témoings.*[44] Such nomenclature follows the tradition of biblical translation, of Greek *martus* and *marturia/marturion* into Latin *testis* and *testimonium* and from Latin into the vernaculars.[45] The testimony of such martyrs consists in the very fact of their public suffering, but they may also speak out to openly declare their belief; finally, the details of their suffering may become eloquent corporeal signs.[46] Hence the martyr's achievement, if I might appropriate Ronsard's words from another context: "Faisant son sang le tesmoing de sa Foy" [Making his blood the witness of his faith].[47] The suffering body is a witness.

And, perhaps most pertinently, a third sort of testimony lies at the heart of Protestant historiography and martyrology, which show a keen sense of duty to the memory of the victims. The historian's act of witnessing combats the attempts of orthodoxy to impose forgetfulness—and I am not referring to attempts in any vague sense. A formula that recurs in at least two of the peace treaties during the civil wars calls for the following: that the memory of past atrocities (for example, Saint Bartholomew's Day) "demeurera esteincte et assoupie, comme de choses non advenues" [will be annulled and suppressed, as if they had never happened].[48] Those texts are recorded in Agrippa d'Aubigné's *Histoire universelle;* and of course, his *Tragiques* is obviously and explicitly an epic of witness, particularly in the central books "La Chambre dorée," "Les Feux," and "Les Fers," with their catalogues of injustice and their visual appeal. In this last variety, literary witness, we find the text itself as *témoin.*

Hence, three subjects of witness: God, the martyr, and the writer. Hence also, two principal media of witness: the body and the text, whether that text be scriptural or historiographic/poetic. Protestant literary practice typically mingles these varieties, but the ultimate object of witness remains the same: Christian truth. Ronsard's myth also contains a divinity and a suffering and signifying body. On the other hand, his account obviously lacks the element of univocal signification; as I began by noting, contradictory interpretations open and close the narrative of "Le Pin." Semiotic similarities and hermeneutic differences connect Ronsard's Attis with the contemporary discourse of witnessing.

In the course of the 1560s it became clear that the Queen Mother was a persecutor of Protestant witnesses. I would suggest that the widespread polemic image of Catherine as the castrating Mother (as in L'Estoile) is based on the pun, usually hidden, that confounds *testes* with *testes, témoin/testicle* with *témoin/witness.* On the other hand, Ronsard's own opposition to the Protestants, as voiced in his *Discours des misères,* is based on a suspicion of the potency of witness unbridled by tradition or social norms. The poet's orthodoxy amounts to a politicization of the myth interpretation offered by the emperor Julian: Attis's castration represents "the checking of the unlimited" (*epoche tes apeirias).*[49] The common Catholic reproach, that Luther and Calvin opened the door to scriptural interpretation by everyone, voices a fear of excess, figurable both conceptually and corporeally.

That the integrity of *témoins* in the physical sense was an important political principle can be seen in an anecdote told by d'Aubigné. The gentleman Villandry was almost put to death for playfully grabbing Charles IX by "les parties honteuses." Such an action constituted a capital crime according to the laws, "qui ostent la vie à tous ceux qui prennent leur Souverain en tel endroit" [which condemn to death all those who take hold of their sovereign in such a place].[50] Villandry was saved from execution through the intervention of Admiral Coligny, who was himself later castrated as part of the ritual mutilation of his corpse on Saint Bartholomew's Day.[51] The perceived deviations of the body politic could be expiated on real bodies. Those real bodies, as martyrs bearing witness, could subsequently become textual bodies of peculiar power; a tendency exemplified strikingly by the hagiography of Coligny and his fellow victims of 1572.

The process can be summarized abstractly: the threat of a dangerous excess of witness, followed by the suppression of that witness, followed by its textual recuperation. Such a pattern hinges on what must be paradoxically called the productive role of castration.

Putting it that way may at first appear irrelevant to Ronsard. Attis is a figure of the poet.[52] As I earlier expressed it in Ronsard's words, "[les] escris sont tesmoins," and what Attis loses are explicitly called *autheurs* (v. 52). The Queen Mother deprived Ronsard of his *escris/tesmoins* by imposing silence. This she did by forbidding any more polemic pamphlets after the peace of Amboise in March 1563, and so, it might be claimed, putting an end to the series of *Discours des misères.* However, that gesture of negation does not mean simply silencing the poet. If we follow Daniel Ménager in reading the *Discours* as realizing the dead end of historical discourse, and their suspension as the return to "pure" poetry (that is, to an apparently nonpolemical poetry), we can see the Queen Mother's decree equally well in another light.[53] She is, in a sense, the one to thank for the mythological delirium of the four seasonal *Hymnes* as well as the other poems of the 1560s attesting to Ronsard's turn away from political poetry.

True, for some of Ronsard's contemporaries, as might be expected, castration constitutes an unambiguous image of censorship. Such is the case in the anecdote shared by Béroalde de Verville in *Le Moyen de parvenir* and d'Aubigné in *Les Avantures du Baron de Faeneste,* in which the artistic representation in a church of an excessively well endowed devil is subsequently deprived of his obscene feature by a censorious orthodoxy: painterly or sculptural castration.[54] In a similar vein, Montaigne recalls how Pope Paul IV "chastra" ancient sculptures in Rome "pour ne corrompre la veue" [in order not to corrupt sight].[55] For Ronsard, however, the gesture is more complex. He takes the Attis myth to mean "Un Philosophe sage / Doibt... estre un home sauvage: / Se faire un Pin, c'est frequenter les bois," and so forth [A wise philosopher (and thus a poet) must be a wild man; to become a pine tree is to haunt the woods] (133–35). What is constituted by the castration and metamorphosis of Attis is, so to speak, the forest of Gastine. The resemblance of "Le Pin" to the late elegy "Contre les bûcherons…" is based on similar phrasing early in both poems, their common perception of mythological figures beneath the *écorce* of nature, and their common positing of such a forest as the locus for poetic inspiration.[56] Ronsard recalls Ovid's allusion to the transformed Attis, where the Latin poet includes the pine in an enumeration of all the trees flocking to hear the poetry of Orpheus.[57] That Ovidian scene presents an enduring and much-imitated image of the supreme power of poetry.[58]

The pine tree becomes part of the locus of poetry through Attis's mutilation, but this is only part of a larger phenomenon. Poets may in fact be constituted by a radical lack. Ronsard's biographer Claude Binet calls the deafness which changed his poet's life "ce malheur bien-heureux," and makes an explicit parallel between that handicap and Homer's blindness.[59] Du Bellay takes the same tack in his "Hymne de la Surdité," addressed to Ronsard. Like Binet, he considers his friend's good fortune to consist in the necessary abandonment of a courtier's life. The place opposed to the court and, of course, far friendlier to poetic inspiration, is a woodland setting. This redirection from the court to poetry resembles the blessing that the Queen Mother's command of political silence bestowed on the poet of the *Discours des misères*.

Ronsard goes further in his "Responce aux injures," where he makes blindness a cause of the greatness of the primordial poets such as Homer, Thamyras, and Stesichorus. He takes his own example and Du Bellay's to show that what held true in archaic times for blindness holds true for deafness in the present day, in a sort of *translatio* of handicaps.[60] This homology between deafness and blindness as sources of poetry is relevant for several reasons. First, in Ronsard's case the visual element of witness takes over from the lost sense of hearing. As Binet puts it: "il pensa de transferer l'office des oreilles aux yeux par la lecture des bons livres" [it occurred to him to transfer the ears' office to the eyes by reading good books].[61] The poet's deafness is the image of ocular maiming (Ronsard = Homer), and it finds compensation in the seeing that generates texts: literary practice as *témoignage* of an absence. Moreover, we might listen to Freud, whose anthropological speculation proposes blinding as a substitute for castration (Oedipus, for example).[62] Such a substitution provides a new dimension for the maiming that founds poetry.

Some form of self-emasculation and inspiration are associated in Ronsard's poetry as early as the declaration in the 1552 *Amours:* "Je suis semblable à la prestresse folle" [I am like the mad priestess].[63] It may be that Ronsard accentuates gender ambiguity most in his erotic poetry,[64] but a similar process turns up elsewhere. In his "Dithyrambes" for Jodelle's "Pompe du bouc" and in the "Hymne de Bacus," Ronsard includes himself among the inspired followers of Dionysus/Bacchus. In the first case he establishes a parallel between the Bacchic triumph and the procession of Cybele and her followers, while in the second he repeatedly refers to the female gender of the Bacchantes, his companions.[65] What this amounts to in both poems is an assimilation of the poet to the castrated or female devotees of the god(s); he becomes a transvestite spying on mysteries like Pentheus, but sympathetic and undetected.

Ronsard concludes "Le Pin" with a reference to the fever from which he currently suffers, and a recognition that "La Muse peut alleger le soucy"[66] [The muse can lighten cares]. This bald commonplace takes on new meaning when we notice just how frequently the poet refers to his illness in the Sixiesme and Septiesme livres des Poëmes, and how intimate the link is between illness and poetic creation. Amadis Jamyn's liminary sonnet to the Sixiesme livre introduces Ronsard's sudden burst of composition as the direct result of a god-given quartan fever.[67] Many allusions in both books reaffirm an association between febrile illness and febrile creativity.[68] In the present poem and the collection that first contains it, with an explicit autobiographical note and in the cherished setting of Saint-Cosme, Ronsard plays variations on the theme of poetry as pathology or maiming.

What is more, although "Le Pin" narrates the story of a mortal and a goddess, which translates most obviously to an allegory of royalty and its dependent, the productivity of castration also exists in the intertextual realm. When Ronsard uses these terms in accusing his Protestant opponent, "Tes escris sont tesmoins que tu m'as desrobé," he is speaking metaphorically but not at all vaguely. The Protestants robbed him most clearly in the two Palinodies which appeared anonymously in 1563. These consist mostly of Ronsard's own verses, from his "Elégie à Guillaume des Autels" and the "Discours à la Royne," so that he was certainly justified in accusing them of stealing his textual potency.[69] Ronsard also suffered in later years what might be considered hermeneutical theft. A Protestant pamphlet of 1574, Le Réveille-matin des François, cited and interpreted certain passages in the fourth book of the Françiade as using figures of the dreadful Merovingian dynasty to refer to members of the reigning Valois family.[70] The epic poet was thus interpreted as subverting the royal authority that his poem had aimed to legitimize. On the other hand, from the Protestant point of view, Ronsard's problem was that he had already lost the power of witness by betraying what had previously seemed promising to adherents of the Reformation.[71] Their mockery of him as "Grand Prestre de Cybele" condemns, first, a poet who wastes his time with pagan mythology and, second, one who has sought to advance his career through the unnatural occupation of cleric.[72] By both deeds, which both amount to self-mutilation, he has declined to testify.

So the gesture of mutilation, of oneself or another, stages an interplay among powers in the intertextual, ideological, and political realms. And that interplay is literarily fertile.[73] Likewise, a process takes place in Ronsard's imaginary. The castration of Attis leads to the erection of the pine tree, and provides the condition necessary for the pursuit of wisdom (which means being a poet); on the other hand, the cutting down of the forest of Gastine entails the death (or at least the dispersal) of poetic inspiration at the same time it inspires the poet to lament that fact. However violent the clash, it is not a matter of a simple opposition between cornucopian/genital fecundity on one side and sterility on the other.

Ronsard's second, positive interpretation of the Attis myth (cited above) continues with this quasi-Platonic distinction:

(151) L'home est Centaure: en bas il est cheval,

(152) Et home en haut, d'embas vient tout le mal,

(153) Si la raison, qui est l'home, ne guide

(154) Cet animal & ne luy tient la bride.[74]

(151) [Man is a centaur. Below he is a horse,

(152) Human above. All evil comes from below,

(153) If reason, which is human,

(154) Does not guide this animal and hold it reined in.]

The image of the rein of reason needed to control a double human nature, which comes from the *Phaedrus,* should not obscure what is different and troubling in Ronsard's version. First, of course, there are not two horses in question as for Plato, but one creature simultaneously man and beast. This more intimate association of good and bad is joined to a neat corporeal distinction: "en bas...en haut." In these lines, as in a quite similar passage of the prose discourse, "Des vertus intellectuelles et morales," there is nothing surprising in finding the lower body condemned as the locus of base sensuality.[75] Nor is it incongruous that the interpretation represents as discipline (*guide, tient la bride*) what the myth represents as castration, or irreversible negation. But it turns out that both reason and madness perform the same function of purification. The effect of Attis's *fureur* ends up as the effect of reason—what makes humanity truly human.

What makes the poet a poet, what makes man human; finally, it is the same act that also creates human society. After all, Attis is a lawgiver. His cultic activity takes place in public, and his defining gesture has social circumstances and consequences. The social paradox of Ronsard's Attis myth is encapsulated in a formal element, as are the paradoxes of poetics and anthropology. The poetic cliché reads: madness at the inception of poetry; the anthropological cliché: a man becomes truly human by taming his irrational impulses. "Le Pin" serves as a reminder of the corporeal violence underlying those clichés. In particular, the striking rhyme near the end (133–34) sharpens the point: *sage/sauvage*. As for the social dimension, consider the startling parataxis of lines 39–40: "Premier, [Attis] & loix & statutz leur donna, / Et ses tesmoings d'un caillou moissonna" [Attis was the first to give them laws and statutes, and reaped his *tesmoings* with a flint]. That mysterious *et,* apparently so feeble as it connects the two clauses, provides the link between private and public, violence and construction, the intimate body and the body politic. It holds in balance the possible meanings of simultaneity (both...and) as well as temporal sequence (first...then). It suggests a connection between intimate violence and the foundation of civilization, but avoids being explicit. That minimal conjunction is a microcosm of the relationship between Ronsard's pun in "Le Pin" and the larger dialectic of witness contemporary with his text. There is no question of causality or precedence between the two realms, although they do share a common dynamic structure: excess (madness), suppression (castration), recuperation (text). Ronsard's poetic practice, placed in its context, reminds us of the physical destruction as well as the poetic fecundity that crisis may bring about. It is no longer possible to ignore the social dimension of textual maneuvers, or to ignore the force behind signification.[76]

The fate of Attis's—and Ronsard's—*tesmoings* poses a problem of excess meaning. The fate of *et* in line 40 possesses, in this connection, at least a symbolic importance. In the 1584 edition of Ronsard's *Œuvres*, the distich reads: "Loix et statuts ministre leur donna, / Puis ses tesmoins d'un caillou moissonna." The excision of *et* and its replacement by *puis* means a reduction of ambiguity and the promotion of a clearer narrative chronology: first, the productive religious/social activity, then the private violence. The aging poet, revising for the final collective edition before his death, cuts along with *et* some of the semantic excess from his poem. Nevertheless, much flourishes still beneath Attis's blow.

Notes

1. I cite the first edition: Pierre de Ronsard, *Œuvres complètes,* ed. Paul Laumonier et al., 20 vols. (Paris: Société de Textes Français Modernes, 1914–75), 15:178–85. All volumes of the Laumonier edition will be indicated as Lm. For the version in the 1584 *Œuvres,* see Pierre de Ronsard, *Œuvres complètes,* ed. Jean Céard, Daniel Ménager, and Michel Simonin, 2 vols. (Paris: Gallimard, 1993–94), 2:735–39. This edition will be indicated as Pl. The revisions are not numerous, especially after about v. 40.

2. For the equation Cybele = Nature, see the posthumous "Preface sur la Franciade"; Lm. 16:355; Pl. 1:1179.

3. As in such expressions as "Je faux"; for example, *Sonnets pour Helene* 2:30; 2:49 (1584) (Lm. 17:271; Pl. 1:404), or "Mais non," for example, in the poem that becomes the liminary sonnet for the 1584 *Œuvres* (Pl. 1:3; modified from the Lm. 4:85). See also Alex L. Gordon, *Ronsard et la rhétorique* (Geneva: Droz, 1970), 169–72; Marc-Antoine de Muret, *Commentaires au premier livre des Amours de Ronsard,* ed. Jacques Chomarat et al. (Geneva: Droz, 1985), 94ff.

4. See Terence Cave, "Ronsard's Mythological Universe," *Ronsard the Poet,* ed. Terence Cave (London: Methuen, 1973), 181–208, esp. 200–201 on "Le Pin"; Ann Moss, "New Myths for Old?" in *Ronsard in Cambridge,* ed. Philip Ford and Gillian Jondorf (Cambridge: Cambridge University Press, 1986), 55–66, esp. 61–64.

5. Julian, Oration 5, "To the Mother of the Gods"; for Ronsard's possible acquaintance with it, see Géralde Nakam, "Le mythe de Cybèle ou la terre et l'arbre dans l'oeuvre de Ronsard," *Ronsard et la Grèce 1585-1985,* ed. Kyriaki Christodoulou (Paris: Nizet, 1988), 89 n.; Lucretius *De rerum natura,* 2:600–660; Augustine *De civitate Dei* 7.24 (citing Varro). The first offers a metaphysical allegory, the latter two a naturalist one.

6. Lm. 15:180. According to *A Dictionarie of the French and English Tongues,* ed. Randall Cotgrave (1632–), *tesmoings* "are (sometimes) a man's testicles, or stones." He cites the proverb "Tesmoing passe lettre," as does Littré, who gives both nouns in the plural.

7. J. N. Adams, *The Latin Sexual Vocabulary* (London: Duckworth, 1982), 67.

8. *Pasquinate romane del Cinquecento,* ed. Valerio Marucci et al., 2 vols. (Rome: Salerno, 1983), 1:311–12; Matteo Bandello, *Tutte le opere,* ed. Francesco Flora, vol. 1 (Milan: Mondadori, 1934), 838, 843; Agnolo Firenzuola, *Le Novelle,* ed. Eugenio Ragni (Milan: Salerno, 1971), Giornata prima, novella quarta, secs. 35 and 44. The pun turns up again in Tassoni, *La Secchia rapita* 5.13.

9. Des Périers, *Nouvelles* 15 and 60. The use of the pun in the novella tradition concerns a stock situation (a trapped adulterer forced to castrate himself in order to escape) already imagined by Horace, *Serm* 1:2:45–46. For the stock situation, cf. no. 85 of *Les Cent nouvelles,* and nouvelle 26 of Nicolas de Troyes, *Grand parangon.*

10. Plautus, *Miles Gloriosus* 1426 in *Comoediae,* vol. 2, ed. W. M. Lindsay (Oxford: Oxford University Press, 1904). Cf. Curculio 31: "quod amas amato testibus presentibus."

11. Jean-Antoine de Baif, *Le Brave,* ed. Simone Maser (Geneva: Droz, 1979), vv. 3992–93. Ronsard participated in the premiere of this play, composing verses for one of its entr'actes (Lm. 14:201–2; Pl. 2:1122–23).

12. Lm. 11:117; Pl. 2:1044.

13. Michael Riffaterre, *Semiotics of Poetry* (Bloomington: Indiana University Press, 1978), 94. Riffaterre draws his main example from Francis Ponge's use of *artificier* (with the latent Latin *artifex*) in one of his *Douze petits ecrits.*

14. Riffaterre, *Semiotics of Poetry,* 95.

15. Catullus is named at v. 30. For the background of this intertext, see Mary Morrison, "Ronsard and Catullus: The Influence of the Teaching of Marc-Antoine Muret," *Bibliothèque d'Humanisme et Renaissance* 18 (1956): 240–74.

16. Boileau, *Art poétique,* 1:126.

17. Pierre de L'Estoile, *Registre-Journal du règne de Henri III,* ed. Madeleine Lazard and Gilbert Schrenck, vol. 1 (Geneva: Droz, 1992), 172. "Rognons de coq" were thought to be an aphrodisiac; see "La Bouquinade" attributed to Ronsard (Lm. 18:394; Pl. 2:1238).

18. L'Estoile, *Registre-Journal,* ed. Lazard and Schrenck, 172. I make what seems a necessary correction in the last line.

19. L'Estoile, *Registre-Journal,* ed. Lazard and Schrenck, 189. In 1586 the chronicler records another pasquinade which mentions Cybele and declares: "Vrai est qu'on ne vit onques Poule / Tant de braves Coqs commander," but he specifies in a note that Poule refers to Henri III; L'Estoile, *Journal pour le règne de Henri III,* ed. Louis-Raymond Lefèvre (Paris: Gallimard, 1943), 474, 477.

20. Cf. L'Estoile, *Journal pour le règne,* ed. Lefèvre, 174.

21. *De rerum natura* 2:600–643; *Aeneid* 6.784–87.

22. *The Royal Tour of France by Charles IX and Catherine de' Medici: Festivals and Entries 1564–66,* ed. Victor E. Graham and W. McAllister Johnson (Toronto: University of Toronto Press, 1979), 114.

23. *Royal Tour of France,* ed. Graham and Johnson, 177, 182, including this distich for a statue of Cybele (referring to the Trojan origin of the French monarchy): "Alma Phrygum Cybele, Phrygio de sanguine creto/ Effundo Regi pleno mea munera cornu.'

24. *The Paris Entries of Charles IX and Elisabeth of Austria 1571,* ed. Victor E. Graham and W. McAllister Johnson (Toronto: University of Toronto Press, 1974), 188.

25. *Paris Entries,* ed. Graham and Johnson, 189: "Foelix prole parens, qualis Berecenthia mater / Invehitur curru Phrygias turrita per urbes, / Laeta deum partu, centum complexa nepotes." The Virgilian passage (*Aeneid* 6.784–86) begins "felix prole virum," but is otherwise identical.

26. *Paris Entries,* ed. Graham and Johnson, liminary sonnet by Bouquet to the Queen Mother, 101, and sonnet by Guy du Faur de Pibrac, 124.

27. See also Jean Dorat's verses, cited in *Paris Entries,* ed. Graham and Johnson, 62.

28. Lm. 7:35; Pl. 1:726.

29. Lm. 12:157; Pl. 2:218. Lm. 13:97; Pl. 2:154. Lm. 13:277; Pl. 2:1121. During the reign of her husband, Henri II, Catherine was understandably more often represented as Juno; see Edouard Bourciez, *Les Moeurs polies et la littérature de cour sous Henri II* (Paris: Hachette, 1886), 177, 183–85.

30. Baif, *Euvres en rime,* ed. Ch. Marty-Laveaux, 5 vols. (Geneva: Slatkine, 1966), "dedication" of *Le Premier des Meteores,* 2:3, and *Troisieme livre des Passetems,* 4.365.

31. Lm. 9:195; Pl. 2:283.

32. Cf. Guy Demerson, *La Mythologie classique dans l'oeuvre lyrique de la Pléiade* (Geneva: Droz, 1972), 331–32.

33. As Nakam, "Le mythe de Cybèle," 90, comments, "La Franciade doit tout a Cybele."

34. For the texts, see Hugo Hepding, *Attis: Seine Mythen und sein Kult* (Berlin: A. Topelmann, 1967), 37–45, 47–51, 64–67.

35. Lm. 5:24; Pl. 1:297. Lm. 1:252; Pl. 1:711. Lm. 5:61; Pl. 1:563. Lm. 7:275; Pl. 1:202. Not to mention Joachim Du Bellay, *Œuvres poétiques,* ed. Henri Chamard and Geneviève Demerson, 8 vols. (Paris: Société des Textes Français Modernes, 1908–85), 1:135, 5.10, 7.83. In the last of these poems ("Epigramma 2") Du Bellay, like L'Estoile's texts, plays on *Galli/Galli* and the opposition between French virility and oriental (whether Italian or Phrygian) "semivirility." There exists a Virgilian intertext for this Cybele and her procession as for the "high" version: *Aeneid* 9.614–20.

36. Lm. 7:275; Pl. 1:202. The less-than-tragic use of the myth is evident in Belleau's coy comment on this sonnet: "Il celle un autre point duquel il lui [= Attis] voudroit moins resembler," as he refers to Catullus's account; Remy Belleau, *Commentaire au second livre des* Amours *de Ronsard,* ed. Marie-Madeleine Fontaine and François Lecercle (Geneva: Droz, 1986), 47. Cf. Demerson, *La Mythologie classique,* 377.

37. This has already been done, albeit briefly, by Donald Stone, "Poetry and the Attis Legend," *Studi di letteratura francese* 12 (1986): 143–58; and by Nakam, "Le mythe de Cybèle."

38. See Maarten J. Vermaseren, *Cybele and Attis: The Myth and the Cult* (London: Thames and Hudson, 1977), 9–11.

39. Lm 5:21–29; Pl. 1:295–99. Cf. a violent poem in French against the Queen Mother, recorded by L'Estoile, *Registre-Journal,* ed. Lazard and Schrenck, 188, which apostrophizes her as "Catin." These verses and four subsequent Latin epigrams are glossed in the margin thus: "Katin" (187–90).

40. Lm. 12:157; Pl. 2:218. For other examples of Catin as a pastoral character, see Belleau, *Bergerie.*

41. Etienne Jodelle, *Œuvres complètes,* ed. Enea Balmas, 2 vols. (Paris: Gallimard, 1965), 1:205.

42. Jean Calvin, *Institution de la religion chrestienne,* ed. Abel Lefranc et al. (Paris: H. Champion, 1911), 565.

43. Calvin, *Three French Treatises,* ed. Francis M. Higman (London: Athlone Press, 1970), 143

44. See also Catharine Randall Coats, *Embodying the Word: Textual Resurrection in the Martyrological Narratives of Foxe, Crespin, de Bèze, and d'Aubigné* (New York: Peter Lang, 1992).

45. See for example the important uses in Rev. 1:4–5 and 1.9. One of the Protestants who engaged Ronsard in the polemic of the *Discours des misères* makes the identification *tesmoin = martire;* see *La Polémique protestante contre Ronsard,* ed. Jacques Pineaux, 2 vols. (Paris: Didier, 1973), 423.

46. Theodore Agrippa D'Aubigné, *Les Tragiques,* provides the clearest examples. In addition to the numerous uses of *tesmoin* as "martyr" and *tesmoignage* as "martyrdom" in the martyrological book, "Les Feux" (vv. 605, 625, 741, 746, 1097, 1130, 1155), see "La Chambre dorée," 651–52: "Que Dieu a ses tesmoins a donné maintesfois, / La langue estant couppée, une celeste voix"; see Theodore Agrippa D'Aubigné, *Œuvres,* ed. Henri Weber et al. (Paris: Gallimard, 1969).

47. Lm. 15:104; Pl. 2:393 (revised).

48. Theodore Agrippa D'Aubigné, *Histoire universelle,* ed. André Thierry, 10 vols. (Geneva: Droz, 1981–99), 4.143, 7.242.

49. Julian, *Oration 5,* "To the Mother of the Gods," 167C.

50. D'Aubigné, *Histoire universelle,* 3:301.

51. See Simon Goulart, *Mémoires de l'Estat de France sous Charles Neufiesme,* 3 vols. (Mendelbourg: H. Wolf, 1578–79), 1:209r.

52. See I. D. McFarlane, "Aspects of Ronsard's Poetic Vision," *Ronsard the Poet,* 56. Nakam, "Le mythe de Cybèle," 98, sees the three elements of the myth as symbolizing the moments of poetic creation: Cybele, "la fécondité de l'inspiration"; the Corybantes (with Attis), furor; the pine, "l'écriture créatrice."

53. See Daniel Ménager, *Ronsard: Le Roi, le Poète et les Hommes* (Geneva: Droz, 1979), 187–274, esp. 253, 266, 270.

54. D'Aubigné, *Œuvres,* 804; Béroalde de Verville, *Le Moyen de parvenir,* ed. Hélène Moreau and André Tournon, 2 vols. (Aix-en-Provence: Publications Université de Provence; Marseille: Diffusion Jean Laffitte, 1984), 2:118–24. Cf. Catharine Randall Coats, "The Devil's Phallus: Humanistic vs. Theological Notions of Writing in Béroalde de Verville and Agrippa d'Aubigné," *Stanford French Review* 13 (1989): 37–48; and Michael J. Giordano, "Transgression and Castration in *Le Moyen de parvenir:* A Reading of 'Chapitre General' (1.29)," *Studies on Béroalde de Verville,* ed. Giordano (Paris: Biblio 17–Papers on French Seventeenth-Century Literature, 1992), 109–38.

55. Michel de Montaigne, *Œuvres complètes,* ed. Albert Thibaudet and Maurice Rat (Paris: Gallimard, 1962), 837 (*Essais* 3:5).

56. "Elegie," 24 (Lm. 18.143–47; Pl. 2:408–9). Cf. "Le Pin," vv. 9–10, and "Elegie," 1–2 (similar structure and vocabulary already noted by Laumonier 15.178 n.); "Le Pin," 16–17, and "Elegie," 4 (the myth of Erysichthon); "Le Pin," 21, and "Elegie," 22 (nymphs beneath the bark); "Le Pin," 23–34, and "Elegie," 41–48 (poetry and tree[s]). For Ronsard's forest as a place of inspiration, cf. the ode "A la forest de Gastine" (Lm. 1:243–45; Pl. 1:703–4); the sonnet "Sainte Gastine..." (Lm. 4.128; Pl. 1:111); Elizabeth Armstrong, *Ronsard and the Age of Gold* (Cambridge: Cambridge University Press, 1968), 185–88.

57. Ovid *Metamorphoses* 10.86–105 (103–5 for the pine).

58. For example, "L'Orphee," vv. 347–49 (Lm. 12:142; Pl. 2:363); "Hymne de France," 9 (Lm. 1:24; Pl. 2:647); or "A son luc," 122–24 (Lm. 2:162; Pl. 1:965).

59. Claude Binet, *La Vie de P. de Ronsard (1586),* ed. Paul Laumonier (Geneva: Slatkine, 1969), 7–8. Cf. the verses by Dorat cited by Pierre de Nolhac, *Ronsard et l'humanisme* (Paris: H. Champion, 1966), 82n.

60. Lm. 11:129–30; Pl. 2:1049. Is it only a coincidence that he adduces Du Bellay's example thus: "Tesmoing est du Bellay qui comme moy fut sourd"? His Protestant opponents also make the comparison between him and Thamyras, Homer, etc., albeit mockingly; see *La Polémique protestante,* 356–57.

61. Binet, *La Vie de P. de Ronsard,* 9.
62. Sigmund Freud, *Totem and Taboo,* trans. James Strachey (New York: Norton, 1950), 161.
63. Lm. 4.31; Pl. 1:38.
64. See Lawrence D. Kritzman, "Le corps de la fiction et la fiction du corps chez Ronsard," *Sur des vers de Ronsard 1585–1985,* ed. Marcel Tetel (Paris: Aux Amateurs de Livres, 1990), 71–83.
65. Lm. 5.53–76; Pl. 1:560–69, esp. vv. 103–7, 138; and Lm. 6.176–90; Pl. 2:594–601; esp. vv. 179–210, a graphic description of his own divine furor.
66. Lm. 15.179, v. 168.
67. Lm. 15.14.
68. In the *Sixiesme livre,* see: "Le Chat," vv. 91, 110; "Les Parolles que dit Calypson," 150, 263; "La Salade," 34; "L'Ombre du cheval," 85. In the *Septiesme livre,* see: "Elegie au seigneur Pierre du Lac," 17; "Le Soucy du jardin," 29, 85–90; "Le Pin," 165–70; "Le Rossignol," 79–81. See also sonnets 1, 2, 3, and 5: "Elegie, ou Amour oyseau," 1–26; "Elegie: Pour vous aymer," 1–4; "Elegie à A. Jamyn"; "Elegie: Seule apres Dieu," 43–52. As noted by D. B. Wilson, *Ronsard Poet of Nature* (Manchester: Manchester University Press, 1961), 108n, Ficino in his *De triplici vita* suggests that the *"fiebvre quarte* is a disease particularly appropriate to the *studieux."*
69. Ronsard, cited in *La Polémique protestante,* 5–27. The second *Palinodie* is addressed—like Ronsard's "Discours"—to the Queen Mother. For the response to this accusation (Ronsard had already stolen the riches he accuses others of taking from him), see *La Polémique protestante,* 236, 369–72.
70. See Eusebe Philadelphe, *Le Reveille-matin des François et de leurs voisins* (Edinburgh: Jaques James, 1574), 109–16; Ménager, *Ronsard: Le Roi,* 289 and nn. 88–90. Cf. the extended comparison of Catherine to Brunehaut in the *Discours merveilleux de la vie, actions & deportemens de Catherine de Medicis Royne mere,* in Simon Goulart, *Mémoires de l'Estat de France,* 3:345r–349r (as in *Le Reveille-matin*).
71. See Ménager, *Ronsard: Le Roi,* 250–51.
72. For the "Grand Prestre de Cybele," see *La Polémique protestante,* 296, 507; cf. p. 517 to see what Ronsard has cut or will cut in order to advance himself in the church. The declaration in that polemic (336) that Ronsard knows the galliambic meter, of which Catullus's *carmen* 63 is the sole extant example, not to mention a reference to the ancient custom of castrating priests (342), also allude to the poet's involvement with the matter of Attis.
73. Note the vocabulary of both play and fertility in the lines that introduce Ronsard's retelling of the Attis myth, vv. 32–34: "Et moy François en me joüant apres / Je la diray, afin que telle histoire, / En tous endroitz fleurisse par memoire" [And I, a Frenchman, in playing hereafter / I will tell it, so that such a story, / May flourish everywhere in the memory].
74. The passage 151–54 is the only one in the poem, apart from 129–30, to be set apart by sententious quotation marks.
75. Lm. 18.456; Pl. 2:1191.
76. See Jacques Derrida, *L'écriture et la différence* (Paris: Seuil, 1967), 9–49.

Mother's Milk
from Father's Breast
Maternity without Women
in Male French Renaissance Lyric

Kirk Read

La société humaine est une anti-physis: elle ne subit pas passivement la présence de la nature, elle la reprend à son compte. Cette reprise n'est pas une opération intérieure et sub-jective: elle s'effectue objectivement dans la praxis.

—Simone de Beauvoir, *Le Deuxième Sexe*[1]

The poetry that inspired this study, its curious title, and the convening of sources as diverse as Pierre de Ronsard's odes and Simone de Beauvoir's *The Second Sex*, employs an image that unsettles the modern reader for its supposed unnaturalness. The concept of the breast-feeding male is arresting, even comical. Accustomed as we are to centuries of discourse on the natural processes of the nursing mother and to a small industry of recent scholarship by social historians on the subject, the suggestion of a lactating father in her stead elicits shock—a strange oxymoron that would appear to have a decidedly small field of investigation.[2] The evidence from humanists of sixteenth-century France, however, disproves this. The nursing father was a common topos, employed in a variety of literary settings to different effect. As such, a study of this curious, albeit rather common, literary convention whereby male authors appropriate such a highly female-defined function offers important insight into prevailing attitudes towards gender and literature in early modern Europe. This study may prove the extremes of de Beauvoir's critique of historical materialism: human nature (*la société humaine*) does not heed a monolithic natural law—and in the context of this chapter we shall gender this resistance male. Indeed, men such as those quoted in this analysis do not stop short of co-opting the woman's nursing body as their own, consuming her, becoming her, and transforming her (*[Il] la reprend a son compte!*) to pro-mote and protect what remains a perpetually male literary universe.[3]

The project here discovers what a feminist critique of canonical male authors can tell us of how gender informs the praxis of men's writing of the Renaissance. Gender studies have revealed much about the literary strategies of early modern women writers and their inscription of gendered conventions and traditions in their works. With copi-ous and diverse responses to de Beauvoir's legacy with regard to women writers now in mind, men's writing seems ripe for reappraisal. Ann Rosalind Jones's groundbreaking article on this period, "Assimilation with a Difference," insightfully reveals the ways in which women writers strategize with male literary conventions to express a distinctly female condition. This work will present a converse operation with regard to their male counterparts: men as assimilators of women—their bodies, their domain, and their language—striving to construct a startlingly self-sufficient paradigm of literary sustenance and reproduction.[4]

For the French Renaissance male poet, the maternal metaphor was an exceedingly attractive one for all it suggested in terms of rebirth and nourishment vis-à-vis a revered classical past. And so, just as Jones explored women's *bricolage* with male-defined convention and rhetoric, so this essay will propose gendered readings of canonical male writers who masculinize maternity in order to empower their writing—co-opting women and women's roles to further the cause of the French literary tradition, and perhaps more importantly, their own quest for immortality. As they scavenge through Rome for edifying allusions and precedent, so do they pillage the female gender for all that it may afford their glorious project: assimilation, as it were, with a vengeance.

Two examples of maternalized mentorship in the poetic works of Pierre de Ronsard present and pull into focus this peculiar dynamic: first, an *elogia* to his teacher Jean Dorat; second, a recasting of the same issues of praise and male nurturance with regard to a returning French statesman. Dorat, a renowned Renaissance Hellenist known as the father of a group of poet luminaries named the Pléiade, and Ronsard, its most shining member, leave intriguing literary traces of their mentor-disciple relationship, publicized most memorably in Ronsard's early poem "A Jan Dorat."[5]

Ronsard's tremendous sense of privilege and personal mission combined with his consummate facility with the literary conventions of his day make him a fruitful primary subject for an analysis focused on issues of appropriation and masculine control.[6] Ronsard's poem begins:

Puissai-je entonner un vers
Qui raconte à l'univers
Ton los porté sus son aile,
Et combien je fus heureus
Sucer le laict savoureux
De ta feconde mammelle!

[Could I but intone a verse
Which would tell the world
Your glory carried on its wing,
And how fortunate I was
To suckle the savory milk
Of your fertile breast!

Sur ma langue doucement
Tu mis au commencement
Je ne sçai quelles merveilles,
Que vulgaires je randi,
Et premier les épandi
Dans les Françoises oreilles.[7]

Upon my tongue sweetly
Did you place at first
Indescribable marvels
Which I rendered into French,
The first to pour them
Into French ears.]

Not surprisingly for those familiar with Ronsard, this ode penned ostensibly to honor his beloved teacher Dorat is ultimately about Ronsard himself. This narcissism is common throughout Ronsard's works, most notably in the *Amours* where his praise-weary lovers Cassandre, Marie, and Hélène stand in as models for his personal literary agenda. In "A Jan Dorat," he begins: "Puissai-je" [Could I] and rarely refocuses attention objectively. Dorat becomes a pretext for talking about Ronsard's greatness. The back-and-forth between Ronsard and Dorat in this poem is a structuring mechanism indeed: "puissai-*je*" – "*ton* los" / "*je* fu heureus" – "*ta* mammelle" / "*ma* langue" – "*tu* mis", and so on, but the emphasis clearly is on the success of Ronsard. The poem ends, not with direct praise of Dorat, as in, "you are so knowledgeable and wonder-ful," but with "Voi m'en ci le temoignage" [See in me the witness of this greatness]—literally, "Look at me!" Ronsard's practice of co-opting the subjects of his works and employing them for personal gain—be they lovers, mothers, and/or mentors—is deeply relevant to Ronsard's poetics and emblematic of the same impulse one finds in his contemporaries. A summary of the remainder of the poem should make clear Ronsard's intentions.

It is the duty of a student, he explains in the next two stanzas, to pay homage to one's teacher—emphasizing again "le miel de *ma voix*" [the sweetness—honey—of *my voice*] and his own laureled head. At the midpoint in stanza five, Ronsard returns to the imagery of the opening, in slightly modified terms. Again, "si j'ai du bruit" [if I am famous] then concedes it is because of his preceptor's fine tutoring—a teacher who found him thirsting (*Tout alteré me treuva*) and gave him drink (*m'abreuva*)—"de l'une et l'autre fontaine" [from both fountains/sources]. This reference to the two fountains of the muses, Castalia and Hippocrene, harkens back to the breasts from his opening lines and, metaphorically, to Greek and Latin, the languages of antiquity so key to Ronsard's apprenticeship in letters. Stanza six reiterates the name of the mother as mentor to the apprentice who, while young, may please the common public (*les bandes rurales*), yet who when fully formed, targets the more discerning, more educated, and as in "mains liberales," more remunerative royal court. The Ronsard-Dorat relationship is then recast in the Olympian context—Dorat as generous minister or Phoebus Apollo to Ronsard's grateful, adoring muse—which leads to a final, self-interested description of how contented and proud Dorat must feel to have suckled a child such as him (Ronsard), a witness to Dorat's greatness which now firmly belongs to them both. So concludes this poem written ostensibly to praise the mentor, but working simultaneously to immortalize the apprentice as well.

Some twenty years later, Ronsard offered another version of the nursing male, this time describing Monseigneur le Connétable (the uncle of his addressee, the cardinal de Chatillon) as wet nurse to an adoring, thirsting nation.[8] What appeared in the poem to Dorat as supporting a literary agenda is reworked here into a political message. Monseigneur le Connétable returns to his countrymen as a bountiful mother whose breast will nourish and warm his hungering charges. The thirst for knowledge that is slaked in his earlier poem is here conflated with a thirst for leadership and moral authority:

(1)	… Comme un petit enfant que sa nourrice avoit	(1)	[Like a baby whose wet nurse had
(2)	Allaité longuement pleure s'il ne la voit,	(2)	Suckled him for so long who cries should he not see her,
(3)	De ses petites mains au berceau se tourmente,	(3)	His little arms flailing vainly from the cradle, inconsolable
(4)	En soupirant l'appelle, et toujours se lamente	(4)	Sadly calling out to her, continously crying
(5)	D'une voix enfantine, et ne veut s'éjouir	(5)	In his infant voice, and who refuses to rejoice
(6)	Jusqu'à tant qu'il la voie ou qu'il la puisse ouir…	(6)	Until he can see or hear her…
	………		………
(9)	Elle en ses bras l'échauffe, et depuis le matin	(9)	She warms him in her arms, and from morning
(10)	Soigneuse jusqu'au soir le pend à son tétin:	(10)	Until night, carefully holds him to her nipple:
(11)	Ainsi toute la France à l'heureuse venue	(11)	Such is France's joy at the most happy
(12)	De ton oncle captif joyeuse est deve- nue….[9]	(12)	Return of your captive uncle.]

France, here depicted as the hungry male child, awaits the return of its wet nurse, again a male, who will suckle his adoring countrymen back to health and contentedness: this from a poet whose epic verse, however unsuccessfully, attempted to rival the bellicose strains of Virgil's *Aeneid*. The mother soon disappears, however; men, even warriors, now suckle their sons. One sees here how the image of the nursing male remains a powerful metaphor for Ronsard across genres and within the various paradigms of desire, consumption, and satiety that these literary configurations entail. In a literary milieu obsessed with the celebration and rebirth of classical origins for the purpose of legitimizing and nourishing the French vernacular tradition, Ronsard strives in a variety of ways to transform and implicate the male spirit and body as part of the imaginings of creation and sustenance of national leadership and literary prowess. In this masculinist poetics, Ronsard appropriates for men the role of bountiful mother who may dispense and impart at will to disciples, peers, and countrymen an abundance of maternal warmth and fecundity exacted from their idealized female others. As subsequent examples demonstrate, Ronsard's strategy of appropriation was not unique: male glorification and edification via maternal discourse was common to a variety of contemporaneous writers. Having presented one poet's particular versions of this theme, however, some preliminary suggestions as to the provenance and general currency of the maternal male are in order. Investigation of the logic of such seemingly unusual poetic rhetoric is illuminated by an analysis of both literary convention and precedent and other, more literal, scientific suppositions of the early modern period. What emerges is a set of conveniently crafted assumptions about gender, production, and reproduction that persistently favor male dominance and control—a preponderant iconography of men vested with women's maternal functions, supported and sustained in both poetic and anatomic constructs.

Just as Ronsard's lovers served his self-interest as *porte-paroles* of his changing literary agenda, so is the mother co-opted in quite similar ways by the opportunistic lyricist. The poet's engagement with Petrarchan poetic convention easily repermutates from one female role to another. Ronsard's relation both to female lovers and maternal figures betrays a more generalized appropriation of the female persona in order to better totalize his literary control. Philippa Berry's study of male Petrarchan poets and their relation to the female lover resonates well with practices of the same group of writers with regard to mothers, and responds quite appropriately to the specific case of Ronsard's poem:

> This figure [of the beloved] was usually little more than an instrument in an elaborate game of *masculine* "speculation" and self-determination, for the philosophical enterprise common to both Petrarchism and Renaissance Neoplatonism used woman as a "speculum" or mirror of masculine narcissism. The hypothesis that a chaste woman could serve as a bridge between the material world and an invisible spiritual dimension enabled Petrarchan poet and Neoplatonic philosopher to elaborate a new *concept of masculine wholeness and self-sufficiency* through or across her idealized figure. By this means, they affirmed Renaissance man's conviction that he could achieve a godlike control, not just over his own nature, but over his environment as well.[10]

By focusing on another female role that is exploited and appropriated by male writers, this poetry suggests that men were not constrained entirely within the realm of the chaste and idealized body of the Platonic, female lover in order to achieve masculine wholeness and self-sufficiency, but worked through or across—and indeed as or within—the maternal body in order to further this godlike control over their own nature and environment: shades of de Beauvoir come to mind—*elle ne subit pas passivement la présence de la nature, elle la reprend à son compte.* By expanding the paradigm that Berry uses in her analysis, we shall see in Ronsard and his contemporaries a vision of the male poet as ever more controlling, his agenda perhaps only more insidious and predatory. The desire for the female lover becomes conflated with the desire for creative control, an ideal more logically centered in the female breast and womb than in the heart.

Berry's exploration of masculinist control of women and nature as witnessed in their manipulation of Petrarchan conventions appears only more keenly relevant to

Ronsard and Dorat when paired with theories of male homosociality. The discussion of the female lover and her conflicted role as essential to male creativity yet ultimately irrelevant or incommodious is the subject of Eve Sedgwick's treatment of Shakespeare.[11] Sedgwick illuminates this recurring image of male poets bonding over the ubiquitous female object of desire and consumption in a way that is only further expanded by examining men as observers and consumers of mothers. Sedgwick defines the process of female inclusion and eventual effacement within the male literary world as programmatic, even normative. Like Berry's, Sedgwick's claims are for a male-female erotic love construct—"the compulsory routing of homosocial desire through heterosexual love more or less as a matter of course."[12] The refiguring of their paradigms with respect to mothers as opposed to lovers disturbs little the economy of their desire for immortality. Just as in Shakespeare's sonnets where the poet and his rival joust and bond over the Dark Lady (as in Sedgwick's Girardian configuration), so do Ronsard and Dorat raise the specter of woman, only to absorb her, that is, embody her, and continue on unfettered. Women become the site for male union and then dematerialize or rematerialize in their poetic works as masculinized mothers.

In terms of homosocial theory, Ronsard plays out the paradigm in a way that is at once more expansive and more efficient than the triangular configuration originally suggested. In Ronsard's poem, we know Dorat to be at once a collaborator or mentor to Ronsard as well as, in this instance, a muse. Dorat's reputation as a crafter and teacher of poetic verse is collapsed into his inspirational role, here expressed through a depiction of him as mother. He thus performs double duty in the male-female-male triad, a feat accomplished by Ronsard's supernatural suggestion of his mentor as endowed with maternal capacities. Ronsard thus configures and controls both his muse and his modes of production, engaging in and imparting roles traditionally reserved for women. Woman is most certainly still implicated in Dorat and Ronsard's poetic enterprise; she is, however, entirely absorbed. The praise that in most other Petrarchan situations belonged at least ostensibly to the lover is here clearly that of the men.

The question of men's working within the maternal body to assume literary control of their poetic subjects is echoed in the sixteenth-century literature on human anatomy. Recent scholarship on early modern conceptions of sex and gender brings to light a vision of male and female conflation that suggests what Ronsard imagines is grounded in the physiological reality of the time. In the Renaissance worldview, Dorat was already more maternal than later critics might give him credit for. Physicians from as early as Galen to the more contemporaneous Ambroise Paré explained sex and gender under the assumption of anatomical sameness, the woman's genitalia being merely undescended. Thomas Laqueur's analysis of prevailing conceptions converges on the view of an "oxymoronic one-sex body":

> It is a ... body whose fluids—blood, semen, milk, and the various excrements—are fungible in that they turn into one another and whose processes—digestion and generation, menstruation, and other bleeding—are not

so easily distinguished or so easily assignable to one sex or another.... This "one flesh," the construction of a single-sexed body with its different versions attributed to at least two genders, was framed in antiquity to valorize the extraordinary cultural assertion of patriarchy, of the father, in the face of the more sensorily evident claim of the mother.[13]

Within this paradigm, then, with regard to sex, the process of appropriation had already been suggested to men. Notions of what the male body was capable of and how it functioned allow for a somewhat less perplexed reaction to Ronsard's depiction of his nursing mentor. Men had been making their milk and drinking it too, so to speak, since antiquity. The "extraordinary cultural assertion of patriarchy," expressed by Laqueur, conveniently and convincingly mirrors the "godlike control of nature" proposed in Berry's literary paradigm. Thus, Ronsard expresses literarily what Laqueur sees as a powerful cultural impulse to control and define a male hegemonic code. Medical, scientific discourse sets in place a view to man's naturally androgynous physical being, which finds expression in these literary imaginings. Male breast-feeders speak to a condition that is less appropriation than expression, or perhaps exploitation, of an already integrated body capable of male and female functions.

What is clearly important is that this quasi-hermaphroditic conception of the body for men is worked consistently to their advantage. Men do not become weakened or effeminized by dint of their embodiment of both male and female properties; on the contrary, they become ever more male, ever more perfect. Here, medical and literary imaginings of the Renaissance diverge in interesting ways. Ambroise Paré, the royal surgeon to the French court, includes a chapter in his 1573 *Des Monstres et des Prodiges* [Of monsters and prodigies] entitled "Histoires Memorables de Certaines Femmes Qui Sont Dégénérées en Hommes" [Memorable stories of certain women who changed into men]. Paré relates indeed quite memorable and fantastic stories from the past of women who, when their natural processes of heat exhalation are blocked, may well, with a sudden jolt, experience an expulsion of their previously internalized genitalia. The story made famous by Montaigne of Marie-Germain, whose sex changed as she jumped the stream while chasing her pigs, is the author's final dramatic example. Paré concludes his physiological explanation with the following observation:

Or, comme telle metamorphose a lieu en Nature par les raisons et exemples alleguees, aussi nous ne trouvons jamais en histoire veritable que d'homme aucun soit devenu femme, pour-ce que nature tend tousjours à ce qui est le plus parfaict, et non au contraire faire que ce qui est parfaict devienne imparfaict.[14]

[So, just as this metamorphosis takes place in nature for the reasons and in the examples here alleged, we never find, thus, a reputable story of any man become woman, for nature evolves always to that which is more perfect and does not, on the contrary, make that which is perfect imperfect.]

And so, though the single sex theory of anatomy implies a fungibility of fluids and a certain indeterminacy of sexual identity, Paré is quick and sure to offer a misogynist truism that points to inevitable transformation toward that which is perfect and male and away from the cold, troubled humors of the female. What Ronsard imagines in his poem, however, is not so much that Dorat abandons his perfect sex, but rather enjoys a literary transvestism of sorts that affords him the control of body and of word, a praxis, as de Beauvoir would have it, that does not passively submit to nature's laws. He indeed subverts them. The masculinist voice is only more empowered for the surplus of imagined maternal capacities. Dorat may don all that the mothering male may afford him and shed it at will, certain of his status rejoined to the fraternity of poets he has spawned.

Given this contextualization of Ronsard's poetics of maternal appropriation, there remains an array of similar literary texts where the recurrent image of men as mothers further illuminates this masculinist agenda. The "père nourrisseur" [nourishing father] surfaces in the writings of many of Ronsard's peers, both secular and religious. The following examples reveal a variety of ways in which other male writers engaged the maternal figure on their behalf, further expanding our appreciation of the popularity of this image for men across decades, literary genres, and political agendas. These poets' inscription of the maternal male also plays into and transforms many of the poetic conventions of their male literary tradition—all of them converging on a common view to male glorification and a concomitant, gradual effacement of the female body which they put into temporary poetic service.

Ronsard's fellow Pléiade member Rémy Belleau, in his *Amours et Nouveaux Eschanges des Pierres Précieuses* of 1576 [Love poems and new works on precious stones], speaks of paternal nourishment, transforming a common literary convention in which traditionally female or maternal imagery is thoroughly masculinized. Belleau writes in geological metaphor of the rivers, characterized as masculine, which nourish and form the material *galactite* (perhaps the mineral known as talc):

(77) Le Nil et l'Achelois, grands fleuves de la terre,

(78) Dans leur sein limmoneux nourrissent ceste pierre,

(79) De couleur blanchissante et de mesme saveur

(80) Que le lait, des enfans le pere nourrisseur.[15]

(77) [The Nile and the Achelois, great rivers of the earth

(78) In their silty breast nourish this stone

(79) Of whitish hue and of the same taste

(80) As milk, (this stone) the nourishing father of children.]

Belleau participates here in a common literary trope for writers of his century, that of poetic allusion to regional rivers that flow through the writers' birthplaces and are honored for having inspired and, in a metaphysical sense, produced them. The Loire and Loir garnered much praise from Ronsard and Joachim Du Bellay for having borne, nourished, and inspired their vastly productive poetic careers. Similarly, the confluence of the Rhône and Saône rivers in Lyon is worked into the strains of many of that city's writers, most consistently by Maurice Scève, who depicts the felicitous joining of the two rivers into one as symbolic of both male-female romantic union and the resultant fertility of the Lyonnais environs which produces and inspires its renowned poets. Scève declares in dizain 17: "Plutôt seront Rhône et Saône déjoints / Que d'avec toi mon coeur se désassemble" [Sooner would the Rhône and Saône disunite / Than would my heart from yours break away].[16]

That Belleau revises this topos in a way that does away with the female influence is telling, and quite compatible with similarly male-defined paradigms penned by his peers. Mother Nature cedes to "père nourrisseur". And, as if to underscore this miraculous, male coup de force, the mineral produced by this fecund father river—the "*père/pierre nourrisseur*"—is said by Belleau to assist in the production of milk when applied to the breast.[17]

Just as the father's breast might signal goodness and nourishment, so might it convey the opposite and be the source of corruption. Another Pléiade member, Pontus de Tyard, in his "Du Socratique," ode 3, also masculinizes the maternal breast in his depiction of male nourishment and influence when speaking of Epicurus, this time portraying the counterexample, the "*père nourrisseur*" gone bad:

(10) Luy, comme les inhumains,	(10) [He, like those barbarians
(11) Qui feirent au Ciel la guerre	(11) Who make war with heaven
(12) Pour l'egaler à la terre,	(12) To reduce it to earthly dimension
(13) Sentit les divines mains	(13) Felt the divine hands
(14) Assommer les discours vains	(14) Break asunder the vain discourse
(15) Dedans sa poitrine infecte,	(15) Within his filthy breast
(16) Qu'encor depuis ont teté	(16) From whence have suckled
(17) Les nourrissons de la secte	(17) The disciples of this sect
(18) Qui souille la Deité.[18]	(18) Which sullies God.]

While the pure, male, nursing breast can pour forth the milk of human kindness and true compassion, so might its polluted twin—the "poitrine infecte"—pass on evil and degeneration. While Ronsard and Belleau insist on the positively idealized qualities of the mothering breast and exploit it to express a miraculously masculinized version of fecundity and nutriment, Tyard plays on the more physical and, therefore, dangerous suppositions of women's corporeal nature: bodies as changeable, polluted, and vulnerable to nefarious forces of corruption. As Juan Luis Vives admonishes in his contemporaneous *Education of a Christian Woman:* "I pray thee, understand thine own goodness maid, ... shut up both body and mind, and seal them with those seals that none can open."[19] And so it is that Tyard puts into play the notions of pollution and degeneracy that issue from the mother; he then transfers this deplorable threat onto a male nursing figure, here depicted as corrupted instead of glorified by association with the maternal body. The maternal breast could be appropriated in completely opposite ways depending upon the poet's agenda—an arbitrariness comparable to the fate of poetic lovers. If Ronsard's Marie could be praised as the hallmark of a new *style bas,* so could she later be cast off as too simple, a vestige of a previous poetic agenda. Likewise, in these poetic appropriations of the maternal role, the nursing mother may stand in for divine bounty or contaminated vessel of sin and corruption at the whim of the scribe. Women, whether lovers or mothers, are, in the universe of these male lyric poets, malleable and ultimately disposable.

The authors examined thus far hail from the literary fraternity of Pléiade poets, whose maternal fantasies exhibit a common rhetoric of infinite control over the content and the destiny of their writing. While these men had individual—and at times rival—agendas, their poetics have been seen as functioning within a homosocial dialectic that edifies male production and self-sustainment. These male poets assume the natural processes of women, exploiting and explaining them in ways that praise (Ronsard and Belleau) or caution (Tyard) regarding the powerful effects of male mothers. In the remaining examples, the analysis moves within and beyond the Pléiade sphere to explore how the use of the maternal metaphor transformed larger, commonly held literary and iconographic depictions of poetic creation, here again invoking the maternal and gendering it male. Readings of Rabelais, Agrippa d'Aubigné, and Du Bellay push our analysis from breast to womb, furthering the vision of the totalizing control of women's bodies enacted by this generation of male writers.

One of the better known examples of maternalized mentorship among male humanists is that of François Rabelais's 1532 letter to Bernard Salignac—whose true addressee was Erasmus. Having referred to Erasmus as "Pater mi Humanissime," Rabelais continues:

> Patrem te dixi, matrem etiam dicerem, si per indulgentiam mihi id tuam liceret. Quod enim utero gerentibus usui uenire quotidie experimur, ut quos nunquam uiderunt fœtus alant ab aërisque ambientis incommodis tueantur.... Qui me tibi de facie ignotum, nomine etiam ignobilem sic educasti, sic castissimis diuinae tuae doctrinae uberibus usque aluisti, ut quidquid sum et ualeo, tibi id uni acceptum.[20]

> [I have called you "father," I might say even "mother," if you would indulge me in this sentiment. In fact, pregnant women nourish a foetus that they have never seen and protect it from the perils of the outside world.... You have never seen my face, even my name was unknown to you and yet you educated me, you have not ceased from nourishing me with the irreproachable milk of your holy knowledge; what I am, what I am worth, I owe entirely to you.]

Again, as with Ronsard and Dorat, we see the praise of a mentor figure which employs a maternal metaphor in order to describe the apprenticeship and growth of the learner. In some translations, the "divinae tuae doctrinae uberibus" is rendered from Rabelais's

Latin "uberibus" as, logically, "mamelles" or teats. The English translation of *uber* connotes richness, fruitfulness, fertility, and alternately, breast, teat, udder, or dug.

Several influences appear to be at work in Rabelais's epistle. Rabelais is in dialogue here with his mentor in ways that bespeak an intertextual relationship as well as a common view of Renaissance poets' conception of indebtedness to classical precedent. The concept of pairing the nursing breast with the dispensing of knowledge, whether divine or humanist, held great currency in the sixteenth-century literary milieu. Child-rearing manuals and scholarly ruminations concerning the imbibing of milk and of knowledge are consistently wont to link the two activities as one. Conduct books, such as Vives's *Education of a Christian Woman,* admonish women to breast-feed their own children and cultivate their minds simultaneously as the two phenomena are interdependent.[21] Erasmus himself was similarly convinced, and he replicates much of this text (and its classical precedent which is most surely Plutarch's "On the Training of Children") in his own "On the Education of Children," suggesting the conflation of men, nursing, and learning presented more tacitly in his predecessors. Having concluded his remarks on nurses, Erasmus turns to the timely selection of a tutor. Contrary to popular thought, which advises indulging children in their carefree youth, he claims:

> Instead, you should straightaway begin to search for a man of good character and respectable learning to whose care you may safely entrust your son to receive the proper nourishment for his mind and to imbibe, as it were, with the milk that he suckles, the nectar of education.[22]

If it was suggested before in the case of Ronsard and Dorat that feminization precedes appropriation, it appears that remasculinization of the mentor and disciple is an equally important part of this dialectic. Further iconographical evidence may offer some insights.

For the learned Renaissance audience, this maternalization of the mentor bespeaks as well an attachment to the highly recognizable theme of innutrition or nourishment which characterized the Pléiade poets' relationship to knowledge and inspiration in general, and to their Latin and Greek ancestors more precisely. Du Bellay, another Pléiade member, describes this perhaps most clearly in his *Deffence et Illustration de la Langue Françoise* of 1535 wherein he speaks of emulating the Romans, whom he describes as

> ...immitant les meilleurs aucteurs Grecz, se transformant en eux, les devorant, & apres les avoir bien digerez, les convertissant en sang et nourriture, chacun selon son naturel.[23]

> [...imitating the best of the Greek authors, transforming oneself into them, devouring them, and after having well digested them, converting them into blood and food, each one according to his own style.]

Images of appropriation and oral sustenance seem keenly applicable. The process of transforming, digesting, and being reborn is entirely suggestive of the phenomenon of maternalization and subsequent appropriation—seen here as devouring—that these authors are enacting. Not only do these writers become and devour their literary ancestors, however; this same transformation and consumption pertains to women. Feeding off women (just as Du Bellay would have it described of the Greeks), the Renaissance writer empowers his poetry with all that his opportunistic pen can glean. The comment "chacun selon son naturel" only further emphasizes the convenience and adaptability of this poetic strategy. Thus, the works of Du Bellay and his male contemporaries, however conflicted in their relation to the past, express highly similar impulses to biologize, and more specifically to maternalize, the process of the creation of a viable French literary agenda. Their theses are predicated on the notion of maternal language, of naturalness of expression passed on through evolving generations of writers indebted to but distinct from a Greek and Latin past that cannot respond fully to their emerging sense of national identity.

Thomas Sébillet in his *Art Poétique* maps out this generational ancestry most exhaustively, and the absence of female participation or inclusion is revealing. In a passage redolent of Old Testament rhetoric, he intones the "begats" of literary precedent: "from Apollo and Orpheus came Homer...from whence came Hesiod, then Pindar...from whence Plautus...after whom Virgil, Ovid, Horace...then the Italians...Dante and Petrarch and finally the French...Jean de Meun and Jean Lemaire de Belges."[24]

The mothers in this poetic process have vanished. Sébillet's genealogy is a male poetic conceit that suggests female absorption into what remains an entirely masculine descent. If Ronsard and his peers suggest the means by which this is possible, Sébillet simply expresses the ends: male writers, male tradition, male reproduction.

With Sébillet and Ronsard particularly in mind, Du Bellay's famous sonnet 9 from *Les Regrets* provides a telling commentary on conceptions of gender and literary ancestry evoked by writers of his century:

France, mere des arts, des armes, et des loix,	[France, mother of arts, mother of arms and laws,
Tu m'as nourry long temps du laict de ta mamelle:	You gave me suck from your abundant breast:
Ores, comme un aigneau qui sa nourrice appelle,	Now like a lamb crying for what is lost
Je remplis de ton nom les antres et les bois.	I fill the rocks and forests with my call.
Si tu m'as pour enfant advoué quelquefois,	If at one time you admitted I was yours,
Que ne me respons-tu maintenant, o cruelle?	Why are you silent now, why are you cruel?
France, France, respons à ma triste querelle:	France, oh France, answer me mercifully!

Mais nul, sinon Echo, ne respond à ma voix.[25]	But the echo only brings back my own words.][26]

Du Bellay depicts himself here as a helpless lamb/child, wandering the Roman countryside in search of the breast of his mother, his mother's milk, the *langue maternelle* that can sustain him and which, not inconsequentially, he has fought to define and defend. If "France, mother of arts," places woman at the center of this maternal personification, the evidence gleaned from contemporaneous accounts suggests the transparency of this claim. Ronsard has maternalized Dorat, the father of Renaissance court poetry, and claimed Monseigneur le Connétable as *nourrice* to his country; Sébillet's genealogy clearly marks the effacement of female involvement; Tyard even suggests that maternalized males are as capable of corruption as women themselves. Indeed, Du Bellay's regrets and sense of abandonment during his sojourn in Italy where his poems are penned harken back not so much to this idealized Mother France as to a group of male poets whose celebrity and favor with the court threaten to outstrip him.

The implication of a male presence and tradition in control behind the façade of the mother country is more explicit later in Du Bellay's poem where he evokes lupine imagery and a mythological account of parenthood and nurturance quite fitting to this discussion: "Entre les loups cruels j'erre parmy la plaine" [I am left to wander among hungry wolves]. The poet/lamenter depicts himself orphaned, wandering about the countryside, in search of sustenance, and in the presence of wolves. Du Bellay begs comparison with the Roman sucklers par excellence, Romulus and Remus, a reprise of Rabelais's "uber"—the breasts, dugs, or teats. And images return of Ronsard, found thirsting by a Dorat qua Faustulus, the shepherd who discovered the abandoned twins, suckled by a she-wolf. Du Bellay's sonnet is an elegant depiction of his conflicted relationship with two mothers, two "sources": that is, France and Rome. France, the good wolf/mother, is absent and Du Bellay wanders Rome, tormented, agonizing as he does textually throughout the *Regrets* and *Deffence* about his relationship to the Roman legacy, alluded to as the roving, carnivorous, "bad wolf."[27]

This nursing wolf challenges our conceptions of maternity in much the same way as Ronsard's depiction of Dorat. Suckling at the breast of an aging male mentor and alternately under a wild she-wolf seem at first glance to be similarly unnatural, inappropriate activities. If it is Dorat's gender that unsettles the reader, it is the wolf's animality, an animality accentuated by a visual code that is clearly, again, masculine. The most famous icon of Roman lore is the Capitoline Wolf, a bronze visited like a shrine during the Renaissance by legions of enthralled humanists, drinking, or nursing, at the source, as it were, of their reborn world of letters. Bernard Andreae's popular description of the statue from *The Art of Rome* expresses most efficiently the gender flux at work in the poetic renderings of this image:

> The forelegs are rigidly blocked in place, as if the animal had stopped short. The back legs with their muscular shanks are supplely relaxed but ready, at an

instant's need, to swing the body around to face an aggressor from any direction. The wedge of the body culminates in the half-open muzzle with its bared fangs. The dilated nostrils sniff the air for an enemy scent, tense veins shoot across the muzzle, the folds above the eyes are sharp.... Wide open, erect, the ears emphasize the impression of alertness. The tightly superimposed curls of the mane are like flames, and they continue in a crest along the back all the way to the tail (a later restoration), circling the entire forepart in a tight girdle just behind the shoulders. The flanks of the lean but powerful beast are sucked in, its ribs protrude....[28]

As this description rather unsubtly suggests, the image of the Roman she-wolf is highly masculinized, with its female features quite consciously reconstrued—the dugs themselves, given the sucked-in flanks and protruding ribs, appear more phallic than maternal. If Du Bellay, Ronsard, and their contemporaries were searching for a male model of maternal sustenance, this icon would appear to serve the purpose well. The strangeness of the twins suckling at this phallic, bestial mother resonates with and neatly prepares the image of the young male poet suckling at the breast of his mentor. Natural, maternal functions are conveniently revised. The iconography circulating at the time suggested a fluidity of gender, leaving it to Renaissance male writers to incorporate and transform its power and meaning.

The opening to d'Aubigné's *Tragiques* provides appropriate material for a conclusion to this study in that it pushes the concept of male appropriation of the maternal body to its most powerful end: the male poet who produces his own, textual, progeny and is then suckled by this child-become-mother. From "L'Auteur à son Livre":

(1) Va Livre, tu nes que trop beau	(1) [Go, my book, you are too beautiful
(2) Pour estre né dans le tombeau	(2) To have been born in this tomb
(3) Duquel mon exil te delivre;	(3) Into which my exile has delivered you;
(4) Seul pour nous deux je veux perir:	(4) Alone, I shall perish for us both:
(5) Commence, mon enfant, à vivre	(5) Begin, my child, to live
(6) Quand ton pere s'en va mourir.	(6) When your father goes to die.
(7) Encores vivrai-je par toi,	(7) I shall live again through you,
(8) Mon fils, comme tu vis par moi;	(8) My son, as you were given life by me;
(9) Puis il faut, comme la nourrice	(9) Thus you must, like the wet nurse
(10) Et fille du Romain grison,	(10) And daughter of the Roman prisoner,
(11) Que tu allaicte & tu cherisse	(11) Suckle me and cherish
(12) Ton pere, en exil, en prison.[29]	(12) Your father, in exile, in prison.]

D'Aubigné, engaging another relevant literary topos popular among his literary peers, addresses his book as his child that he has created and who he hopes will outlive him and continue to give testimony to his worthiness as a writer.[30] D'Aubigné illustrates this convention with an allusion to the legend of the Roman girl who visits her famished father in prison and breast-feeds him through the bars to keep him from starving. D'Aubigné thoroughly masculinizes the story to speak of his own tightly controlled universe of literary production. *La nourrice* becomes *mon fils,* a son begat, in effect, by literary parthenogenesis. Furthermore, as in Ronsard's regendering in "La Nourrice," the original legend cited by Garnier and Plattard in their edition of *Les Tragiques,* tells the story of a mother, not a father, who is imprisoned and subsequently nursed by her daughter.[31] In d'Aubigné's version then, once again, the women vanish. There is no woman's body left in his story and we are left with the recurring image of men suckling men.[32] With d'Aubigné, the maternalized homosocial triad that was streamlined in the case of Ronsard and Dorat is entirely collapsed into one utterly self-sufficient and self-sustaining paradigm. D'Aubigné is the birth father of his own son, who subsequently enjoys the same powers of supernatural gender fluidity that allow him to suckle his starving father in return. How much simpler, one cannot help observing, for d'Aubigné to have suggested the book as daughter; simpler, yet unwelcome in a genealogy of female erasure and exclusion and male poetic control.

If the image of men's nursing their literary progeny is more rarely invoked, the idea of their giving birth was certainly not: miraculous male births were a commonplace. Indeed, the thesis about breast-feeding males might easily be seen as a subset of a much broader phenomenon of men as childbearers. The "children of the spirit" privileged by Renaissance readers of Plato's *Symposium* were commonly cited, and it is that source that certainly informs the scenarios of suckling mentors discussed within this study. Perhaps the most famous Renaissance practitioner of literary male birthing was Michel de Montaigne, whose "De l'affection des peres aux enfans" [On the affection of fathers for their children)] offers pertinent and often-quoted observations that show the extent to which women—their bodies, their functions (both physical and social)—can be appropriated and effaced within a male literary agenda:

> [C]ar ce que nous engendrons par l'ame, les enfantemens de nostre esprit...sont produicts par une plus noble partie que la corporelle, et sont plus nostres; nous sommes pere et mere ensemble en cette generation.

> Et je ne sçay si je n'aimerois pas mieux beaucoup en avoir produict ung, parfaictement bien formé, de l'acointance des muses, que de l'acointance de ma femme.[33]

> [For what we engender by the soul, the children of our mind...are produced by a nobler part than the body and are more our own; we are father and mother both in this generation.

> And I do not know whether I would not like much better to have produced one perfectly formed child by intercourse with the muses than by intercourse with my wife.][34]

D'Aubigné simply extends the metaphor that much further by allowing this nobler enterprise to continue to nourish its own without the messy interventions of "l'acointance de [l]a femme." The "nous" and "notre" ["we" and "our"] are clearly the rhetoric of a male literary bond that indicates a perpetually masculine privilege enthralled with maternal functions to the extent to which they can be transformed and owned by men.

Ronsard and his contemporaries' relationship to the maternal was identical to the very process of imitation and apprenticeship they sought to express. Just as Homer, Ovid, Petrarch, and others are *devoured, digested, and converted* (to borrow Joachim Du Bellay's terminology), just as the wisdom of Dorat is sucked from his breast and made manifest in the "body" of writing penned by Ronsard, so is the mother consumed and transformed by these still unquestionably male appropriators. As these diverse variations of the mothering male have shown, the plundering of maternity was the not-uncommon modus operandi of this generation of writers bound for glory. Controlling nature through women's bodies on their own behalf, as de Beauvoir's rhetoric suggests at the beginning of this essay, male writers of the French Renaissance birthed a self-sustaining literary tradition unencumbered by natural mothers.

A brief epilogue is provided here in conclusion to a study that dwells so relentlessly on female exclusion and silence in a male literary tradition. Louise Bourgeois, midwife to the French court in the late sixteenth and early seventeenth centuries and friend and follower (with her husband) of Ambroise Paré, authored several works on her experiences in the profession of assisting real women in real births, most notably Marie de Médicis. Her prefatorial writing in the work *Observations diverses, sur la stérilité, perte de fruiet, fœcondité, accouchements et maladies des femmes et enfants nouveau-naiz* [Various observations on sterility, miscarriage, fertility, birthings, and illnesses of women and newborn children] provides a welcome antidote to the masculinist verse that plays at maternity yet may willfully avoid its "acquaintance."[35] She begins her "Au Lecteur":

> Ami lecteur, cet enfant de mon esprit…ne s'étale point à tes yeux pour se faire admirer en la vanité du langage. Il te dit pour une de ses maximes véritables, qu'il n'a point le fil d'une Ariane pour te conduire avec un plaisir doucement trompeur, parmi les contours d'un labyrinthe de paroles. Aussi ne lui ai-je donné pour tout fard que la vérité, pour raison que l'expérience, et pour témoin tout notre sexe, qui ressentant en soi-même ce que j'en écris ne démentira jamais ma plume.

> [Friendly reader, this child of my spirit…is not displayed before you to be admired for the vanity of its language. It holds as a truth that there is no Ariadne's thread that can guide you with sweet deception among the twists and turns of a labyrinth of words. So have I given it no mask but the truth, no reasoning but experience and as witness all those of our sex, who, able to feel within themselves that which I write about will never repudiate my writing.]

Louise Bourgeois's words might indeed be the opening of the complementary chapter to this study. The "notre sexe" suddenly and clearly refocuses the attention on women, whose maternal potential or actual experience presents a radical revisioning of what this "child of the spirit" entails. Claiming to be suspicious of rhetorical tricks or literary imaginings (such as those, we might conjecture, that would make mothers out of men), Bourgeois pens prose that is literally life-giving and sustaining. Bourgeois comes out of the dark shadows of male imagination and dismissal and bears witness to her own experience in poetry, in anecdotal accounts of her birthing experiences and remedies, and in cautionary, epistolary prose to her own daughter. Her "observations" are a link to a tradition of women's writing borne of women's bodies, a tradition thoroughly elided in the Renaissance, male poetic agenda.

"A Jan Dorat"
Pierre de Ronsard

(1) Puissai-je entonner un vers

(2) Qui raconte à l'univers

(3) Ton los porté sus son aile,

(4) Et combien je fu heureus

(5) Sucer le laict savoureus

(6) De ta feconde mammelle.

(7) Sur ma langue doucement

(8) Tu mis au commencement

(9) Je ne sçai quelles merveilles,

(10) Que vulgaires je randi,

(11) Et premier les épandi

(12) Dans les Françoises oreilles.

(13) Si en mes vers tu ne vois

(14) Sinon le miel de ma vois

(15) Versé pour ton los repaistre:

(16) Qui m'en oseroit blasmer?

(17) Le disciple doit aimer

(18) Vanter et louer son maistre.

(19) Nul ne peut montrer devant

(20) Qu'il soit expert et sçavant,

(21) Et l'ignorance n'enseigne

(22) Comme on se doit couronner,

(23) Et le chef environner

(24) D'une verdoiante enseigne.

(25) Si j'ai du bruit, il n'est mien,

(26) Je le confesse estre tien

(27) Dont la science hautaine

(28) Tout alteré me treuva,

(29) Et bien jeune m'abreuva

(30) De l'une et l'autre fontaine.

(1) [Could I but intone a verse

(2) Which would tell the world

(3) Your glory carried on its wing,

(4) And how fortunate I was

(5) To suckle the savory milk

(6) Of your fertile breast!

(7) Upon my tongue sweetly

(8) Did you place at first

(9) Indescribable marvels

(10) Which I rendered into French,

(11) The first to pour them

(12) Into French ears.

(13) If in my verse you see

(14) Only the sweetness of my voice

(15) Pouring forth to spread your glory:

(16) Who would dare to blame me?

(17) The disciple must love

(18) To exalt and praise his master.

(19) No one can teach, before

(20) He becomes expert and knowledgeable

(21) Ignorance does not teach,

(22) Just how to honor oneself,

(23) To crown oneself

(24) With the laureled wreath.

(25) If I have fame, it is not mine,

(26) I confess it to be yours

(27) Whose great learning

(28) Found me thirsting,

(29) And quite early in my youth gave me drink

(30) From both fountains.

(31) De sa Mere l'apprentif

(32) Peut de son luc deceptif

(33) Tromper les bandes rurales:

(34) Puisse avenir que ma vois

(35) Atire et flatte des Rois

(36) Les grandes mains liberales.

(37) L'honneur nourrist le sçavoir:

(38) Quand l'oeil d'un Prince veult voir

(39) Le ministre de la Muse,

(40) Phebus lui fait ses leçons,

(41) Phebus aime ses chansons,

(42) Et son Luc ne lui refuse.

(43) On ne se travaille point

(44) Aiant un disciple époint

(45) A vertu dés son jeune age,

(46) En peu de jours il est fait

(47) D'apprentif maistre parfait,

(48) Voi m'en ci le temoignage.

(31) The apprentice can learn from his mother

(32) Aided by the tricks of his lyre

(33) How to fool the common public:

(34) Oh, that my voice might some day

(35) Attract and flatter the great

(36) And generous hands of kings.

(37) Honor nourishes knowledge:

(38) When the eye of a prince wants to see

(39) The muse's minister,

(40) Phoebus gives him his lessons,

(41) Phoebus loves his songs,

(42) And does not refuse him his lute.

(43) One does not worry at all

(44) Having a keen disciple

(45) So virtuous from such an early age,

(46) In little time he is formed perfectly

(47) From apprentice into master,

(48) See in me the witness of this greatness.]

Notes

1. "Human nature is an antiphysis—in a sense it is against nature; it does not passively submit to the presence of nature but rather takes over the control of nature on its own behalf. This arrogation is not an inward, subjective operation; it is accomplished objectively in practical action," Simone de Beauvoir, *The Second Sex,* trans. H. M. Parshley (New York: Vintage, 1974), 58. All translations in this essay, unless otherwise noted, are my own.

2. For illuminating contemporary treatment of this subject, see in particular Londa Schiebinger, *Nature's Body: Gender in the Making of Modern Science* (Boston: Beacon Press, 1993), esp. chap. 2, "Why Mammals Are Called Mammals"; see also Mary Jacobus, "Incorruptible Milk: Breast-feeding and the French Revolution" in *Rebel Daughters: Women and the French Revolution,* ed. S. Melzer and L. Rabine (Oxford: Oxford University Press, 1992), 54–75; and Ruth Perry, "Colonizing the Breast: Sexuality and Maternity in Eighteenth-Century England," in *Forbidden History: The State, Society, and the Regulation of Sexuality in Modern Europe,* ed. John C. Fout (Chicago: University of Chicago Press, 1992), 107–37. Thomas Laqueur, *Making Sex: Body and Gender from the Greeks to Freud* (Cambridge: Harvard University Press, 1990), a more-in-depth, panhistorical treatment of the pre-Rousseauian discourse on the breast, with several mentions of lactation in males.

3. For a study of this question in the English Renaissance, see Katharine Eisaman Maus, "A Womb of His Own: Male Renaissance Poets in the Female Body," in *Sexuality and Gender in Early Modern Europe: Institutions, Texts, Images,* ed. James Grantham Turner (Cambridge: Cambridge University Press, 1993), 266–88.

4. Ann Rosalind Jones, "Assimilation with a Difference: Renaissance Women Poets and Literary Influence," *Yale French Studies* 62 (1981): 135–53.

5. Pierre de Ronsard, *Œuvres complètes,* ed. Jean Céard et al. (Paris: Gallimard, 1993), 987–88; see also appendix for text and translation. See the complete poem, appended to the end of this chapter.

6. Ronsard's 1550 preface to the *Odes,* his first publication, conveys quite concisely his less-than-modest level of self-esteem:

> Mais quand tu m'appelleras le premier auteur lirique François, et celui qui a guidé les autres au chemin de si honneste labeur, lors tu me rendras ce que tu me dois, et je m'efforcerai te faire apprendre qu'en vain je ne l'aurai receu.
>
> [Yet when you shall call me the first French lyric author, and he who has guided others in the path of such honest labor, then you shall render unto me that which you owe, and I shall work hard to prove to you that your praise was not unwarranted.]

7. Ronsard, *Œuvres complètes,* 994.

8. Pierre de Ronsard, "La Nourrice" from "Scènes et Croquis" in *Poésies Choisies,* ed. Françoise Joukovsky (Paris: Classiques Garnier, 1969), 384–85.

9. See Ronsard, *La Franciade* (1572) and *Œuvres complètes,* 1011–1159.

10. Philippa Berry, *Of Chastity and Power: Elizabethan Literature and the Unmarried Queen* (London: Routledge, 1989), 2, emphasis added.

11. Eve Kosovsky Sedgwick, *Between Men: English Literature and Male Homosocial Desire* (New York: Columbia University Press, 1985).

12. Sedgwick, *Between Men,* 160.

13. Laqueur, *Making Sex,* 19–20.

14. Ambroise Paré, *Des Monstres et Prodiges,* ed. Jean Céard (Geneva: Droz, 1971), 30.

15. Rémy Belleau in *Poètes du XVIe siècle,* ed. Albert-Marie Schmidt (Paris: Gallimard, 1953), 659.

16. Maurice Scéve, *Délie,* ed. Françoise Charpentier (Paris: Gallimard, 1984), 61.

17. Schmidt, 658; Belleau writes:

| (41) Or cest pierre donc qu'on appelle Laicteuse | (41) [So this stone that is called milky |
| (42) Fait enfler le tetin de l'humeur gracieuse, | (42) Fills the teat with that grace-giving fluid, |

(43) Qui arrose en maillot la lèvre des enfans,	(43) Which waters the lip of infants in their swaddling
(44) Et qui les nourrisant fait accroistre leurs ans.	(44) And which in nourishing them, increases their years.]

18 Pontus de Tyard, "Ode III: Du Socratique" from the *Livre des Vers Lyriques* (1573) in Schmidt, *Poètes du XVIe siècle*, 380.

19. Juan Luis Vives, *A very fruteful and pleasant boke callyd the instruction of a Christen woman...*, trans. Richard Hyrde (London: Thomas Berth, 1541); this treatise was originally published in Latin in the 1530s.

20. François Rabelais, *Œuvres complètes*, ed. Guy Demerson (Paris: Seuil, 1973), 947–49.

21. For a useful edition of the Vives treatise, see the *Livre de l'institution de la Femme Chrestienne*, trans. Pierre de Changy (1542), reprinted with preface and glossary by A. Delboulle (Le Havre: Lemale et Compagnie, 1891); see also Foster Watson, *Vives and the Renascence Education of Women* (New York: Longmans, 1912), for extensive reproduction and translation of the text.

22. Desiderius Erasmus, *De Pueris Instituendis in Collected Works of Erasmus*, ed. J. K. Sowards (Toronto: Toronto University Press, 1985), 299.

23. Joachim Du Bellay, *La Deffence et Illustration de la Langue Françoyse*, ed. H. Chamard (Paris: Société des Textes Français Modernes, 1970), 42.

24. "De la (Apollo, Arion, Amphion, Orphée) Homère, de la Hesiode, de la Pindare resentirent entre les Grecz admiration et louenge.... De la Livius Andronicus, de la le père Ennius, de la le plaisant Plaute trouvarent nom et faveur entre les Romains: et apres euz Virgile, Ovide, Horace, et autre infinis, furent enrichis, favoris...se releva entre les Italiens, retenans encor quelque vestige de ce florissant empire par le moien d'un Danthe et d'un Petrarque. Puis passant les mons, et recongnue par les François auz personnes de Alain, Jan de Meun, et Jan le Marie, divine de race, et digne de roial entretien...," Thomas Sébillet, *Art Poétique*, ed. F. Gaiffe and F. Goyet (Paris: Nizet, 1988), 13–14.

25. Joachim Du Bellay, *Les Regrets*, ed. Françoise Joukovsky (Paris: Garnier Flammarion, 1971), 64–65.

26. Du Bellay, *Les Regrets*, trans. C. H. Sisson (Manchester: Carcanet Press, 1984), 26–27.

27. Du Bellay's sonnet, "Une Louve je vy," from his collection *Songe* (Paris, 1558) complements the version in the *Regrets* with a more literal rendering of the story (the French gender distinction expressed by "loup"-"louve" is decidedly less clumsy than the English translation), Joachim Du Bellay in Schmidt, *Poètes du XVIe siècle*, 433:

Une Louve je vy sous l'antre d'un rocher	[A she-wolf I spied in a rocky cave
Allaictant deux bessons: Je vis à sa mamelle	Nursing two twins: I saw at her breast
Mignardement *joüer* ceste couple jumelle,	This twin couple gently playing
Et d'un col allongé la Louve les lecher....	As the she-wolf stretched back her neck and licked them....]

28. Bernard Andreae, *The Art of Rome*, trans. R. E. Wolf (New York: Harry N. Abrams, 1977), 37.

29. Agrippa d'Aubigné, *Les Tragiques*, ed. A. Garnier and J. Plattard (Paris: Société des Textes Français Modernes, 1990), 17.

30. See as well Ronsard, "A Son Livre" (*Mon fils, si tu savais ce qu'on dira de toi...*), *Œuvres complètes*, 167–72.

31. "L'origine de cette légende est une anecdote de Valère-Maxime (*Factorum ac dictorum memorabilium libri*, au livre V, chap. IV, 7), chez qui d'ailleurs *c'est une mère, et non un père*, qui est ainsi allaitée par sa fille." *Les Tragiques*, 17, emphasis added in note.

32. For an extended discussion of d'Aubigné's relation to the maternal as it evolved over his entire career, see Kathleen Perry, "Motherhood and Martyrdom in the Poetry of Théodore Agrippa d'Aubigné," *Neophilologus* 76 (1992): 198–211. D'Aubigné's maternity works not only in the service of his own poetic immortality, but as representative of a larger agenda of Protestant salvation and sacrifice: "He [D'Aubigné] sees the ultimate role of the poet as a maternal rejection of violence

through literary creation.... It is the poet's maternal role to give new life out of the fire to these martyrs, to restore their voices in the hope of putting an end to sacrifice"; ibid., 209–10.

33. Michel de Montaigne, *Essais,* livre 2, ed. Alexandre Micha (Paris: Garnier-Flammarion, 1969), 71, 73.

34. Michel de Montaigne, *The Complete Essays of Montaigne,* trans. Donald Frame (Stanford: Stanford University Press, 1976), 291, 293.

35. Louise Bourgeois Boursier, *Observations diverses, sur la sterilité, perte de fruict, foecondite, accouchements, et maladies des femmes, et enfants nouveaux naiz* (Paris: Melchior Mondière, 1626).

Montaigne *moqueur*
"Virgile" and Its Geographies of Gender

Tom Conley

Almost fifty years have passed since Simone de Beauvoir reserved for Montaigne a privileged rank among women writers in the French pantheon. The author of *Le deuxième sexe* noted that the essayist, if he did not write androgynously, at least refused to respect Christian hierarchies that had conceived of woman as a botched creation in the order of things. The confusion of gender, the multiplication of points of view, and meditations on the collusion of classical and Christian practices of sexuality are studied everywhere in the *Essais,* but are nowhere better summarized or organized than in the exhilarating rhapsody, "Sur des vers de Virgile" [On some lines of Virgil] (3.v). No other chapter plays with or takes such pleasure, if Thomas Laqueur's formula is fitting, in "making sex" of its own writing. In this short chapter I would like not so much to add to a pullulating number of readings of the essay than to draw the issue of gender away from what Montaigne remarks about the limits of human perception in the "Apologie de Raimond Sebond" [Apology for Raimond Sebond], the monstrous essay of 1580 in which he states that in view of the world and cosmos before its eyes, humankind discovers its own absurdity. If humankind has no reason to be alive, how does it get redeemed and configured in a universal play of shapes in the great rhapsody of 1588 on love, gender, and writing? How does the praise of generative force become the matter of poetry that supplies a provisional answer to the dilemma that figures at the center of Montaigne's creative enterprise?

"Nous n'avons aulcune communication à l'estre" [we have nothing to do with being], Montaigne states in the "Apologie."[1] When recalled in light of the reflections on sexuality in "Virgile," a blatant paradox emerges. He who virtually "becomes-woman" in the tortuous meanders of the later essay's style nonetheless admits that no effort can allow a man to know, feel, or live the life of anything or anyone outside of himself—much less the affective world of another man or woman. Any empathy that motivates a man's desire to become female is based on the shortcomings of a will unable to overcome the gap between itself and the narcissism of wanting to be something other.[2] The meaning of Montaigne's pronouncement in the "Apologie" does not imply, however, that he later essentializes the female as a personification of Being or Life itself, or that by the simulation of writing he can be all that he can be. The impossibility of assailing the difference becomes the very ground for a chapter that comes as close as any single effort has ever come in conflating or collapsing sexual differences into a movement of style. Just as "De l'exercitation" [Of practice] (2.vi) had exploited the "spiritual automatism" of writing to move into a world of death and to return to life, the machinery of "Sur des vers de Virgile" rides in a groove of difference that confuses things male and female.

The essay owes erotic force to the indistinction it fashions through its own convolutions, in its own bending and twisting of inherited stereotypes of love. The way that the chapter crafts a space of its own determines its erotic complications. The space it creates becomes the site of a polymorphous erotic practice. Now space, noted the anthropologist Claude Lévi-Strauss, is a socially constructed entity.[3] To the creative writer and to the tactical subject at large, male or female, is assigned the task of inventing "manner" or "styles" of *producing space* that codes of conduct—in books of civility, pedagogical treatises, urban plans—cannot prescribe or control. "Sur des vers de Virgile" evinces an "invention" and a "practice" of spaces that it creates through multiple confusions and distortions of gender. The reanimation of its confusions that takes place in the hardly innocent act of reading the essay pertains to its force and to the political actuality that de Beauvoir had discovered in it earlier in the twentieth century.

The spatial reading that follows will tie signs of gender to two different geographical places, or plot points, that appear to inform the physical character of the essay. "Virgile" seems to be constructed by simultaneously discursive and schematic or perspectival modes. On the one hand, the essay is an itinerary that starts from a title and proceeds to "decline" or explicate its connotations. On the other, it is drawn as an ellipse that is built from a double axis of quotations on the coupling of Mars and Venus by Virgil and by Lucretius. The discussion moves within the saturnal area defined by the geometrical figure, an anamorphic view of a circle, that resembles a projective mechanism in the cartographical tradition.

Two hypotheses can be tendered at the outset: First, the spatial allegory lures the reader into seeking a central or axial truth that would be found at a hypothetical plot point, meridian, or vanishing point. At the same time, because of the physical character of the essay's ellipsis, the allegory, reiterating the same truth everywhere along its way, bends, turns, and defers any convergence of its reflections upon a centrally located moment or *vrai-lieu*. The geography of the discourse prevents arrival at a conclusion or final formulation. Second, when the essay approximates a cartographical genre by using verbal fragments to map out an anamorphotic gridding of observations, the projective system of the essay causes their contradictions or oppositions to flow into and through each other. Oppositions are collapsed into differences within the form of the essay. The latter thus deconstruct the very grammar that would create or sustain oppositions of gender.

In a certain way the essay resembles a topography of fluvial lines engraved in topographical maps that ramify and diffuse different orders, whether of geography, genealogy, or even sexual difference.[4] In that form—which Montaigne discovers, it seems, when he compares the movements of the river Dordogne, whose meanders resemble his own style, to those of the cosmos at the outset of "Des cannibales" [Of cannibals]—a sense of endless passage and renewal weds the reflections on love, marriage, and intimacy to the art of confession, to the creation of a physical itinerary, and a labyrinthine miniature of social space. The "I" of the essay works its way through a sort of fluvial and amniotic map embedded in the very itinerary. The overall design of the greater projection can be glimpsed when the reader looks at the text in two ways at once, as a discourse or a meditation that creates space as it advances, and as a map that has already folded the extension of the limits of its topography—often erotic in contour—into the difference inhering in its printed vocables.

In guise of an explanation of these two points and as a first segment of analysis it is instructive to follow the way the author charts his reflections on love in terms of tourism that pertain to the 1580s.

> Isocrates disoit que la ville d'Athenes plaisoit, à la mode que font les dames qu'on sert par amour: chacun aymoit à s'y venir promener et y passer son temps; nul ne l'aymoit pour l'espouser, c'est-à-dire pour s'y habituer et domicilier. (p. 950)

> [Isocrates used to say that the city of Athens offered pleasure in the way of women who are served by love: every man loved to come therein to walk about and spend good time; no one loved the place in order to be married to it, in other words, to get used to it and to live within it.]

Greek and Latin sites are explicitly construed to offer a mode of whoring, which might otherwise be summed up as *voir et visiter.*[5] Love and marriage are mapped, as it were, onto a gloss of an imaginary masculine tourism of classical Athens as it would be practiced in Montaigne's time. Touristic, commercial, and erotic spaces convey a topos that compares the residency in a town or country to marriage, the inverse of the cosmopolitan ethos of continuous displacement or pleasure gained by grazing on different customs. The comparison draws attention to itself at once because it is synchronous with the growth of touristic cartography (for example, Braun and Hogenburg, Münster, Ortelius, cosmographical books and atlases that Montaigne reputedly knew of or had consulted during his voyage to Italy) and because the overlay of the cliché, historical space, and contemporary practices of misogyny indicates that the printed surface of the text of "Virgile" may well be of a different, much more manifold, character than what it purportedly represents.

Two more cartographical instances convey the same conundrum. Following the first of two major sighting points in the essay, a quotation of Virgil's rendition of Mars and Venus entwined, Montaigne notes that Aristotle proffers keen advice for harried husbands who ought not to confuse Eros and Economy. "Il faut, dict Aristote, toucher sa femme prudemment et severement, de peur qu'en la chatouillant trop lascivement le plaisir la face sortir hors des gons de raison." [A wife, Aristotle says, must be touched prudently and severely for fear that, in being tickled too lasciviously, pleasure might cause her to jump off the hinges of reason] (p. 951). When the authority of Aristotle is respected it gets perverted. *Raison,* compared to a hinge, brings into view the very

Tom Conley

emblem of fornication that medieval currents of naturism had invested in the "con-gress" of male and female, in this case the oarlock and its socket or a shutter and its moveable joint. But the text also might be eliciting a graphic echo of the Greek *gonê* to underscore what the latent image of a bolt or a doorpin might produce when the text is itself "too lasciviously tickling" a metaphor that undoes the "severity" of Aristotle's prudent words.

In this area of the essay the *gons* turns into a mapped coordinate in the spatial net-work of the text. In extending the discussion to ancient taboos that forbade people of different social classes even to rub or touch one another, Montaigne imagines that the interdiction can be translated into what had become a touristic space for a Frenchman, like himself, who had recently visited Italy. Ignoble subjects are required to shout as they walk, "comme des gondoliers de Venise au contours des ruës pour ne s'entreheur-ter" [like the Venetian gondoliers at the bends of streets to avoid bumping into one another] (p. 951). In the imagination of Venice two social surfaces are overlaid. Untouchables and outcasts yell out to avoid making contact with others while they ambulate in the public space, while Venetian gondoliers do the same on the watery canals of the city of 138 islands. The Aristotelian oarlock, hinge, or lever of reason is now loosened. The gondolier pushes and pulls his freely detached rod as he navigates through the crowded waters of Venice. *Gondolier* evokes a highly touristic space that the gondola had already afforded to foreign visitors. But its own history as a word, "cette piece estrangiere iointe à la chose" [this foreign piece joined to the thing] (p. 697) beckons its root in the Greek *gondy,* or "vase" that is likened to the erotic vessel—or metaphor—that conveys its meaning as it moves. As the author's seductive turn of style implies, the *contour des ruës* embodies a canal, or an fluvially erotic shape caressed by the very gondolier's shaft as he shouts to avoid bumping into other vessels.

Geographical and historical registers are in play with the inherited figure of Eros. The former bend and twist the latter. The effect elicited in the comparison prompts the reader to glimpse erotic surfaces all about the graphic character of the essay—the "con-tour" of its surface—that both interrupts and, like the gondola, conveys the multiple forms of meaning in the ripples of spatial play. The articulation of eros, geography, con-fession, and trickery are most clearly advanced in the celebrated comparison of the essayist to a clump of mistletoe on a dead tree. "Puisque c'est le privilege de l'esprit de se r'avoir de la vieillesse, autant que je puis, de le faire: qu'il verdisse, qu'il fleurisse, ce pendant, s'il peut, comme le guy sur un arbre mort" [Because the mind bears the priv-ilege of getting back at old age, so do I, as best I may: let it green, let it flower, none-theless, if it might, like mistletoe on a dead tree] (p. 942). Wit eroticizes where it parasitizes. An old writer with a dead branch needs prosthetic assistance to display his leaves. As it greens and blossoms in the mind of the writer, like tufts of holly in the limbs, the floating appositive, "ce pendant" [nonetheless, however, etc.] transmogrifies into *ce pendant,* this pendant member of the essayist. The wit of the pun is what brings the organ to life. Mistletoe varies on many other figures that liken the essays to second-ary forms that live in symbiosis with greater forces in the world. Yet by comparing the essay on love to a false shape that would inspire the identification of a mere spacing, an appositive "however" in the name of a limp organ, the text opens onto a geography of desire that plots the space of a popular world onto that of a classical past.

The *arbre* of the comparison implies that mistletoe, a parasite, is to a tree as wit relates to an inherited body of knowledge. The latter can be the *Essais* themselves reflected throughout the chapter, notably in the passages on eros and language. As if preempting Saussure's concept of the arbitrary nature of the linguistic sign long before its formulation in the chapter on the "Nature of the Linguistic Sign" in the *Course on General Linguistics,* the "tree" becomes the sign of a highly conventional view of language. Unless they are "motivated" by the erotic play of the signifier, signs remain neutral—but not natural—in respect to the speaker, interlocutor, reader, or writer. For Saussure the "arbitrary" quality of the sign was indirectly motivated by the printed image of an oak next to the word, in bold characters, that spells *arbor.* Things "arbitrary" were "motivated" in their adjacent image by being treelike.

In view of the mediation on the relation of eros to the motivation of conventional signs, an implicit feminism in "Sur des vers de Virgile" takes root in an anecdote that relates how the author's daughter was redressed in the course of a botany lesson. Reading a French book, she happened upon a vernacular name of a tree. The author witnessed how the governess pruriently "motivated" the sign in a gesture of censure:

> Ma fille (c'est tout ce que j'ay d'enfans) est en l'aage auquel les loix excusent les plus eschauffées de se marier; elle est d'une complexion tardive, mince et molle, et a esté par sa mere eslevée de mesme d'une forme retirée et particuliere: si qu'elle ne commence encore qu'à se desniaiser de la nayveté de l'enfance. Elle lisoit un livre françois devant moy. Le mot de fouteau s'y rencontra, nom d'un arbre cogneu; la femme qu'ell'a pour sa conduite, l'arresta tout court un peu rudement, et la fit passer par dessus ce mauvais pas. Je la laissay faire pour ne troubler leurs reigles; car je ne m'empesche aucunement de ce gouvernement: la police feminine a un trein mysterieux, il faut le leur quitter. Mais, si je ne me trompe, le commerce de vingt laquays n'eust sçeu imprimer en sa fantasie, de six mois, l'intelligence et usage et toutes les consequence du son de ces syllabes scelerées, comme fit cette bonne vieille par sa reprimande et interdiction. (pp. 957–58)

[My daughter (she is the only remaining child of mine) is in the age in which laws excuse the most heated women from getting married; she is of a tardy complexion, meager and mushy, and was raised by her mother much in the same manner, in a retracted and particular fashion: and only now is she beginning to get out of the grip of the naïveté of childhood. She was reading a French book in front of me. She happened on the word *fouteau,* the name of a known tree; the woman she had to direct her suddenly stopped her, somewhat abruptly, and made her skip over this pernicious passage. I let the woman do so in order not to call their rules in question, because I'm not ready to get involved in this way of doing things; feminine governance has a mysterious way about it, and it must be left to them. But if I'm not mistaken, the talk of twenty lackeys over six months could never have printed in her fancy the intelligence, the usage, and all the consequences of the sound of these scabrous syllables as did this little old lady through her reprimand and interdiction.]

Like Saussure's appeal to an image that motivates the arbitrary qualities of language, the censuring agency itself promotes what it so avidly seeks to repress. As in the earlier figure of the tuft of mistletoe growing in the crotch of the branches of a dead tree, here the "nom d'un arbre cogneu" is arbitrary as would be any other, even species less familiar than an *hêtre* or beechtree.[6] The passage is cited extensively because it draws through a series of reversals the outlines of the poetic space of the essay. The episode is set against the background of a language of convention to show, it appears, how sexual difference is a socially motivated, but also an ideologically laden phenomenon. The other side of the text, its own unnameably forceful dimension, draws energy from both natural and conventional views of the relations of words to their referents.

In the complex theater of this reading scene the author sees the daughter reading. A male, he notices a female reader catching a word that another (barely) female reader might misconstrue. *Fouteau* is "met" as if the word were neither a grapheme nor a mass of phonemes and morphemes, but something base and ignoble, like the untouchable in the street or the prow of an advancing gondola in the waters of Venice, that needs to be physically circumvented or skipped over (the governess "la fit passer par dessus ce mauvais pas"). As willful outsider who will not trouble women or their *reigles,* Montaigne takes care to report that he minds his own business. The beechwood seen in this French book prompts the woman to betray the very prurience that the essay takes so much pleasure in mocking. The text satirizes the imagination that it observes by producing a configuration of sounds and shapes of letters that is simultaneously arbitrary and motivated. "Mai*s, si* je ne trompe ["if I am not fooled," but also, "if I do not 'herald,' 'trumpet,' or 'blow out' what follows"], le commer*c*e de vingt laquay*s* n'eu*s*t *s*çeu imprimer en *s*a fantasie, de *s*ix moi*s,* l'intelligen*c*e et u*s*age et toute*s* le*s* consequence*s* du *s*on de *ses* *s*yllabe*s* *s*celerée*s*"(p. 958).

This passage, as well as the introductory remarks that sketch a portrait of the daughter Eleonore (probably fifteen years old), attests to a conspicuous hypertrophy of a "poetic effect." The accolades that end in *s,* "ces syllabes scelerées," are preceded by other, different consonants of a liquid but "masculine" shape. Of a complexion "*m*ince et *m*olle," she was "par sa *m*ere eslevee de *m*esme d'une for*m*e retiree et particuliere: si qu'elle ne com*m*ence en*c*ore qu'à se des*n*iaiser de la *n*ayveté de l'e*n*fance." These signs of a difference obtained by two alliterative series run contrary to the mute impression that strikes the governess when she imagines Eleonore imagining what she herself might wish to see in *fouteau,* "nom d'un arbre cogneu."

Imagination and impression, knowledge and phantasy, are at loggerheads. Matter so commonly known, *cogneu,* such as the *hestre,* only "strikes" the eyes when it is seen other than it is, or when shaded with other meanings being invested into it. What makes the *fouteau* so common and so arbitrary is that it is being struck or happened upon, *cogneu,* as if the perceiving subject bumped into it. A host of cognate associations with *cogner* and *coigner* are anticipated, dissimulated, and then dissipated in the orthography. And the very somatic quality of a meeting or encounter of two different forms is underscored in the event where the word has met the eyes, where it "s'y rencontra."[7]

The anecdote stages an inopined and impardonable meeting where impressions are brought forth and no sooner radiated from an oscillation. A process of cognition takes place where bodies strike each other, an action contrasted with a surface tension of forms that caress each other, and that yield a battery of effects by the generative force of paronomasia. The action of sticking or striking that would be conveyed by *foutre* beneath the reflective surface of *fouteau* is scattered, attenuated, diffused, but also multiplied.

A sentimental geography informs the anecdote. What kind of book was Eleonore reading? A guide to common French trees or an herbal, a French counterpart to something like John Gerarde's *Herball or Generall Historie of Plantes* (1597)? Geofroy Linocier's *Histoire des plantes*? Charles Estienne's *Agriculture et maison rustique* (1564)? Antoine Mizauld's *Le jardin medicinal* (1558)? A pastoral novel? Beyond all shadow of a doubt it was a French work, and its field of reference extends to things seen and encountered in *Gallia* at large. No matter what the title, the reading scene maps out an uncommon relation of body and gender with private and public space. The male author does *not* report having seen or gazed upon the event. The daughter reads and he listens. Excluding himself "pour ne troubler leurs reigles" ["not to disturb them in their ways"—but also, it is suggested, "in their rules or menstrual patterns"] he implies that in the home a private space, a space in which writing and reading take place, is feminized. Further, the public world of male banter, ineffectual to the extreme, is entirely isolated from "la police feminine" with its mysterious codes of conduct.[8] Yet the space that Montaigne fashions for himself throughout "Virgile," both in and as the essay itself, carries the very same, feminized, private valence of intimacy that the form of the book turns into the paradox of a "public confession." "Ce chapitre me fera du cabinet," he notes, admiring women's "commerce un peu privé" [This chapter will be my closet, it will sneak a glance at privy business] (pp. 940, 946, 947).

If the essayist assimilates himself into a private space that is generally inflected as feminine, the public nature of the printed report requires that an endlessly "hidden" or nuanced dimension of the writing be allowed at once to emerge from and to disappear into the printed characters and their serial configurations. *Fouteau,* the vanishing mark of the picture of feminine commerce, conveys not only a sign of a popular stratum of French but also a sign of *ramification* that connects, as would the branching forms of a tree or a map of rivers, the many different—but never contrary—aspects of things. It might be said that the emblem of the beech tree in the ladies' salon concretizes the *accouplage* or coupling of male and female, of castes high and low, and of life both organic and inorganic. "Tout le mouvement du monde se resoult et rend à cet accouplage: c'est une matiere infuse par tout, c'est un centre où toutes choses regardent" [all the movement of the world is resolved by and given to this coupling: it is a matter everywhere infused, it is a center when all things are held in view] (p. 959), except that in the fabulous labor of the essay the centers proliferate everywhere for the eyes and ears of the reader that see and hear the process in the printed substance. Later in the essay, praising his propensity to debate even the most banal of all topics—"[t]out argument m'est esgallement fertille" [for me every argument is equally fertile] (p. 951), he notes that with his mercurial will (*une volonté autant volage*), he can begin anywhere he pleases, "car les matieres se tiennent toutes enchesnées les unes aux autres" [for the materials are held entirely linked to each other] (p. 981). The concatenation is anchored in oak, guaranteeing that the material which so much upset the governess is naturally related to the *chesne* that holds together the diversity of things that comprise the world and language.

In the secret dimension of the text the related presence of the *hestre,* the *chesne,* and the *guy sur l'arbre mort* serves to configure a moving image of space both male and female, that is both national and individual, both abstract and corporeal, and experienced at once in the essayist's report and in the transverse itinerary the reader constructs from the diverse verbal and pictorial material strewn about the chapter. The universal "accouplage" depends on a nature that extends from the forests and rivers about Montaigne to those in the very substance of the ink and paper below one's eyes:

> Pour ce mien dessein, il me vient aussi à propos d'escrire chez moy, en pays sauvage, où personne ne m'ayde n'y me releve, où je ne hante communéement homme qui entende le latin de son patenostre, et de françois un peu moins. J'eusse faict meilleurs ailleurs, mais l'ouvrage eust esté moins mien; et sa fin principale et perfection, c'est d'estre exactement mien.... Quand on m'a dit ou que moy-mesme me suis dict: Tu es trop espais en figures; Voilà un mot du creu de Gascoigne. Voilà une frase dangereuse (je n'en refuis aucune de celles qui s'usent emmy les rues françoises; ceux qui veulent combatre l'usage par la grammaire se moquent). (p. 979)

> [For this design of mine it happens also to be likely for me to write in my domain, in a savage country, where no one either helps me or takes over, where I commonly never meet a man who can understand the Latin of his paternoster, and French even less. I would have done better elsewhere, but the work would be less of my own hand; and its principal and perfection is to be exactly my own.... When they say to me or when I myself have muttered: "You're too thick in figures; there's a word of Gascon vintage. There's a dangerous sentence (I never refuse any of those used in the midst of French streets; those who want fight usage with grammar are mocked).]

In this famous dialogue that erupts in the discussion of the style of the *Essais* in view of Lucretius's description of Mars and Venus that leads to the writer's recognition that "tout le monde me reconnoit en mon livre, et mon livre en moy" [everyone recognizes me in my book, and my book in me] (p. 979), the avowed design is to write in nature, in a savage place. "'Tu es trop espais en figures'" means that Montaigne is being accused for being not merely overly poetic, or just plain "thick," but for being *es-pais,* in the countryside of *Gascoigne,* a toponym that contains its own reproductive virtue in itself, in what its proverbially male character complements by the presence of the feminine organ seen within its form. The *coin,* the slit of the world, and the *con,* the unnameable name of *une partie honteuse,* resides in the center of the place-name.[9] As he here admits, laws of grammar are unable to repress the drives that allow the writer and speakers to see or hear language otherwise: they are mocked by the very force of different practices that elude the order they wish to impose on language when they force it to mean what they want it to mean.

The nascent geography of a savage place, Gascony, in which the book is written, is coextensive with what the governess of Montaigne's daughter feared the adolescent would see in *fouteau.* When the two passages are superimposed, a space of intimacy and of universal force comes into view, where there prevail paradox, dialogical movement and countermovement, and, if one of Jean Starobinski's readings can be recalled, a "thermodynamics" of poetry and desire.[10] An object indicated can also be seen, beyond the law of grammatical usage, as a veil cast over something else. The "treasons" of removing the ordinary and constant imperfections of style can be seen as the labor of translating them into what, as is visible elsewhere, can disappear and be shown at once. For this reason the capital terms applied to the dupes of Montaigne's work— grammarians—need to be mercilessly mocked. They are the culprits who fix and erect the laws of gender.

In the overall register of the chapter, *se moquer* serves as a cardinal plot point in the overall treatment of space, time, desire, and sexual differences. No other essay uses the verb either so often, or with such care, or, I should like to argue, with such a drive to inform the erotic matter of the essay at large. At the bottom of the essay, in the 1588 stratum, the chapter ends itself in a black figure of mockery:

> Pour finir ce notable commentaire, qui m'est eschappé d'un flux de caquet, flux impetueux par fois et nuisible ... je dis que les masles et femelles sont jettez en mesme moule: sauf l'institution et l'usage, la difference n'y est pas grande.... Il est bien plus aisé d'accuser l'un sexe que d'escuser l'autre. C'est ce qu'on dict: Le fourgon se moque de la poele. (p. 1005)

> [In order to finish this notable commentary, that has escaped me in a flow of cackle, an impetuous and sometimes harmful flow ... I say that males and females are thrown into the same mould: except for education and usage, the difference is not great.... That's what they say: the pot calls the kettle black.]

Taking up a timeworn cliché, "the pot calls the kettle black," or "the mortar mocks the pestle," Montaigne would seem to end on a jest, a *boutade,* that resembles the fishtail design at the terminus of the grotesques that his fabled painter used to terminate the decorative whorls in the surrounds of the paintings commissioned for Montaigne's château:"Desinit in piscem mulier formosa superne" [With a handsome feminine body ending in a fishtail] (p. 218).

At the end of "Virgile" the geography of gender might be more complex than what the passing joke implies. The end of the essay refers back to a central area in its landscape, near the passage that praises the hills and valleys of Gascogne, where Platonic chickens and eggs are satirized. "Je fais volontiers le tour de ce peintre," he had noted in self-mockery, "lequel, ayant miserablement representé des coqs, deffendoit à ses gar-çons qu'ils ne laissassent venir en sa boutique aucun coq naturel" [I willingly use the ploy of this painter who, having represented roosters miserably, forbade his boys from bringing any natural rooster into his studio] (p. 979). Better that the *Essais* be simula-tions than representations of real things. In question are eggs, roosters, and chickens, figures bearing on mimesis in general, that are taken up again within the network of associations in the final sentences. The chapter has escaped the author's pen *d'un flux de caquet*, in a way that the text reports a "cackling" that comes when, like an egg, the essay is laid. Its obscure, dark virtue—that is labelled as *nuisible*—becomes the light of day that signals the birth of the essay at its end.

Would it be wrong to see in the flow that has escaped (*eschappé*) the author (the reminder of the *chappon* or capon who has written a form, because it is inert and can only be animated by a living, gendered, and eroticized recipient) has a both codeless and an androgynous aspect? Would the essayist be the *indifferent* mould that forms shapes which are not easily differentiated in sexual terms? If the answer is to the affir-mative, then the last piece of mockery, "le fourgon se moque de la poele," all of a sud-den gains inflections that would otherwise be repressed by the immediately oral sense of quid pro quo signalled by the proverb-cliché.

Thus *la poele* is not just a kettle or a pail—a female shape that receives something that fills it—but it is also a variant on a *poule* and a *poele,* a hen and a heated space (with geographical connotation of northern climes that Montaigne elucidates later in the third book) that generates animation.[11] One space in which things are engendered challenges what its counterpart can produce. But as is usual in the choice of words throughout the third volume, an enigma is invested into their shape and form. If *poele* refers to a hen, a pail, and a heated room, then *fourgon* must be used for similar polyvo-cal ends. Would there be in the word the reminder of the Greek *gon* that in the *Cratylus* is used to mark growth and generation? And would it contain a particle of *fou-* that recalls the *fouteau,* the mistletoe, and the general folly basic to love and generation in general? Finally, would it also be the phallic stick that Cotgrave registers as "An Oven-forke, (tearmed in Lincolnshire a Fruggin) wherewith fuell is both put into an Oven, and stirred when it is (on fire) in it"? The text invites the reader to go so far as to hear in "ce qu'on dict" the mirrored reversal of a *dict-on,* such that the "qu'on dit" echoes a "gon dit," a spoken sign of a sexed organ, at the same time the grapheme *q,* the hom-onym of the male member, masks—hence blackens, shades, and mocks—the *c* that is within and below it, the letter that indicates the female organ?

In the graphic arcana of the text it cannot be denied that the mockery extends to this outrageous degree. The reason for affirming that it does is contained, as the essayist remarks in the beginning of the chapter that follows (*Des coches*), in the production of enigmas, *dictons,* and other innocuous shapes that solve the very riddles that they convey. The most important device of that type is contained in the allusively emblematic shapes that crown the essay and respond to the questions posed at the bottom. Hence, in the frame between the end of "De la diversion" and "Virgile," the reader sees the following configuration, an *emblema triplex,* that is written in Latin and French and that bears a mathematical cipher:

O prima infoelix fingenti terra Prometheo!
　　Ille parum cauti pectoris egit opus.
Corpora disponens, mentem non vidit in arte;
　　Recta animi primum debuit esse via.

Chapitre V
Sur des Vers de Virgile

A mesure que les pensemens utiles sont plus plains et solides, ils sont aussi plus empeschans et plus onereux. Le vice, la mort, la pauvreté, les maladies, sont subjets graves et qui grevent. (pp. 938–39)

[O primal clay, so ill-fashioned by Prometheus!
　　He has brought little wisdom to the making of his work!
He only has the body in his art without being taken by the mind;
　　however, it is with the mind that he should have begun.

Chapter 5
On Some Lines of Virgil

As useful thoughts are more full and solid, so also are they onerous and impede. Vice, death, poverty, and illness are subjects grave and grievous.]

The text begins after a quotation from Propertius (3.v)and then seems to slide in a dreamlike way into the oneiric realm of thoughts (*pensemens*) on Eros. In the graphic register the letter *v* is graven into the surface of the text, from the *via* that ends "Diversion," to the Roman numeral *V* that inaugurates the work announced "on" the lines of Virgil. Since the essayist avows that the names of his chapters do not always embrace their matter (p. 1115), and that they are now and again set beneath "quelque embleme supernumeraire" [some supernumerary emblem] (p. 1079), it would not be wrong to see in the cipher of the title the figure of the place in the *Essais* where gender gets lost and confused.

It is where travel to an area of a utopian androgyny begins. In *V* we behold the emblem of the cutting stylus of a burin that etches matter, that grooves the lines of itinerary and travel in and about words. But also, in *V* we are invited to glimpse the shape of the female sex, the pubis, that elsewhere the essay caresses and describes without naming. In this allusive and elliptical way the essay is written under the sign of a conflation of sexual difference, and its entire body of signifying form seems to transform the oppositions of gender and of body and mind into a rich and alternative area—printed poetry—that cannot be theorized in the codes assigned either to male or to female. In its blackest expression, the process might be called a poetics of mockery.

The figural contours of the printed letters are drawn into the dialogue on difference. They are indeed inert shapes, "pendant" forms that are motivated through the style of the essay. In the groove or rut of the writing, sexual oppositions are conflated and differences multiplied and generated. An art of "mockery" prevails in the penchant for citation, in a tactics of disposition, and in a textual geography that turns the landscape of the essay into a handsome body that welcomes the reader's gaze. Like the author watching his daughter's governess balk at the sight of the *fouteau* on the printed page, the essay seems to mock the reader wherever he or she would too easily distinguish things male from female.

Notes

1. Michel de Montaigne, *Essais,* ed. Albert Thibaudet (Paris: Gallimard-Pléiade, 1950), 679. Subsequent references will be made to this edition and cited in the body of the text. English translations are mine.

2. Jean-François Lyotard, "Oikos," in *Political Writings,* trans. and ed. Bill Readings and Kevin Paul Geiman (Minneapolis: University of Minnesota Press, 1993), 102–3, notes that every human feels that he or she has been "dropped" into life, having come too late into the world, and that the task of living entails having to "learn something that is already here. We have to learn what it is to live, what it is to die, what it is to be female or male." He develops further de Beauvoir's psychogenetic inflections about "becoming" as opposed to "being" the gender with which one is born (or that one eventually seeks to change). Imaginary representations, he adds, are everywhere available for everyone to use in contending with these questions. "Sur des vers de Virgile" constitutes a welter of interrogations about how a subject is born into gender, and how he or she mediates it through the imaginary dedifferentiation experienced in writing. The remarks are pertinent for bringing an empirical perspective to the work of Thomas Laqueur, *Making Sex: Body and Gender from the Greeks to Freud* (Cambridge, Mass.: Harvard University Press, 1990). Lyndal Roper, *Oedipus and the Devil* (London: Routledge, 1994), 16, does just that when she underscores how much "what Laqueur is actually describing is the discourse of medical theory. It is not apparent that it was by means of such theory that early modern people understood their bodies." Deeply enracinated apprehensions, of the kind that Lyotard describes here, cannot easily be put into writing since, as Roper adds, structures of sexual difference "are not fully conscious, and cannot be articulated with the same transparency as medical theory."

3. Claude Lévi-Strauss, *La pensée sauvage* (Paris: Plon, 1962), chap. 1.

4. Many early modern maps confuse the shape of a river, the anatomy of a human body, and a "tree" so as to bring together family history, the self, and geography. A *fleuve* leads from its tributaries, that are branches, back to a trunk which is the area where it opens onto the sea. I have ventured a reading of Licino Guyeto's map of the Anjou in Maurice Bouguereau, *Le théâtre françoys* (Tours, 1594), from this perspective in Tom Conley, *The Self-Made Map* (Minneapolis: University of Minnesota Press, 1996), chap. 6. See esp. Josef Konvitz, *Cartography in France, 1648–1848* (Chicago: University of Chicago Press, 1987), 109–10.

5. "Pour avoir le plaisir [of Tupinamba culture], il faut les voir et visiter en leur pays" [to enjoy Tupi culture one must see and visit the people in their country], noted Jean de Léry about the Brazilian natives he said he met in his travels. The cliché of "seeing and visiting" is already anchored in sixteenth-century tourist writing, as notes Michel de Certeau, *L'Ecriture de l'histoire* (Paris: Gallimard, 1982), 246 n. 62.

6. When the text elicits the reader to find other forms camouflaged within and about itself, or to see different words folded in single words, it also invites the reader to move in an endless process of comparison that modifies the terms that are being concatenated. In the tale surrounding the *fouteau,* the "real" common name being elicited, the *hestre,* invokes being, or *estre,* a sign hidden in the figure of the tree to which everyone's attention is drawn. A play of particular and general qualities is in endless tension.

7. *A Dictionarie of the French and English Tongues,* ed. Randall Cotgrave (1632–?), suggests that *rencontre* envelops at least three semantic fields: physical, military, and linguistic. *Rencontre* is an adventure (hence an event, something that happens) that goes into space and thus produces an effect of a body moving into what it defines by that movement—a sudden battle of adversaries—a piece of wit, implied to be caused by the unforeseen meeting of two very different signs: "Rencontre: f. A leap, or adventure; also, a meeting, or encounter (as of adverse troopes, which on a suddaine, or by chaunce, fall foule one on the other; an accidentall getting, obtaining, or lighting on; also, an occurrence; also, an apt or unpremeditated ieast, conceit, wittie saying." He adds that a *mot de rencontre* is an "apt or unpremeditated ieast," whereas a *nom de rencontre* is "a good, acceptable, honest, or happie name." Montaigne's text clearly displays all of these inflections.

8. The latent cartographical implications in this anecdote take clearer form in "De la vanité," where domestic and worldly space are delineated in terms of household and world economy, *oikonomia*. The woman controls the world from inside the house. "Selon que l'experience m'en a apprins," he says in order to take distance from the female, "je requiers d'une femme mariée, au dessus de toute autre vertu, la vertu oeconomique" [According to what experience teaches me, I require of a married woman, above all other virtues, economic virtue] (Essais, 1092). In the shadings of the text the female can rule the world at large. The apparent misogyny of the following sentences, especially the remark that notes, "[I]l est ridicule et injuste que l'oysiveté de nos femmes soit entretenuë de nostre sueur et travail" [it is ridiculous and unjust that the idleness of our women be upheld by our sweat and labor], is undone by the male's being always absent or errant, and thus the female's assuming the political and administrative tasks for which the male does not have discipline enough to be responsible.

9. The relation of the male "Gascon" to the "French" female was articulated in "De la praesomption" [Of presumption]. "Il y a bien au-dessus de nous, vers les montaignes, un Gascon que je treuve singulierement beau, sec, bref, signifiant, et à la verité en language masle et militaire plus qu'autre que j'entende; autant nerveux, puissant et pertinent comme le François est gratieus, delicat et abondant" [Above us, towards the mountains, there is a Gascon that I find singularly comely, clear, concise, meaningful, and in truth more a male and military idiom than any I have heard; as quick, powerful, and pertinent where French is gracious, delicate, and abundant] (721). In Tom Conley, "Montaigne's *Gascoigne:* Textual Regionalism of the *Essais*," *MLN* 92 (1978): 710–23, I tried to argue that a verbal force of regeneration of the *Essais*, especially in "Des boyteux," derives from a medieval residue of shapes copulating within the words themselves. "Virgile" is, however, a much more extensive and compelling proof of the same process.

10. Jean Starobinski, "Dire l'amour," in *Montaigne en mouvement* (Paris: Gallimard, 1982), 223–56. The chapter originally appeared in the *Nouvelle Revue de Psychanalyse* (1980).

11. "Un Aleman me fit plaisir, à Auguste, de combatre l'incommodité de nos fouyers par ce mesme argument dequoy nous nous servons ordinairement à condamner leurs poyles. Car à la verité, cette chaleur cropie, et puis la senteur de cette matiere reschauffée de quoy ils sont composez, enteste la plus part de ceux qui n'y sont experimentez; à moy non"; Montaigne, *Essais,* 1213 [In Aosta a German afforded me the pleasure of fighting the inconvenience of our foyers with the same argument we usually use to condemn their heated rooms. For in truth, this stagnant heat, and then the stench of this heated matter with which they are built goes to the head of most of the people who have known them; but for me, not at all]. It should be added that "De l'experience" also begins with the example of eggs in order to weigh issues of resemblance and difference; see Montaigne, *Essais,* 1195.

Jacques Duval
on Hermaphrodites

Kathleen Long

The early seventeenth century saw a continuation of the rivalry between professors of medicine and surgeons who were increasingly literate and publishing their own treatises. This rivalry had already revealed itself in a court case concerning publication of the works of Ambroise Paré (1510–90). Professors at the Sorbonne felt that Paré had exceeded his limits and had written on matters beyond the scope of a mere surgeon. Increasingly, surgeons were presenting themselves as authorities on matters of medicine, with their power based on practical experience instead of knowledge of ancient texts.[1] Thus, in the court case as well as in exchanges of vituperative pamphlets and medical treatises, an early version of empirical science was vying with the old, bookish ways of understanding the human body. For the professors of the Sorbonne, the issue was no less than potential loss of power over the profession itself.[2]

During this contentious period, control of childbirth was transferred from the hands of midwives to those of male surgeons.[3] Even as the surgeons began to succeed in defining themselves as dignified practitioners of medicine, they took over tasks formerly assigned to women. Their treatises argue the necessity of control of the disruptive and disrupted female body by more rational male doctors. Jacques Duval's treatise, *Des Hermaphrodits, accouchemens des femmes, et traitement qui est requis pour les relever en santé, & bien élever leurs enfans* (1612) [On hermaphrodites, childbirth, and the treatment that is required to return women to health and to raise their children well] is illustrative both of this rivalry between professors of medicine and practicing surgeons and of the concomitant impulse toward men's control of all medical practices. Duval was a well-educated surgeon who practiced at Paris and Rouen, and who contended with Jean Riolan, a well-published professor of medicine from an established academic family. The bone of contention was the celebrated case of Marin le Marcis, a Rouen man who had been raised as a girl. Duval's work represents a sort of fault line in the history of science in France, privileging empirical observation and clinical examination over traditional academic modes of training. Strikingly, Duval also privileges the sense of touch over sight, since in childbirth the crucial information is unavailable to view. This shift in emphasis represents a clear break from the treatises that present copious illustrations of the infant's position in the womb and a clear turning away from the lecture hall to the hospital ward.

While asserting the importance of the male doctor's control over the woman's body in the process of childbirth, inconsistencies in Jacques Duval's text reveal that this control is not complete, and that female anatomy remains something of a mystery to the men writing about it. Duval seems particularly concerned with the unruly quality of female sexuality, and although he links the power of naming with power over the body, his own assertions are unconvincing in light of the clinical cases he discusses. He also focuses on cesarean section—surgical incision of the abdomen and uterus for delivery of offspring—a procedure that provides the opportunity for doctors to control the process of childbirth, but his failure to save the life of his own wife in childbirth signals the limited success of this kind of control. The issue of power hovers over the entire treatise: power over the body, control of women, and power within the profession of medicine. But precisely because this power is at risk, it is asserted continuously, because one must contend for it. Intertwined with this contention, I would argue, is the status of masculinity itself, now scrutinized in detail in Duval's passages on the excellence of the penis and the perfection of sperm, now protected against the dangers which women present, whether in illness or in professional rivalry.

Although reminiscent in many ways of the work of Ambroise Paré and Caspar Bauhin,[4] Jacques Duval's work represents a turning away from Bauhin's relatively skeptical and pluralistic views, towards Hippocratic models of gender and generation as well as towards a positivistic belief in the power of empirical science.[5] Like Bauhin, Duval is interested primarily in the question of sexual difference, that which distinguishes the female from the male. For both authors, the hermaphrodite becomes the source for discussion of the complexities and problems inherent in this distinction. Whereas Paré's and Bauhin's discussions of hermaphrodites seem focused on the various ways of knowing and on the variety of discourses used to define hermaphrodites, Duval seems intent on one manifestation of gender in particular, sexuality, and in his view its necessary consequence, reproduction. His discussion of the hermaphrodite is, therefore, much narrower than Bauhin's, and his conclusions seem much more rigid in terms of designation of gender identity. A man is revealed to be perfectly male only when he engenders life, that is, becomes a father. Duval's accompanying definition of womanhood is effaced from the treatise (even though the work ostensibly concerns itself with childbirth) in favor of establishing unequivocal proofs of maleness. Thus, although he reiterates many of Bauhin's arguments, Duval creates a treatise that represents a backlash against Bauhin's pluralism and a return to more clearly hierarchical notions of gender.

An even more significant difference between Bauhin's treatise and that of Duval is their views of how knowledge is acquired and passed on. For Bauhin, working within the context of the Renaissance revival of Pyrrhonian skepticism, no sense impressions hold particular validity for the acquisition of knowledge; all possible perceptions are unstable, affected as they are by the various conditions of the perceiving subject, the perceived object, and the circumstances that bring the two together. In this context, poetry and myth have the same value as clinical reports and legal precedents. Unlike Bauhin, Duval clearly feels that certain forms of clinical observation must be accepted as more accurate than others. In particular, he privileges the sense of touch as a more direct means of understanding, or reading, the body. Appearances, when judged merely by the sense of sight, easily can deceive. The sense of touch reveals underlying forms which, precisely because they are tangible, hold greater validity for the doctor. This is particularly true in the case of childbirth, where much necessary information is accessible not to view, but only to touch. It is also true in the case of Marin le Marcis, where feminine characteristics that are more easily apparent are contradicted by internal structures observable only upon invasive internal examination that proceeds by means of touch. This is the other aspect of Duval's work that is striking: knowledge is obtained by penetration of the body, an invasive interference in the body's workings. Duval seems quite aware of the intrusive nature of internal medicine, and of the fact that knowledge is a sort of violation, albeit one that often prevents worse violations such as execution, imprisonment, or death in childbirth.

For Duval, direct knowledge of the body is better communicated by words than by visual representations. Language is the means of mastery of knowledge that is acquired indirectly, and in its performative guise it mimics the tangible but fluid nature of the body. Language is thus invasive, and even transforming. Here, Duval elaborates a theory of the body and its representation that is more complex than those fueled by skepticism. He asserts that there are underlying structures to the body which are more real, or at least should be read as more indicative of the sex of a person, than the surface presentations. He admits that there is a gap between the surface presentations of sex/ gender and their underlying structures; these two aspects of a person may even contradict each other. He links the surface presentations of sex/gender to notions of sex that we might call performative—that is, behavior, dress, gesture, even environment— which can alter our understanding of a person's sex. And he argues that these performative aspects can, to some extent, alter the underlying structures. He sketches out, somewhat tentatively, a complex relation between body and environment (mostly in social context) that is based on mutual interaction. In postmodern terms, Duval recognizes neither performative nor essential notions of gender as ideal modes of understanding the body, but describes how organic structures of the body can be altered over time by certain practices and situations, and how the body in turn can transform, even if only slightly, those practices.

Marin le Marcis

Jacques Duval is best known for his involvement in the case of Marin/Marie le Marcis, discussed at some length by Lorraine Daston and Katharine Park.[6] Duval opens his treatise with a brief version of this story,[7] claiming this case as the inspiration for his work:

> ... [U]ne fille nous a esté represené: Laquelle ayant esté baptisée, nommee, entretenue, élevee & tousiours vestue comme les autres filles de sa sorte, iusques à l'aage de vingt ans, à esté finalement recognue homme: & comme tel à plusieurs & diverses fois eu habitation charnelle avec une femme, qu'il avoit fiancee par paroles de present, avec promesse du mariage futur.

Nonqu'on peust appercevoir en ce subiect les marques & particules destituez aux deux sexes, telles qu'on recognoist ordinairement aux Hermaphrodits: tant en ceux qui sont entiers & parfaicts, qu'en ceux auxquels on peut noter quelque marque d'imperfection, comme il advient plus souvent. Ou bien que la nature feminine fust totalement obliteree, pour ceder à la masculine, si qu'il n'en restast vestige quelconque, comme il se voit pratiqué aux gunaneres ou filles-hommes.

Mais par une merveilleuse dexterité de ce grand ouvrier, le membre viril obtenoit telle situation, qu'il se pouvoit monstrer & sortir actuellement, pour l'exercice & action qui en est requise, tant à rendre l'urine, que semence genitale: souvent aussi s'absconcer et cacher, en retrocedant à l'interieur. (A4v–A5)

[We had been told about a girl who, having been baptized, named, nourished, raised, and always clothed like the other girls of her lot, until the age of twenty, was finally recognized to be a man, and as such had carnal knowledge of a woman, many and different times, to whom he had become engaged by his word before witnesses, with a promise of future marriage.

Not that one could perceive in this subject the marks and parts assigned to both sexes, such as one ordinarily finds in hermaphrodites: as much in those who are complete and perfect, as in those in whom one can note some sign of imperfection, as occurs more often. Or that the feminine nature has been totally effaced, ceding to the masculine, so that no vestige at all remains, as one can see occurring in *gunaneres,* or girl-men.

But through the marvelous skill of this great worker, the male member was so placed, that it could show itself and actually protrude, for the required exercise and action, whether to urinate or to ejaculate, but it could also often conceal and cover itself, by withdrawing into the body.]

The case is difficult, since Marie/Marin is not clearly a hermaphrodite or a man. Her male genitalia are hidden, yet functional. Duval is called, together with other doctors, to decide this case. The reports of the other doctors are "diametralement contraires" to his own conclusions, and the unfortunate hermaphrodite is condemned to death for her apparent sexual misconduct:

...[C]e pauvre gunanthrope qui avoit encouru condemnation de faire amende honorable, tout nud, la torche au poin, en divers endroits, de la ville de Monstiervillier, puis d'estre conduit au lieu patibulaire, pour la estre pendu estranglé, & finalement son corps reduit en cendres. (A5v)

[... (T)his poor woman-man who had incurred condemnation to make honorable amends, completely naked, torch in hand, in several places, in the town of Monstiervillier, then to be led to the place of execution, to be hanged, strangled, and finally his body reduced to ashes there.]

The author heroically prevents this evil fate by means of further examination of the subject in question, discovering the hidden member and its capacity to urinate and ejaculate. As Duval suggested in other parts of his treatise, a functional penis is the sign of masculinity. It must be noted that this examination resembles a violation; the hermaphroditic body, in order to be recognized or categorized, must be dissected or otherwise invaded and its secrets revealed. The other doctors shrink from such an act; but Duval files a dissenting opinion and saves the life of the accused. Marin/Marie must live in limbo, dressed as a woman, for four years, until one or the other sex (gender) becomes clearly dominant (A6v). Ten years after the trial, Marin is bearded and living as a man:

> ... [C]e gunanthrope est de present rendu en meilleure habitude virile qu'il n'estoit auparavant, & que qualifié du nom de cadet de Marcis il exerce son estat de tailleur d'habits, entreprend, faict, execute tous exercices à homme appartenans, porte barbe au menton, & à dequoy contenter une femme, pour engendrer en elle.... (A7)

> [... (T)his womanly man is now restored to an even better manly state than he had before, and that under the name of Marcis the younger, he is practicing the profession of man's tailor, and undertakes, performs, and completes all duties pertaining to a man, he has a beard on his chin, and has that which is necessary to content a woman, and to beget children by her....]

Marin is self-defined as a man by external attributes and actions; he is self-constructed as a man and is apparently accepted as such by society. Duval justifies this designation by referring to Marin's sexual prowess, even claiming that the young man can beget children; but as in the case of Paré's hermaphrodites, the external attributes of gender that are acquired performatively, that is, by the very exercise of those attributes, define the person as much as any physical characteristics. It is ironic that Marin is a "tailleur d'habits," creating the very signs of gender that were once so problematic (since he was forced to wear women's clothing), but which now help to establish his identity.[8]

Duval repeatedly designates Marie/Marin as a "gunanthrope" (Dd3) and a "gunanere" (Bb5), terms he has established to describe a predominantly female being who has some male characteristics, but in whom, generally, the male reproductive organs do not function.[9] Duval places his paradoxical defense of Marie/Marin le Marcis within the context of the heterosexual and reproductive imperative that he has chosen to advance. Occasionally, he has observed, such a woman is revealed to be a man. Still, Duval does not describe Marin le Marcis as unequivocally male, even though the court demands that a clear gender designation be made and even though Marin's life depends upon his male identity being established legally. Duval firmly believes Marin to be a hermaphrodite, but one who has that one important masculine characteristic: a functioning penis. He concludes that Marin's gender (*sexe*) is ambiguous, but that he could function as a male. This refusal to assign a clear role is unusual for the period. The court accepts this ambiguity to some degree, requiring that Marin dress as a woman until the age of twenty-five, but allowing for the possibility that Marin will choose to live as a man after that (chap. 80, Ff4v).

Duval's reasons for humane conduct in this case are clear throughout the narration. The sanctity of life that is attached to the reproductive imperative, which Duval emphasizes in the remainder of the treatise, extends to all human beings. Duval adopts the view that the diversity of nature is a sign of divine power, not that which sees any deviation from an established norm to be monstrous: "… [N]ature n'a rien formé en vain, & n'a fait aucun animal ou partie d'iceluy quelque vilaine qu'elle semble estre ausquels elle n'ait inseré une grande perfection" [… (N)ature has formed nothing in vain, and has not made any animal or part thereof, however lowly it might seem to be, into which she has not placed great perfection] (chap. 68, Cc8v). Duval also argues that this diversity is present in all men and women, and therefore should be seen as normal in hermaphrodites: "Or d'autant que telle diversité n'est specifique en tous les autres hommes & femmes, elle n'est tant remarquable & considerable, comme en ceux du sexe desquels nous somme incertains" [Inasmuch as such diversity is not limited in all other men and women, it is not so remarkable or noteworthy when it is found in those about whose sex we are uncertain] (Dd6). Nature continually practices these variations, so that a model of sexual difference other than a simple male/female binary must be proposed: "… [D]effaillant la propre difference, nous soyons munis sinon de ce qui depend en tout de ce qui est propre à tout le moins de l'amas de beaucoup d'accidents communs…" [… (I)n the absence of a clear-cut difference, we might arm ourselves if not with that which occurs or is appropriate to all, at least with an accumulation of common instances…] (Dd6). Thus, difference and resemblance are not clear and absolute, but cumulative impressions of similarities.

For Duval, the condemnation to death of someone who does not fit neatly into the constructed categories of male and female is a violation of the sanctity of life and a patent absurdity, since none of us fits neatly into those categories. While his fellow doctors shrink from the contamination they might endure from contact with the hermaphrodite's body, Duval condemns their deadly negligence: "… nous demeurerions chargez & contaminez du sang de ce pauvre garçon si nous ne faisons deuë visitation pour cognoistre la verité du fait" [… we would remain covered and contaminated with the blood of this poor boy if we do not make a proper investigation to understand the truth of this matter] (Dd1v). This difference of opinion and approach also marks the confrontation between empirical forms of medical investigation—including dissection and invasive internal examinations—and more traditional, and distant, forms of observation based on ancient traditions. The impact of early forms of internal medicine, practiced on living beings, is hinted at in Duval's discussion of the external appearance and internal structure of Marin's body as well as in his discussions of the pregnant body and of the body during labor:

Auquel apres plusieurs signes exterieurs qui se sont submis à la veuë, nous tirions premierement consequence que ledit Marin estoit fille…non obstant que les signes exterieurs donnassent grande occasion de la iuger fille, si toutefois il estoit homme muni de membre viril, suffisant pour la generation & propagation de son espece.… (Dd2v)

[In the course of which [examination], after observing numerous external signs, we came to the preliminary conclusion that the said Marin was a girl …but notwithstanding the fact that external signs give great reason to judge her a girl, nonetheless, he was a man armed with a male member sufficient for the generation and propagation of his species.…]

Note that Marin's appearance passively *submits* (the term used of proper female sexual conduct in this period) to examination, but his male member is more defiant, a munition of sorts; and so the very description evokes his hermaphroditic nature. The pronouns used to designate Marie/Marin oscillate between the masculine and the feminine, according to the context in which they appear. Such textual instability suggests that while Duval recognizes the public nature of gender, he does not abandon the belief in a body that may not conform absolutely to socially acceptable gender roles, even as it is shaped and molded by those very roles.

This more complex notion of gender and sex is elaborated in an exchange between Duval and a court official who wonders why Marin's penis has not been observed even once by his captors, although he has been in jail for some time (and one notes the absolute lack of privacy revealed by this question). Duval's response marks the early seventeenth century's position as the meeting ground between medieval and modern notions of physiology. First, Duval points out that Marin's humoral "complexion" is more feminine than masculine—that is, cold and moist instead of hot and dry. But the heart of his answer is a long speech on the emasculating effect of disempowerment. He points out that Marin has had to endure several invasive, even hostile, physical examinations; indeed, for his hidden penis to be located, he had to endure penetration, the stereotypically feminine role of the time. He is now no longer free, but lives in hardship and pain. He cannot exercise in fresh air, but languishes in a small space. He does not eat well and drink good wine, but is fed meager amounts of bread and water. He cannot enjoy the company of the beautiful widow Jeanne Le Febvre, but must pass the day alone. In short, he is leading a confined and passive existence, and thus is rendered effeminate by the conditions in which he is living (Ffv–2v). For Duval, it is clear that these conditions shape the body to some extent. But Marin's penis is still there; the body cannot be entirely transformed by external influences. Nonetheless, it can appear to be radically different from what it was before. Duval underscores his recognition that the relationship between a body and the culture with which it interacts is not straightforward or easily categorized. Given this complexity, the only absolute which Duval asserts is the sanctity of life: Marin's life must be spared, precisely because his gender is indeterminate.

Gender and Generation

The hermaphrodites in Duval's treatise are the pretext for discussion of a more wide-spread, immediate, and serious issue: the difficulties of childbirth and how they might be overcome. Thus, hermaphrodites are set, once again, in the context of heterosexual reproduction. Duval's treatise might be seen as far more practical, and far less about hermaphrodites, than that of Bauhin, as Duval prescribes methods for ensuring the survival of mother and/or child. Duval justifies his project of establishing the parameters of sexual difference by arguing that it is necessary to understand and recognize the genitalia of either sex in order to determine such complex cases (A5v). He claims that his work is a legal manual for surgeons involved in deciding cases of sex, sexuality (defloration), birth, and so forth (A6). Thus, from the opening pages of this treatise, sexuality is strictly linked (even in the case of Marin) to the question of reproduction within marriage. The author particularly wishes to avoid the high infant mortality rates that have plagued France (A6v). He denies any lascivious interest in this subject (a denial that seems severely undercut by the text itself), and argues that he has many children (*heureuse lignee*) and a long, happy marriage (A7). But he hopes that the gaiety of the subject will encourage midwives to read this book and learn the methods contained therein. Certainly, the largest portion of the book is devoted to questions of childbirth:

> Si donc recreant & delectant la pensee des hommes, (quoi que ce ne soit mon but principal) par l'exposé des richesses viriles, & representation de utensiles reconces aux plus secrets cabinets des femmes: en l'usage desquels les uns & les autres se donnent carriere de delectation: J'eleve tellement la pensee de celles qui se disent obstetrices & matrones... qu'elles puissent vrayement estre rendues sages femmes, dont le monde à tant de besoin.... (A8)

> [If then, in amusing and pleasing men's thoughts (although this is not my principal goal) by the description of the treasures of manhood, and the representation of the hidden utensils in the most secret chambers of woman, in the use of which each gives the other a full range of delight, I enhance the understanding of those who call themselves obstetricians and matrons... so that they might truly be made wise women ... whom the world so greatly needs....]

Duval thus admits his use of hermaphrodites to draw the reader into what he deems to be a more serious discussion of reproductive issues. Duval's discussion also privileges men over women as the superior sex, and it places women in the purely reproductive role, accepting unquestioningly the clichés of women as disorderly beings governed by their womb.[10] In keeping with this spirit, Duval's assertion of the need for more and more demanding training of midwives implies a desire to assert masculine control over the process of childbirth. This book can be seen as a step in the development of greater supervision over midwives by male doctors, a move which led eventually to the suppression of midwifery in favor of deliveries controlled at every stage by male doctors.[11] Thus, science is being called upon here to confirm traditional attitudes toward the sexes and traditionally prescribed roles. The woman is seen as almost pure physicality, upon whom the male doctor works his magic.

Duval also, from the beginning, associates mastery of discourse with mastery over the body, contrasting his eloquence to the ineptitude of those doctors who opposed his examination of Marin le Marcis:

> Deslors ie fis curieuse recherche de plusieurs belles histoires & graves authoritez, avec ample discution de diverses causes & raisons qui pouvoyent concurrer à l'entiere cognoissance d'un si rare subiect. Lesquelles ie sceus tant bien disposer & naïvement representer, que cooperant l'ayde du tout puissant qui me daigne dessiller les yeux, & lever le bandeau d'ignorance en cette part, ie rendis ce qui en estoit, tant cler & manifeste, par l'exposé qui i'en fis à la Court, sur ce que nous fusmes faits entrer à la chambre, pour rendre & dire les raisons de la diversité de nos rapports.... (A5)

> [On this occasion I researched carefully many pleasant stories and stern authorities, with detailed discussion of diverse causes and reasons which could lead to a full understanding of such an esoteric subject. Which I knew how to put forth so well and present so earnestly, that with the help of the all-powerful one who deigned to open my eyes, and lift the band of ignorance concerning this matter, I made the case so clear and evident, by means of the report I made to the court, that we were called into the chambers, to give and explain the reasons for this difference of opinion in our reports.]

He wishes to share this discursive mastery with his readers, among whom he includes patients, so that "those who need to consult doctors...might respond competently to that which is proposed to them" (A6). He also wishes to aid surgeons and midwives who might be asked to pronounce on legal matters, and to pass on his mastery of the process of childbirth to surgeons so that they might deliver skillfully, when the midwife is not equal to the task (A6). Childbirth has been transformed in this text from a natural process to an art; this art requires knowledge of signs and forms instead of knowledge of the body, which might nonetheless present some of those signs. Accession to knowledge of this art will save the lives of infants. Thus, mastery of discourse is mastery of life itself (A6v).

This mastery is linked to masculinity, as Duval makes clear in subsequent discussions of "ce qui est en l'homme de plus plaisant & voluptueux: c'est la semence genitale, qui y est tellement copieuse & abondante, que le docte Fernel n'a fait doute de dire que *homo totus semen est*" [that which is most pleasant and pleasurable to man, which is semen, so copious and abundant in him, that the learned Fernel did not hesitate to say that *man is entirely semen*] (A7r–v). Nevertheless, the mastery of language over the body is factitious at best, as Duval concedes in his discussion of the genitals:

Mais aussi elle (nature) à par ie ne sçay quel instinct, concedé une tant volup-
tueuse titillation & libidineuse amorce, lors que par la nomination, ou seule
signification, l'esprit est attiré à s'y encliner, que quand i'userois de lettres
Hierogliphiques empruntees des Egyptiens, ou seulement de signes expressifs
repetés de l'Anglois Taumaste, pour les designer, sans autrement les nommer:
encores ne pourrois-ie rescinder cette naïfve gayeté dont nature a voulu deco-
rer & orner leur commemoration. (A7v)

[But also nature, by some instinct, has granted such pleasurable titillation and
libidinous power, that by the naming or simple representation, the spirit is so
drawn to this inclination, that if I were to use hieroglyphics borrowed from
the Egyptians, or merely expressive signs (hand gestures) taken from the
English Thaumaste, in order to signify them, I would never be able to prevent
that naïve happiness with which nature has wished to decorate and embellish
their memory.]

Words or signs can prompt the body to do that to which it is already inclined, but they
cannot undo this inclination or action. The performative power of words has its limits,
but it is the sole form of mastery that can be conveyed by a book, and so it is what
Duval wishes to pass on to midwives and surgeons, so that they might save lives:

... [P]ar ce traité, estant bien entendu, ie retranche le chemin à un grand
nombre de mauvais rapors, & à la perte d'une quantité d'ames presque infi-
nie, qui sans avoir la commodité de iouyr de la lumiere de ce monde, pour
rendre graces & louange à la maiesté divine, sont contraintes de rebatre
promptement la mesme piste que le souverain Createur leur avoit fait tenir.
Et ce à cause de l'ignorance des obstetrices, qui pour n'estre capables de lire
ny entendre des livres de plus grand consequence.... (A7v)

[... (B)y means of this treatise, if it is well understood, I will block the way to
a large number of bad results, and the loss of an almost infinite number of
souls who, without having the capacity to enjoy the light of this world, so
that they might render praise and thanks to the divine majesty, are constrained
to return by the same road that the sovereign Creator made them take in the
first place. And this because of the ignorance of women obstetricians, who
because they cannot read or understand books of greater importance....]

The midwives are cut off from mastery of the techniques of childbirth by their illiter-
acy, and are replaced, even in the text, by male barbers and surgeons (A7v). These latter
often do more harm than good, "[c]e qu'ils ne feront Dieu aydant pour l'advenir, s'ils
se rendent dociles à l'intelligence de ce présent traicté" [which they will no longer do
in the future, God willing, if they submit themselves to the wisdom of this present trea-
tise] (A8). Duval thus renders himself master of the entire discipline, directing his "doc-
ile" pupils.

In this context, Duval reviews various ways of knowing, for the most part linked to discourse. Both orators and philosophers use primarily discursive modes of knowing, orators cite authorities in order to confirm their assertions, and philosophers construct arguments (B–B1v). Pure discourse is fine for generalizations, "Mais quand ils descendent au particulier & individu, ils sont souvent contraints laisser arriere les arguments, pour venir à l'authorité des sens ausquels Aristote, en son second livre de l'ame, veut que pleine foy soit adioustée" [But when they descend to the particular and the individual, they are often compelled to abandon these arguments, and turn to the authority of the senses to which Aristotle, in his second book on the soul, wishes full faith to be granted] (B1v). Faced with individual cases, empirical methods, which rely heavily on the senses, are preferable. Gone from Duval's treatise are the strong skeptical doubts concerning the validity of observations or sense perceptions, such as those expressed in Bauhin's work. Modern science depends in large part on faith in the accuracy of perceptions; Duval already expresses this faith clearly in his accounts. It should be remembered, however, that appearances can deceive, as in the case of Marin le Marcis, and that informed observers will look beyond the obvious to find underlying truths.

Here, then, is a clearer break than is apparent in previous work with the traditional epistemological methods, particularly as used to acquire knowledge of the body, that predominated well into the sixteenth century. Generally, in the period preceding Duval's work, medical treatises were quite dependent on citation of classical and medieval authorities rather than on dissection or other forms of observation of the body. Duval asserts that such authorities do not recognize the existence of someone like Marin le Marcis; certainly, they discuss hermaphrodites, but do not acknowledge diversity even among hermaphrodites. Because of the boundless diversity of creatures, nature is the sole authority to which Duval will accede. Or so he claims. He does cite Aristotle, Galen, Hippocrates, and others constantly, but reserves the right to criticize their theories and counter them with examples from nature.

Nonetheless, Duval retains traditional views of the male/female binary when he asserts that all knowledge is meaningless when divorced from masculinity/virility. In his chapter praising genitals (chap. 2, B2vff.),[12] Duval links them with both rationality and immortality. He claims that genitals create heat in the body and are superior to the heart, which merely enables one to live, not to propagate. This is perhaps an extreme example of defining masculinity purely by means of the penis, and this argument seems to echo Galen's theories of heat as well the predominant view of the hierarchy of sex in which the cooler woman remains subservient to the hotter man.[13] Deprived of their reproductive organs, eunuchs show a degradation of intellect, Duval claims: "Nous y trouvons des moeurs perverses, & tres mauvaise ratiocination, & qu'à peine on peut trouver un Eunuque de bonne loy & iugment solide" [We find in them perverse morals, and very poor reasoning, and hardly ever can one find a eunuch of good behavior and sound judgment] (B3v). One wonders, of course, what his statistical sample was, and to what extent he really does rely on direct observation for some of the arguments he presents in the treatise. But at least in his mind, the phallus is associated with law and reason, and further on, with the divine itself:

> Ie ne craindray de dire, qu'en l'usage de ces parties consiste non seulement la plus utile & necessaire action de toutes, mais aussi la plus noble & excellente: d'autant qu'au compliment d'icelle concurre manifestement la faveur du verbe Divin, qui seule s'est reservé la puissance d'engendrer, disant l'Evangeliste Saint Jean, "Omnia per ipsum facta sunt, & sine ipso factum est nihil." (B3 v)

> [I will not hesitate to say, in the use of these parts consists not only the most useful and necessary action of all, but also the most noble and excellent: all the more for the fact that in support of this activity the favor of the Divine Word concurs openly, which has reserved to itself alone the power to engender, as Saint John the Evangelist says, "Everything is made by him, and without him nothing is made."]

The male role in procreation is compared to divine creation by means of the Word, and is judged to be the most noble of human actions. Duval lists various terms used to designate the penis, and he observes that this organ is frequently presented as life itself, or the sole source of life (B4).[14] By means of procreation, man leaves his image (*son image vif*) on life. Duval repeats the divine mandate to "be fruitful and multiply" (B5 r–v). He makes it clear that marriage is the context of this entire discussion. Most striking, however, is the extent to which creation, and even procreation, are linked to the divine *logos* (*le verbe divin*), that is, to rationality and discursive mastery. He defends language with the same ardor that fuels his praise of masculinity, attacking the hypocrisy of scandalmongers in a manner reminiscent of Reason's discussion of words and things in the *Roman de la Rose:* "Mais laissant arriere ces hypocrites ensouffrez, qui s'efforcent de blasmer de paroles, ce qu'ils mettent en usage tant voluptueusement..." [But leaving behind these sulphurous hypocrites, who strain to condemn those words which they use with such pleasure...] (B4 v). Duval even plays on the Latin term for testicles, *testes,* which also means "witnesses": "ils donnent tesmoignage de la virilité" [they give proof of virility] (C2). The parts of the body speak, act, reason, and thus represent the whole. This synecdochical dynamic of the part standing for the whole is most picturesquely evident in Duval's description of sperm "comme pleine de petites clochettes, dans lesquelles sont enclos les esprits ouvriers, scientifiques batisseurs & edificateurs du corps humain" [as full of little bells in which the worker-spirits are enclosed, knowledgeable builders and fabricators of the human body] (D2). This is a slightly different version of Paracelsus's *homunculus* (C4).[15] Here, the little men are not merely tiny reproductions of the father, but participate actively in the construction of those reproductions.

This proliferation of images of busy body parts, from talking testicles to industrious sperm, might remind the reader of the passage in which the limitations of discursive and rational power are considered (A7 v). The masculine body is not entirely subsumed into an integral self, controlled by the intellect or reason, but consists of various parts which follow their own inclinations. They can be prompted by words to do that to which they are already naturally inclined; dissuading them from these inclinations is another matter altogether. Thus, the insistence on masculine rationality and discursive power is mitigated by the depiction of automatalike body parts that follow a preprogrammed agenda.

Into this scene of turbulent activity steps yet another disruption: the "petit monde inferieur" [little inferior world] that is woman. Obviously, man is the "petit monde superieur." Duval cites Paracelsus's argument that inferior worlds cannot influence superior ones, but counters with the observation that they can indeed, by means of "la communication des pisse-chaudes, chancres, poulains & verole…" [by transmission of venereal diseases, cankers, sores, and pox] (D3). Thus, woman is presented as the carrier of disease, and most significantly of those diseases which disrupt the procreative process. He has repeated several times his belief that the seed which creates a female is produced by the left testicle (B8, C2r–v).[16] This belief confirms the notion of woman as sinister and menacing, as do the allusions to menstrual taboos in Duval's accounts of the engendering of hermaphrodites.

Rather than declare sexuality a disorderly, messy process that defies reason, Duval reasserts the superiority and dominance of the penis, devoting a chapter to its praise. In the name of the penis, he reasserts discursive control over sexuality:

> …Plus un instrument est cognu, remarqué, desiré & souvent mis en usage par l'un & l'autre sexe (indice de sa plus grande excellence, noblesse & dignité) tant plus grande varieté de noms luy est attribuée. Or n'y en à il en quoy cela soit plus frequent qu'en cette partie.…" (D3)

> [The more a tool is known, remarked upon, desired, and often put to use by one and the other sex (an indication of its greater excellence, nobility, and dignity), the more names are attributed to it. So, there is no part more frequently in this situation than this one (the penis).…]

A long list of names is offered, in epic fashion, to prove the importance of the penis. Again, mastery of language covers over the impossibility of mastery of the body.

Duval similarly glorifies male anatomy and male sexuality, claiming that the testicles, although themselves cold, render the body warm and robust. Therefore, a well-endowed man is a healthy man. He spends some space elaborating on the importance of ejaculation (and one remembers that this was the proof positive of Marin's masculinity), and describes the penis in some detail:

> C'est une partie de l'homme longue & prominente, souvent pendante, molle, ridee & flache, quelquesfois aussi tendue, roide, ferme, & dure, lors principalement qu'elle est preste & bien disposee à l'excretion de la semence genitale, dans le fertile & avide champ du genre humain. (D4)

[This is a part of man which is long and protruding, often hanging, soft, wrinkled, and limp, sometimes also erect, stiff, firm, and hard, principally when it is ready and well-disposed for the excretion of semen, in the fertile and eager field of the human species.]

Thus, masculinity is not only defined in terms of the reproductive organs, but of the reproductive capacity itself. A man who does not propagate is seen by Duval as less than a man. Duval comes very close here to designating the woman as mere vessel, even though he does not fully accept this Aristotelian theory of generation. She is depersonalized, and becomes a mere field, albeit an "avid" one.

After a long discussion of male anatomy, Duval embarks on a similar discussion of female anatomy. Proof of some adherence to a one-sex theory is the illustration of the chapters on the "Parties genitales de la femme" [The female genitals] (E2v). The organs depicted do not seem in any way to resemble a man's organs, but the terminology used is largely derivative of male anatomy: "la veine spermatique," "vaisseaux spermatiques," "rameaux spermatiques," "les testicules feminins," "les vaisseaux eiaculatoires" [the spermatic vein, the spermatic vessels, the spermatic branches, the feminine testicles, the ejaculatory vessels] (E3, E5v–E6). So the female organs are being described as analogies to male ones. The vagina is simply translated from Latin into French, and becomes the "gaine du membre viril" [the sheath of the male member]. All female reproductive organs become subject to the law of male sexuality. They are subject to the law of categorization and language as well. Duval offers a multiplicity of names used for the labia, pudendum, and clitoris, as he did for the penis (E4v, E8v). In this discussion of female genitalia, Duval cites a sermon by Anne de Joyeuse on their corrupting influence, and then cites a series of names and authoritative sources that link these genitalia to hell. The names that he lists for the clitoris hint at the reasons for this perception of a menace: "En français elle est dite tentation, aiguillon de volupté, verge feminin, le mespris des hommes; Et les femmes qui font profession d'impudicité la nomment leur *gaude mihi*" [In French it (the clitoris) is called temptation, the goad of pleasure, the female rod, the disdain of men. And women who make a living off of immodesty call it "my delight"] (E8v). Several of these names hint at the possibility of independent female sexuality, at the superfluity of the masculine member, and at contempt for men. Fear of this independent sexuality and this contempt may have driven the courts of the time to forbid one woman with an enlarged clitoris ever to use that body part (E7v–E8); this notion of the superfluity of men is also why Marin le Marcis's case caused such an uproar and why his punishment upon condemnation was so severe. This is also why Duval contends that in chaste women, the clitoris is scarcely visible, while in "indecent" women, it is more evident. It is most probably this fear of an independent, unregulated feminine sexuality which motivates Duval's lengthy and repeated discussions of the signs of virginity (ten pages in the thirteenth chapter, repeating points made earlier from E4v–E7).

Thus, parts of the woman's body seem to escape male domination. Duval discusses a "barre feminin," which creates a barrier to penetration and which he claims "tribades" and "subigatrices" (two of a number of names for lesbians) use. He does not clarify whether these women use their "barre" to prevent penetration by a male, or whether they use it for their own pleasure. The clitoris seems to guarantee male access to the female body: contact with it apparently renders all women "submises à la volonté de celuy qui les touche: leur causant l'attrectation d'icelle, une si grande titillation, qu'elles en sont amorcees & ravies, voire forcees au deduit venereen" [subject to the will of him who touches them: causing the stimulation of this part, and such great titillation, that they are pushed and carried away, even forced to venereal pleasure] (E8). Duval's use of the word *forcees* would seem to equate seduction with rape; yet he recommends this method for controlling unruly women. The clitoris can also be forbidding: "Mais en quelques unes ledit cleitoris s'est trouvée si grand, qu'il y à eu des femmes ausquelles il representoit la grandeur & grosseur d'un membre viril dressé & disposé à la culture: dont elles abusoyent les filles & femmes" [But in some the said clitoris has been found to be so large, that there have been women in whom it resembled an erect penis in length and size, one ready for cultivation, with which they abused girls and women] (F). Because these parts did not ejaculate, they were not male. Duval takes this opportunity to denounce lesbian practices (lesbians were called *tribades*, *subigatrices*, *frictrices*, and *ribaudes*, among other names). The fact that he returns to this topic suggests that this independent female sexuality is obviously a source of irritation for the author (F2v).

The need to control this sexuality is the author's justification for the Islamic practice of clitoridectomy:

> En Egypte cette maladie est vulgaire presque en toutes filles, ausquelles on est contraint faire couper cette barbole, quand elles sont prestes à marier, de peur que venant à dresser lors du coit, elle n'en oste le plaisir tant à elles qui les portent, qu'à leurs maris. (F2v)
>
> [In Egypt this illness is common to almost all girls, from whom it is necessary to cut this little rod, when they are ready to marry, for fear that if it rises up during coitus, it will prevent pleasure as much for the women who have them, as for their husbands.]

Apparently, it was believed at the time the Egyptian women were particularly "hot" in nature, and that their genitalia were consequently enlarged, sometimes to the point of resembling a male member. These phallic women, rivaling male anatomy as they do, are presented as unacceptable and monstrous. Even though Duval takes pains to defend similar characteristics in Marin le Marcis, he can only accept this conformation by designating it as male. So, when the woman's body threatens male dominance as well as male sexual activity, the menacing part is seen as an illness and is to be cut away, actualizing the myth of woman as castrated or lacking.

Further complicating the difficulties of controlling feminine sexuality is the belief (and Duval quotes Paracelsus on this matter) that the uterus is a separate entity, which he calls *animal*, and for the maintenance of which the rest of the female body was formed. Thus, just as the male is subsumed into his penis and testicles, rather than the reverse, the female is subordinated to her womb. For this reason, most of the remainder of the treatise is devoted to the governance of pregnant women and of delivery. Some of these pages contain rules of conduct: women should avoid violent emotions (M4), and women should avoid too great an interest in visual images, which might affect the form of the child (M4v). And again Duval notes the diseased nature of woman as he discusses the signs of imminent death in the mother (O7).

Thus, the largest portion of Duval's treatise is devoted to pregnancy and child-birth, from "the formation and nourishing of the infant in its mother's womb" (K2v), to the possibility and causes of monstrous births (K6), to the appropriate behavior for an expectant mother (chaps. 18, L7v). Most detailed of all is his description of child-birth in the chapter "Comment il faut accoucher une femme" [How to deliver a woman] (M6vff.). In spite of the obvious passivity of the woman, who is supplanted by the heroic doctor in this event, much of the advice seems quite enlightened for the period. For example, Duval suggests that women should exercise during pregnancy in order to simplify the process of labor (N4v).

Duval offers a section on natural childbirth (M6v–O6) and one on artificial or assisted births (chap. 21–24, O6v–Q5). The techniques for assisted births include turn-ing the infant by hand inside the womb, the use of hooks, mirrors. In such complicated cases, the loss of the mother was a real threat, and Duval lists the warning signs, so that at least the baby might be saved. But in the section on cesarean birth, he details the treatment of the mother after the procedure, to assure her better recovery. In the chap-ter on "How a woman should be governed after she has delivered" (chap. 25, Q5vff.), he offers sensible dietary rules, bed rest (R6), and gives guidelines for breast-feeding. A large section, "What must be done for the newborn," is also devoted to the care of the infant (R7v–T3v). Duval is clearly concerned with the very real effects of heterosexu-ality, and with what he sees as the necessary outcome of this sexuality. Clearly, there is a gap between his cultural biases concerning gender and the practical advice he offers on the very real bodily event of childbirth (chap. 21–24, O6v–Q5).

This portion of the treatise is a heroic account of the virtually divine control the doctor exercises over these unruly bodies, one that reads almost as an appropriation of the parturiant maternal role, as is clear from the comparison of the work of the doctor to a bear licking her new cub into form, an image which echoes a belief still held in the Renaissance. The doctor can even vanquish unruly nature in this divinely hermaphro-ditic role of mother and father:

> … [L]es anciens Payens ont attribué honneurs divins aux Medecins: veu qu'il est besoin qu'ils se monstrent avoir plus de force & energie que la nature mesme, quoy que procedante directement de la main & toute puissance de Dieu eternel. … Voire mesme un Dieu remplissant & parfaisant le tout par son actuelle presence. (P1v)

[The ancient Pagans attributed divine honors to doctors: seeing that it is necessary for them to demonstrate more force and energy than nature herself, even though she proceeds directly from the hand and omnipotence of eternal God…truly, even a God fulfilling and perfecting everything by his effective presence.]

Once again, the doctor assumes Godlike control through his superior knowledge; this role is to be contrasted with the deadly ignorance of midwives, due to their unwillingness to communicate their knowledge: "Because rarely do they wish to transmit their secret and precious experiences one to another" (E2). Again, mastery of discourse conveys mastery of nature. One of the more brutal images of mastery is offered in Duval's exhortation to tie the woman in labor down, so that she will not move during an internal examination (and possible rotation of the child) (P3); as necessary as the procedure might sometimes have been, the image is striking.

This discourse of mastery is revealed to be overcompensation, at least to some extent, in the following chapters on cesarean sections. In his justification of the procedure, Duval reveals that he lost his own wife and child, because the infant's head was too large for natural delivery. His in-laws refused to allow a cesarean section, so after his wife had been in labor for four days, Duval had to pull the dead infant out of its mother, in pieces. Duval's wife died eight days later (P4v). This example, as Duval himself admits, shows the extent to which nature still eludes mastery. He makes clear that, to some degree, any cesarean section is an admission of defeat as well. He asserts that this procedure should be used only as a last resort, when the mother is dead or dying, but the child is still viable (P6v). Yet he describes the great care with which a cesarean section must be performed, each layer of tissue cut separately and carefully so that the least possible amount of damage might be done,;and the care with which the mother must be treated after this procedure. He also lists and describes specific instances of this procedure, cases in which the mother survived and even went on to bear more children (Q2v–5). Clearly, the goal for Duval is not merely to save the child at the expense of the mother's life; in his experience, this choice is rarely successful.

Singular in a midwifery manual of this period is the lack of illustrations representing the pregnant uterus or the fetus itself. Duval instead uses extremely vivid and detailed descriptions of what physiological phenomena the doctor might encounter; he is particularly effective in communicating what certain conditions and parts of the body might feel like. As the illustrations Karen Newman has selected demonstrate, representations of an independently active fetus, although they may serve a particular ideological agenda, are in fact useless for facilitating successful childbirth.[17] A doctor in seventeenth-century Europe would not be able to see the fetus before birth and would have wanted to know the meaning of what he was feeling. Duval is correct in his assertion of the importance of mastery of language; obstetrical practice of the time was only partly reliant on visual cues, and it more often proceeded by touch. Duval describes with great care how various vital organs feel (so that a surgeon performing a cesarean section might avoid damaging them) as well as how to judge by touch the various difficult presentations of the fetus. His words guide much more effectively than illustrations of the period would have; strangely, for all his proclamation of the mastery of language over the body, Duval's words exhort and signal a responsiveness to bodily cues that can be read only in the most direct and physical fashion. And although still normative to some extent (the surgeon is to feel for certain muscles that should be aligned in a specific way), this emphasis on verbal representations of touch allows for greater variations in physiology, in that the doctor must locate organs and muscles for himself rather than assume their location based on crude visual representations. Duval's detailed descriptions of the complications of childbirth and of cesarean sections demonstrate an understanding of the range and variety of anatomy in pregnant women; this is in keeping with the awe he expresses at the range of physical presentations nature has concocted in hermaphrodites. This appreciation of difference, instead of a more normative approach, is crucial to the successful practice of medicine.

Thus, the sense of touch and language are described as jointly conveying mastery, just as they were in the chapters on sexuality. But, once again, touch and language must be sensitive to the natural dispositions and inclinations of the body. They convey mastery only to those who are willing to submit to the laws of the body and understand what realistically can be done. The godlike qualities of the doctor, all affirmations of his mastery over nature notwithstanding, are incessantly effaced by the power and variety of nature.

The Generation of Hermaphrodites

After some discussion of the proper care of the newborn and of the new mother (the word most frequently used is *gouvernance*, implying the relationship of ruler and subject), Duval turns again to his discussion of female anatomy and its role in conception, in order to prepare for his tale of the hermaphrodite Marin le Marcis. He rejects the Aristotelian notion of the active male principle and the passive female receptacle, in favor of Hippocratic theories of generation:

> Ie sçai qu'en ce i'aurai repugnance des peripaticiens sectaires d'Aristote, qui ne veulent admettre deux principes actifs. L'un provenant de l'homme, & l'autre de la femme....
>
> Nature n'a rien fait en vain. Elle a formé les parties seminales aux femmes. C'est donc pour engendrer la semence. S'il n'y avoit semence genitale que du masle, le seul masle seroit engendré. Or la femelle est aussi engendree par une faculté qui se trouve au sang, lequel n'est qu'excrement, comme veut l'Aristote. Et par conséquent il ne peut donner la faculté specifique de la femelle. (T7 v–8)
>
> [I know that for this reason I will hold in repugnance those peripatetic partisans of Aristotle, who do not wish to acknowledge two active principles; one coming from the man, and the other from the woman....

Nature has made nothing in vain. She has formed seminal organs in women. They are thus to form seed. If there were only male seed, only the male would be engendered. The female is also engendered by a faculty which is found in the blood, which is nothing but excrement, according to Aristotle. But logically, this cannot endow the specific conformation of the female.]

Duval rejects Aristotle's explanation from *The Generation of Animals,* of the generation of females, as irrational and self-contradictory. Nonetheless, he seems primarily concerned with reaffirming the distinctions between the sexes:

Les sexes establis selon le commun & frequent usage de celle qui dispose de nos corps, dont tous les climats du monde sont pour le iourd'hui habitez, depuis un pole iusques à l'autre, sont l'homme, dit en Latin *Vir,* en Grec *anur,* & la femme, dicte des Latins *mulier,* des Grecs *gunu.* L'un & l'autre aussi sont nommey *homo,* en Grec *anthropos,* usurpant ces deux dictions tant au masculin, que feminin genre....

Ceux qui ont devié des plus frequentes & ordinaires configurations, sont l'Hermaphrodit, homme-femme, femme-homme, dictions rendues en Grec *hermaphroditoi, andraguny & gunanur.* Desquels il nous convient traicter separement, en faisant & constituant trois especes diverses. (V)

[The sexes established according to common and frequent usage of her who governs our bodies (nature), which inhabit all of the zones of the world today, from one pole to another, are man, called *Vir* in Latin, *andros* in Greek, and woman*, mulier* in Latin, *gynon* in Greek. One and the other are also known as *homo,* in Greek *anthropos,* these two terms encompassing the masculine as well as the feminine gender.

Those who have deviated from the most frequent and ordinary configurations, are the hermaphrodite, the manly woman, and the womanly man, terms rendered in Greek *hermaphroditoi, androgyni,* and *gynanyr.* Which should be discussed separately, since they form three diverse species.]

Duval's discussion seems convoluted: sexual difference is established by "common and frequent usage," but, he claims, this usage is that of nature. This sexual difference is both universal and necessary for the population of the world. Duval thus oscillates between the notion of sexual difference as a practice and such difference as a state of being. This ambiguity is in keeping with his discussion of Marin le Marcis's gender, and the way in which it is effected by his environment.

This problematic argument is further complicated by Duval's insistence on the importance of language for designating gender and by his immediate retreat into literary and mythological examples of hermaphrodites, accompanied by an avoidance of scientific discussion of any actual cases. He begins his list of hermaphrodites with the tale of Hermaphroditus and Salmacis (V–V2v), retelling the Ovidian tale as well as the story of the Carians and Lelegians, who were civilized by the waters of the fountain Salmacis (V2). Duval does suggest in his version of the Ovidian tale that the hermaphrodite is a "demi-homme," and defines it as "un homme nay au vice de composition, portant nature d'homme & de femme" [a man born of imperfect form, containing both male and female natures] (V). This suggests that Duval still perceives the male as the ideal sex, and the female as merely a defective or lesser male; certainly the outcome of the Ovidian tale echoes this view of sex.

Nonetheless, the hermaphrodite creates a confusion about sex or gender, effacing the distinction between male and female, as Duval admits:

> … [L]es instruments ou particules servantes à l'un ou à l'autre sexe, sont telle-ment configurez, qu'on ne peut distinguer, si on doit dire du subiect qu'il soit homme ou femme, dont parlant Iean Soter d'un Hermaphrodit qui estoit dedans un baing d'eau tiede, il dict:

> [… (T)he instruments or parts serving one or the other sex, are so configured, that one cannot distinguish whether one should say of the subject that he is man or woman, as Jean Soter said of a hermaphrodite in a tepid bath:

Cypris me nomme femme, Hermes homme me dit,	Cypris calls me woman, Hermes man,
Mon corps estant noté, de tous les deux ensemble.	My body was marked by both together,
Ce n'est donc sans raison, qu'ils m'ont Hermaphrodit	So it is not without cause that they placed me
Mis en ce baing, dont l'eau est chaude et froide ensemble.	A hermaphrodite, in the bath of hot and cold water.]

(V3)

The image of tepid water suggests a mixing of two disparate elements that do not retain their identity, but create a third, yet again different, element. This third state is neither one nor the other, but somehow both.

Duval then reverts to stories of hermaphrodites that are more reminiscent of the journalistic or popular style of Pierre Boaistuau than of scientific analysis.[18] The insistence on mastery has dissolved in these accounts. He rehearses the ancient stories of hermaphrodites told by Bauhin (chap. 33, V4r–v), and then offers an odd chapter on "Histoires des enfans Hermaphrodits, desquels le parfait sexe n'a peu estre remarqué, à raison de leur bas aage & mort subite" [Stories of hermaphroditic babies, for whom the correct sex could not be discerned, because of their young age and sudden death] (V5–6). He tells of a mother who died giving birth to 364 hermaphroditic children, who also died. Those designated as boys were baptized Jean, those as girls, Elisabeth; one wonders, if their sex could not be determined, how they were so baptized, but this is one of the many contradictions in Duval's arguments. He in fact repeats this error in yet another story, claiming that the sex of the child was determined by the functions (in urination) of the external genitalia:

> L'an mil six cens à sainct Sever prés cette ville de Rouen, la femme d'un nommé Roland accoucha d'un enfant qui avoit marque des deux sexes, & sur la question du baptesme, sçavoir s'il seroit presenté pour fille, ou fils: Ils observerent par laquelle des natures il rendoit l'urine, voyant qu'il l'avoit rendu par le conduit muliebre, il fut baptisé pour fille, & ne fut jouissant de longue vie. C'est enfant fut receu par Catherine Mahom obstetrice qui me l'a ainsi affermé. (V6)

> [In 1600, at Saint Sever near this town of Rouen, the wife of a man named Roland gave birth to a baby with the marks of both sexes, and on the matter of baptism, and whether he would be presented as a girl or a boy, they observed by which of the parts he urinated, and seeing that he did so by the feminine conduit, he was baptised a girl, but did not enjoy a long life. This child was delivered by Catherine Mahom the midwife who swore this was true.]

The language betrays the certainty of the conclusions drawn concerning this child. Even though the child is designated a girl by the authorities, Duval insists on using the masculine pronoun, even when "he" is baptized as a girl. This insistence is made possible by use of the masculine noun *enfant*, but it is particularly odd given the flexibility of usage in Duval's narration of the case of Marin le Marcis. Perhaps Duval in fact wishes to hint at some doubt about the infallibility of this straightforward method; perhaps he is preparing the way for the dramatic story of Marin, which he will retell at the end of his treatise.

Although he has suggested that most hermaphrodites are essentially male, Duval turns to a discussion of "perfect" hermaphrodites, "qui peuvent tirer usage de l'un & l'autre sexe" [who can make use of one or the other sex] (chap. 35, V6–V8v). In this chapter, he repeats the accepted notion of sex roles: women submit, men act. He also reviews the notion that Adam was the first hermaphrodite, and offers the usual Neoplatonic reading of Genesis:

> Quand à ceux lesquels sont designez avoir eu leurs parties genitales tant viriles que muliebres, tellement complettes & decentement constituees, qu'ils ont peu accomplir & parfaire les œuvres naturelles, tant agissant avec les femmes, que se submettans aux hommes. D'iceux le pere Adam à esté le premier....[19]

> [As for those who are designated as having male as well as female genitalia, so complete and properly formed, that they have been able to undertake and complete natural duties, acting upon women as often as they submit to men.... Of these, father Adam was the first.]

Most of the examples of perfect hermaphroditism that Duval offers are from less threatening and more remote sources, such as the distant past, distant places, and the animal kingdom. He echoes Augustine's contention that some animals are naturally hermaphroditic, and Pliny's affirmation that there is a race of androgynes in Africa (V7v).

Still, in his opinion, the existence of hermaphrodites is indisputable and this existence tests many theories of generation. So, he is particularly concerned with establishing the truth of the existence of "double" hermaphrodites—that is, those who can beget and bear children:

> J'ay cogneu un Hermaphrodite ... [qui] fut marié à un homme, auquel il engendra quelque fils & fille, & ce nonobstant il avoit accoustumé monter sur les chambrieres & engendrer en icelles. (V8)

> [I knew a hermaphrodite who was married to a man, by whom he conceived several sons and daughters, and this notwithstanding, he was accustomed to mounting the chambermaids and begetting children by them.]

Although he recognizes that, for social reasons, these hermaphrodites must choose one role or another, Duval argues that such double beings do exist. Their existence is crucial for his argument against Aristotle's theories of generation; the fortieth chapter is devoted to a refutation of these theories (X6r–v). Duval points out that these theories are incoherent and are inconsistent with each other, and then he takes them on one by one. For the theory that too much material (provided by the mother) causes the generation of hermaphrodites, he argues that this excess should cause other "deformities" at the same time. Why is the location of the "deformity" so specific? Duval seems particularly offended by Aristotle's description of "the female as mutilated and imperfect." He makes the logical point that if the woman does not contribute anything but "material" to generation, then why is the male seed not entirely to blame for malformations?

Duval also rejects theories that link hermaphrodites to pollution taboos, among them Avicenna's theory that hermaphrodites are conceived in the eighth to eleventh days after the last sign of menstrual flow, and Lemnius's theory that hermaphrodites are caused by the presence of menstrual blood (V8v–X2v). In his rejection of Democritus's theory (that when the timing of the joining of seed is off, so that it does not join perfectly, a hermaphrodite is created), Duval suggests that the hermaphrodite is not a monster, but some sort of super being: "Comment pourra estre engendré l'Androgyne, ou la crase & mistion n'aura esté complette? Veu que ce n'est un corps imparfaict, mais qui à perfection d'un sexe & plus?" [How could an androgyne be born, when the formation and mixture has not been complete? Seeing that it is not an imperfect body, but one which has one perfect sex and more?] (X5). Here, he is returning to the Neoplatonic notion of the androgyne as the perfect being, as his vocabulary indicates. He is guiding the reader away from theories that would brand hermaphrodites as monstrous (that is, unnaturally so) towards those that reinscribe them in the orders of nature. But Duval reserves his harshest criticism for Aristotle, even if he retains some Aristotelian biases about the superiority of men. He accuses Aristotle of vagueness: the philosopher believed that monsters were the result of too much seed. Yet rather than the result of multiple births, some obstacle prevented normal conception; Aristotle does not explain the nature of this obstacle.[20] Duval, probably rightly, accuses Aristotle of complete lack of understanding of the function and inner workings of the uterus (X6v). He even rejects Aristotle's designation of the female as monstrous, even though he does believe in the superiority of the male.[21] He continues to refute Aristotle in the following chapter, and declares the superiority of Hippocratic theories.[22] Duval astutely observes that if the feminine matter were passive in conception, then it would not affect the process in any way (X8), yet Aristotle is so intent on crediting conception entirely to the male, that he begs the question:

> Mais il ayme mieux attribuer retusion en la faculté residente en ce spermeviril, comme provenant de ce sang informe, que de conceder un principe formel en la femme, par le moyen de la semence qu'elle fournit au coit. (X7v)

> [But he prefers to attribute any flaw in the faculty residing in the male sperm to this formless blood, rather than concede a formal principle to the woman, by means of the seed she provides in conception.]

Duval then argues that both male and female seed join to form any infant, and chastises Aristotle for not following the opinions of the wiser Hippocrates:

> Combien eust il esté meilleur à ce subtil Philosophe ne se departir de l'authorité des plus signalez personnages, ains suivant l'opinion du sage Hippocrate constituer les deux principes tant actif que passif à la semence genitale, qui procede tant du masle que de la femelle. (Y)[23]

> [How much better would it have been for this subtle philosopher not to depart from the authority of more significant figures, thus following the opinion of wise Hippocrates who establishes two principles, active and passive, to generative seed, which proceeds as much from the female as the male.]

He even accuses Aristotle of stealing his best ideas from Hippocrates. Yet the final opinion which Duval expresses varies only a hair from Aristotle's theories: he attributes conception of a male to more active and "robust" seed, that of a female to more passive seed (Y2v). Seed from the father tends to be more robust; seed from the mother tends to be weaker. Both come together, and whichever is present in greater quantity dictates the sex of the child. This model still ascribes greater perfection to the male, although Duval does add that both men and women carry stronger and weaker seed. Duval's own argument seems self-contradictory: both men and women have male and female seed, yet the seed from a man, because of its superiority, engenders a boy more often than does that from a woman. Duval, who corrected Aristotle's similar mistaken notions only a few pages earlier, falls into the same trap of presumption of male superiority (even though he does attribute some effective action to the maternal matter):

> Or quand il vient plus de sperme du corps de l'homme que de la femme ce part est mieux formé, & semblable au pere, mais quand il en vient plus de la femme, ce corps est plus beau & plus semblable à la mere & nullement au pere.... (Y3)

> [So when more sperm comes from the body of the man than from that of the woman, this part is better formed and resembles the father, but when more comes from the woman, this body is more beautiful, and resembles more the mother, and not at all the father....]

This passage echoes Duval's early pronouncements on reproduction as *self*-propagation and thus immortality. But it creates a basic flaw in his argument, similar to the flaw he used to destroy Aristotle's seeming logic: if the male seed is superior, why can it not vanquish the unruly but clearly inferior female seed? If there is in fact a hierarchical relation of male to female, by which the female is merely a defective male, then the "defects" of the female seed should be effaced by the perfect male seed, in the same manner as Salmacis's identity is effaced when she is joined to Hermaphroditus. Any hierarchical explanation of generation cannot in fact account for hermaphrodites.

At the same time that he is trying to assert male superiority in his accounts of conception, Duval rejects any theory of the origin of hermaphrodites that denies the mother an equal role in the generation of the child. He has adopted instead a slightly more complex theory based on Hippocrates's claim that both mother and father carry strong and weak seed. As we have seen, when "robust" seed predominates, a boy is conceived; when weak seed is present in greater quantity, a girl is conceived. But if one or the other does not predominate, a hermaphrodite is born. Since the issue is one of variable quantities, a whole spectrum of genders can be explained: from the manly man to more effeminate men, through a range of hermaphrodites, to vigorous women, and to very feminine women. This spectrum fits in well with the great variety in nature that Duval has remarked upon elsewhere in the treatise. While retaining the superior value of the masculine in his theories, Duval has managed to mitigate at least a bit of the misogyny and vehement prejudice against hermaphrodites present in the work of the "partisans of Aristotle" (T7v). In fact, the most coherent part of Duval's argument simply echoes Paré's explanation of hermaphrodites, which did not assign higher or lower values to either sex[24]:

> Dont resulte facilement, que s'il advient que la semence genitale soit rendue en égale quantité & qualité, tant de l'homme que de la femme...l'une ne cede à l'autre, mais apres deue mission agisse en patissant, patisse & endure en agissant mutuellement & esgallement l'Hermaphrodit sera engendré.... (Y3v)

130 ■ *High Anxiety*

[So it occurs easily, that if it happens that the generative seed is given in equal quantity and quality from the father as well as from the mother...one does not give way to the other, but after proper mixture, acts while submitting, submits and endures while acting mutually and equally, the hermaphrodite will be conceived....]

The concepts of *agir* and *patir,* used so often in discussions of sexual roles, are at play even at the moment of conception in this theory. But the notion of equal mixtures, equal roles, and equal power granted to each type of seed belies the constantly assumed superiority of the male which informs most of Duval's treatise.

After establishing an acceptable (to him) theory of the origin of hermaphrodites, Duval once again turns to mythological and astrological accounts. He claims that the positions of the Sun and Moon, Venus and Mercury, are particularly important. He lingers for quite some time on the figure of Mercury, calling him a prophet and linking him to Theuth (Y7), the Egyptian god of language, with all of the implications of mastery and loss of mastery that this form of divinity might contain.[25] Mercury was often portrayed in alchemical treatises as being of ambiguous gender, and in mythology as the father of Hermaphroditus, thus linking hermaphrodites to eloquence and rhetoric. He daringly describes Mercury as the Divine Logos (again echoing alchemical treatises)[26]:

Mais ils parlent en ces livres là d'une parole ou verbe energique & actuel, lequel ayant pour sa Venus cette masse elementaire, qui estoit lors confuse en un cahos, à creé le ciel, la terre, & tout ce qui est enclos sous la voute de ce grand temple celeste, auquel ce verbe Divin doit estre adoré avec toute humilité. (Y6v)

[But they speak in these books of an energetic and effective word, which having as its Venus this elemental mass which was previously mixed together in chaos, created the sky, the earth, and all that is encompassed under the vault of this great celestial temple, in which this Divine Word should be adored with all humility.]

Note that Mercury, often portrayed as an androgynous divinity, is here cast as the male principle which organizes and forms the chaotic female matter, represented by Venus. This cosmology echoes Aristotelian notions of generation, Platonic notions of the union of spirit and matter, and alchemical depictions of the process of conjunction (concepts which overlap in large degree). Mercury is then depicted as tricephalous, a representation of the trinity, but also of the pagan god's intellectual characteristics of memory, intelligence, and providence, which inform the triple-headed figure of Prudence in Renaissance iconography.[27] Duval also elaborates on Mercury's nature as the serpent killer, vanquisher of Satanic forces. But Mercury as the Divine Logos is ineffective without the material upon which to work; bodily reality meets linguistic mastery in this image as well. So, Duval discusses Venus's qualities, and tells some mythological stories about the two (Y7v–Z); but his main concern remains with Mercury as the image of salvation, propagation, and immortality. In astrological accounts of the generation of hermaphrodites, the influence of the planet Mercury is seen as key (Z1). These accounts thus place hermaphrodites in a stereotypically masculine role, one that involves mastery of discourse and control over others.

In his examples, Duval does seem concerned primarily with masculine hermaphrodites and with establishing their social role as men, even though he has argued in theory for a continuous spectrum of genders. For hermaphrodites with two sets of genitalia, of which only the male organs function, he uses the term *Androgyne,* arguing that "la plus excellente partie obtenant le premier lieu en la nomination" [the most excellent part obtains the first place in the name] (Z2). *Gynanders* are hermaphrodites in whom the female reproductive organs function, but the male do not; sometimes these people pass as men, but are eventually discovered to be women (Z2v). As was the case in Duval's opening arguments, here the primary criterion for designating a male is his reproductive capacity:

> Car la perfection du sexe ne se doit iuger par l'excretion de l'urine seulement mais par l'orgasme, & emotion de nature, s'inclinant d'avantage aux particules desquelles l'Hermaphrodit peut user, en l'habitation & copule charnelle, pour le fait de la generation. (Z3)

> [Because the perfection of a sex should not be judged only by urination, but by the orgasm and natural feeling, inclining more to the parts the hermaphrodite can use, in the sexual act and in coupling for the purposes of generation.]

Neuter hermaphrodites can fulfill neither the active nor passive role (Duval's terms), neither beget nor bear children (Z5v). Thus, gender identity is linked only to reproductive capacity. This limitation of criteria is crucial to Duval's defense of Marin le Marcis, who by all appearances is female but for her fully functioning penis.

When Duval admits the possibility of unstable or transformed gender, the only examples he gives are mythical or animal. He offers the example of Tiresias, and later mentions the hyena's apparent capacity to change sex (Aa1v). Any transformations that may have occurred in recent history are explained away as misobservation in the initial determination of sex. In the reign of Louis XI, a man from Auvergne gave birth to a child (Z7.) In 1575 in Paris, a young man (an altar boy) was discovered to be a girl, and allowed to live as a woman (Z7v). Duval becomes concerned that his (apparently male) audience may feel threatened, and reassures them:

> …[L]es hommes formez tels en la vulve maternelle, ne deposent iamais leur nature virile, & ne retourne arriere vers le sexe feminin, d'autant que toutes choses tendent à perfection, & n'ont regres à ce qui est moins parfaict. Or est la nature de l'homme plus parfaicte que celle de la femme. (chap. 51, Z8)

> [… (M)en formed as such in the maternal womb never lose their virile nature and do not regress towards the feminine sex, since all things tend

towards perfection, and do not degenerate into that which is less perfect. So, the nature of man is more perfect than that of woman.]

The social construction of male superiority, which certainly would guarantee a strong desire to remain male, is here taken as a natural or biological fact. Duval seems torn between his understanding of female anatomy and biological functions and the cultural biases he has received, more from philosophical treatises than from any other source. His powers of scientific observation remain in conflict with the received attitudes towards sex that his society has dictated. For Duval, the hermaphrodite becomes the site of his own intellectual conflicts concerning sex and/or gender.

It is for this reason as well that Duval emphasizes the extent to which our perceptions of external signs lead us to misjudge the sex of a person. He offers examples of men who have been discovered to be women, arguing that these men cannot have become women, but were women who merely seemed to be men. He emphasizes the social pressures that favor masculinity: "Il advint aussi qu'un Hermaphrodit estant produict sur terre, les parens plus curieux d'elever un fils, qu'une fille" [It happens as well that a hermaphrodite appearing on earth, the parents are more eager to raise a boy than a girl] (Z8v). Such social pressures bear upon the subject, causing her to maintain the masculine role she has been given, but nature will out (this is his own assessment) (Aa1). Similarly, in his accounts of women who were revealed to be men, of which he gives many examples from ancient Rome (Aa6), Duval emphasizes the extent to which appearances deceive and to which social practices may shape those appearances. He asserts repeatedly that it is the functioning of the body, not its appearance, which should be used to designate the sex of a subject.

Throughout these accounts, Duval insists that men cannot become women (Z8), and women cannot become men (Bb2v). In cases where this seems to have happened, the appearance belied underlying function, the only true mark of sex for Duval. Or the subject in question was a hermaphrodite, exhibiting characteristics of both male and female, although one set of characteristics may have remained hidden for some time. As is true in his discussion of childbirth, what one sees is not to be trusted, and it is the sense of touch that reveals the truth. This view dominates the case of Marin le Marcis, and Duval's eloquent presentation of this revolutionary argument will save the young hermaphrodite's life.

For Duval, then, visual cues of gender (*sexe* in sixteenth-century French, and thus indistinguishable from a more essentialist notion of sex) are linked to performative presentations (dress, speech, gesture, comportment, and the like); touch is linked to the underlying body, which he considers more essential or more real than the surface presentations. Duval clearly feels that the structure of the body as established by internal examination, and primarily by the sense of touch, provides a more definitive mark of sex than the surface and social presentations. To some extent, then, he is offering a view of sex that is close to essentialist theories being discussed today. But, as we have seen in the case of Marin le Marcis, Duval not only concedes but elaborately delineates a concomitant theory that environment, and what might be deemed performative practices (dress, level of activity, relative empowerment or disempowerment), can alter bodily reality. The complex interaction between the body and the roles imposed upon it makes it difficult (although not impossible, according to Duval) to determine the sex of some subjects. Duval seems to be arguing that the body itself is mutable and unstable, so that bodily reality can only be factitiously determined by given functions at a specific time. Yet he sets limits on this mutability—men can never become women—in a desperate attempt, it seems, to hold onto traditional gender roles. Duval cannot break free from the traditional misogyny so central to his profession. Yet he seems to remain at the margins of that profession, coming as close as any other author to questioning those very traditions.

The extent to which Duval differs from his colleagues in the subtlety and complexity of his understanding of gender is nowhere more evident than in Jean Riolan's refutation of his work, the *Discours sur les hermaphrodits, où il est démontré contre l'opinion commune, qu'il n'y a point de vray hermaphrodits* [Discourse on hermaphrodites, in which it is demonstrated that, contrary to popular opinion, there are no true hermaphrodites].[28] Riolan argues that there are only males or females, and that the distinctions between them are quite clear. His primary argument is that those who are deemed to be hermaphrodites are in fact sexually deviant women who have enlarged clitorises due to their activities. Although he claims in his opening letter that he wishes to make hermaphrodites loved and accepted, he condemns any sexual difference in the body of his text. The opening lines of his text evoke a horror at the possibility of unbridled sexuality:

> On dit que l'Afrique produit tousiours quelque monstre nouveau, c'est un pays fort sec, arrousé de peu de rivieres, & fertil en bestes sauvages, qui sont contraintes souvent d'aller boire en mesme riviere, où se rencontrans en grand nombre, ils s'accouplent pesle-mesle, & de ce meslange & copulation dissemblable naissent les monstres estranges....[29]

> [They say that Africa always produces some new monster. It is a very dry country, watered by few rivers, and fertile in wild beasts, which are often compelled to drink in the same river, where, encountering each other in great numbers, they couple without order, and from this mixing and diverse coupling are born strange monsters....]

The milder climate of Paris produces no monsters; any oddities that are to be found there have gathered in Paris because of its pleasant situation.[30] Again, we see the association between the animal and unbridled sexuality. This prepares the way for Riolan's condemnation of hermaphrodites as merely overly lustful women:

> Or ceste partie dicte clitoris, representant par sa figure & composition la verge de l'homme, peut croistre & grossir comme le doigt aux femmes voluptueuses

& amoureuses, & en peuvent abuser pour se donner plaisir, en habitant les unes avec les autres.[31]

[So this part called the clitoris, mimicking by its form and its composition the male rod, can grow and thicken like a finger in libidinous and lustful women, and they can abuse it to give themselves pleasure, by living with each other.]

The threat of this form of sexuality is its exclusion of the masculine. This menace is clearly too great for the author to bear, as he displaces this form of sexuality onto distant cultures, claiming almost immediately after this discussion of female homosexuality that it is Egyptian women who are best known for this form of enlarged clitoris.[32] The cure for this condition is "l'amputation des parties superflues" [the amputation of superfluous parts], a suggestion which echoes the more forceful "retrancher ce qui ne leur appartient" [cut away that which does not belong to them] offered earlier in the treatise.[33] Egyptian women are more fertile, probably because their country is hotter, and their genitalia grow overly large, and thus must be cut off (also Duval's explanation for clitoridectomy). These excesses are also linked to the myth of hypermasculinity of Egyptian men. Riolan then devotes a chapter to the history of "the circumcision of women" and how they might be castrated (his term) without risking their lives.[34] In a treatise that is otherwise a fairly conventional recasting of Duval's work, with frequent verbatim repetition, this obsession with excessive female sexuality and its cures as well as the insistence on distancing this sexuality from French culture reveals the extent to which male dominion felt itself to be very vulnerable indeed. The precise vulnerability of this dominion is evident in Riolan's argument that "un homme sans bourses & testicules, s'il a la verge bien formee, ne lairra pas d'estre homme" [a man without scrotum or testicles, if he has a well-formed penis, does not cease to be a man].[35] But if women can be castrated, and indeed if some of them must be in order to assure their femininity, then how sure is masculinity based on this one body part? The fear of castration, of sexual insufficiency, lurks below the surface of this argument, and in his insistence on clear distinctions based on examples that are hardly clear, Riolan destroys all certainty of what is masculine, what feminine. If the penis grants manhood, then the phallic woman is also a man; if the penis can be taken away, then manhood based solely upon it is easily lost.

Riolan's paranoia, along with the sinuous twists and turns of Duval's arguments, reveals the extent to which, although a biological reality, sexual ambiguity was an untenable state in French society of the time. Duval concludes his treatise with a longer narration and discussion of the case of Marin le Marcis (Bb7–Ff7), making quite clear the suffering and fear Marin and his wife, Jeanne, endured. Duval's melodramatic account of their lives underscores the social torment and ostracism involved for a person of indeterminate gender. Thus, he must heroically establish Marin's true nature, not only for his contemporaries, but as an uninterrupted state that already existed at birth. Even transformation was unacceptable; Marin had to be categorized as unequivocally male if he was to survive. Thus, although anatomical observations had established the fact of sexual ambiguity—a whole continuum of sexes and genders, of biological and social identities—this ambiguity was like a dirty little secret that had to be denied and repressed in order for society to function, and for individuals to function in society. Science had advanced somewhat in its understanding of anatomy, sex, and sexuality. Society, however, did not stay in step with these medical advances, but maintained rigid roles, increasingly revealed as fictional or cultural constructs, enforced by means of capital or corporal punishment and public humiliation. The hermaphrodite, recognized at least to some degree by medicine, was repressed mostly by the legal system. But like anything repressed, this figure resurfaced continually in the poetry, novels, and popular pamphlets of the time. Denied existence, the hermaphrodite seemed to be everywhere, invading every aspect of intellectual life. The constant ridicule or repression of such ambiguity revealed intense fear; this fear hints at the power of the hermaphroditic figure for the intellectual and the popular imagination.

Notes

1. See, e.g., Ambroise Paré, *Les œuvres d'Ambroise Pare...: Reueues & augmentees par l'Autheur* (Paris: Gabriel Buon,1585). For a brief discussion of this case, see Jacques Duval, *Des monstres et prodiges,* ed. Jean Céard (Geneva: Droz, 1971), xiv–xix. One point of criticism against Paré was that he did not know Greek. See also *Catholic Encyclopedia*: "at the time of his enrollment in the faculty of the Collège de St-Cosme, in 1554, the faculty made his ignorance of Latin a ground of objection".
2. For an excellent discussion of the Sorbonne and medicine in this period, see Iain M. Lonie, "The 'Paris Hippocratics': Teaching and Research in Paris in the Second Half of the Sixteenth Century," in *The Medical Renaissance of the Sixteenth Century,* ed. A. Wear, R. K. French, and I. M. Lonie (Cambridge: Cambridge University Press, 1985), 155–74.
3. See Jacques Duval, *Des hermaphrodits, accovchemens de femmes: et traitement qui est requis pour les releuer en sante* (Rouen: David Gevffroy, 1612). Page numbers are referenced in the text. This treatise on childbirth seems to indicate that this shift was already occurring by the end of the sixteenth century, somewhat earlier than in England, and earlier than some historians of medicine have noted. See Andrew Wear, "Medicine in Early Modern Europe, 1500–1700," in *The Western Medical Tradition, 800 B.C. to A.D. 1800,* ed. Lawrence Conrad et al. (Cambridge: Cambridge University Press, 1995), 234–35. For a general history of childbirth, see Jacques Gélis, *History of Childbirth: Fertility, Pregnancy, and Birth in Early Modern Europe,* trans. Rosemary Morris (Boston: Northeastern University Press, 1991).
4. Caspar Bauhin was professor of botany and anatomy at the University of Bagel, and author of the treatise *Hermaphroditorum monstrosorum–que parteum hatura* [On the birth of hermaphrodites and monsters in nature].
5. Duval, *Des hermaphrodits,* cites both Paré and Bauhin rather far along in his discussion (Z3 for Paré, Z5 for Bauhin). Katharine Park and Lorraine Daston, "The Hermaphrodite and the Orders of Nature: Sexual Ambiguity in Early Modern France," *Gay and Lesbian Quarterly* 1 (1995): 419–73, argue that this period sees an evolution away from Aristotelian notions of generation, toward Hippocratic views, which often posited a "more equal" role for the woman in the process of generation.
6. Park and Daston, "The Hermaphrodite and the Orders of Nature."
7. Duval, *Des hermaphrodits,* concludes with a much longer and more melodramatic version, Bb7–Ff7.
8. This problematic nature of apparel certainly links the tailor to homosexuality and other marginalized forms of sexuality in English Renaissance literature. See Simon Shephard, "What's So Funny about Ladies' Tailors? A Survey of Some Male (Homo)sexual Types in the Renaissance," in *Textual Practice* 6 (1992): 17–30. Tailors themselves were often portrayed, mostly in the theater, as foppish and effeminate, thus making this the perfect profession for the ambiguous Marin.
9. Duval, *Des hermaphrodits;* this type of hermaphrodite is discussed in chaps. 53 and 54 (A3v–A4).
10. Some of his arguments recall to the modern reader those summarized by Natalie Zemon Davis, "Women on Top," from *Society and Culture in Early Modern France* (Stanford: Stanford University Press, 1975), 124–51.
11. This evolution is traced briefly by Karen Newman, *Fetal Positions: Individualism, Science, Visuality* (Stanford: Stanford University Press, 1996), 48–51.
12. Duval, *Des hermaphrodits,* "Louange des parties genitalles," and by this he means male genitalia.
13. Thomas Laqueur, *Making Sex: Body and Gender from the Greeks to Freud* (Cambridge: Harvard University Press, 1990), 28.
14. This contention is contradicted by his adoption of Hippocratic theories of generation, later in the treatise.
15. Duval quotes Paracelsus earlier.
16. Duval, *Des hermaphrodits,* B8 (*l'emulgente senestre*), C2r–v (*le senestre* thylugonon, *engendreur de femelles*).
17. Newman, *Fetal Positions,* 27–42, for examples and discussion of such illustrations, although she uses them to support a slightly different argument.

18. Pierre Boaistuau, *Histoires prodigieuses* (1561), Wellcome Library for the History and Understanding of Medicine Manuscripts in Facsimile (Milan: Franco Maria Ricci, 2000); continued by Claude Tesserant, *Quatorze histoires prodigieuses* (Paris, 1567).

19. For a detailed account of this myth, see Naomi Yavneh, "The Spiritual Eroticism of Leone's Hermaphrodite," in *Playing with Gender: A Renaissance Pursuit,* ed. Jean R. Brink, Maryanne C. Horowitz, and Allison P. Coudert (Urbana: University of Illinois Press, 1991), 86ff.

20. Here, Duval seems to be discussing Aristotle's *Generation of Animals*; see *The Complete Works of Aristotle,* ed. Jonathan Barnes (Princeton: Princeton University Press, 1984), 770b27–772b34 (1192–96).

21. Duval, *Des Hermaphrodits,* X6v, "Pourquoy il ne se trouverra en cette opinion, comme ie croy non plus de raison, qu'en l'action retuse qu'il veut estre en la semence virile, lors qu'au lieu d'un masle la femelle (dit-il) animal comme mutilé & imparfait est engendrée" [Why there is no reason in this opinion that when the action of the male sperm is blocked, instead of a male, a female is born, a mutilated and imperfect animal].

22. Duval, *Des hermaphrodits,* chap. 41, X7v–Z2, "Suitte de la refutation des opinions d'Aristote touchant la conception des Hermaphrodits, & comme il faut entendre Hippocrate sur le faict de la semence" [Continuation of the refutation of the opinions of Aristotle concerning the conception of hermaphrodites, and how Hippocrates should be understood on the matter of seed].

23. Duval, *Des hermaphrodits,* X. The presentation of the Hippocratic argument by Laqueur, *Making Sex,* 39, is clearer than Duval's and may be of some help here: "Hippocrates argues for pangenesis, the view that each part of the body of each parent renders up some aspect of itself; that the representatives of the various parts form a reproductive fluid or seed; and that conception consists of a blending, in various proportions and strengths, of these germinal substances. Hippocrates abandons any effort to attribute strong or weak seed respectively to actual males or females. Although male must originate from stronger sperm, 'the male being stronger than the female,' both are capable of producing more or less strong seed." See also Hippocrates *On Generation,* in *The Hippocratic Treatises,* ed. Iain M. Lonie (Berlin: Walter de Gruyter, 1981), 7.2.

24. Ambroise Paré, *Des monstres et prodiges,* ed. Jean Céard (Geneva: Droz, 1971) chap. 6, pp. 24–25.

25. Not only is this in keeping with discussions of language previously offered in this treatise, but this figure is analyzed as one of attempted mastery over that which remains elusive in Jacques Derrida, "La pharmacie de Platon," *La dissemination* (Paris: Seuil, 1972), esp. 71–133.

26. In particular, the *Rosarium philosophorum* (1550) compares the alchemical process to Christ's life; see the facsimile edition: *Rosarium philosophorum: Ein alchemisches Florilegium des Spätmittelalters,* ed. Joachim Telle (Weinheim: VCH, 1992), 182–92.

27. Edgar Wind, *Pagan Mysteries in the Renaissance* (New York: Norton, 1968), 260. These triple intellectual virtues also correspond to past, present, and future.

28. Jean Riolan, *Discours sur les hermaphrodits* (Paris: Ramier, 1614).

29. Riolan, *Discours sur les hermaphrodits,* 1, a2

30. Riolan, *Discours sur les hermaphrodits,* 2.

31. Riolan, *Discours sur les hermaphrodits,* 79.

32. Riolan, *Discours sur les hermaphrodits,* 81. Riolan also adds examples of Turkish women.

33. Riolan, *Discours sur les hermaphrodits,* 5, 83.

34. Riolan, *Discours sur les hermaphrodits,* 85, 87, 89.

35. Riolan, *Discours sur les hermaphrodits,* 105.

Molière's Body Politic

Mitchell Greenberg

*En vérité, le monarque nous semble passer une grande partie de son temps sur la chaise per-
cée. Il n'y est question que de purges et de clystéres, de dévoiements de ventre qui durent
parfois plus de vingt-quatre heures; de selles répétées jusqu'à la douzaine....*
　　　　　　　—F. Millepierres, *La Vie quotidienne des médecins au temps de Molière*

*[L]e corps est aussi directement plongé dans un champ politique; les rapports de pouvoir
opèrent sur lui une prise immédiate; ils l'investissent, le marquent, le dressent, le suppli-
cient, l'astreignent à des travaux, l'obligent à des cérémonies, exigent de lui des signes. Cet
investissement politique du corps est lié, selon des relations complexes et réciproques, à son
utilisation économique.*
　　　　　　　　　　　　　　　—M. Foucault, *Surveiller et punir*[1]

Gone from recent discussion of seventeenth-century France is that comfortingly monochromatic and slightly marmoreal image of "le grand siècle." A notable victim of the renewed attention literary critics and theoreticians have brought to the study of the classical age is the hieratically fixed notion of a structured world in which things and people were believed to be neatly arranged in an ordered and organic whole. French society of the period is no longer envisioned as a pyramid, the apex of which would be fixed at Versailles, seen as the shiny apogee of a classical moment more ideal than real. In its place, we are offered a vision of a society in radical transformation. France in the seventeenth century was situated at the crossroads of epochal changes—changes in epistemology, economies, theology, philosophy, and the arts. It appears to us now as a rich, if often extremely violent, culture where political, sexual, and economic differences commingle, divide, and are reconfigured.[2]

In his many provocative and innovative readings of the origins and ramifications of the modern subject, Michel Foucault returns time and again to this conflicted seventeenth century, which he defines as one of the two decisive moments of epistemological change that mark the modern period, a moment in which the parameters defining human subjectivity are decisively realigned.[3] At the same time that Foucault marks off the seventeenth century as a period of radical realignment of epistemology, he also (and this of course is intimately related to epistemology) situates the coming into being—through his mapping of a new "confessional" policy—of sexuality.[4] Impelled by the reconfigurations of the socioeconomic spheres of the seventeenth century, this change in sexuality/ epistemologies informs a corresponding transformation of the family in its physical and metaphysical avatars. The seventeenth century in Europe marks a moment of realignment in the conception of the family, which gradually shifts from that rather large, inchoate definition of people who all live and work under the same (extended) roof, be they servants, kinsfolk, or other dependents, to the more restricted sense of family as that limited group of blood relations (parents and children) that the eighteenth century will come to cherish.[5] It is by this change that the family becomes in the words of Foucault:

> l'échangeur de la sexualité et de l'alliance: elle transporte la loi et la dimension du juridique dans le dispositif de sexualité: et elle transporte l'économie du plaisir et l'intensité des sensations dans le régime de l'alliance.[6]

> [the site of exchange of sexuality and alliance: it transports law and the dimension of the juridical into the domain of sexuality: and it transports the economy of pleasure and intensity of sensations into the system of alliance.]

How are we to understand this meeting of pleasure and law/economics, this alliance, in the conflicting representations that seventeenth-century theater offers of the family? How are we to locate it? How did the seventeenth century locate it, if not by representing this strange configuration—this new configuration, emerging out of and still intimately inextricable from other, older subjective patterns—and incorporating this intermeshing network in/on/as the body? I am speaking of those bodies of the passionate, comic personages that the seventeenth century figures for us, newly ensconced in the family that is born on the stage with all the passion and rage of a deeply conflicted sexuality, and with all its comic hilarity as well.

But what are we to make of these bodies given to us in representation? Is there a reality there that points to anything other than precisely the configuration and reconfiguration of discursive practices? For, and this will be the point of my discussion, the body does not exist, is not available to us in some empirical thereness, but always as a complex nexus of ideological investments. Much work from scholars in various disciplines has been brought to bear on the body in these cultures, so near and yet so removed from us. For instance, in one of the most provocative attempts to circumscribe the site and function of the body in early modern culture, *The Tremulous Private Body: Essays on Subjection,* Francis Barker argues for seeing the body as "not a hypostatized object, still less a simple biological mechanism of given desires and needs acted on externally by controls and enticements, but a relation in a system of liaisons which are material, discursive, psychic, sexual, but without stop or centre."[7] In *The Politics and Poetics of Transgression,* Peter Stallybrass and Allon White insist that the "body cannot be thought separately from the social formation, symbolic topography, and the constitution of the subject. The body is neither a purely natural given nor is it merely a textual metaphor, it is a privileged operator for the transcoding of these other areas. Thinking the body is thinking social topography and vice versa."[8]

In a sense, these works and others I omit owe a great debt, on the one hand, to Mikhail Bakhtin's study of Rabelais and on the other, to the work of the anthropologist

Mary Douglas. Douglas's influential *Purity and Danger: An Analysis of Concepts of Pollution and Taboo* provides a structural account of the social symbolization of the body that is congenial to critics who wish to deal precisely with the body as a symbolic system without appealing to the symbolizing processes of psychoanalysis. Douglas's study of the interpretive strategies at work in archaic and so-called primitive societies where the body is seen as a reflection of the larger world and vice versa has proved particularly useful as a critical tool:

> The body is a model which can stand for any bounded system. Its boundaries can represent any boundaries which are threatened or precarious. The body is a complex structure. The functions of its different parts and their relations afford a source of symbols for other complex structures. We cannot possibly interpret rituals concerning excreta, breast milk, saliva and the rest unless we are prepared to see in the body a symbol of society, and to see the powers and dangers credited to social structures reproduced in small on the human body.[9]

Psychoanalysis, from the beginning, in Freud's studies on hysteria, has also taught us that the body is a symbolic production. By this, it is meant that there is a complex interweave of the physical and psychic functions in which is produced a phantasmic image in each of us of our own corporeality. Our bodily image reflects as much of how we are inserted in the symbolic, signifying systems of our culture, as how that culture is manifested in and as that image.[10] As the French psychoanalyst and critic Guy Rosolato writes,

> la formation de l'image du corps ne peut être abordée sans tenir compte de l'interaction complexe des investissements libidinaux, de la capture imaginaire narcissique et de la potentialité substitutive et symbolique du langage, qui orientent l'identification en général.[11]

> [the formation of the image of the body cannot be undertaken without taking into account the complex interaction of libidinal investments, the imaginary narcissistic capture, and the substitutive and symbolic potentiality of language, which orient identification in general.]

The body is inscribed at the interstice of reality (social, economic, physiological) and fantasy (desire). Furthermore, this split between reality and desire is never unilateral. There is no perception of the body, one's own or others, that can be separated out from the desiring, phantasmic structures into which it is inserted and which it reproduces as its symptoms at the same time that these phantasmic structures bear the impress of exterior social imperatives.[12]

Molière's last play, *Le Malade imaginaire,* the play in which—during the fourth performance—he suffered his fatal attack, was written to be staged in celebration of Louis XIV's triumphal return from his Dutch campaign (1672). The play was first given on 10 February 1673; that is, during carnival. At the very end of the comedy, in the concluding lines of Béralde, Argan's brother, there is a direct reference to carnival and to those liberties that traditionally are permitted during the pre-Lenten festivities:

> Mais, ma nièce, ce n'est pas tant le jouer que s'accommoder à ses fantasies. Tout ceci n'est qu'entre nous. Nous y pouvons aussi prendre chacun un personnage et nous donner ainsi la comédie les uns aux autres. Le carnaval autorise cela. (3.14.454)[13]

> [But, my niece, it is not so much tricking him as accommodating ourselves to his fantasies. All this is only among us. We can each take on a character, and offer each other a comedy. Carnival authorizes this.]

Carnival forms the overarching structure inside of which *Le Malade imaginaire* plays out its farcical attack on seventeenth-century medicine in and across the body of the hypochondriac Argan. These obvious references to carnival and the carnivalesque allow me to fix our attention on two highly invested moments in the history of modern literary-social criticism that form the parameters of my own discussion of Molière: the body and the subject of political modernity. At the one end of my spectrum is Bakhtin and, more precisely, his much commented, highly debated idea of the carnivalesque; at the other, Freud, or rather a certain twentieth-century psychoanalytical vision of the human subject. In between, torn between the one and the other—objects of mediation and change—I will place Molière, or rather his two characters Harpagon and Argan, the protagonists of *L'Avare* and *Le Malade imaginaire*.

Bakhtin's rich use of the term carnivalesque and the carnivalesque, that is, grotesque, body to describe what he believed to be a different, premodern subjectivity, exemplified most notably by Rabelais, has proved to be an extremely fertile concept for contemporary criticism. Bakhtin's description of the carnivalesque body is authorized in *Rabelais and His World* by its dialectical relation to its supposedly historically later other: the closed classical body. As we know, the grotesque is a body that knows no limits. The social activity that corresponds to the grotesque body is the carnival, which Bakhtin tells us cannot be thought of as a function that distinguishes or separates out. Although the concept of the grotesque body may be but one way among many to describe a different subjective imbrication of the human being in an epistemic formation that has become for us but a nostalgic memory, it does seem to correspond, as an image, to the medical science of the late Middle Ages and the early modern period. Recent historians remind us not only of the principles of Galenic medicine but of the enormous patriarchal investments such a humoral conception of the human body both obfuscates and reveals.[14] The early modern English, and we can assume French, subject, according to G. K. Paster, "grew up with an understanding of his or her body as a semipermeable, irrigated container in which humors moved sluggishly. People imagined that health consisted of a state of internal solubility to be perilously maintained often through a variety of evacuations either self-administered or in consultation with a healer."[15] Obviously, in the masculinized ideology that informed such a conception of the body, the male body was the ideal object of creation, being both more hot than the female, and particularly more closed.[16] The female body because of its effluents was famously described as a "leaky vessel," tautologically dangerous for a society that in the seventeenth century was growing increasingly wary of any unbounded system.[17]

On the one hand, therefore, the open, unfinished, female grotesque body; on the other, the classical, closed, male body. And who best represented the shining ideal of bodily and political perfection but the king—the extolled, idolized, and triumphant Louis XIV? Here I recall that *Le Malade imaginaire* was written as part of the ceremonies celebrating Louis's triumphal return from the Dutch campaign of 1672. While the purpose of this military action undertaken by the French with Louis at their head was not ostensibly to enlarge their territory, the campaign must be seen as forming an integral part of the policy of territorial aggrandizement of the French state under both Louis XIII and Louis XIV. The territorial policy of the French crown in the seventeenth century becomes essentially a consistent and organized attempt to secure natural boundaries (natural in the sense of geography or cultural spheres) for the state. These borders, once secured, were thought to protect the state from the vulnerability of openness. By closing off the frontiers—at the Pyrenees, the Rhine, the Atlantic coast—France became a secured, bounded entity. Of course, once this entity was separated out from and defended against external threats, attention could then be directed at securing the internal vulnerabilities of the state.

What I am suggesting is simply that there is a homology working throughout the seventeenth century between the geographic integrity of the realm and the ideal of a classical body which Bakhtin defines in the following way: "The new bodily canon… presents an entirely finished, completed, strictly limited body, which is shown from the outside as something individual. That which protrudes, bulges, sprouts, or branches off… is eliminated, hidden, or moderated. All orifices of the body are closed."[18] Mary Douglas speaks about this analogy between the social body and the physical body in an attempt to demonstrate how the fear of permeable social/political boundaries is reflected by the "anxiety" associated with bodily orifices or margins: "Any structure of ideas is vulnerable at its margins. We should expect the orifices of the body to symbolize its specially vulnerable points."[19] To instill the conception of an integral body politic in the individual subject, an image must be substantiated that is at once familiar and august, both near and distant. The idea of the state must be made to correspond to the image of the individual body, just as the image of the body (of the subject) is made to mediate the distance separating metaphysical ideology from an anchoring in the physical. The body that mediates between the transcendental concept of the perfect state and the physical reality of the body in its evanescence becomes fixed upon the shining body royal, the *corps glorieux* of the king: Louis XIV as he was produced in and as a spectacular embodiment of the ideals towards which the French state moved.[20]

The important point, however, which White and Stallybrass stress, is that the dialectical nature of the grotesque/classical opposition assures that one form (the classical) exists in an inextricable relation to its other (the grotesque):

The classical body splits precisely along the rigid edge which is its defense against heterogeneity: its closure and purity are quite illusory and it will perpetually rediscover in itself, often with a sense of shock or inner revulsion, the grotesque, the protean and the motley, the neither/nor, the double negation of high and low which was the very precondition for its social identity.[21]

So, although the glorious body royal becomes an icon too sacred to be touched, that remains incorruptible even into advanced old age, the king's surrogate, the father, the king of his family, lends himself to more ambivalence, to the ambivalence of the clash of cultural codes and values, in a way that is both more tragic and more comic than the hieratic image of the "Père du peuple" could ever be.[22]

Borrowing the term *oikodespotès* from Jürgen Habermas, who uses it to describe familial-economic organization in Greek society, I suggest that the word fits admirably into our own purposes as a way of introducing the sociosexual dimension of the role of the father in Molière's comedy.[23] It combines both the etymological connotations of house, home (and by extension husbandry, household economy) with the term for controller, ruler. This latter term echoes with the proleptic resonance of despot, tyrant, and dictator, and in this sense sends us back to the metaphorical conundrum uniting father and king in seventeenth-century culture. The father remains, for seventeenth-century patriarchy, the central figure in familial economy. I think it would be best to map the economic change—the change that is written on the bodies of these men. This is, I suggest, interestingly perverse because in the classical period we are discussing, men and bodies have become almost mutually exclusive terms. In the emerging redistribution of patriarchal monarchies that marks the introduction of the modern, it is men who are the arbiters of value and meaning, who are at work in the chancelleries, in the learned societies, in the amphitheaters where anatomical dissections and lessons are carried out more and more readily. In this context, the split between the body and the soul, the body and the mind, becomes, true to its roots in Aristotelian thought, even more the split between male and female, between masculine and feminine. In this split, women become *le sexe* for the men who, although they may have a sex, certainly refuse any notion that they are "le sexe."[24]

Having examined *Le Malade imaginaire,* we look now at *L'Avare* (1668), written and performed five years earlier, and we find repeatedly stamped in its very center that other, diluted, Bakhtinian category, the fair. In his attempts to court Mariane, Harpagon enlists the services of Frosine, a go-between. On Harpagon's behalf, Frosine has arranged for Mariane to pay a visit to Elise, Harpagon's own daughter, and while waiting to dine with Harpagon's family, to accompany Elise to the fair:[25]

> H. C'est que je suis obligé, Frosine, de donner à souper au seigneur Anselme; et je serais bien aise qu'elle soit du régal.

> F. Vous avez raison. Elle doit après dîner rendre visite à votre fille, d'où elle fait son compte d'aller faire un tour à la foire, pour venir ensuite au souper.

H. Hé bien! elles iront ensemble dans mon carrosse, que je leur prêterai. (2.5.346-47)

[*H:* It's that I am obliged, Frosine, to invite Seigneur Anselme to supper, and I would be pleased if she took part in the festivities.

F: You are right. She should visit your daughter after dinner, from where she plans to go to the fair and look around, and so that she can then come to supper.

H: All right, then! They will go together in my carriage, which I will loan to them.]

I point to this apparently inconsequential plot device because, as marginal as it seems, it indicates for us another inscription of a public economic locus that in its contrast to the invocation of carnival in *Le Malade imaginaire* is revelatory of at least a competing economic sphere existing simultaneously in Molière's theatrical universe. The presence of the carnival context signals extravagant expense (*dépense*), while the fair suggests a more contained and regulated mercantilist exchange. So, in the one case, at least at the very outset, we have a comedy, *Le Malade imaginaire,* that with its reference to carnival would seem to be, economically speaking, backwards looking, while the other, *L'Avare,* with its reference to the fair, would appear to be pointing towards the capitalistic future, at least insofar as the realities of seventeenth-century life seem to intrude within the confines of the play. This division is only a heuristic device; quite clearly what we have is the coexistence in Molière's theater of the transitional moment, the moment that contains both systems, without choosing between them.[26]

Argan, the hypochondriacal father of *Le Malade imaginaire,* is evidently a wealthy bourgeois who, as the introductory scene shows us, is, even in the throes of his mania, very close to his *sous.* The play begins with Argan sitting on his *chaise percée,* counting his different medications and calculating their cost:

Trois et deux font cinq, et cinq font dix et dix font vingt. Trois et deux font cinq. "Plus, du vingt-quatrième, un petit clystère insinuatif, préparatif, et rémollient, pour amollir, humecter, et rafraîchir les entrailles de Monsieur." Ce qui me plaît de Monsieur Fleurant, mon apothicaire, c'est que ses parties sont toujours fort civiles: "les entrailles de Monsieur, trente sols." Oui, mais, Monsieur Fleurant, ce n'est pas tout que d'être civil, il faut être aussi raisonnable, et ne pas écorcher les malades. Trente sols un lavement: Je suis votre serviteur, je vous l'ai déjà dit. Vous ne me les avez mis dans les autres parties qu'à vingt sols, et vingt sols en langage d'apothicaire, c'est-à-dire dix sols; les voilà, dix sols. (1.1.388)

[Three plus two is five, plus five is ten, plus ten is twenty. Three plus two is five. "Furthermore, from the twenty-fourth, a little enema, insinuating, preparing, and softening, to soften, humidify, and refresh Monsieur's entrails."

What pleases me about Monsieur Fleurant, my apothecary, is that his bills are always so polite: "Monsieur's entrails, thirty *sous*." Yes, but Monsieur Fleurant, it is not everything to be polite, one must also be reasonable, and not flay the sick. Thirty *sous* for a washing. At your service, as I already told you. You have only charged twenty *sous* for them in the past, and twenty *sous* in the language of an apothecary means ten *sous*; here we are, ten *sous*.]

Argan is ill, so he believes, and because he is ill with a sickness unto death he desperately tries to restore his health, or at least maintain it in its precarious equilibrium by fetishistic ministrations to his bowels, ministrations for which he pays dearly. But although from the very beginning the comedy establishes a running equation between the economy of the body and the economy of the marketplace, the laughter of this play is generated by the former rather than the latter. The entire play's comedy turns around the obsessive references Argan makes to his excretory functions. He is continually administering to himself or having others administer to him, purges, enemas, *clystères*. Of all the works in the French canon, including those of Rabelais, no other is so persistently scatological, no other, as A. Glucksmann reminds us so insistently, rubs our noses in shit.[27]

For a twentieth-century audience, Argan's obsession with his bowels appears much more symptomatic than what a contemporary seventeenth-century public would notice, at least at first. In seventeenth-century Europe (where a humoral concept of the body prevailed) purges were a daily familiar treatment. The desired effect of these purges was to reestablish a harmonious equilibrium in the body that illness had disturbed. Clearly, however, Argan's attention to his bowel functions, his obsessive interest in maintaining a constant ebb and flow of intake and output, goes beyond the socially accepted limits of his time and places him in the realm of the scatological and outrageous.

If Argan focuses obsessively on his bowels, it is precisely because in any society that puts a high price on order, on closure, on a complete, integral structure (in any society, in other words, which views the father as embodying a totalizing fantasy of corporate integrity—in patriarchy, in sum) the anus is that bodily orifice that first comes in conflict with the social imperatives of renunciation.[28] The control of bodily excretions becomes the locus of a continuing battle between the internal economy of the child and the external law of his world. It is a battle whose consequences, so Freud tells us, have repercussions on the entire future sociosexual life of the individual. In his *Three Essays on the Theory of Sexuality*, Sigmund Freud first describes the importance of the anal zone:

It is to be presumed that the erotogenic significance of this part of the body is very great from the first. We learn with some astonishment from psychoanalysis of the transmutations normally undergone by the sexual excitations arising from this zone and of the frequency with which it retains a considerable amount of susceptibility to genital stimulation throughout life.[29]

It is this "genital excitability" that is, once again according to analytic theory, like all forms of infantile pleasure, so difficult to renounce. Under the pressure of society it is the anal zone that becomes the object of the child's first struggle with the law, the law that says "no": no to his/her pleasure, no to what is quickly defined as dirty, bad, and unacceptable. For Melanie Klein, continuing the theoretical speculations of Karl Abraham, the fixation of the anal stage is marked as sadistic in that there seems to predominate an aggressively hostile attitude toward the world—the desire to dominate and destroy the ambient social locus through the manipulation of—in attempts to control—the anal muscles and the control of the contents of the intestines.[30] The struggle between the child's pleasure and social injunction is an early and deciding factor in the child's relation to his own body, to the psychic image the child has of her own body, and consequently to other peoples' bodies, and to the law:

> The process of defecation affords the first occasion on which the child must decide between a narcissistic and an object-loving attitude. He either parts obediently with his feces, "offers them up" to his love, or else retains them for purposes of auto-erotic gratification and later as a means of asserting his own will.[31]

But Argan's fixation on his bowels is only a symptom of his larger problem, hypochondria. What—and this will come as no surprise—underlies Argan's obsessive anal fixation is fear of and desire for control. Argan wants order in his world. From the very beginning, the play underlines the points of intersection between chaos/order, passivity/activity, loss of control/mastery, and the mounting anxiety that is produced when one side of the dichotomy (chaos, passivity, loss of control) seems to Argan to be gaining the upper hand. In the first speech there is a growing crescendo of anxiety, marked by the comic buildup of the maniacal economies of Argan, that leads to his anxious outburst, "Il n'y a personne: j'ai beau dire, on me laisse toujours seul.... Ils n'entendent point, et ma sonnette ne fait pas assez de bruit.... Ils me laisseront ici mourir" [No one is here: it is useless to ask, they always leave me all alone.... They do not hear, and my bell is not loud enough.... They are going to let me die here] (1.1.390). We can assume this to be an eruption of the heart of his anxiety and which can be translated as the underlying cry, "I am defenseless, I am vulnerable, I am a helpless infant in distress," which forms the underside—the nonarticulable underside—to the public persona that Argan, as *pater familias,* is expected to project to the world: "I am strong, I am the father (king), I am one and invincible." Here, Argan's angst, which he focalizes on his bowels, represents his desire to create a perfect economy of control, to render his body, in its *creaturlichkeit,* unthreatening to his fragile sense of security and integrity. We could see this personal angst (but also this so spectacularly public angst) as expressing the larger ambient insecurity of boundaries of the emerging nation-states that on another level the play is purportedly celebrating. It would seem that neither the nation nor the ego is as yet securely buttressed by firm definition. Argan's angst is the anxiety of conflict, the conflict between a pull towards a system into which he (and we may assume the father in general) does not dovetail but whose lure nevertheless entices him.[32]

In other words, in whatever code we desire to place his symptoms—the humoral code of the seventeenth century, or the analytical code of ours—Argan's initial presentation at the beginning of the play, with the heavily underlined emphasis on the body (the leaky, grotesque body of Galenic theory, or the hypochondriacal, anal-sadistic [psychic] body of analysis), places him as a father at odds with the ambient (emerging) ideology of masculinity. In both instances, Argan is not integral. For the humoral theory, he is split by the constant quiddity of his lower bodily stratum that represents a female intrusion into what should be a male subject. His integrity is constantly sundered by the apertures, the flux of excreta, in which he delights, and which constantly call attention to him as an open, effluent body. In Freudian terms, Argan would be split between a narcissistic attention to his own body (a sign which Freud considers to be a particularly feminine attitude) and what it is opposed to: normatively masculine object-love.[33] At the same time, Argan's delectation in his anality would also in a more complex fashion indicate that he is—that the carnivalesque body is—in a schema of oedipal sexuality, in a pregenital stage: a stage that refuses castration and therefore the law of difference, a stage that refuses the construction of a self that would define itself off from its/an other.[34] So, in the first instance, what marks Argan as comic, beyond the scatology, beyond the tirades for or against the medical profession, is the copresence in the father of what seventeenth-century psychology, medicine, theology, and esthetics would suppress: the body, and more particularly the body coded as feminine and thus vulnerable.

Although Argan's attention to his excretory functions is, like all psychic phenomena, anchored in the physicality of the body and in ambient bodily practices, this obsession obviously exceeds these social realities. His own internal economy has only a tenuous relation to external reality.[35] It does, on the other hand, have quite a rich and forceful influence on the members of his household. Marriage forms the central conundrum of Molieresque comedy because it is a heavily overinvested locus where social and political economies meet with and are inseparable from personal sexual economies. This extremely enchafed locus produces equally the tragic and comic scenarios of familial/social conflict in seventeenth-century drama. In *Le Malade imaginaire* we have two negative types of marriage: the proposed marriage of Angélique to Thomas Diafoirus, and the actual marriage of Argan and Béline. Both, I suggest, are indentured to Argan's anal economy in which the passive and aggressive sides of his anality take precedence over any genital economy that would supersede it.

Although we might suggest that Argan's hypochondria fixes him in a pregenital relation to sexuality, a relation marked by a desire to control, it interferes with the sexual fulfillment of the other members of his household—particularly that of his daughter, Angélique. While Argan's anality attempts to control his household economy by an obsessive attention to the free flowing of his intestinal tract, this enforced fluidity leaves his daughter *bouchée* (dammed up):

... [I]l n'est rien de plus fâcheux que la contrainte où l'on me tient, qui bouche tout commerce aux doux empressements de cette mutuelle ardeur que le
Ciel nous inspire? (1.4.393)

[... (T)here is nothing more annoying than the constraints in which I am
held, which block all access to the sweet attentions of this mutual passion
which the heavens inspire in us?]

Both father and daughter envisage the same type of therapy for this problem of being
blocked or backed up—marriage. But here, once again, despite his invocation of
nature, the difference between Argan's anal economy and the more natural economy of
Angélique brings them into conflict. Angélique desires to marry the young, bright,
good-looking Cléanthe, who has been courting her, while Argan, entirely possessed by
his hypochondriacal mania, wishes to use his daughter as part of his economy, wishes to
secure through her—that is, through a bartering of her sexuality—a closed circuit
where symptoms and on-site medical aid exist in a copresent cycle of need and fulfillment. Argan wants a live-in physician, present *à demeure,* to minister to his every
demand:

Ma raison est que, me voyant infirme et malade comme je suis, je veux me
faire un gendre et des alliés médecins, afin de m'appuyer de bons secours
contre ma maladie, d'avoir dans ma famille les sources des remèdes qui me
sont nécessaires, et d'être à même des consultations et des ordonnances.
(1.5.395)

[My reason is that, seeing myself infirm and ill as I am, I want to make myself
a son-in-law and allies who are doctors, so that I might support myself with
good support against my illness, that I might have in my own family the
sources of remedies which are necessary for me, and to be on the spot for
consultations and prescriptions.]

Argan's desire to possess Angélique, to use her as but an extension of his body, represents the sadistic totalizing side of his anality. In a sense, we can interpret Argan's
tyrannical abuse of his daughter as but one more metaphor for the control of his feces
that is so vitally important to him—staving off as it does the undoing of his being, its
total collapse into chaos. On another level, a level that Freud also analyzes and that we
have already seen operative in Argan, his interest in feces is displaced (but only partially)
onto that other currency: money.[36] Argan, although wealthy in his own right, has not
forgotten what this exchange of his daughter for a doctor son-in-law will also bring
him financially. This obsessive intrusion of Argan's anality into the general economy of
marriage as it was practiced in the seventeenth century (an unnatural institution, in
Molière's terms, as they are repeated in comedy after comedy), is precisely society's
desire to confuse the libidinal (that is, natural) economy with the economy of the marketplace. In his defense of young lovers against aged, maniacal fathers, Molière at first

appears to be defending a liberatory position, which is radically disruptive of the patriarchal economy of his day. Argan's case is complex, however; in either its passive or active forms, his anality clearly situates Argan on the near side of phallic sexuality, the sexuality of the emergent bourgeois family.[37] Although by his insistence on the continued heartless exploitation of his daughter he participates in an economy of patriarchal aggrandizement, this very economy is corrupted by the intrusion of his lower bodily stratum into the integrity of his position as father. It undoes the orthopedic rigidity necessary to support the economic law of marriage he would, as *oikodespotès*, impose. We might say that his own fascination with his bowels, with his anal economy, precludes his phallic valorization as father; that is the *aufhebung* by which biology (Argan as *genitor*) becomes one with ideology (Argan as *pater*).[38]

When we step back in time to *L'Avare*, written and performed five years prior to the *Malade*, we appear to have advanced in the development of the bourgeois family and its precapitalist milieu. This step back from the carnival to the fair indicates, it seems to me, a certain cultural indeterminacy that lends itself equally to different comic treatments. For although it has been claimed that *L'Avare* is a very physical comedy, for our purposes this earlier play seems to be already situated on the far side of the divide where the body in its quiddity is no longer present.[39] What we have in its stead is precisely classical representation, in which and for which the body exists, if at all, as an object of discourse, as a discursive, that is absent, reality.[40] In its place we find, however, an entire play structured around the symbolic systems of exchange—sex and money—which although they never make any direct mention of the physicality of the body, all bear, in one way or another, its impress.

I would like to propose simply that when the grotesque body of free-flowing excreta is suppressed, what is repressed returns in the sublimated, symbolized form of another currency. When we pass from Argan's "chaise percée" to Harpagon's *cassette*, the feces that was so amply apparent in the carnivalesque world of *Le Malade imaginaire* continues to exist in the libidinalized fetishization of money (*trésor*) of *L'Avare*. The anal economy of Molière's last play resurfaces in/as the classical economy of representation of *L'Avare*, where the symbol stands in for (thus kills) its missing (repressed) referent. As we have already mentioned, one of Freud's most shocking but by now sufficiently banalized insights suggests that in the unconscious there exists a contiguous relation between feces and money. When we move in Molière's universe, a convoluted, conflicted, and often contradictory universe, from the farces to the high (that is, classical) comedies, we move, in a sense, from a subaltern to a hegemonic discourse. Ideologically speaking, the classical (despite the resistances to it) was becoming the master narrative of the emerging absolutist/mercantilist state. But, as Stallybrass and White point out, the grotesque remains the hidden underside informing classicism's self-definition.

In a series of essays, Freud returns to the problem of anality, to the importance of the anal zone in the development of our sexual (in the widest sense) subjectivities. In both "Character and Anal Erotism" and "On the Transformation of the Instincts with Special Reference to Anal Erotism," Freud turns his attention to the anal stage to suggest how certain character traits met with in adults—traits of "orderliness, parsimony, and obstinacy"—can be seen as the result of a particularly ill-navigated passage from (in his own normative description of sexual chronology) the predominance of the anal to the genital zone. This "ill-navigation" (another term for which would be neurosis) can take several different forms in the constitution of the mature character: "…the permanent character-traits are either unchanged prolongations of the original impulses, or sublimations of them, or reaction-formations against them."[41] In the case of our protagonist we have no trouble recognizing both parsimony and obstinacy, which seem to predominate, while orderliness can be seen clearly peering through his tyrannical desire for control of his children and household. They are all intertwined with his retentive delight in acquiring and holding onto his money.[42]

The relation that Freud draws between feces and money, as shocking and seductive as it may seem, is only but one small part of a complicated chain of symbolic displacements that can, he hypothesizes, exist in the unconscious of the infant, and that later continue to exist in sublimated form in the adult. In the essay "On the Transformation of Instincts with Special Reference to Anal Erotism," Freud continues to refine, this time with relation to the object (feces) of anal erotism, the symbolic displacement from infancy to adulthood. Here, Freud suggests that for the infant, at a very early stage of his development, a chain of symbolic displacements is elaborated, infused already with erotic pleasure wherein the equations "feces (money, gift), child, and penis are seldom distinguished and are easily interchangeable."[43] Freud goes on to offer a distinct evolution of this signifying chain for the normal development of women and men. Here, I would like only to focus on what he has to say about masculine evolution:

> A different series of relations can be observed much more distinctly in the male. It is formed when the boy's sexual curiosity leads him to discover the absence of a penis in women. He concludes that the penis must be a detachable part of the body, something analogous to feces, the first bodily substance the child had to part with. Thus the original anal defiance enters into the composition of the castration complex.[44]

I. Reiss-Schimmel glosses Freud's dense essay to point out the following predominant traits: feces as it is transformed into gift already bears the impress of desire—the child's desire to please its mother and receive her love in return; as such, the object (feces/gift) is already an ambivalent object.[45] Freud's symbolic chain of displacements is established, she says, on an analogy of separation that is only understandable in relation to an originary fantasy of castration, which alone allows for the substitution of one element for another. Underlying (for the male subject) this substitutive chain is, as we have seen, the castration complex, which will retroactively determine the libidinal intensity of the invested object ("money," "penis").[46]

In his study of the "wolfman" (*From the History of an Infantile Neurosis*), Freud returns to his speculations on anal sexuality and its effects on psychic life, and offers the following summary:

Since the column of feces stimulates the erotogenic mucous membrane of the bowel, it plays the part of an active organ in regard to it; it behaves just as the penis does to the vaginal mucous membrane, and acts as it were as its forerunner during the cloacal epoch. The handing over of feces for the sake of (out of love for) someone else becomes a prototype of castration; it is the first occasion upon which an individual parts with a piece of his own body in order to gain the favor of some other person whom he loves. So that a person's love of his own penis, which is in other respects narcissistic, is not without an element of anal erotism. "Feces," "baby," and "penis" thus form a unity, an unconscious concept (*sit venia verbo*)—the concept, namely, of "a little one" that can become separated from one's body.[47]

For our present purposes, what is particularly important to retain is, first, the idea of psychic transmutability—that is, feces = money, and second, the inherent fear of losing a part of one's self, a part that is highly invested with narcissistic libido.

While it was Argan's anality that presided over his familial economy, the Harpagon household seems, at first, to be firmly situated in a mercantilist economy with a correlative dominance of oedipal (that is, genital) sexuality. *L'Avare* appears as probably the most glaringly "oedipal" of Molière's many conflicted familial comedies. The rivalry between the father and son for the sexual prize (Mariane), as comically ludicrous as it might appear to the audience, provokes at the same time as laughter a sense of unease. Sexuality reveals its hostilely aggressive side in the rivalry of Harpagon and Cléante, a rivalry intensely marked by death wishes on both sides. It is in fact this mortiferous rivalry between father and son that forms the central plot device of the play. Only once we understand that this desire, the disruptive intrusion of the body into the world of mercantilism, is inseparable from the economy of the marketplace, can we understand that *L'Avare,* even at this early date, presents us with a world where people are already in Marx's terms "fetishized commodities," and thus can we understand the seamless interweave between sexuality and avarice as structurally necessary in this comedy of the oedipal family.[48]

The comedy configures a clear sexual symmetry between the young members of the household—both of Harpagon's children are in love and wish to marry—and then immediately triangularizes that symmetry through the rivalrous relation between Harpagon and his son Cléante, and by the censorious pressure Harpagon brings to bear on Elise. The mediation for this triangularization of desire is financial. From the very outset, the desire of the children is frustrated by the avarice of the father.

Cléante's opening declarations to his sister, while couched in terms of desire and frustration, are also and as fully imbricated in an economy of mercantile exchange in which his desire for Mariane can, he knows, be mediated by his family's wealth. His desire comes up against the severe thriftiness of his father and is consequently frustrated. In a simple sense, therefore, the oedipal rivalry between father and child is mediated in and through money—the new law of emerging capitalist France. It is the "no" of the father, but here it is transcoded as a question of financial tyranny. In this play, Harpagon's controlling the family purse strings effectively controls the son's "bourses" [genitals, testicles] as well. Elise, faring no better with her father than her brother, becomes a bartered bride given to the least expensive.

Clearly it is the fear of loss that is at the very heart of Harpagon's mania. From his first entrance on stage, Harpagon appears obsessed with the thought that everyone is trying to get the better of him, which becomes in his fantasy the idea that everyone is trying to rob him. The anxiety of being robbed is exacerbated for comic effect by the presence in the home of a large sum of money that Harpagon received the day before. He is frantically trying to hide it from all those prying eyes he imagines around him:

> Certes ce n'est pas une petite peine que de garder chez soi une grande somme d'argent; et bienheureux qui a tout son fait bien placé, et ne conserve seule-ment que ce qu'il faut pour sa dépense. On n'est pas peu embarrassé à inven-ter dans toute une maison une cache fidèle; car pour moi, les coffres-forts me sont suspects, et je ne veux jamais m'y fier: je les tiens justement une franche amorce à voleurs, et c'est toujours la première chose que l'on va attaquer. Cependant je ne sais si j'aurai bien fait d'avoir enterré dans mon jardin dix mille écus qu'on me rendit hier. Dix mille écus en or chez soi est une somme assez.... (1.4.331)

> [Surely it is no small trouble to hold a large sum of money in the house; and happy is he who has all of his earnings well placed, and only keeps what he needs for his expenses. One is quite confounded in his search to find a safe hiding place anywhere in the house; because for me, the safes are suspect, and I do not want ever to trust them: I think of them rightly as obvious bait for thieves, and it is always the first thing they would try. Nonetheless, I do not know if I did well to bury the ten thousand ecus I received yesterday in my garden. Ten thousand gold ecus is a large enough sum....]

Harpagon has buried the money, locked in the famous *cassette,* in his garden. For the time being I only want to point out the obvious: if we can, for the moment, accept Freud's chain of equivalencies (feces = money), Harpagon's choice of cache is particu-larly rich in analogies. He buries his money, out of sight, in the ground. The only safe place he can find for his treasure is in the *bowels* of the earth. But even here, of course, the hiding place is not entirely secure; other eyes can peer into the center of the earth, discover and carry off the precious *cassette.* What is intriguing in Harpagon's mania is its monolithic intensity. In a sense, Harpagon's avarice, which reduces the entire world to a series of things that can be possessed (and therefore, at the same time to a series of things of which one can be dispossessed), reflects a totalitarian psychic system that would constantly attempt to enclose the world in the same way the body is phantasmat-ically desired as sealed. If we remember that the original choice of the infant in relation to his bowel is presented as a dichotomy, either to retain his feces in the autoerotic enclosure of narcissism or to surrender it as a love offering to an object (person) in the world, we see that we are presented with a choice between closing in on the self or opening the self up to the world. We can understand the enormous tension that exists in Harpagon—the comic tension of a character who is situated on the horns of this one very crucial dilemma. He is presented as a totally self-enclosed (but paranoid) narcissist, a position that would seem to parody in a negative reversal the ideal of corporate/ bodily integrity that underpins the evolution of absolutist patriarchy; yet at the same time he is tempted by the opening up of this enclosed, defended structure as it reaches out for object-love.

What could be more comic than a desirous *barbon*? What more perverse than the spectacle of a wizened, maniacal old miser who nevertheless is presented as concupiscent? The body returns, elliptically, in this comedy as that which resists the retentive psychic economy of sublimation. It is the conflict between the desire of the body and the resistance of sublimated retention that forms the comic nexus of the play.

We witness the reappearance of the body most pointedly in the interchanges between Harpagon and his *entremetteuse,* Frosine. Although La Flèche warns her that she is dealing with a particularly obstinate case, that Harpagon is, as he strategically says, "le plus dur et le plus serré" of men [the toughest and most tight] (2.4.345) (and I would suggest that there is in the French *serré* the same sense we have in the English term, "tight-assed"). She maintains that she, desire's spokeswoman, knows how to loosen up the most obdurate. Frosine's description of herself as an expert in catering to men's innermost secrets is couched in terms of opening up the enclosed body of adult males. In a sense, therefore, she (Molière) creates the analogy which equates the *jouissance* of the body to openness. Pleasure, the body's desire to be opened, to be available, to be made, so to speak, like a woman, is positioned as a feminization, and thus as the inverse of what the dominant ideology says a man must be: closed, *serré,* bounded.

Desire, when it announces itself in this play in the body of Harpagon, declares itself as precisely what patriarchal absolutism, as it evolved towards ideological hegemony, had to suppress. It signals, quite unconsciously, that what it desires is the presence, as pleasure, of (once again in Bakhtin's terms) the grotesque (as female), of precisely what it has had to repress. It is this persistence in the dominant discourse of the fantasy of its own obverse that is being played out in the tension between Harpagon's retentiveness and the desire that is bred in that retention for release—the classical body's yearning for its own grotesque.[49]

Any attempt to divorce sexuality (love) from economy is already precluded from the ideological universe of the play. Although there is a yearning for their separation especially in the gesture that would place passion on the side of the natural (that is, youth, heterosexuality, and so forth) and economy on the side of perversion (that is, avarice), in truth this is an untenable dichotomy in a world totally immersed in the bourgeois culture of the seventeenth century. For that (still primitive) bourgeoisie, marriage remains the most overinvested institution for the exchange of financial and sexual economies. It is for this reason that the plot of *L'Avare* can crescendo to a dizzying height of comic misprisions in the dialogue between Harpagon and Valère, the former panic-stricken over the loss of his *cassette,* the latter pleading his love.

How can we understand the immensely comic (for us) displacement of lust onto his *cassette* if not precisely by seeing it as the highly overdetermined instance where libidinal energy is captured and fixed on a symbolic object of psychic exchange? The scene of Harpagon's distress upon discovering the theft of his *cassette* is among the most hilarious in Molière's repertoire. It is a bravura piece of writing (and of acting) that focuses in so concentrated a fashion all of the lines of contradictory tensions (between market and libidinal economies) in the play into this one paroxysmic moment where the symbolic systems of finance and the body come to rest in and on the miser's anguish over his loss—a distress that is figured most poignantly and most comically as a loss of one's self. Harpagon cries that his body has been attacked, that he has been murdered:

> Au voleur! au voleur! à l'assassin! au meurtrier! Justice, juste Ciel! je suis perdu, je suis assassiné, on m'a coupé la gorge, on m'a dérobé mon argent.... Mon esprit est troublé, et j'ignore où je suis, qui je suis, et ce que je fais. Hélas! mon pauvre argent, mon pauvre argent, mon cher ami! on m'a privé de toi, et puisque tu m'es enlevé, j'ai perdu mon support, ma consolation, ma joie; tout est fini pour moi, et je n'ai plus que faire au monde: sans toi, il m'est impossible de vivre. C'en est fait, je n'en puis plus; je me meurs, je suis mort, je suis enterré.... (4.7.374)

> [Thief! Thief! Assassin! Murderer! Justice, just heavens! I am lost, I am murdered, they have slit my throat, they have stolen my money.... My spirit is troubled, and I do not know where I am, who I am, and what I am doing. Alas! My poor money, my poor money, my dear friend! They have deprived me of you, and since you have been kidnapped from me, I have lost my support, my consolation, my joy; all is over for me, and I have nothing left to do in the world: without you, it is impossible for me to live. It is over, I cannot continue; I am dying, I am dead, I am buried....]

In the high comedy of this scene, Harpagon describes the disintegration of his self. But, curiously, this disintegration is metaphorized in a highly symbolic fashion, a fashion that I suggest allows us some entry into the phantasmatic system that underpins Harpagon's anxiety. He tells us that he has been "murdered," but this murder is significantly couched in particularly symbolic terms, "on m'a coupé la gorge" [they have slit my throat], a cry that is immediately coupled with "on m'a dérobé mon argent" [they have stolen my money]. I would propose that the equation of having one's throat cut and having one's money stolen allows us some insight into why Harpagon's psychic trauma is so comically intense and why, finally, it leads us back into the conflict between anal and genital sexuality that we have been tracing through the two comedies.

In a simple way, if we take into account the "economic" phenomenon of psychic displacement discussed by Freud in relation to dream interpretation, we will be able to unravel what is at work in Harpagon's mania. In analytic theory an affect can be detached from its source and displaced onto another psychic or physical structure. In Harpagon's case, I think we can assume that what we have is a "vertical displacement" from the lower bodily stratum to the higher—from the genitals to the throat (neck, head). In another searingly funny cry, Harpagon reveals the profound investment at work in this psychic configuration, when after referring to the theft in abstract, that is, in legal-social terms, calling it "un guet-apens," "un assassinat," in which "les choses les plus sacrées ne sont plus en sûreté," he returns to the physicality of his attachment, referring to his treasure as "mon sang," "mes entrailles" [my blood, my entrails] (5.3.379). He constantly oscillates from the abstract to the body, from the higher to the lower. In his impassioned cry that his throat is slashed, I think we can hear a more primitive castration anxiety, an anxiety that returns us once again to the confusion we have already alluded to in Freud's discussion of the symbolic displacements of anality. But in this case, both the displacements and the affect are stronger and more complicated than we might first imagine.

On one level, I think it is reasonably clear that in the passage from anality to genitality, from Argan to Harpagon, from grotesque to classical, Harpagon represents a snag in any clearly defined, unproblematic navigation from the one to the other. Let us recall one of the associative chains Freud proposed in his discussion of the persistence of the anal stage in the character traits of a mature individual—that is, feces = penis = money. Then let us also remember that the passage from the anal to the genital stage is intimately connected to the castration complex and to the different traumatic avatars of this complex for the psychosexual development of the male child. Although it would be unproductive to offer an analysis of Harpagon, who is, after all, not a real psychic entity (not a person) but merely a character in a play, I think that by considering Harpagon as a nexus of conflicting and conflicted social, sexual, and economic vectors we can see how, by a personal analysis, we can arrive at a sociohistorical description.

Harpagon, in his obsessive miserliness, would represent a misplaced investment of libidinal energy onto his bowels—onto, that is, the pleasure of the retention of his bowels, onto money. Or we could turn this around and say that, inversely, there is the invasion of genital sexuality by the misplaced intensity of anality. In either case, the vehemence of this displacement is explicable only if we concede that the intermediary term in the associative chain—penis—has been displaced. It has been consigned to the unconscious, resurfacing as concentrated affect, the fear of loss, the fear of self-destruction, the fear of death. This fear of loss—the representative of the castration complex— has been, I believe, sutured into the psychic construction of Harpagon by and through the insistence on still another displacement, the metonymic displacement from money (namely, penis) to *cassette* (from a part to a whole, from contained to container). The *cassette* functions, on one level, as a fetish object, which allows Harpagon to have his money (feces/penis) and to relinquish it too (transform it into, in a sense, object-love). The vehemence of his attachment to his money box (O *ma chère cassette* [O my dear money box]) takes on the lure of another man's (Valère's, for example) attachment to a woman. In *The Theme of the Three Caskets,* Freud offers a reading of the casket (box or *cassette*) as a symbol of "the essential thing in woman, and therefore of a woman herself...."[50] He goes on, however, to show how in folklore, fairy tales, and the like, this "woman herself" is an ambiguous construction where the "casket" does not just represent woman in general, but a particular ambivalent projection of woman, both the figure of *Atropos,* a symbol of death, and (reaction formation) the image of woman as the youthful, life-giving goddess of love.[51] It is this ambivalence functioning bivalently that acts as the hinge between the sexual and financial economies in the play, allowing their mutual displacement. As we have seen, especially in the stichomythia that opposes Harpagon and Valère, this ambivalence (essentially on the level of linguistic economies, between metaphor and metonymy) relays the sexual into the linguistic, creating the comic quid pro quo of the double misprision in the dialogue, the sexual/economic chiasmus of woman and money.

But, as this dialogue also makes clear, while Valère talks about his love in more traditionally metaphorical terms, Harpagon only understands these metaphors metonymically because for him, first and foremost, the *cassette* represents a displaced part of himself. So, on one level we can see that the *cassette* might represent a woman, but for Harpagon this is a special phantasm of a woman, the fetishistic "woman-with-a-penis." And it is, I would suggest, to this final displacement that Harpagon is so attached that he cannot give up. This displacement finally presides over his divesting himself of his genital/oedipal desire for Mariane, a desire in which, as in all desire, he risks (or so it appears to him) his annihilation in the woman-as-other (the woman as object and proof of castration—for the male psyche) and remains in the protected, self-enclosed narcissistic position where as long as he has his beloved *cassette* he is protected from loss, protected from castration, protected from death.

With restitution of his *cassette,* the play can end, as all comedies do, with the promise of marriage—the marriage of the children. On an important level, therefore, the comedy ends by reaffirming a familial model of oedipal genitality. While the stage is cleared by the exits of all the characters gone off to share the news of their impending weddings, Harpagon returns to his obsession, returns to the position from which he was almost displaced. This possibility of movement proved too threatening, too great a breach in his closed economy. He alone returns to the contemplation of what completes and assures him of his integrity; he reverts to the closed circle where, with his *cassette,* he retains an entire libidinal economy, protected from the anxiety of risk and loss.

L'Avare and *Le Malade imaginaire* form a chiastic economy of their own, emblematic of the conflicted and contradictory economies—libidinal and financial—that Molière's theater mediates. On the one hand we have the predominance of the farce, of the carnivalesque, grotesque body, the open, effluent body of Argan; on the other, the high comedy of classicism with its sublimation of the body, its disappearance in an economy of retention and symbolization. This dichotomy, of course, is too rigidly opposed here to account fully for the overlaps, exchanges, and interconnections that unite rather than oppose the multiple economies that coexist within Molière's theater and which finally come to rest in that ultimate economy, the economy of laughter—the laughter of the spectators of these, and other Molieresque, comedies. How are we to understand this laughter, this "sideration of the body" in its voluptuous abandonment to its own pleasure? The history of laughter, of the comic, is long and complex. As a coda, I would only like to add a small note on what I believe is the role of the laughter spawned by Molière's comedy, spawned by Harpagon and Argan.

If we return to Bakhtin, who comments extensively on carnivalesque laughter, he tells us that the laughter of the marketplace, the laughter of the premodern, nonindividuate ego is:

> ...first of all, a festive laughter. Therefore, it is not an individual reaction to some "comic" event. Carnival laughter is the laughter of all the people. Second, it is universal in scope; it is directed at all and everyone, including the carnival's participants. The entire world is seen in its droll aspect, in its gay relativity. Third, this laughter is ambivalent: it is gay, triumphant, at the same time mocking, deriding. It asserts and denies, it buries and revives.[52]

Bakhtin's description of laughter, although nuanced at the end, remains nevertheless like most of his description of the carnivalesque, a paean to some utopian notion of the people. What is repressed from his enormously rich contribution to the study of laughter, of the carnival, is precisely, as Stallybrass and White point out, the negative, destructive side of the grotesque, which, rather than empowering, as often as not authorizes itself by degrading and demeaning society's outcasts while maintaining its own complicitous relation with the dominant social structures.[53] Although Freud in his essay on humor claims that "Humour is not resigned; it is rebellious. It signifies not only the triumph of the ego but of the pleasure principle,"[54] the question for Molière remains, it seems to me, undecidable, situated somewhere between the unavowed repression inherent in Bakhtin's carnival and the structuring of the modern ego—as much a product of what has been unconsciously repressed as what is consciously expressed.

What generates the laughter, the mirth of the spectators in the comedies we have been discussing? On the one hand we might say that it is the mania—the hypochondria—the fixation of Argan on his bowels, or the avarice of Harpagon fixated on his *cassette* (his money, and therefore also his bowels). In both cases we are made to laugh, and our laughter is spawned by an *écart,* a split in the image we have of the main character, the father and head of the household (*oikodespotès*). In the patriarchal world of seventeenth-century France, in this world which ideologically tends ideally toward the order of the absolute, the order of the one—which is embodied most tellingly in the persona of the king and of all his paternal declensions, declensions that span the celestial and terrestrial realms from "God the Father" to the king, "father of his people," and finally to the father, head of each individual household—the unacceptable, the monstrous is precisely a split in this unitary fantasy. For, as we have seen, in either the Galenic or Freudian schema the split in the subject (the subject not integral) is the sign of the intrusion into the world of masculine perfection of the other—the other coded as feminine.

We laugh at Harpagon/Argan precisely because in the context of their world they are excessive, split by their monomania, which rather than confirming them as absolute has the contrary effect of revealing their flaw and thus the flaw of their world. They reveal what all seventeenth-century culture in its hegemonic drive would keep hidden—that the king, the father, is not one, but two: that in other words under the austere reverence of the One is the many, the multifarious, and this many is the other—the children, the wily servants, the submissive (and the plotting) women.

So, on one hand, this laughter can be seen, as it often has been, as liberatory or rebellious, and Molière can be seen as the underside of classicism's repression. But, on the other hand, we must also bear in mind the thought that the carnival and Molière are inextricably involved in the dominant political narratives of their time, narratives in which his (their) social, economic, and sexual interests are invested. We might then think that instead of being disruptive of social order, the laughter spawned by his plays is simply recuperative rather than rebellious. For, when we look at the target of our laughter—Argan/Harpagon—we realize that what we are laughing at is the bad father, the father as *pharmakos,* the ritual victim led out onto the stage of our own repressive fantasies and sacrificed to them. But this sacrifice, like all sacrifice, tends finally to maintain in place an entire worldview: when we laugh at the bad father, when we see Argan/Harpagon as risible, feminized, and maniacal, we do so only because we can compare them, as failed fathers, to that image of the ideal father, the absolute father, who continues, in this comparison, to reign in our thoughts, in our repressions, in our fantasies. How else can we explain both the benign patronage of Louis XIV laughing at the antics of Molière's preposterous bourgeois, and the more enchafed reactions of the archbishop of Paris for whom Molière and his cast of characters represented a threat to the well-run order of seventeenth-century France? Both were surely right, but to his credit, Louis XIV was probably more sanguine about the effects of Molieresque laughter, directed as it was at those imperfect bodies of the father, knowing, in his own splendid isolation, in the impervious isolation of his body royal, that the real father, the state, Louis, could only be enhanced by the raucous laughter spawned by the debasement of his imperfect earthly simulacra.

Another version of this essay appears in my book, *Baroque Bodies: Psychoanalysis and the Culture of Absolutism* (Ithaca: Cornell University Press, 2001), 22–61. I wish to thank Cornell University Press for permission to reprint this essay.

Notes

1. Translations:

   > To be truthful, the monarch seems to spend a large part of his time on the chaise percée. We constantly hear of purges and enemas, of intestinal irritations that sometimes go on for an entire day; of bowel movements repeated up to a dozen times.
   > —F. Millepierres, *The Daily Life of Doctors in Molière's Time*
   > The body is also directly involved in a political field; power relations have an immediate hold upon it; they invest it, mark it, train it, torture it, force it to carry out tasks, to perform ceremonies, to emit signs. This political investment of the body is bound up in accordance with complex reciprocal relations with its economic use.
   > —Michel Foucault, *Discipline and Punish*

2. I refer in this brief opening paragraph to the idea of a crisis of the seventeenth century—the century seen as a period of radical, even revolutionary change that we see expressed in works by historians, philosophers, and literary critics. For the broad general ideas, see *Crisis in Europe, 1560–1660*, ed. Trevor Aston (New York: Doubleday, 1967). See also Michel Foucault, *Les Mots et les choses* (Paris: Gallimard, 1966), and idem, *Histoire de la folie à l'âge classique* (Paris: Gallimard, 1967).

3. "Or, cette enquête archéologique a montré deux grandes discontinuités dans l'épistémologie de la culture occidentale: celle qui inaugure l'âge classique (vers le milieu du XVIIe siècle) et celle qui, au début du XIXe marque le seuil de notre modernité"; Foucault, *Les Mots et les choses*, 13 [So, this archeological investigation has revealed two great discontinuities in the epistemology of occidental culture: one which inaugurated the classical era (towards the middle of the seventeenth century) and that one which, at the beginning of the nineteenth century, marked the entry into our modernity]. All translations in this chapter are my own.

4. Michel Foucault, *Histoire de la sexualité*, vol. 1, *La Volonté de savoir* (Paris: Gallimard, 1976).

5. For a more detailed discussion of this transformation, see Mitchell Greenberg, introduction, *Subjectivity and Subjugation in Seventeenth-Century Drama and Prose: The Family Romance of French Classicism* (Cambridge: Cambridge University Press, 1992), 16–23.

6. Michel Foucault, *Histoire de la sexualité*, 143.

7. Francis Barker, *The Tremulous Private Body: Essays in Subjection* (London: Methuen, 1984), 12.

8. Peter Stallybrass and Allon White, *The Politics and Poetics of Transgression* (Ithaca: Cornell University Press, 1986), 192.

9. Mary Douglas, *Purity and Danger: An Analysis of the Concepts of Pollution and Taboo* (London: Routledge and Kegan Paul, 1966), 115.

10. For example, for a feminist psychoanalytic reading of hysteria see Monique David-Ménard, *L'hystérique entre Freud et Lacan: Corps et langage en psychanalyse* (Paris: Editions universitaires, 1983); translation: Catherine Porter, *Hysteria from Freud to Lacan: Body and Language in Psychoanalysis* (Ithaca: Cornell University Press, 1989).

11. Cf. for example these preliminary remarks of Guy Rosolato, "Recension du corps," *Lieux du corps, Nouvelle Revue de Psychanalyse* 3 (1971): 17. Elaborating even more explicitly on this same idea, F. Gantheret, in his "Remarque sur la place et le statu du corps en psychanalyse," p. 142 in the same issue, writes:

    > Le corps ne devient symbolique que lorsque, se substituant comme symbole au refoulé, il entre dans une relation de sens avec d'autres éléments. Il n'y a symbolisation que lors de la rencontre entre une série associative et un ancrage dans un système signifiant; que lorsque la série imaginaire, s'épinglant sur un réel biologique, acquiert valeur de signe, élément d'un système.

[The body does not become symbolic until, offering itself as a symbolic substitute for the repressed, it enters into a relation of senses with other elements. There is no symbolization until the encounter between an associative sequence and an anchoring in a signifying system; until the imaginary sequence, pinning itself to a biological 'real,' acquires the value of a sign, an element in a system.]

12. For the important possible distinction in psychic life between reality and fantasy, cf. J. Laplanche, *Problématiques* (Paris: Presses Universitaires de France, 1980), esp. 2, "Castration, symbolisations," and 3, "La sublimation."

13. See Molière, *Œuvres complètes*, ed. Georges Mongrédien, vol. 3, *Le Misanthrope; Le Médecin malgré lui; Mélicerte; Pastorale comique; Le Sicilien ou l'Amour peintre; Amphitryon; George Dandin ou le Mari confondu; L'Avare; Monsieur de Pourceaugnac* (Paris: Flammarion, 1965), and vol. 4, *Les Amants magnifiques; Le Bourgeois gentilhomme; Psyché; Les Fourberies de Scapin; La Comtesse d'Escarbagnas; Les Femmes savantes; Le Malade imaginaire; Poésies* (Paris: Flammarion, 1979). All references to Molière are to vol. 3, *L'Avare*, and vol. 4, *Le Malade imaginaire*. Here, 3.14.454.

14. Caroline Walker Bynum, *Fragmentation and Redemption* (New York: Zone Books, 1992), esp. chaps. 3, 4, and 6; Marie-Hélène Huet, *Monstrous Imagination* (Cambridge: Harvard University Press, 1993); Thomas Laqueur, *Making Sex: Body and Gender from the Greeks to Freud* (Cambridge: Harvard University Press, 1990); G. K. Paster, *The Body Embarrassed: Drama and the Disciplines of Shame in Early Modern Europe* (Ithaca: Cornell University Press, 1993).

15. Paster, *Body Embarrassed*, 8.

16. Bynum, *Fragmentation and Redemption*, 109, succinctly sums up the patriarchal ideology of Galenic medical theory in the following manner: "Ancient biology, especially in its Aristotelian form, made the male body paradigmatic. The male was the form or quiddity of what we are as humans; what was particularly womanly was the unformed-ness, the stuff-ness or physicality, of our humanness. Such a notion identified woman with breaches in boundaries, with lack of shape or definition, with opening and exudings and spillings forth. But this conception also, we should note, put men and women on a continuum. All human beings were form and matter. Women were merely less of what men were more."

17. Paster, *Body Embarrassed*, 25, "Representations of the female body as a leaking vessel display that body as beyond the control of the female subject, and thus as threatening the acquisitive goal of the family and its maintenance of status and power."

18. Mikhael Bakhtin, *Rabelais and His World* (Cambridge: MIT Press, 1969), 320.

19. Douglas, *Purity and Danger*, 121.

20. For a lengthy discussion of the idea of the king as a representation and "spectacle," see Jean-Marie Apostolidès, *Le Roi machine* (Paris: Minuit, 1981), as well as Louis Marin, *Le Portrait du Roi* (Paris: Minuit, 1981), and idem, *La Parole mangée* (Paris: Klincksieck, 1986). The classic study of medieval theologicopolitics that underlies these works is, of course, Ernst Kantorowicz, *The King's Two Bodies: A Study in Medieval Political Theology* (Princeton: Princeton University Press, 1956).

21. Stallybrass and White, *Politics and Poetics*, 113.

22. For Marin's discussion of the "body" of Louis XIV in Rigaud's regal portrait, see "Le Corps glorieux du Roi et son portrait" in *La Parole mangée*, 195–226. For an analysis of the declension, so important for absolutism, of the slippage the word "father" precipitates from God the father, to the king as "father of his people," to finally the father, head of the individual household, see Greenberg, introduction, *Subjectivity and Subjugation*.

23. Jürgen Habermas, *L'Espace public*, French translation by de Launay (Paris: Payot, 1985), 13–17.

24. Barker, *Tremulous Private Body*, 100, talking of this same split, writes: "It is with an identical gesture that the modern structure…excludes the body from the proper realm of discourse and simultaneously genders that very structuration…. For if the new regime in inaugurating itself deploys a pattern of speech and silence, a semiosis in which the discoursing 'I' is held to be constitutive then it is clear that the designated woman is positioned extraneously to the constitutive centre where the male voice speaks. The woman is allotted to the place of the body outside discourse and therefore also outside the pertinent domain of legitimate subjecthood."

25. Paris had, of course, several important fairs, among them the foire St. Germain and the foire St. Laurent. Molière does not clarify to which of these fairs he is referring.

26. But is this really so? Why then the qualitative difference of esthetic judgment? Why is *L'Avare* a "grande comédie," while the *Malade* is but a "farce"? Does not this hierarchy already speak for the capitalist future instead of for the carnivalesque past?

27. André Glucksmann, *La Bêtise* (Paris: Grasset, 1985), 233: "Il n'y a pas plus osé dans le répertoire occidental. *Le Malade imaginaire* contraint, lui, le spectateur à 'y mettre le nez' tout au long. Jamais avant, jamais après, le théâtre n'a présenté une telle putréfaction flottant dans une moiteur aussi nauséabonde" [There is nothing more daring in the western repertory. *Le Malade imaginaire* forces the spectator to "put his nose into it" throughout. Never before, never after, has theater presented such a putrefaction floating in such a nauseating liquefaction].

28. Norbert Elias, *The Civilizing Process*, trans. E. Jephcott (New York: Urizen Books, 1978), is the classic sociological study of the history of the laws of propriety and manners. Starting with Erasmus, Elias traces the history of bodily policing in western Europe.

29. Sigmund Freud, *Three Essays on the Theory of Sexuality*, vol. 7 of the Standard Edition (London: Hogarth, 1953), 185.

30. "Some Theoretical Conclusions regarding the Emotional Life of the Infant," in *Developments in Psycho-analysis*, ed. Joan Riviere (London: Hogarth Press, 1952), 198–236, esp. 227 ff.

31. Sigmund Freud, *On the Transformation of the Instincts with Special Reference to Anal Erotism*, vol. 17 of the Standard Edition (London: Hogarth Press, 1953), 130.

32. Douglas, *Purity and Danger*, 124: "Here I am suggesting that when rituals express anxiety about the body's orifices, the sociological counterpart of this anxiety is a care to protect the political and cultural unity."

33. Sigmund Freud, *On Narcissism: An Introduction*, vol. 14 of the Standard Edition (London: Hogarth Press, 1953), 88: "A comparison of the male and female sexes then show that there are fundamental differences between them in respect of their type of object-choice....Complete object-love of the attachment type is, properly speaking, characteristic of the male....Women, especially if they grow up with good looks, develop a certain self-contentment which compensates them for the social restrictions that are imposed upon them in their choice of object. Strictly speaking, it is only themselves that such women love with an intensity comparable to that of the man's love for them."

34. For a detailed analysis of this refusal, see Julia Kristeva, *Pouvoirs de l'horreur* (Paris: Seuil, 1980), esp. the chapters "De quoi avoir peur," and "De la saleté à la souillure."

35. D. Anzieu, *The Skin Ego*, trans. C. Turner (New Haven: Yale University Press, 1989), 96: "Every psychical function develops by supporting itself upon a bodily function whose workings it transposes on to the mental plane."

36. "In reality, wherever archaic modes of thought predominate or have persisted—in ancient civilizations, in myth, fairy-tale and superstition, in unconscious thoughts and dreams, and in neuroses—money comes into the closest relation with excrement"; Sigmund Freud, *Character and Anal Erotism*, vol. 9 of the Standard Edition (London: Hogarth Press, 1953), 175.

37. Kaja Silverman, *Male Subjectivity at the Margins* (London: Routledge, 1993), 34, writes on the different possibilities of male subjectivity that would not be based on a phallic (that is, oedipal) model, all the while defining "phallic model" as the dominant cultural mode of sexuality in patriarchal modern culture: "Our present dominant fiction is above all the representational system through which the subject is accommodated to the Name-of-the-Father. Its most central signifier of unity is the (paternal) family and its primary signifier of privilege the phallus."

38. For this interesting distinction within the economy of patriarchy of "genitor/genitrix" and "pater/mater," see Jean-Joseph Goux, *Freud, Marx, Economie et symbolique* (Paris: Seuil, 1973), esp. "La génération matérielle," 239–56.

39. Will Moore, *Molière, a New Criticism* (Oxford: Oxford University Press, 1949), 30, underlines what is for him the physicality of the play: "*L'Avare* is full of concrete illustrations of moral qualities; nothing is described, everything is shown in any physical acts: Harpagon searches his man's clothes, runs after his money, wears glasses and a ring on his finger, crawls under the table."

40. Barker, *Tremulous Private Body,* 62: "The carnality of the body has been dissolved and dissipated until it can be reconstituted in writing at a distance from itself."
41. See Freud, *Character and Anal Erotism,* 175.
42. Freud, *Character and Anal Erotism,* 170: "As infants they seem to have been among those who refuse to empty the bowel when placed on the chamber, because they derive an incidental pleasure from the act of defecation; for they assert that even in somewhat later years they have found a pleasure in holding back their stools.... From these indications we infer that the erotogenic significance of the anal zone is intensified in the innate sexual constitution of these persons."
43. Freud, *On the Transformation of the Instincts,* 204.
44. Freud, *On the Transformation of the Instincts,* 208.
45. Reiss-Schimmel, *La Psychanalyse et l'argent* (Paris: O. Jacob, 1993), 57: "Le cadeau ne véhicule donc pas que des sentiments d'amour mais peut aussi être investi de désirs hostiles" [The gift not only conveys feelings of love, but can also be invested with hostile desires].
46. Reiss-Schimmel, *La Psychanalyse et l'argent,* 76–77: "Pour Freud, ce sont les modalités d'intégration de l'érotisme anal qui déterminent la valeur symbolique de l'argent" [For Freud, it is the modalities of integration of anal erotism that determine the symbolic value of money]; and "la valeur symbolique que l'individu attribue à l'argent est fonction de son niveau d'organisation libidinale" [the symbolic value that the individual attributes to money is a function of his level of libidinal organization].
47. Freud, *From the History of an Infantile Neurosis,* standard edition, vol. 17, 84.
48. For Marx's classic definition of "fetishism," see Karl Marx, "The Fetishism of Commodities and the Secret Thereof," in *Capital* in *The Portable Karl Marx,* ed. E. Kamenka (London: Penguin Books, n.d.), chap. 1, sec. 4, pp. 437–61, "Commodities."
49. On the imposition of classicism in England in the eighteenth century, see Stallybrass and White, *The Politics and Poetics,* 105: "The production and reproduction of a body of classical writing required a labor of suppression, a perpetual work of exclusion upon the grotesque body and it was that supplementary yet unavoidable labour which troubled the identity of the classical. It brought the grotesque back into the classical...as a vast labour of exclusion requiring and generating its own equivocal energies. *Quae negata, grata*—what is denied is desired."
50. Sigmund Freud, *The Theme of the Three Caskets,* vol. 12 of the Standard Edition (London: Hogarth Press, 1953), 65.
51. Freud, *Three Caskets,* 72–73: "The goddess of Death was replaced by the goddess of Love." Freud goes on to generalize from these speculations: "The great Mother-goddesses of the oriental peoples,...all seem to have been both founts of being and destroyers: goddesses of life and fertility, and death goddesses."
52. Bakhtin, *Rabelais and His World,* 11–12.
53. Stallybrass and White, *Politics and Poetics,* 19: "The politics of carnival: its nostalgia; its uncritical populism (carnival often violently abuses and demonizes *weaker,* not stronger, social groups—women, ethnic and religious minorities, those who 'don't belong'—in a process of *displaced abjection*); its failure to do away with the official dominant culture, its licensed complicity."
54. Freud, *Humour,* vol. 21 of the Standard Edition (London: Hogarth Press, 1953), 160.

A Curious Study
in "Parallel Lives"
Louis XIV and the Abbé de Choisy

Virginia M. Marino

C *ross-dressing has become a fashionable avenue* of critical exploration. Studies such as Marjorie Garber's *Vested Interests* and Madeleine Kahn's *Narrative
Transvestism* offer readings in literary history that push the boundaries of thinking about transvestism further into the realm where sexual politics are played out
through narrative strategizing. Works like Vern L. and Bonnie Bullough's *Cross-Dressing,
Sex, and Gender* and Richard Docter's *Transvestites and Transsexuals: Toward a Theory of
Cross-Gender Behavior* document medical and psychological thinking about cross-
dressing. Judith Butler, Thomas Laqueur, Diana Fuss, and many others contribute
important arguments in the essentialist versus constructionist debate about sex and gender.[1] The combination of these approaches broadens our understanding of the cultural
and biological bases on which gender has come to be built.

Underlying these arguments stands a post-Freudian psychological model in which
we as a culture are heavily invested, as witnessed by the dominance of Robert Stoller's
"phallic woman" model in explaining both actual and literary manifestations of transvestism.[2] Despite weighty evidence that transvestism derives its significance from its
cultural and historical context, postmodern perspectives seem to have less impact than
they should towards clearing broader critical thinking about the significance of transvestism and the resurgence of interest in it at particular historical moments.

This essay has at least two purposes. First, to explore exactly where the combination of narratological and psychodynamic models have left us in understanding cross-
dressing; that is, to set limits on the usefulness of the "phallic woman" model and psychodynamic theory in general in order to open a much needed path for broader
sociohistorical thinking. Both cross-dressing (literal and metaphorical) and psychodynamic theory must find their fuller significance within the context of the social and
historical conditions that produce them. Second, in order to make an opening that
will lead to a more contextual consideration, this essay offers a reading of a late seventeenth-century text, the *Mémoires pour servir à l'histoire de Louis XIV* by François
Timoléon de Choisy.[3] This work provides a key because of its historical situation
within what can be called a moment of crisis in the intelligibility of the symbolic. In
other words, the travesty of Choisy's *Mémoires,* which duplicates itself both in terms of
gender ambiguity and as an ironic parallel drawn between Choisy and Louis XIV,

stands as a metaphorical representation of the androgynous instability that is the true nature of the symbolic. As the metaphor of transvestism allows the repression of the feminine in the symbolic to be lifted, we can better read the limits of psychodynamic explanations as products of their sociohistorical context.

❧ ❧ ❧

The abbé de Choisy, who enjoyed the reputation of scholar, memorialist, and member of the Académie française in his own day, fascinates critics today because of his transvestite adventures. Critical studies have generally concentrated on reading limited biographical details in the context of psychodynamic structures, with little more purpose, it seems, than to justify a belief in the universal validity of our post-Freudian view of the psyche. Little attention has been paid to Choisy's writings, except to those moments of his discourse that supposedly help prove the validity of the psychological and psychodynamic models—models employed to organize a reading of the texts in the first place. However, both Choisy's memoirs and psychocritical readings of them are constructed products of a broader sociohistorical phenomenon. Specifically, the larger significance of Choisy's androgynous portrait of the historical actor highlights an important paradox in the configuration of power under Louis XIV, and of power through discursive systems in general.

Choisy characterizes his history of Louis XIV's court as *l'histoire particulière,* particular (not private) history. Faith Beasley has gathered together classical definitions of history such as Charles Sorel's and Antoine Furetière's, noting that "particular history" was generally understood to be the narrative life of great and less important personages, the narrative of memorable events, histories of provinces, and the like.[4] Choisy's are more precisely a subcategory known as the *mémoire particulier,* a significant point because he specifically casts the piece as a hybrid, a combination of history and autobiography. This category of works was largely the province of women authors determined to memorialize a perspective on events and institutions that would necessarily differ from that of their male counterparts. Although they inscribed their own political participation into the record of history, these women memorialists generally did not concern themselves with what we would now call the private sphere.

Choisy, by contrast, offers a curious case. A history of his manuscripts uncovers that he originally intended much of what are now gathered under the title *Mémoires de l'abbé de Choisy habillé en femme* [Memoirs of the abbé de Choisy, dressed as a woman] to be part of the historical work on Louis XIV.[5] Many of those details originally intended for inclusion would have undermined the formal convention that the autobiographical aspect of a *mémoire particulier* constitute a history of the public, not private, self. Although some of the pages of Choisy's own transvestite adventures remain circumscribed within the memoirs on Louis XIV, most were edited out after Choisy's death. Nevertheless, the original plan remains apparent in several ways.

Choisy articulates the project of the *Mémoires* as a pleasant pastime, a memorial with a sense of humor that he can reread with amusement in his old age; he warns the reader:

> [E]n écrivant la vie du Roi j'écrirai aussi la mienne, à mesure que je me souviendrai de ce qui m'est arrivé. Ce sera un beau contraste, mais cela me réjouira; et je veux bien courre le risque qu'on dise: Il joint à tous propos les louanges d'un fat à celles d'un héros. (p. 25)

> [(I)n writing the biography of the king, I will also write my own, to the extent that I will remember what has happened. This will form a striking contrast, but it will also please me, and I am willing to take the risk that people will say: He is uniting under any pretext the praises of a fool to those of a hero.]

Through a playful rewriting in the tradition of Plutarch's *Parallel Lives of the Greeks and Romans,* Choisy's historical persona and its discursive representation were meant to contrast with and/or complement that of the king, although in what way remains to be uncovered by the reader. A brief excursion into the abbé's biography against the background of various psychocritical readings provides a guide to this larger set of questions.

Choisy on the Couch

Recall the main thrust of Stoller's "phallic woman" theory.[6] Stoller elaborates upon the standard interpretation that transvestism is defined at least in part by a fetishistic relation to objects—namely, female garments. He sketches the following profile of the cross-dresser (for Stoller, all cross-dressers are male):

> Let us define adult male *transvestism* as completely pleasurable; it is fetishistic, intermittent cross-dressing in a biologically normal man who does not question that he is a male—that is, the possessor of a penis.

> [T]he man..., in addition to the above criteria, has learned a woman's role so well that he can or wishes to successfully pass undetected in society as a woman; when he does so, the activity alternates with living most of his life in a man's role....

> He is...constantly aware of the penis under his woman's clothes.... The pleasure of tricking the unsuspecting into thinking he is a woman...is not so much erotic as it is a proof that there is such a thing as a woman with a penis. He has identified with a "phallic" woman (mother) and consciously senses himself to be a phallic "woman." He therefore can tell himself that he is, or with practice will become, a better woman than a biological female if he chooses to do so.[7]

For Stoller, then, the transvestite male is delighted to be male; his transvestism is a mere cover for a more aggressively virile personality that his ruffles and frills cannot extinguish. He masters the oppressive other, the oppressive mother, the female who sought, out of her raging penis envy, to castrate the vulnerable son.

Stoller's transvestite is no transsexual; he does not believe he is a female psyche in the wrong body. For Stoller, transvestism is an internal battle of the sexes whereby the male takes pleasure in the knowledge and enactment of his vanquishing capacity.[8] If we were to apply this theory to the case of Choisy, we would have to conclude, as his biographers do, that Choisy's mother usurped for herself, through the personal and political sacrifice of her feminized son, a position of greater power within her patriarchal culture.

For Richard Docter, who expands on some of Stoller's work, cross-dressing is an enormously complex phenomenon. He states:

> The spectrum of cross dressing encompasses nine behavior patterns, some of which have much in common and some of which are quite unique. The five heterosexual variations are: fetishism, fetishistic transvestism, marginal transvestism, transgenderism, and secondary transsexualism (TV type). The four homosexual variations are: primary transsexualism, secondary transsexualism (homosexual type), drag queens, and female impersonators.[9]

This passage is fascinating for its elaborate categorization scheme, reminiscent of some mad scientific attempt to put every last detail into a neat classification box whose tight lid would prevent conceptual slippage into a confusing experience of the real. It also suggests fundamental links between aspects of human behavior and biology that may not necessarily be connected: for example, a hidden connection between the body's sex and its experience of physical objects (that is, a tie between one's sex and/or gender and the sensual experience of fabrics and garments; or an essential connection between sex/gender and the impulse, or the degree of intensity of the impulse, to ornament the body). Paradoxically, the positive side of Docter's minute scheme is its underlying suggestion of fluidity—of behavior, of gender. A real range of possible gender configurations imposes itself, along with the sense that this spectrum belies the notion of sexual binaries to which we stubbornly cling and the cultural significance we entrust to that binary.

Where does the abbé de Choisy fit into this scheme? Can he fit neatly into one of these categories? The youngest child of Jeanne-Olympe de Choisy, the abbé was first swept into court life as a transvestite in order to gain the favor of Louis XIV's brother, Philippe d'Orléans, who was also made to cross-dress as a child and who later continued the practice extensively. Choisy reveals his awareness of the calculation behind this behavior in the following passage:

> On m'habillait en fille toutes les fois que le petit Monsieur venait au logis, et
> il y venait au moins deux ou trois fois la semaine.... [T]out cela se faisait,

dit-on, par l'ordre du cardinal, qui voulait le rendre efféminé, de peur qu'il ne fît de la peine au Roi. (p. 219)

[They dressed me as a girl every time the little Monsieur came to the apartment, and he came at least two or three times a week.... All this was done, so they say, by order of the cardinal, who wished to make him effeminate, for fear that he might otherwise harm the (King).]

Choisy's biographers maintain that, to his detriment, his early political education was dominated by his mother's aggressive authority. Indeed there is repeated anxiety on the part of Choisy's biographers which surfaces in their representations of her influence in the son's life. Implicitly or explicitly, the modern interpreter seeks to blame the mother—especially since she was a woman of great ambition and influence—for her victimized son's transgressions of the law of the father, the law that would secure for him the phallus, his stable identity, and masculine control. Geneviève Reynes concludes that François Timoléon was used, was the child of an unfulfilled schemer experiencing a midlife crisis:

Cet enfant inattendu, tardif, né longtemps après les autres, fait vibrer chez Jeanne-Olympe une fibre maternelle qu'elle n'avait peut-être jamais connue. Elle se prend pour lui d'une passion exclusive, surprenante chez une femme qui jusqu'alors n'avait paru occupée que d'elle-même....

Cet enfant qui va la combler, au sens où il va remplir son vide intérieur, elle va le vivre comme un prolongement d'elle-même.... Comment s'étonner alors qu'elle l'utilise....[10]

[This unexpected child, latecoming, born long after the others, made vibrate in Jeanne-Olympe a maternal fiber that she had perhaps never known before. She was taken with a passion formed exclusively for him, something surprising for a woman who up to that time had not seemed concerned only with herself....

This child which would fulfill her, in the sense that he would fill her internal emptiness, she would experience him as an extension of herself.... How then could one be surprised when she used him....]

The abbé recalls that his mother took him everywhere, since having a small child with her made her feel beautiful and young. This, too, Reynes interprets as a lack in the mother; in fact, she believes Jeanne-Olympe needed him as "la preuve qu'elle est toujours une femme" [the proof that she is still a woman].[11]

This interpretation, with its irksome view of maternity and a rhetorical pretense of knowledge of the essence of womanhood, is itself the product of our own configuration of the symbolic (communication and meaning itself) as the domain of the father, to be accessed upon renouncing the original ties to the mother. But what if the symbolic itself were an illusory stability? Judith Butler raises the essential questions in *Bodies That Matter:*

> Here it seems crucial to ask where and how language emerges to effect this stabilizing function, particularly for the fixing of sexed positions. The capacity of language to fix such positions, that is, to enact its symbolic effects, depends upon the permanence and fixity of the symbolic domain itself, the domain of signifiability or intelligibility.[12]

On this pivotal issue—whether the symbolic constitutes a static or a changing domain—depends the nature of sex categories, since we attribute to that domain the power to assign meaning and identity. Assuming, contrary to Jacques Lacan, that the symbolic is not a static realm but an ever-changing one, we must conclude that when there is a crisis in the symbolic order, in the "identity-conferring function of the name, ... [so will there be a crisis] in the stabilizing of bodily contours according to sex allegedly performed by the symbolic."[13]

Object-relations theories, although useful to a point in explaining transvestism, eventually break down in applicability. Assuming a stable configuration for the symbolic order, they posit transvestite behavior as rooted in an unresolved crisis during the crucial individuation-separation period. Instead of splitting from the mother, the child internalizes or "cannibalizes" the mother, thus creating a second self, an internal duality. As A. Beitel describes it, the child becomes his own "self object."[14] Nicholas Abraham and Maria Torok also elaborate this "duplicité" [doubling or splitting of the self], which engenders guilt feelings and which is tied to linguistic expression.[15] This "abnormal" introjective identification, which Abraham and Torok call "incorporation," is the way to cling to the mother's protection for the duration of adulthood, or as Lionel Ovesey and Ethel Person (respected theorists of gender dysphoria) call it, a "holding on" to the mother.[16]

To be sure, Choisy's historical works betray these obscured boundaries of the mother/child identities, although their power is more aesthetic than literal. Furthermore, the aesthetic configuration of the relation emerges to reconfigure the traditional identities associated with mother and transvestite son. An interpretation through the lens of object-relations theories would hold that during the abbé's periods of transvestism, he introjects the person of the mother, in fact becomes the mother, repeatedly acting out a troubled and exaggerated symbiosis with her. However, the symbiosis Choisy exhibits does not work toward sustaining latent aggression towards the mother. He describes the mother-child relationship in mentoring terms. For example, in one passage he recalls: "A l'age de dix ans, elle me faisait écrire tous les matins deux ou trois heures au chevet de son lit" [When I was ten, she made me write every morning, for two or three hours at her bedside] (p. 25).

Choisy symbolically plays out in the *Mémoires pour servir à l'histoire de Louis XIV* the incorporation of the mother into himself as an act of emulation and creative imitation. At one point we find him playing the role of scribe, writing her words as if they were his own: "et moi, j'étais toujours avec elle. Tous les matins j'écrivais au chevet de son lit toutes les lettres qu'elle écrivait aux plus grandes princesses de l'Europe" [and I was always with her. Every morning, at her bedside, I wrote all the letters she wrote to the greatest princesses of Europe] (p. 218). The psychic dualism that becomes manifest in the narrative voice of the *Mémoires* bears witness to Choisy's early acquisition of an intimate knowledge of female circles that would grow indispensable to him. It is worth noting that the female sphere in question was both private (in the sense of the behind-the-scenes maneuvers for which the *précieuses* especially are well known) and public (as in knowledge of manners and customs appropriate to different social situations; the letters he learns to write, for example, consist of royal correspondence). This expanded perspective could only be an advantage, not a hindrance, to any memorialist.

Whatever one concludes about Jeanne-Olympe de Choisy herself, it is likely, judging by her son's explanations, that she considered cross-dressing him as a potentially flattering and productive imitation of Philippe's behavior, a way to secure his eventual political power and influence. As for Choisy, he seems mostly preoccupied with the political utility of the measure. Recognizing that masculinity has a long tradition of being linked to political, especially royal, power in France,[17] he understood that cross-dressing Philippe was meant to marginalize him and would ultimately distance Choisy, too, from the locus of governmental power. Cross-dressing the king's brother was an exaggerated but parallel gesture to the feminization of the nobility, a point that is taken up below.

Choisy's comments about his transvestism in the *Mémoires* focus not on any emotional or psychological detriment, but on its ramifications in the political sphere—that is, how it was interpreted by others whose approval he needed for upward social mobility. The assessment is purely pragmatic. On the one hand, Choisy points to his mother's strategic failure to gauge accurately Philippe's future governmental role, and therefore the political practicality of François Timoléon's transvestism. Her overall political sense, however, is not questioned. He notes: "[M]a mère était de tous les secrets de la cour.... Mon père ne savait rien de tout cela" [(M)y mother knew all the secrets of the court.... My father knew nothing of all that] (p. 222). Choisy's father, though, presents a more serious case of missed opportunity and lack of due recognition. The son reports: "[M]on père avait eu beau représenter ses services et son ancienneté, il n'avait pu obtenir qu'une place de semestre" [(M)y father recounted his services and his long-standing role in vain; he could only obtain a position for one term] (p. 75). For those who would blame the mother through a mother-child psychological development gone amiss, the memoirs emphasize that both parents ultimately worked unwittingly against the political advantage of their progeny.

Again taking object-relations theories to the limits of their applicability, the reader finds Choisy the historian organizing his sources into two broad categories: firsthand information and things learned secondhand. However, the category "I" is no sooner uttered than it doubles, expanding into two narrating selves in order to encompass the female persona. The opposition becomes I/mother (as the inner world) versus everyone else outside. Choisy explains:

> Pour moi, voici comme je m'y prends pour écrire mes Mémoires; j'écris d'abord tout ce que je sais par moi-même, et tout ce que ma mère m'a dit; ensuite je fais des questions aux gens par les mains de qui les affaires ont passé. (p. 35)

> [As for me, here is how I go about writing my memoirs: first I write all that I know from my own experience, and all that my mother told me; then I ask questions of those men by whose hands these events occurred.]

Thus, once the boundaries of the narrative voice free him to encompass multiple perspectives from both gender worlds, Choisy realizes his own success story. Both the body proper and its text as substitute encompass the rich, symbolic ambiguity of the androgyne. Like the king's insight into the power of symbolic reconfiguration, Choisy's transvestism afforded him access to the power of the symbolic; he realized the potential of this aesthetic tool to empower himself through historical memorialization.

What of Choisy's place within the patriarchy? Psychodynamic theories call for a distant, passive, or absent father. Reynes interprets Choisy's situation in these very psychological terms, claiming that the mother attempted, unconsciously or otherwise, to usurp the father's role and substitute herself as the paternal origin. Such an interpretation, troubling because of the negative judgment carried in its rhetoric, implies an inappropriate power dynamic wielded by the mother who claims the fruits of her generative role. In terms of the "phallic woman" model, the transvestite as historiographer would have to shed the mother's voice in order to assert his phallic power, thus reestablishing the appropriate configuration for the allegedly male-dominant symbolic. In other words, as writer, Choisy would be the mother's troubled child; as the character of his own literary creation, he would become a worthy son of his father's house. However, this interpretation of the narrator is not supported by the text.

In the *Mémoires,* the dynamic ambiguity of the androgynous narrator becomes the real source of power; he negotiates between mainstream representational practice (for example, traditional histories such as the style of the "parallel lives," or the official historiographic and media representations commissioned by the king) and the rhetoric of *l'histoire particulière* (such as the unofficial, often subversive female authors' memoirs). Pushing to the limit the symbolic configuration of the historical text, Choisy subverts the constraints of gender as well as those of official historiography. Employing many of the same strategies as women memorialists of his time, Choisy constructs his discursive historical body as a mirror reflecting the fullness of androgynous representation.[18] Here, rhetorical theories that consider the cultural context of speech acts become more valuable than psychodynamic models we have considered thus far.

Choisy's biographers point out that his periods of cross-dressing, although dispersed throughout his life, were nevertheless continuous when they occurred and were designed to let him pass as a woman. However, this construction of an identity dependent on the binary model was one the abbé came to accept, not one he would necessarily have adopted for himself. Although he was made to cross-dress as a child, he tended first only to ornament his male garb as an adult, which elicited a mixed reception from his contemporaries. In a piece entitled "La Comtesse des Barres," Choisy recounts an unsettling reaction from La Rochefoucauld and Mme de Lafayette when he wore women's jewelry and *mouches* to ornament his male garments. He writes:

> Il arriva même que madame de Lafayette, que je voyais fort souvent, me voyant toujours fort ajusté avec des pendants d'oreilles et des mouches, me dit en bonne amie que ce n'était point la mode pour les hommes, et que je ferais bien mieux de m'habiller en femme. (p. 324)

> [It even happened that Madame de Lafayette, whom I saw quite often, seeing me quite "done up" with earrings and beauty spots, said to me as a good friend that this was not the style for men, and that I would do much better to dress myself as a woman.]

The reception of Choisy's transvestism is beyond the scope of this essay; however, two striking points merit notice. First, the discomfort with what constitutes a kind of hermaphroditic appearance. Mme de Lafayette's statement seems to suggest that societal norms require the individual to choose a category and stay within it, although Choisy's practice of adorning his religious garments with women's accessories became a habit, he tells us, that the church itself permitted. Second, although Choisy does recount incidents where he was chastised by family members for his cross-dressing, his contemporaries' willingness to accept his gender-bending was the overwhelming response. As he indicates in the *Mémoires de l'abbé de Choisy habillé en femme,* it was tolerated at worst but more frequently was the object of fascination and admiration. These varied responses point to a crisis in gender configuration and representation.

Understanding this vast expanse of gender play requires contextualizing it within the Baroque aesthetic. Much has been written about the Baroque, and even by the time Johan Huizinga first published in 1944 his now classic study *Homo ludens,* he notes that the significance of the term "Baroque" had expanded into a vast field of applicability. Certainly more thorough investigations into the Baroque have been made since the publication of *Homo ludens,* but we return to this text because of Huizinga's genius in highlighting an often forgotten element—that of the centrality of play in the elaboration of this aesthetic of excess. Huizinga states:

> The general tendency to *overdo* things, so characteristic of the Baroque, finds its readiest explanation in the play-content of the creative impulse. Fully to enjoy the work of Rubens, Bernini or that Dutch prince of poets, Joost van den Vondel, we must be prepared at the outset to take their utterances *cum grano salis.* This is probably true of most art and poetry, it may be objected; if

so, it affords yet another proof of our main contention—the fundamental importance of play. For all that, the Baroque manifests the play-element to an altogether striking degree. We should never enquire how far the artist himself intends for his work to be perfectly serious....[19]

Reading the transvestite body within the context of the play element produces a very different interpretation from one derived from a psychoanalytic model. For example, Choisy's minutely detailed account of his clothing and accessories in "La Comtesse des Barres" appears as an obsession, a fetish as it is read through the psychoanalytic filter.[20] Nevertheless, such an elaborately detailed description becomes the verbal equivalent of a Baroque portrait, and even appears modest if compared to, say, the discursive excess of one of the king's carousels. Choisy also provides an inventoried description of his home furnishings, the remains of his mother's estate, and the most minute details of numerous public events, thereby conforming to contemporary expectations of excess in representation. Understood as a particular dialect within its particular social and political context, such minutiae move from fetishistic to eloquent or modish. To attribute psychological abnormality to the player-creator of this discursive representation would be to misunderstand entirely its cultural significance. Reynes expresses surprise that his contemporaries' references to the abbé do not even mention his transvestism; however, their reaction supports the view that a vast field of play was available to the Baroque player, and was so pervasive as to appear unremarkable. Reynes writes:

> D'ailleurs, avec le roi, c'est toute la société de son temps qui a pour ses incartades une extrême indulgence: son travesti semble partout comme "mis entre parenthèses." On ne se contente pas de l'excuser, tout simplement on ne le "voit" pas. Il est curieux de remarquer en effet que les témoignages qui nous sont parvenus (anecdotes, historiettes, lettres de ses amis et de ses connaissances) n'en parlent *jamais.*[21]

> [Furthermore, as concerns the king, the entire society of his time was extremely indulgent towards his escapades: his transvestism seemed everywhere to be "put in parentheses." Not only were people content to excuse it; quite simply, they did not see it. It is interesting to note that in effect the accounts which have reached us (anecdotes, short histories, letters from his friends and acquaintances) never speak of this.]

Given that the customary and familiar are often taken for granted, an indifference to the abbé's fascination with ornamentation should suggest that it posed neither an anomaly nor a threat to the seventeenth-century aristocratic viewer, who read it as play within the bounds of the rules. Travesty as a literary theme is prevalent throughout the entire century; travesty even on the part of the king who played male and female roles in theatrical productions was a matter for popular applause; travesty during the elaborate royal *fêtes* and in propagandist media representations were regularly available for consumption. In short, travesty served as an integral metaphorical language of the age.

Dressing Up for History

In his *Mémoires pour servir à l'histoire de Louis XIV,* Choisy offers the embodiment of both literal transvestism and the metaphorical use of cross-dressing that informs the construction of textual and social/historical power plays.[22] Baring his personal experience of transvestism and exploring the limitations born of gender distinctions become inseparable from his role of author. In these *Mémoires,* as in Choisy's various "confessional" pieces, the abbé narrates events in such a way as to betray an androgynous rhetoric: easy, fluid, intimate prose, moments of "innocence" in his *récit* stand alongside moments of tension, violence, and "knowledge." As noted above, there is an expansion of the narrative voice which comes to incorporate male and female personae. This reconfiguring of traditional and stereotypic gender attributes points to an impasse in the intelligibility of the late-seventeenth-century symbolic, a sense of confusion in reading the "overcharged" rhetoric of the Baroque.

Choisy's biographers claim that Jeanne-Olympe de Choisy used her child as an extension of her own desires. Whether or not this is true, the son incorporates rather than despises the mother's desire and ambition; he willingly takes into himself her strengths and writes them into a kind of legitimized, "feminized" patriarchy, an aspect of the text that mirrors and then subverts the androgynous bond that ties the masculinity of the king as sole guardian of, for example, military and economic power, to the deliberately feminized (disempowered) aristocracy. As a rehabilitating imitation of this symbolic model, Choisy has the dynamics of his mother-child symbiosis become the driving rhetorical and political force behind the construction of an androgynous historiographic discourse. Here, the mother functions symbolically as a positive feminine voice, a power that allows him to rival the king in reaching the limits of intelligible significance.

It is well known but bears repeating that Louis XIV assured for himself absolutist power not only through the reorganization of the mechanisms of government and the so-called feminization of the aristocracy, but also by controlling the media. For example, official histories of the Sun King's reign emphasized mainly his military exploits and achievements. The nobility were stripped of their birthright to military glory and reassigned to a kind of "domestic" position as they gave up their residences to remain by the king's side at court. Like a stereotypical 1950s housewife, the nobles stayed home and constituted beautiful, decorative proofs of the power of the ruler to act independently of them. Jean-Marie Apostolidès reminds us of the castrated fate of the seventeenth-century male nobility:

> Le noble désarmé voit d'ailleurs sa vocation naturelle de guerrier singulièrement compromise pendant le règne de Louis XIV.

…L'aristocratie désarmée, dépossédée de ses coutumes, privée de ses prérogatives militaires, se mue alors en une caste spectaculaire. Toujours privilégiée, elle trouve d'imaginaires compensations dans des cérémonies où elle figure aux côtés du roi.[23]

[The disarmed noble sees, furthermore, his natural vocation as a warrior singularly compromised during the reign of Louis XIV.

…The disarmed aristocracy, dispossessed of its customs, deprived of its military prerogatives, transforms itself into a class of spectacle. Still privileged, it finds imaginary compensations in ceremonies where it is represented at the side of the king.]

Choisy usurps this privilege of mastery from the king by narrating events that show himself to be in control whereas the king was not.

One well-documented advantage resulting from this political maneuver of marginalizing the feminine was its rehabilitation through the translation of formerly negative associations into desirable qualities. Carolyn C. Lougee documents this "leveling tendency" of polite societies, underscoring how early feminist arguments capitalized on the occasion to influence the direction of politics and letters by turning feminine weaknesses into feminine strengths.[24]

The king, too, acquired virtues formerly held to be feminine qualities, an air of tranquillity and grace that suggested international peace, for example. His physical appearance in numerous paintings, as in the famous portrait by Hyacinthe Rigaud painted around 1700, or the 1670 allegorical painting of *The Family of Louis XIV* by Jean Nocret, undoubtedly conveys an impression of androgyny. The symbolic body of the king was an ever-changing one that would absorb everything positive its culture had to offer. In her colossal study of *L'Image de Louis XIV dans la littérature française de 1660 à 1715,* Nicole Ferrier-Cavenvière sums up the collective myth that was Louis XIV:

> Il est en quelque sorte la concrétion d'une culture, une formidable oeuvre d'art collective. Entre la littérature et ce Louis XIV, il existe un perpétuel échange, une véritable osmose même parfois, qui font qu'il n'y a pas d'un côté un homme-reflet et d'un autre côté des reflets imaginaires. Le mot même de miroir qu'implique celui d'image ne renvoie nullement à un objet possédant sa corporéité propre, sa réalité sans vie, radicalement indépendante de l'image qu'elle reflète.[25]

[This myth is in some way the concretization of a culture, an amazing collective work of art. A perpetual exchange, at times a veritable osmosis even, exists between the literature and this Louis XIV, which makes it so that there is not on the one hand a man-reflection and on the other imaginary reflections. Even the word *mirror,* which implies that of image, does not refer at all to an object possessing its own corporeality, its reality without life, radically independent of the image it reflects.]

Ferrier-Cavrière emphasizes the humanist dynamics of the mirror as the locus of exchange, encounter, confrontation, and knowledge. In the *Mémoires pour servir à l'histoire de Louis XIV,* Choisy confronts the royal image and plays an interesting mirror game within the broad field of gender and power display open to him.

Faith Beasley, in her excellent study entitled *Revising Memory: Women's Fiction and Memoirs in Seventeenth-Century France,* argues that memoirs constituting *l'histoire particulière* are marked as gender specific, the primary indication of their feminine rhetoric being the addition of the autobiographical aspect. For Beasley, the woman memorialist "locates this deviation in her transgression of a number of conventional boundaries—specifically, those separating the self and history, two spheres usually opposed as private and public."[26] Beasley further claims that memoirs can be tagged as written by women because they show a number of elements that are specifically characteristic of women's writing, essentially proposing the female memoir of the seventeenth century as the strategic equivalent of the twentieth century's *écriture féminine.*

Beasley includes the following strategies in her list of maneuvers specific to women's memoirs:

1. usurping narrative space that should belong to the king for detailing female portraits and women's participation in political events;
2. elevating women's accomplishments to a position superior to that of their male contemporaries;
3. limiting their accounts of male-dominated spheres such as warfare to their psychological components;
4. inscribing their own stories and those of their ancestors onto the pages of history;
5. because of their privileged vantage point, including information unlikely to be found in official histories.

These five elements are certainly characteristic of most women authors' memoirs in seventeenth-century France. Choisy's memoirs employ the same strategies. It remains to consider to what purpose he would inscribe himself within this tradition.

Choisy announces his lack of desire to write the "grande histoire" of Louis XIV's reign; he prefers to concentrate on the "particularités de la vie du Roi" [the specific details of the king's life] (p. 22), to follow the king's daily routine in dealing with his ministers and courtiers. Thanks to his privileged view of court life, his history reveals the underside of government unknown to most: "Je passe légèrement sur tous les événements publics, on les trouve écrits partout; et je ne veux m'arrêter que sur de certaines choses ignorées du commun des hommes" [I pass lightly over all of the public events, one can find them written up everywhere, and I only want to linger on certain matters unknown to most men] (pp. 90–91). In other words, Choisy presents himself as privy to behind-the-scenes events. Like the king's official historiographers, he is in a position to admire and praise Louis XIV. Unlike them, he may evaluate the Sun King's personal faults and political mistakes if he so chooses.

Choisy takes advantage of his unofficial position to criticize political positions he does not approve; this is not surprising. However, the particular events are chosen for the parallelism they afford Choisy in the enhancement of the autobiographical aspect of his memoirs. Consider these examples.

As unofficial memorialist of the king, Choisy notes a military victory Louis missed against William of Orange because he used poor judgment in taking the bad advice of an overcautious minister. In his account of the French crossing the Rhine, a military success inflated to mythic proportions by Louis's official historiographers, Choisy undermines all contemporary accounts of the event.[27] He paints an almost comical scene, noting why Louis failed to lead his troops across the Rhine in true heroic fashion. Choisy recounts:

> [Il n'a] pas passé le Rhin à la nage après le comte de Guiche, à la tête de ses gardes du corps. Il y avait peu de danger à courre, et une gloire infinie à acquérir...il le voulait, mais M. le prince, qui n'osait mettre le pied dans l'eau à cause de sa goutte, s'y opposa. Comment eut-il osé passer en bateau, le Roi passant à la nage?[28]

> [(He did) not swim across the Rhine after the count de Guiche, at the head of his bodyguard. There was little risk of danger, and infinite glory to be won...he wanted to, but M. the prince, who did not dare put his foot into the water because of his gout, opposed this plan. How would he have dared to cross in a boat, had the king been swimming?]

This rendition, hardly conveying military glory, deflates the rhetoric of heroism. This is a typical strategy employed by subversive histories in general. In Choisy's case, such subversions include either redistributing or reattributing, through rewriting, the glory of historical events that had been conspicuously contrived, through discursive propagandist paradigms, to inflate the power of the actor.

In Choisy's *Mémoires,* where Louis XIV's personal errors are "des ombres, des taches dans le soleil" [shadows, spots on the sun], Choisy himself glows in the limelight of his own version of history. On one military expedition, when the king was unable to locate the priest who was to say Mass, Choisy comes to the rescue and saves the day: "j'y étais présent, et même j'eus le plaisir de faire ce jour-là une chose fort agréable au Roi: je lui fis entendre la messe" [I was present, and I even had the pleasure of doing the King a great kindness: I had him hear Mass].[29] A broad, playful distance separates the relative unimportance of the event and the supposed magnanimity of the response to it.

A further example of how Choisy employs rhetoric which Beasley associates with women's memoirs is the psychological lesson he is able to draw from his wartime experience. Contrary to the glorification of death in war as a sign of everlasting glory,

Choisy's memoirs record the pain of facing the spectacle of wasted life. Upon seeing the dead body of his friend Longueville, Choisy ponders:

> Non, je ne crois pas avoir jamais été ni pouvoir jamais être aussi touché que je le fus. Mais ce qui est fort singulier, j'étais encore jeune, grand joueur, assez peu attaché à mes devoirs ecclésiastiques … et cependant j'allai m'enfermer … et je priai Dieu pour M. de Longueville, à genoux, avec des larmes et une contrition de coeur que je voudrais bien avoir pour mes péchés.[30]

> [No, I do not think that I was ever, nor could I ever be, so moved as I was then. But what was very unusual, I was still young, a great lover of games, not very attentive to my ecclesiastical duties … and still I went to shut myself in … and I prayed to God for M. de Longueville, on my knees, with tears and contrition in my heart that I would have liked to feel for my own sins.]

As memorialist, Choisy might have revered the occasion of an honorable death. By choosing to lament a young life that could have been spared—that is, by emphasizing the psychological dimensions of war—Choisy inscribes his discourse within that of many women memorialists. This passage also highlights another dimension of Beasley's analysis of women's memoirs: relating the public event to oneself, telling one's own story while telling that of the public event. Here, Choisy brings his own situation within the scope of reflection, taking a personal, spiritual lesson from the event that uncovers the glory of war as nothing more than an artful construction designed to seduce posterity. But he goes further, for the vivid portrait of himself kneeling, in tears, redistributes the emotional impact of the moment, bestowing it upon his own response as he substitutes his own body for that of the dead soldier.

This progressive movement in the objective account of public events toward a discussion of autobiographical concerns (the memorialist builds a number of branches onto the Choisy family tree) ennobles the narrator, especially as he continues to accumulate a list of political gaffes and atrocities committed by the king's government. The dynamics of Choisy and Louis XIV as parallel lives gains its fullest realization in the following final example that weaves Choisy's story into the history of the king: his recounting in the greatest detail his own part in the diplomatic mission to Siam during the period when Louis revoked the Edict of Nantes.

As elaborated in book V of the *Mémoires,* Choisy tells all "sans déguisement" (p. 142). In fact, the memoirs leave void the seventeen-year period between 1661 and 1678–79 precisely so that Choisy may hasten the recollection of this relatively minor political embassy. He resumes his narrative thread with the events of 1678 because it is the year of the Revocation, "l'origine de la plus cruelle guerre qui ait affligé la France depuis un siècle" [the origin of the cruelest war that had afflicted France for a century], but also and more importantly, he hastens to add, "J'ai aussi des raisons particulières de choisir cette année-là: mon voyage à Siam s'y rencontre" [I also have personal reasons for choosing that year: my voyage to Siam took place then] (p. 113). Just as Louis XIV leads France into its moment of darkest despair, Choisy brings about the culmination of the historical inscription of the Choisy line into history, thereby keeping lit the flickering candle of the glory of the Sun King's reign. While in Siam, when Choisy finally realizes that his role is likely to be a "zéro en chiffre" [nonexistent], he manipulates the chevalier de Chaumont, for whom he serves as aide, in an attempt to make himself indispensable. Upon learning that Chaumont is to deliver a speech before the king of Siam, Choisy clandestinely composes his own speech which he hopes to deliver should Chaumont fall ill. Choisy's text of course was never delivered, but it replaces Chaumont's speech in the memoirs: the memorialist quotes his secret composition in its entirety in the pages of the history of Louis XIV. Choisy substitutes his own voice in the place of the one that made official history.

The negative parallelism of the inspired missionary (Choisy) and the misguided persecutor (Louis XIV) provides the subtext for every detail of the account, particularly as Choisy evaluates the Siam embassy as having inspired and satisfied an "ambition apostolique d'aller au bout du monde convertir un grand royaume" [apostolic ambition to go to the end of the earth to convert a great kingdom] (p. 143). Is Choisy really blissfully ignorant of the king's real motives to expand commercial trade through this embassy? Does he really believe Louis's actual intention was to convert the Siamese ruler to Christianity? Perhaps Choisy as mirror image is Louis's only hope of rehabilitating the monarch's tarnished image after the heinous Revocation. Perhaps Choisy revels in the humor that his method of rivaling the king's reputation turned out to be a good story.

A more fundamental question is whether the abbé's use of typical strategies employed by female memorialists challenges Beasley's model of gendered rhetoric. To be sure, the elements she uncovers do constitute strategies employed by female memorialists, but they are not employed out of psychosexual necessity; rather, they have been demonstrated, through the example of Choisy's memoirs, to represent the acquired behavior of the socially and politically disempowered. Choisy's *histoire particulière* incorporates these linguistic strategies as an act of narrative transvestism, and places them within the mirrored discursive body of the king, thereby reconstituting them as a locus of legitimized power.

Choisy's work clears an opening through which to read gender as a discursive system that was reconstructed in seventeenth-century France. In symbolic terms, the official production of an androgynous historical body for the king makes plausible the notion that the symbolic order, that which confers our identities, constitutes a linguistic field characterized not by gender stability, but by the free play of gender as representation. Inasmuch as this androgynous representation of the king's body suggests a crisis in the symbolic order, the power it holds would then be destabilizing, or at least unable to provide stability. An explosion of gender configurations offers the historical subject in seventeenth-century France a free range of possible, even changing, identities. Transvestism, by expanding the limits of intelligibility of the connection between sex and gender, provides a metaphorical key to seeing that the symbolic does not necessarily represent a static field, but more likely is continually culturally and historically (re)constructed.

Notes

1. Of the numerous studies of transvestism in literature, psychology, and medicine, I find the following works, despite the appearance of more recent ones, to be the most pivotal in current discussions of transvestism in literary criticism: Vern L. Bullough and Bonnie Bullough, *Cross-Dressing, Sex, and Gender* (Philadelphia: University of Pennsylvania Press, 1993); Victor Burgin, James Donald, and Cora Kaplan, eds., *Formations of Fantasy* (New York: Routledge, 1989); Judith Butler, *Gender Trouble: Feminism and the Subversion of Identity* (New York: Routledge, 1990); idem, *Bodies that Matter: On the Discursive Limits of "Sex"* (New York: Routledge, 1993); Richard F. Docter, *Transvestites and Transsexuals: Toward a Theory of Cross-Gender Behavior* (New York: Plenum Press, 1988); Diana Fuss, *Essentially Speaking: Feminism, Nature, and Difference* (New York: Routledge, 1989); Marjorie Garber, *Vested Interests: Cross-Dressing and Cultural Anxiety* (New York: Routledge, 1992); Sandra M. Gilbert and Susan Gubar, "Cross-Dressing and Re-Dressing: Transvestism as Metaphor," in *No Man's Land: The Place of the Woman Writer in the Twentieth Century*, vol. 2 (New Haven: Yale University Press, 1989), 324–76; Madeleine Kahn, *Narrative Transvestism: Rhetoric and Gender in the Eighteenth-Century English Novel* (Ithaca: Cornell University Press, 1990); Thomas Laqueur, *Making Sex: Body and Gender from the Greeks to Freud* (Cambridge: Harvard University Press, 1990); Robert Stoller, *Sex and Gender: On the Development of Masculinity and Femininity* (London: Hogarth Press, 1968) and idem, *Representations of Gender* (New Haven: Yale University Press, 1985).

2. See Stoller, *Sex and Gender* and *Representations of Gender*. Stoller did not invent the "phallic woman" theory, although his name is often associated with it thanks to his extensive elaboration of it.

3. These were first published posthumously by Choisy's friend, the abbé d'Olivet, in 1727. Throughout this chapter, I cite the modern edition of *Mémoires de l'abbé de Choisy*, ed. Georges Mongrédien (Paris: Mercure de France, 1983). Mongrédien presents in this edition both the *Mémoires pour servir à l'histoire de Louis XIV*, which I sometimes refer to simply as Choisy, *Mémoires*, and also the *Mémoires de l'abbé de Choisy habillé en femme*. All page references to Choisy's work are to this edition. All translations of Choisy's work and of critical work in French are my own.

4. Faith Beasley, *Revising Memory: Women's Fiction and Memoirs in Seventeenth-Century France* (New Brunswick: Rutgers University Press, 1990), 20–31. My debt to Faith Beasley is obvious throughout this essay.

5. See Georges Mongrédien's introduction to *Mémoires de l'abbé de Choisy*.

6. Stoller's theoretical discussion does not overlap with those such as Marcia Ian, *Remembering the Phallic Mother: Psychoanalysis, Modernism, and the Fetish* (Ithaca: Cornell University Press, 1993); that is, works that explore the symbolic value of concepts such as the phallus. Stoller's reading is more literal, less abstract, easily lending itself to the charge of misogyny.

7. Stoller, *Sex and Gender*, 176–77.

8. Stoller, *Sex and Gender*, 179–80.

9. Docter, *Transvestites and Transsexuals*, 37–38.

10. Geneviève Reynes, *L'abbé de Choisy ou l'ingénu libertin* (Paris: Presses de la Renaissance, 1983), 21.

11. Reynes, *L'abbé de Choisy*, 29

12. Butler, *Bodies That Matter*, 138. In a footnote accompanying this passage, Butler refers the reader to Teresa Brennan, *History after Lacan* (London: Routledge, 1993), for an argument objecting to the so-called unchanging nature of the Lacanian symbolic.

13. Butler, *Bodies That Matter*, 138.

14. A. Beitel, "The Spectrum of Gender Identity in Disturbance," *Gender Dysphoria*, ed. Betty W. Steiner (New York: Plenum Press, 1985), 189–206.

15. See esp. Nicolas Abraham and Maria Torok, *L'écorce et le noyau* (Paris: Flammarion, 1987).

16. Ethel Person and Lionel Ovesey, "Transvestism: New Perspectives," *Journal of the American Academy of Psychoanalysis* 6 (1978): 304–22, also discussed by Bullough and Bullough, *Cross-Dressing, Sex, and Gender*, 219. Docter, *Transvestites and Transsexuals*, 44, also recognizes the value of their contribution, noting: "Their view of the transvestite is anchored by self theory and they see the 'full-

blown syndrome' as involving two different personalities—one male and one female. 'The feminine personality may be perceived as "fighting" with the male personality and crowding it out.'"

17. This would be obvious to any educated man of the time, but it bears noting that Choisy, in his histories of the early years of the nation, makes a point of commenting on Salic Law that disempowers women. He could not have been a proponent of such marginalization of women, since he rehabilitates them in his versions of the early history of France, detailing their heroic military exploits.

18. Mirror representation was a common motif throughout the ages, as in "mirror of princes" literature, for example. It was also a popular propagandist strategy under Louis XIV, studied by numerous scholars. The post-Freudian obsession with this theme and Lacanian discussions of it, too numerous to recount here, are beyond the scope of this essay.

19. Johan Huizinga, *Homo ludens: A Study of the Play Element in Culture* (Boston: Beacon Press, 1955), 182; Huizinga's emphasis.

20. "La Comtesse des Barres," *Mémoires de l'abbé de Choisy*, 329, 331-32.

21. Reynes, *L'abbé de Choisy*, 75; Reynes's emphasis.

22. The abbé's own transvestism is not the only travesty of which he speaks in his memoirs. Besides those he himself orchestrates, he provides other examples as well. His accounts of the usefulness of disguise are interesting; see the *Mémoires pour servir à l'histoire de Louis XIV*, 225-26, for example.

23. Jean-Marie Apostolidès, *Le roi-machine: Spectacle et politique au temps de Louis XIV* (Paris: Editions de Minuit, 1981), 45-46.

24. Carolyn C. Lougee, *Le Paradis des Femmes: Women, Salons, and Social Stratification in Seventeenth-Century France* (Princeton: Princeton University Press, 1976).

25. Nicole Ferrier-Caverivière, *L'Image de Louis XIV dans la littérature française de 1660 à 1715* (Paris: Presses Universitaires de France, 1981), 14.

26. Beasley, *Revising Memory*, 91.

27. See Peter Burke, *The Fabrication of Louis XIV* (New Haven: Yale University Press, 1992), 76-78.

28. Choisy, *Mémoires pour servir à l'histoire de Louis XIV*, 32.

29. Choisy, *Mémoires pour servir à l'histoire de Louis XIV*, 32.

30. Choisy, *Mémoires pour servir à l'histoire de Louis XIV*, 33-34.

Pig or Prince?
Murat, d'Aulnoy, and the Limits
of Civilized Masculinity

Lewis C. Seifert

Quel monstre n'est-ce pas, en effet, qu'un grand seigneur qui n'a point de civilité?[1]
—Antoine de Courtin, *Nouveau traité de la civilité qui se
pratique en France parmi les honnêtes gens*

F ew books in early modern Europe were to enjoy the success of conduct manuals. Beginning in the sixteenth century, works such as Castiglione's *Il Libro del Cortegiano* (1528), Erasmus's *De civilitate morum puerilium* (1530), della Casa's *Il Galateo* (1558), and Guazzo's *Civil conversazione* (1574) became instant best-sellers that defined the ideals of polite interaction across all of Europe until the French Revolution, if not beyond. Especially in France, the impact of these books was profound and immediate. In the sixteenth century, civility—in both its Christian moralist and courtly varieties—received considerable discussion and debate.[2] Yet the explosion of writings on civility in the seventeenth century not only quickly outnumbered the previous century's efforts, it also tailored the foreign, largely Italian, models to the particular needs of city and court elites. Treatises by the likes of Faret, Grenaille, Du Bosc, and Caillères—and later in the century by Courtin, La Chétardie, Chalesme, and Goussault—were designed specifically to facilitate success in the *monde,* and especially at court.[3]

In our own time, the history of what Norbert Elias termed the "civilizing process" has received considerable scholarly attention.[4] But surprisingly little has been made of the fact that the vast majority of conduct manuals are addressed to men, something made clear by the titles of many of these works, for example, *L'Honnête homme ou l'art de plaire à la Court* (Faret, 1630), *Traité de la fortune des gens de qualité et des gentilshommes particuliers* (Caillères, 1658), and *Le Portrait d'un honnête homme* (Goussault, 1692). To be sure, important texts were published for women, and these have proven to be invaluable for the history of women.[5] However, the fact that far more conduct manuals were composed for men than women has spurred only scattered attempts to explicate the ways that the civilizing process constructs masculinity.[6] Of the numerous studies of *honnêteté,* for instance, most either explore it as an aesthetic theory or adopt the universalizing masculine perspective of the texts they consider. It is undeniable that any code of good manners presupposes an aesthetic theory and that doctrines of early modern civility expound ethical precepts applicable to both men and women (for example, the topoi of humility, modesty, and virtue). And yet the pragmatic value of much literature of civility resides in the fact that it is designed for men seeking to gain entrance to and acceptance in the elite circles of court, salon, cabinet, academy, and other public venues. In other words, it is concerned with defining masculine codes of sexual difference: it seeks to enunciate not only the kinds of conduct that are presumed to differentiate men from women, but also elite and/or dominant from common and/or marginalized masculinities. Conceived in this way, civility is no less useful for the historical reconsideration of men and masculinity than it has been for women and femininity.

On the most immediate level, the literature of masculine civility is especially helpful for understanding those men who were potentially but not yet fully established members of the privileged elite. No matter how wide its purported scope, this literature was addressed specifically to men such as these. This is not to say, of course, that those at the top of the social hierarchy were unaffected by the civilizing process. But they were presumed to exemplify par excellence—and by birth—the sort of refinement that the doctrines of civility seek to impart. Accordingly, they are only infrequently the subjects of conduct manuals. When they are, as in a brief chapter of Antoine de Courtin's enormously popular *Nouveau traité de la civilité qui se pratique en France parmi les honnêtes gens* (1671–), the possibility that they would be "incivils" is hardly imaginable.[7] As the epigraph makes clear, such a "grand seigneur" would be monstrous. He would be, following the early modern conception, an abnormal hybrid, a deviation from divinely conceived order. This is all the more the case, says Courtin, because of a built-in advantage:

> Les grands seigneurs peuvent même être civils à bien meilleur marché que les autres, car à l'égard des inférieurs, ils n'ont, sans s'incommoder, qu'à être un peu familiers et caressants, ils passeront pour fort honnêtes et fort civils parce que cette familiarité est obligeante....[8]

> [Members of the high nobility can even be civil with much less effort than others, for with respect to their inferiors, without troubling themselves, they only have to be a bit familiar and attentive, and they will pass for being extremely *honnête* and civil since this familiarity is obliging.]

What was unimaginable for the *grands seigneurs* was even more so in the case of the king. At the pinnacle of the social hierarchy of Old Regime France, he was the incarnation of the res publica and the divine representative for the entire French nation. In both the political and religious domains, his exemplarity was a superlative given. Of course, this exemplarity had particular resonance for the king's male subjects. For fathers throughout the realm, he was the embodiment of paternal authority: they were to govern their families as the king governed his subjects. For noblemen the king's example had another sense as well: since, by tradition, he was first among them, his entire lifestyle was supposed to bespeak the ethos of the second estate, and his bearing, social graces, and language were, ideally at least, to be emulated by all male courtiers. It is well known that the Bourbon kings increasingly used civility and court ceremony as political tools in what amounted to a highly regimented system of potlatch, but it is also the case that the king was both the master of ceremonies and the superior in whose presence the theory and practice of civility met their ultimate test.[9] By this standard, an uncouth or uncivil monarch was an impossibility. Indeed, the entire social and political order was founded on foreclosing the reality of such a possibility.[10]

But what if the monarch were not the model of civility at its most refined, and was instead the very incarnation of nature at its most uncivilized? This is the scenario imagined by two literary fairy tales from the end of the seventeenth century.[11] Henriette-Julie de Murat's "Le Roy Porc" (1699)[12] and Marie-Catherine d'Aulnoy's "Le Prince Marcassin" (1698)[13] rewrite a folkloric tale-type in which a prince, the long-awaited, unique offspring of two monarchs, is born with the appearance of a pig. Neither entirely animal nor completely human, the pig heroes of these two *contes de fées* disrupt the boundaries not only between animal and human, but also between individual instinct and social constraint and, in the end, between nature and culture. Since they are heirs to the throne—and not yet kings—they embody a future threat: they evoke the possibility that their kingdoms, incarnated by a soon-to-be king in the guise of a pig, would fall into the nebulous interstices between nature and culture. The king's exemplarity would thoroughly undo rather than uphold the refined culture at the foundations of his court and his realm. The dubious example of a pig king would also throw into question the very principles of courtly masculinity, based as it is, especially since Castiglione, on bodily and social grace. But in these tales, the prince regains his unequivocal human form before ascending to the throne. What this tale-type and its rewritings accentuate is the process of becoming, the process by which a prince attains both manhood and kingship. What they bring into focus, then, is the impact of the civilizing process on masculine subjectivity. Writing from a doubly marginal position—as women and in a noncanonical genre—Murat and d'Aulnoy take aim at the very central questions of the civilizing process and its effects on royal masculinity. As we will see, the visions these two women offer are considerably different and at times opposing. And yet both revamp, without entirely dismissing, patriarchal models of courtly masculinity. Both invite readers to reconsider exactly what constitutes civilized masculinity and how it is acquired.

Civilizing Plots

Murat and d'Aulnoy each rewrite a sixteenth-century Italian tale found in Giovanni Francesco Straparola's *Le Piacevoli notte* (1550–53) (The facetious nights, night 2, fable 1).[14] Straparola's tale articulates in succinct fashion the motifs (to use folkloristic parlance) that both of the *conteuses* integrate and/or adapt in their much longer narratives:

1. A barren and disheartened queen is visited by three fairies: the first two promise her a handsome and intelligent son, but the third indicates that he will be born resembling a pig and remain so until he has married three women
2. Once born, the pig prince develops a close attachment to his mother

3. He develops human characteristics (for example, speech) without completely eradicating animal impulses (such as foraging in garbage)
4. He marries the first of three daughters of an impoverished mother at court; on their wedding night he kills his bride after learning of her hostile intentions toward him
5. He marries the second daughter of the impoverished mother and, again, kills her on their wedding night
6. He marries the third daughter who, unlike her sisters, gladly sleeps with him
7. The prince's third wife discovers that he sheds his pigskin at night
8. The pigskin is destroyed, revealing a ravishingly handsome young man

Apparent in these motifs are many of the precepts of early modern civility that both Murat and d'Aulnoy interrogate in their rewritings. Perhaps most obvious is the assumption that those of noble blood possess an inherent biological advantage for acquiring courtly civility. Although this assumption is sometimes contested in the seventeenth century, it remains current in theories of polite behavior until well into the eighteenth century.[15] The tales by Straparola, Murat, and d'Aulnoy all play on this assumption by presenting what, at the outset, is its obverse: a prince who ought to have been born graceful in manners and bodily appearance is quite the opposite. Yet this apparent subversion of the superiority of noble blood is undone (at least ostensibly) by the dénouement of these tales, which in turn is guaranteed by the gifts of the two good fairies at the very beginning.

The demetamorphosis of the prince's appearance underscores just how central the graceful body is to the notion of the nobility's essential superiority. From Castiglione on, proponents of civility make the body the synecdoche for the multiple facets of grace, be they linguistic, behavioral, moral, or political.[16] Such a crucial role for the body and, by extension, appearances is what Straparola, Murat, and d'Aulnoy highlight. In each of these tales, attempts are made to repress the animality of the pig prince's body (through accoutrements such as clothing or training), both physical and intellectual (such as hunting, dance lessons, and conversation). The results, as we will see, are mixed at best. The base instincts of the pig cannot be so easily conjured from the prince whose body is not human. The outward rudiments of grace can perhaps be learned, so the logic holds, but its essence can only issue from a body so predisposed, and a body that is of course born noble. What Straparola, Murat, and d'Aulnoy all outline, then, is the path to recovery of the graceful human body.

Although it is true that supernatural destiny is ultimately what effects the transformation from pig to human, the stipulation given by the third, evil, fairy is not insignificant. The prince's three courtships and marriages correspond to the refining influence that women, and especially the love for women, are presumed to effect in men, according to a recurrent topos in the literature of civility and courtliness.[17] Of course, the civilizing influence of women is celebrated throughout animal-groom folkloric tale-types (such as "Beauty and the Beast"). In contrast to many of these allied tale-types, however, the pig prince tales by Straparola, Murat, and d'Aulnoy situate the action squarely at court. Even so, they entrust women with the prince's *Bildung,* and exclude male courtiers from any role whatsoever. Thus, women—fairies, mothers, and brides—assume both the more private civilizing role prescribed for them in doctrines of civility and the more public and advisory roles attributed by the literature of courtliness to the male courtier. However one might account for this feature—and particularly tantalizing is the observation by folklorists that animal-groom tales belonged to the repertoire of female storytelling groups[18]—it accentuates the scrutiny all three literary versions devote to the civilizing influence of women upon the prince, masculinity, and the court at large. It puts the focus of all three tales on the extent to which masculinity is formed by differentiation from and/or by imitation of femininity.

The central role the pig prince tales accord to women as agents of the civilizing process can be explained in another way as well. As conceived by patriarchies, women have one foot in nature and the other in culture, so to speak. They have the ability to show men the way into the plenitude of culture, to take men from where they are (nature) to where they are preordained to be (culture). At the same time, their mediating role points to the interdependence, within the logic of civility, of concepts such as nature and culture, the uncivilized and the civilized, the deformed and the refined. At the heart of the tale rewritten by Straparola, Murat, and d'Aulnoy is the notion that civility can be defined only in opposition to its antithesis: nature, the uncivilized, the deformed. Of course, this interdependence has always been well understood by writers of conduct manuals, who describe the benefits of their rules for polite behavior by spelling out the negative consequences of breaking them. But, unlike conduct manuals—and unlike other stories of pigs and humans, such as the Ovidian Adonis myth— the pig prince tales situate this opposition within the same person.[19] Rather than a polarization of refined-versus-unrefined people, of us-versus-them, the three fairy-tale writers describe a hero split between two contradictory principles. Ultimately, the tales attempt to overcome this split, to show how nature is molded into culture, the uncivilized into the civilized, the deformed into the refined. And yet in none of them is such an outcome necessarily a given. Instead, the tensions within these oppositions, which are in fact tensions within the civilizing process, are revealed to be the driving force in masculine subjectivity.

No less uncertain in these tales is the relation between being and appearances, between interior and exterior. Of course, even as they recognize the capacity of civilized appearances to mask an uncivilized being, most theories of civility set as their ideal the harmonious unity of *être* and *paraître.* To varying degrees and in different ways, Straparola, Murat, and d'Aulnoy all suggest that the correlation between being and appearances is far more difficult to achieve than fairy magic would have it. Questioning instead of reasserting the unity of *être* and *paraître,* these fairy tales cast doubt on the epistemological foundations of the civilizing process itself. If appearances are deceiving, these tales invite us to ask, how can we know if nature has indeed been transformed into culture? If the civilizing process is uncertain, what is the essence of masculinity?

Straparola: Feminine Abjection = Masculine Being

Straparola's pig prince is born to Hermésile, wife of King Galiot of England, after she is visited by three fairies. The first promises the queen that she will have "le plus beau fils du monde" [the handsomest lad in the world]; the second, that her son will have "toutes les vertus et gentillesses qui se puissent imaginer" [all the virtues and kindnesses that can be imagined]; but the third warns that her newborn son will be born "tout couvert de poil de porc, avec les contenances et maintien d'un porc, et ne se puisse jamais changer de tel estat s'il ne prend premierement trois femmes" [completely covered with pig hair, with the expressions and bearing of a pig unable ever to change from such a state unless he first takes three wives].[20] In spite of dirtying everything he touches, the pig-child is cherished by both his parents, but especially his mother. Later, he has his mother arrange for him to wed the eldest of an impoverished mother's three daughters. As they retire to bed on their wedding night, the prince kills his bride after overhearing her wish that he were dead. When the prince demands to marry the second daughter, the queen intervenes again, overcoming the king's objections and paying off the mother. Repulsed by the groom, the bride meets with the same end as her older sister. Finally the prince marries the youngest daughter, Meldine, who discovers a happier fate. Contrary to her sisters, she receives him "humainement" [humanely] in the wedding bed; after he licks her face, breasts, stomach, and shoulders, "elle...le caressoit et baisoit, en s'embrasant du tout d'amour" [she caressed and kissed him, burning with love for all of him].[21] After becoming pregnant and giving birth to a "très beau fils" [a very handsome son], Meldine divulges to the king and queen the secret her husband had revealed to her shortly after their wedding: his piglike appearance is nothing other than a skin that he—in reality a "beau jeune fils" [handsome young man]—wears only during the day. The king orders that the skin be destroyed promptly, and then abdicates the throne in favor of his son, "qui fut couronné avecques grand triomphe, et fut appellé le roy Porc" [who was crowned with great triumph and was called the Pig King].[22]

As Straparola conceives it, the pig prince tale is less one of transformation and more one of revelation. Compared to Murat and d'Aulnoy, Straparola makes no significant concessions to the civilizing process, except to state that the prince "fust nourry et entretenu, non point comme beste brute, mais comme animal raisonnable" [was fed and kept not as a wild beast but as a reasonable animal].[23] He is treated like a domesticated animal, implying that only minimal efforts are made to tame his animal instincts. At first, though, he seems to develop simultaneously as both a human and a pig: "Estant ce petit porc creu, commença à former la parolle humaine, et s'en aller par la ville, et se fourroit par les ordures et immondices comme font les autres porcs" [This little pig being grown, he began to form human speech and to go around the city, and rummaged in the garbage and filth as do other pigs].[24] Contrary to these appearances, however, the tale indicates that the prince's being is in fact unambiguously human. The storyteller in Straparola's frame narrative prefaces the tale with a moral of sorts:

Il n'y a au monde, gracieuses Dames, langue tant eloquente et excellente en
bien dire, qui peust assez suffisamment exprimer combien l'homme est tenu
à son createur de l'avoir fait et formé homme en ce monde, et non point
beste brute.[25]

[In all the world, gracious ladies, there is not a tongue eloquent or excellent
enough in beautiful speech that could express sufficiently how much man is
endebted to his creator for making and forming him man in this world, and
not a wild beast.]

Implicit in this moral is the possibility that humans could have been created indistinguishable in appearance from animals. Significantly, the storyteller does not suggest
that humans and animals could have shared the same essence. Rather, the tale imagines the case of a human born in the form of a pig, an aberration of appearances
designed to celebrate the divine wisdom of differentiating among essences by discrete
outward shapes.

At the end of the tale, the prince himself reveals what turns out to be his fundamentally immutable humanity. Shortly after the wedding, he tells Meldine that if she
promises not to reveal it to anyone, he will disclose "une chose que j'ay tenu secrette
jusques à present" [a thing I have kept secret up to the present]. He then takes off his
"puante et orde peau" [stinking and dirty skin], becomes a beautiful young man, and
"couch[e] toute la nuict estroittement entre les bras de sa chère Meldine" [sleeps snugly
all night long in the arms of his dear Meldine].[26] Conspicuously absent from this
account is any explanation of precisely how the prince born a pig is finally able to shed
his skin. (In both Murat's and d'Aulnoy's versions, the fairies intervene to make this
possible.) Instead, the prince implies that he has always been able to do so, and has simply kept it a secret. By his own suggestion, then, the prince has been a human in the
skin of a pig from the very beginning.

The question we might ask at this point is why he chooses to keep his true appearance a secret. To be sure, the third fairy had stipulated that he must remain a pig until
he has married three women. Yet the narrative never refers to this injunction once it has
been uttered, contrary to what happens in both Murat's and d'Aulnoy's tales. Rather
than obeying the evil fairy's command, the prince's secrecy ultimately has more to do
with an imperative of the text itself. In his pig guise, the prince serves as a way for the
narrative to abjectify the maternal, and more generally the feminine.[27] The queen, who
does not hesitate to display her affection and even prevents the king from having the
prince put to death,[28] must tolerate his stench and filth each time she sees him.[29] The
oedipal relation here is obvious. But in a twist of the classic Freudian account, it is the
mother and not the son who is sullied (both literally and figuratively) by these affective
ties. Not only is she the one who is befouled (repeatedly) by the prince, but she is also
the one who defies the king/father by refusing to allow him to kill their son. In the
end, the dirtied, rebellious mother incarnates the rejection of the post-oedipal maternal
that is perpetrated by many (if not most) patriarchal cultures.

When the prince marries for the third time, his wife Meldine assumes the role played until this point by the queen. She patiently—even lovingly—endures his putrid touch, and the comfort she offers him is absolute. In fact, her acceptance of the prince exceeds even the queen's. On the wedding night, as the couple prepare to retire to their bed, Meldine rejects the queen's advice that she try to resist him and, instead, responds with her own words of advice: never look for what is lost, do not believe what is false or unreasonable, hold dear what is rare and precious.[30] Putting these principles into action, Meldine submits to the prince's defiling touch while transforming it into a "rare et precieuse chose" [rare and precious thing].[31] She assumes onto herself an abjectifying sexuality, but a sexuality that nonetheless leaves her content:

> Le matin, la royne s'en alla vers la chambre de l'espousée, et estimant voir ce qu'elle avoit veu des autres et par le passé, trouva sa belle fille toute joyeuse et contente, et combien que le lict fust souillé d'ordures et d'infections.…[32]

> [The next morning, the queen went to the bride's bedroom expecting to see what she had seen of the others in the past. She found her daughter-in-law so joyful and happy and the bed so completely fouled with garbage and vermine.…]

The morning-after scene discovered by the queen encapsulates in striking fashion a patriarchal maxim that Bruno Bettelheim observes (and endorses) as central to all animal-groom folk and fairy tales: "It is mainly the female who needs to change her attitude about sex from rejecting to embracing it, because as long as sex appears to her as ugly and animal-like, it remains animalistic in the male; that is, he is not disenchanted."[33] Meldine seems to have reaped the benefits of just such an attitude adjustment; but the appearance of the bed reminds us that the initial sexual encounter requires the bride to accept the "ugly and the animal-like" nevertheless. Doing so, as we already have seen, she indeed disenchants the prince.

And yet Straparola remains fixated on this initial encounter when he shifts to the frame narrative at the end of the tale:

> La fable d'Isabelle estoit desjà finie quand toute la compagnie se mit à rire de grand appetit de monsieur le porc tout souillé, qui caressoit sa chère épouse, couchant avec elle tout puant qu'il estoit.[34]

> [Isabelle's story was hardly finished when the whole assembly started to laugh heartily at the thought of Mister Pig covered with dirt caressing his dear wife, sleeping with her stinking as much as he did.]

The reception that Straparola imagines for his own tale diverts attention away from product (the demetamorphosed prince) and back to process (the three marriages). This process, however, bears little resemblance to the civilizing process. The prince does not make a conscious change—except to reveal his own well-guarded secret. If, at the end of the tale, he is transformed, it is because Meldine allows her own body to be transfigured by nature, the deformed, and the uncivilized. Paradoxically, women's civilizing influence leaves Meldine uncivilized, even as it allows the prince to reveal the essence of gracefulness that he has always possessed. All appearances to the contrary, so Straparola insinuates, masculinity is anything but a process of self-discovery, self-development, or self-transformation. Rather, it is a matter of self-assertion—at the expense of women and femininity. It is not the product of transforming or eliminating the animal, nature, or the uncivilized, but instead of transferring them onto women.

Murat: Secrets and Doubles

Murat preserves only the barest outline of Straparola's tale, even though she explicitly acknowledges her debt to *Le Piacevoli notte*.[35] She begins much as Straparola does: three fairies endow a barren queen, who gives birth to a pig prince. But then the narrative takes a dramatically different turn. By a secret pact, the queen hides the birth of her son from the king and allows the two good fairies, Bienfaisante and Tranquille, to raise him away from court. From this point on, everything that happens to the prince is controlled by these fairy godmothers. They begin by partially outwitting the third fairy, Rancune: they allow the hero to shed his skin at night, during which all his subsequent adventures occur. Then, unbeknownst to him, they arrange what could only be called two marriages of convenience: he is wedded to two *grisettes* [commoners], both of whom magically disappear immediately after taking their vows. Never once do thoughts of violence enter his or his wives' heads. Finally, they orchestrate an encounter with the captive princess Ondine, with whom the prince immediately falls in love. Bienfaisante then overcomes several obstacles in order to free Ondine and, in the end, reunites the couple with their long lost parents.

Even this brief summary indicates just how much Murat's tale accentuates women's civilizing influence. And yet it is neither the mother nor the third wife but rather the two good fairies who refine the prince. Typical of many of the late-seventeenth-century fairy tales authored by women, the prominent role played by the fairies magnifies feminine authority even as (or perhaps because) it extracts it from the constraints of the family.[36] Of course, Bienfaisante does not entirely escape—but nonetheless reconfigures—familial structures. She acts as a sort of surrogate mother (a role fairies often play in seventeenth-century *contes de fées*) with the full knowledge and consent of the prince's biological mother. At the same time, she supplants or negates paternal authority first by concealing the prince's existence from the king and then by choosing a mate, a future queen, for the heir to the throne. Having the pig prince raised away from his biological parents and under the tutelage of a supernatural parental figure, Murat's tale dissociates the civilizing process from the oedipal drama and infuses it with the aura of fairy magic.

No matter how magical the fairies' parenting may be, the pig prince is still required to learn, to become civilized.

> Lorsqu'il fut dans un âge raisonnable, [Bienfaisante] luy apprit tout ce qu'un Prince doit sçavoir pour joindre l'esprit & la politesse à la grandeur de sa naissance....[37]

> [When he was of the age of reason, (Bienfaisante) taught him all that a prince ought to know so as to add wit and courtesy to the grandeur of his birth....]

What the prince learns ranges from principles of basic hygiene to sociability. He is raised surrounded by impeccable cleanliness, and he is not allowed to eat "les aliments cochoniques" [piggish food].[38] Early on he acquires the ability to speak and soon "ce qui luy faisoit le plus de plaisir étoit la conversation des belles Dames qui composoient la Cour de Bienfaisante" [what gave him the most pleasure was the conversation of the beautiful women who made up Bienfaisante's court].[39] Quickly he realizes the second fairy's gifts of "tendresse" and "galanterie"—not only because he falls in love with the two *grisettes* and then Ondine, but also because he pursues these courtships with the consummate, effortless grace of the *galant homme,* a figure often synonymous with the *honnête homme* in the seventeenth century.[40] It is hardly surprising, then, that the prince scrupulously avoids mention of his enchantment and his pigskin to Ondine.[41] The *bienséances* would scarcely have allowed him to reveal what he himself, with the help of the fairies, conceals so assiduously. By repressing the prince's animalistic body, the fairies also eliminate the need for him to exact any form of violence whatsoever. The civilizing influence leads to the extreme situation where Bienfaisante herself—and not the prince—rescues Ondine from the clutches of the evil fairy Rancune and her protégé King Pactole. Thus, in contrast to the paradoxical ideal of courtly civility according to which men were to be subdued at court and aggressive on the battlefield, the fairies restrict the prince's training to the first aspect and assume the second for themselves. In the end, he incarnates (what many early modern observers denounced as) the thoroughly "feminized" courtier.[42]

Diegesis, however, is only one facet of Murat's commentary on the civilizing process. Throughout "Le Roy Porc" the recurrence of secrets and structures of doubling extend this commentary to a textual and metaphorical level. So doing, this fairy tale highlights problems central to civility and court culture.

Secrecy or dissimulation is a recognized aspect of sociability, especially in court circles. Beneficial when it signifies concealing from public view the unacceptable in whatever form, it is more often perceived as harmful, a tool used to promote duplicity and falsehood. Not unexpectedly, then, writings on civility seek to circumscribe the proper use and control of secrecy and dissimulation. In Murat's tale secrets are similarly ambivalent, depending on who possesses them. The pig prince keeps secrets for reasons of shame or submission. Such is the case when he hides from Bienfaisante his initial encounter with Ondine, which takes place after he accepts an invitation by a magical carp and a dwarf to lead him to a mysterious underwater kingdom. (He is at first unaware that the carp and the dwarf are in fact the fairy's own creatures.) Later, as we have already seen, he conceals from Ondine the story of his enchantment and his pigskin. Both of these secrets stem from a fear of losing respect in the eyes of the women from whom the information is withheld. They are both, then, effects of the civilizing process: the prince has internalized the constraints of submission and shame and keeps for himself knowledge capable of reexternalizing those constraints.

By contrast, Bienfaisante keeps secrets principally to enhance her own power, and especially her own designs for the prince. When she hides news of the prince's birth from the king, the fact of the prince's first two marriages from the queen, and her arrangement of the first encounter with Ondine from the prince, she avoids potential complications of her plans for the prince. These secrets are not motivated by submission or shame, but by a desire to wield her power in the most efficient way possible. Secrecy, for Bienfaisante, is tantamount to power. And this fact is all the more clear when Bienfaisante prepares for the final liberation of Ondine by retiring to a "cabinet secret où étoient renfermez les secrets les plus occultes de l'art de Féerie" [secret study where all the most occult secrets of the art of fairy magic were kept].[43] The secret study filled with secrets of a magical art is a topographical metaphor for the reality of what is at once women's knowledge and their authority in this tale. Women's secret knowledge, so often castigated by moralists, becomes a legitimate and powerful tool for masculine acculturation.

In addition to secrecy, Murat also employs structures of doubling in her metaphorical commentary on civility. A more general conceptual feature than secrecy, doubling is perhaps the most fundamental epistemological and pragmatic mechanism of civility. With it, civility promotes an understanding of the self and of society that is twofold and split. The self is divided into an interior and an exterior, and the doctrines of civility seek to regulate the latter by bringing it into harmony with the former.[44] On a collective level, society, according to many early modern writers, can be divided into private and public spaces, with specific forms of behavior appropriate to each.

"Le Roy Porc" reveals a veritable obsession with doubles, and, not surprisingly, all of these relate to the prince. Most are part of the process by which he becomes the superlative and triumphant king at the end of the tale: he has two sets of mothers (the queen and the fairies); he has two surrogate mothers (the fairies Bienfaisante and Tranquille); Bienfaisante has two of her creatures (the carp and the dwarf) introduce the prince to Ondine; both Bienfaisante and Ondine must assume a second identity (as sparrows) in order to escape Pactole's captivity; and the testimony of two fairies is necessary to convince the king (the prince's father) of his son's existence. At the end of the tale, it is the hero's very identity that is doubled since he is given two different (and competing) names. He is called "Aimantin" by Bienfaisante, in honor of her rescue of his bride Ondine from the evil fairy Rancune's *Tour d'Aimant* [Magnet tower].[45] But a short while later, the prince succeeds his father "au grand plaisir de tous ses sujets, qui ne peûrent jamais l'appeler autrement que le Roy Porc" [to the great pleasure of all his subjects, who could never call him anything other than the Pig King].[46]

The instances of doubling that occur during the prince's quest to rid himself of the pig enchantment all accentuate women's civilizing influence. Highlighting women's (and particularly the fairies') agency, all of them redouble, so to speak, this influence. More significant still is the fact that femininity itself is represented not as single, but rather as multiple. Indeed, this tale seems to demonstrate Luce Irigaray's association of femininity with multiplicity.[47] Women's power does not emanate from a single source (person), but from several. It is not univocal, but polyphonous if not contradictory (for example, the third fairy Rancune works against Bienfaisante and Tranquille). In the end, though, it is not only femininity that is multiple, but masculinity as well. The recurrent instances of doubling throughout the tale produce anything but an autonomous, self-mastering hero. Instead, he is the result of multiple female influences: his upbringing is a collective female effort; his identity is likewise collective and even ambiguous; his first name, Aimantin, casts him as the diminutive celebration of Bienfaisante's exploit on his behalf; his second name, le Roy Porc, in one sense seems to negate, in comic fashion, the two good fairies' efforts to disenchant the hero. In another sense, though, this sobriquet rejects a conception of the prince's upbringing as singular and linear. "Roy Porc" combines both the past (when the hero, as prince, was required to don the pigskin) and the present (when, as king, he is freed from this spell), and suggests if only humorously that the hero's final transformation is neither definitive nor unequivocal. The masculinity evoked by Aimantin/Roy Porc, like the civilizing process that forms him, is a collective and participatory construction that is multifarious but unstable.

D'Aulnoy: Appearances Undone

Of the three pig prince tales, d'Aulnoy's "Le Prince Marcassin" is the longest and offers the most detailed description of the masculine civilizing process. Closer to Straparola's basic plot than Murat's, d'Aulnoy's tale gives extended narrative description, dialogue, and psychological detail. These textual features, typical of d'Aulnoy's corpus, produce characters who are uncharacteristically multifaceted for a fairy tale.[48] Although the hero, the queen, and the three wives are all endowed with a psychological depth absent from Straparola's and Murat's counterparts, it is the pig prince who receives the most detailed narrative attention. What this scrutiny reveals is a hero beset by a conflict between opposing psychological forces, a conflict set into motion by the civilizing process.

Early on, d'Aulnoy's hero is exposed to the physical and intellectual rigors of a royal upbringing. Throughout it, the goal is to repress the degrading animal within him while enhancing his superlative human qualities. The first challenge is to efface his pig-like appearance: he is given specially tailored clothing, he learns to walk on his two back feet, he is whipped each time he snorts, "enfin on lui ôtait autant qu'il était possible les manières marcassines" [in the end his boarish mannerisms were taken away as much as possible][49] and "l'on n'oubliait rien pour le rendre propre & poli" [nothing was neglected to make him clean and refined].[50] He then is instructed in the more properly human arts of dance, music, horseback riding, and hunting, excelling at all of them. In the end, though, this civilizing program is a failure, most of all for the prince himself: "Il ressentait bien amèrement le ridicule de sa figure marcassine, de sorte qu'il évitait de paraître aux grandes assemblées" [He understood only too bitterly how ridiculous his boarish face looked, such that he avoided appearing in large crowds].[51]

No matter how much training he receives, the prince remains neither fully animal nor completely human. His is an excruciatingly ambiguous state. D'Aulnoy's play with onomastics only heightens this ambiguity. "Marcassin" is often used as a proper noun, yet the hero is also called "le marcassin" [young wild boar] and "le sanglier" [wild boar]. Some designations, such as "le marcassin royal" or "son Altesse bestiole," underscore the undecidability of the hero's being: is he the royals' pig or a royal who just happens to be a pig? a beastly Highness or His Highness the beast? Furthermore, the very choice of "marcassin" and "sanglier" rather than "cochon" or "porc" (used by Straparola and Murat) only serves to accentuate the hero's liminality. The terms "marcassin" and "sanglier"—meaning, respectively, young and adult wild boars—situate the prince's animal instincts squarely outside the domesticated and anthropomorphic realms of the "cochon" and the "porc."[52] Lexically—but also psychologically and experientially—d'Aulnoy's hero leads an existence that is conflicted if not tortured.

Not unexpectedly, Prince Marcassin expresses this conflict through aggression and violence. Ideally the civilizing process would provide a mechanism for restraining these impulses. Such, at least, is its fundamental raison d'être. In the case of d'Aulnoy's hero, however, the situation is considerably more complicated. The civilizing process cannot be brought to completion—his penchant for aggression and violence cannot be eradicated—precisely because his animal instincts overlap with his inborn nobility. "[I]l lui venait des défenses terribles, ses soies étaient furieusement hérissées, son regard fier & de commandement absolu." [He grew terrifying horns, his bristles stuck up incredibly, his countenance was proud and commanding in an absolute sort of way].[53] Linked as they are to his naturally dominating (and thus royal) appearance, the prince's animal instincts are ambiguous. Although his behavior would be laudable on a hunt or in battle, Marcassin commits what is unacceptable at court—overt aggression against his wives. He pushes his first wife, Ismène, to suicide by insisting on marrying her even though she had been promised (by the queen, no less!) to another man. Almost immediately thereafter, he pursues Ismène's sister, Zélonide, whom he stabs to death with his horns when she attempts to strangle him. Finally, having renounced his human existence to lead the life of a *sanglier* in the forest, Marcassin discovers and falls in love with the third sister, Marthésie. Quickly, he breaks his promise to let her come and go as she pleases and holds her captive until she accepts to marry him. Explaining his actions to her, Marcassin invokes his monstrous hybridity, but attributes his faults to his human side:

> Il faut bien…qu'il y ait un peu de l'homme mêlé avec le sanglier. Ce défaut de parole que vous me reprochez, cette petite finesse où je ménage mes intérêts, c'est justement l'homme qui agit: car à vous parler sans façon, les animaux ont plus d'honneur entre eux que les hommes….[54]

[There must be a little bit of man mixed with the boar. The broken promise that you criticize me for, the subtle ruse by which I look out for my own interests are precisely the man at work. Let me tell you plainly: animals have more honor amongst themselves than men.]

Having fled the court and purporting to despise his humanity, the Marcassin who plays the role of the wild boar in the forest distances himself from the civilizing process. At the same time, however, he pursues Marthésie and, by extension, the civilizing effects of her love. Through this contradictory stance, Marcassin reproduces the text's own ambivalence toward the influence of women. Neither abjectified as in Straparola's rendition nor wholeheartedly celebrated as in Murat's, all of the women in d'Aulnoy's tale play a crucial yet ambiguous role in the prince's development. The fairies, to begin with, are more prominent than in Straparola's "fable," but less so than in Murat's *conte de fées*. They are transcendent, omnipotent beings who are nonetheless aloof, even mysterious for the mortals of d'Aulnoy's tale (for example, the third fairy's spell is not even revealed until the very end of the tale).[55] Only in the dénouement do they reappear to work the prince's final disenchantment. The nitty-gritty work of Marcassin's upbringing is left to his mother and, of course, his third wife, Marthésie.

Like Straparola, d'Aulnoy makes the queen a profoundly ambivalent figure. Even more so than Straparola's Hermésile, though, this mother wavers between restraining and acquiescing to the prince's animal urges. When he first asks her permission to marry Ismène, the queen throws up strong resistance, arguing that no one would want him, that his children would be deformed, that Ismène is of low birth, and that he should not marry any woman against her will.[56] But in the end, she gives up and arranges the marriage with the help of Ismène's greedy mother. It is doubtless possible to read this ambivalence as a reflection of the transitional oedipal relation between mother and son, a relation that is implicit in the very word "marcassin," designating a young wild boar that has not yet left its mother. Ultimately—and unlike Straparola's depiction of the mother-son bond—it is the prince and not the queen who is made to feel the effects of this transgressive bond. Profiting from his mother's weakness, he becomes even more deeply torn between his animal and human selves, and even more subject to antithetical psychological impulses. Finding Ismène's body, for instance,

> il pensa mourir de tristesse & de rage; ses sentiments, confondus entre l'amour et la haine, le tourmentaient tour à tour.[57]

> [he thought he would die of sadness and rage; his feelings, somewhere between love and hate, tormented him one after the other.]

Shortly thereafter, of course, Marcassin sets his sights on Zélonide, and the queen once again vigorously contests her son's plans. Although she eventually drops her resistance, it is only after she reminds him once again of his monstrous appearance: "Es-tu plus aimable que tu n'étais, moins sanglier, moins affreux?" [Are you any more handsome than you were before, less a boar, less hideous?],[58] she asks him. In the same conversation, she defends an ideal of courtly behavior that will profoundly impact the prince later on. Responding to her son's claim that everyone at court praises him, the queen reiterates the conventional criticism of courtiers' flattery, asking: "Comment connaître ses défauts dans un tel labyrinthe?" [How can one know one's faults in such a labyrinth?][59] Marcassin retorts that no one enjoys hearing one's faults exposed and that he is in fact grateful "à ceux qui adoucissent là-dessus ma peine, qui me font des mensonges favorables & qui me cachent les défauts que vous êtes si soigneuse de me découvrir" [to those who soften my pain, who tell me soothing lies and who hide the faults that you are so careful to uncover in me].[60] To this, the queen adopts a moralist stance and exclaims, sarcastically:

> Ô source d'amour-propre … de quelque côté qu'on jette les yeux, on te trouve toujours. Oui, mon fils, vous êtes beau, vous êtes joli, je vous conseille encore de donner pension à ceux qui vous en assurent.[61]

> [O source of self-pride … wherever one looks you are always there. Yes, my son, you are handsome, you are good-looking, and, further, I advise you to pay wages to those who tell you so.]

The queen, then, attacks dissimulation and insists on absolute honesty and transparency. In her view, one's inner self-image must match the reality of one's outer persona, and ugliness must be assumed for what it is. In opposition to the queen's doctrine of authenticity (a doctrine that was increasingly prevalent in late-seventeenth-century France), Marcassin endorses a variant of the (earlier-seventeenth-century) notion of "honnête dissimulation," an attempt to transform deceiving appearances into a pleasing truth.[62] He is only too happy to entertain the deceptive self-image created by the flatterers at court, even if he remains conscious of his real appearance.[63]

After the debacle of his marriage to Zélonide, however, the prince adopts his mother's advice, pushing it to its farthest logical extreme. Not only does he accept his own outward animal likeness, he also rejects court life—and the civility upon which it is based—in terms worthy of a La Bruyère.[64] Speaking to a confidant, he declares:

> Je veux abandonner la cour, j'irai au fond des forêts mener la vie qui convient à un sanglier de bien & d'honneur, je ne ferai plus l'homme galant, je ne trouverai point d'animaux qui me reprochent d'être plus laid qu'eux…. Je vivrai plus tranquillement avec eux que je ne vis dans une cour destinée à m'obéir, & je n'aurai point le malheur d'épouser une laie qui se poignarde ou qui me veuille étrangler.[65]

> [I want to leave the court; I will go to the depths of the forest to lead the life of a good and honorable boar; I will not play the perfect gentleman anymore; I will not find animals that criticize me for being uglier than they are…. I will live more tranquilly with them than I have lived in a court destined to obey

me, and I will not have the bad fortune to marry a sow who will stab me or who wants to strangle me.]

Repudiating the animalistic behavior of the (purportedly) fully human members of court, Marcassin hopes to resolve his own ambiguous state by becoming fully animal. This, however, is never quite possible. One day he encounters Marthésie in the forest, immediately declares his love, and insists that he has seen the error of his past ways:

J'ai appris, depuis que je suis habitant de ces forêts, que rien au monde ne doit être plus libre que le cœur; je vois que tous les animaux sont heureux, parce qu'ils ne se contraignent point.[66]

[Since becoming an inhabitant of these forests, I've learned that the heart must be freer than anything in the world. I see that all the animals are happy because they are not bound by constraints.]

Equating freedom with happiness, Marcassin claims to offer Marthésie the choice of whether or not to marry him. But this proposal is simultaneously a rejection of the constraints inherent in the civilizing process. Animals are happy, so he claims, "because they are not bound by constraints." Free from the demands of civility, he too can strive for happiness.

In the brief courtship that ensues, Marthésie defends an opposing perspective on civility. Shocked to find the prince "dans un état si peu convenable à [sa] naissance" [in a state so unsuited to (his) birth], she implores him to return to court.[67] And initially, it is on this condition that she agrees to marry him, expressing disgust at the idea of having only lizards and snails for company and leaving behind all her clothes, ribbons, lace, and jewelry. Marcassin, to the contrary, sees no benefit in sociability and rejects cultivated appearances, asserting:

Quand on a de l'esprit & de la raison, ne peut-on pas se mettre au-dessus de ces petits ajustements? Croyez-moi, Marthésie, ils n'ajouteront rien à votre beauté & je suis certain qu'ils en terniront l'éclat.[68]

[If one is witty and reasonable, cannot one do without those petty adornments? Believe me, Marthésie, they will add nothing to your beauty, and I'm certain that they will dull its splendor.]

Having renounced the pleasures of outward appearances, Marcassin is content to live on *esprit* and *raison*.

Marthésie, however, is not pleased with this conclusion, and continues to insist that they return to court. When the prince then protests that she is driven not by love but by ambition, she diagnoses what she takes to be the cause of his rejection of court (and, at least implicitly, civility), declaring: "Vous avez une disposition naturelle...à juger mal de tout notre sexe" [You have a natural predisposition to misjudge our entire sex].[69]

Misapprehending women, Marcassin cannot hope to form a happy marriage. Even further, through Marthésie, the text insinuates that if he were to accept women's judgment—as the civilizing process requires—he would see the value of court life and his own place within it. When, of her own free will, Marthésie returns to see Marcassin a second time, he seems to have taken her advice to heart, displaying "naturally" refined behavior:

> Dès qu'il l'aperçut, il courut au-devant d'elle &, s'humiliant à ses pieds il lui fit connaître que les sangliers ont, quand ils veulent, des manières de saluer fort galantes.[70]

> [As soon as he saw her, he ran toward her and, bowing at her feet, he showed her that, when they want to, boars can have very polite ways of greeting people.]

As early modern civility prescribes, politeness flows effortlessly from Marcassin when he submits to a woman, and especially to a woman he loves. When he does, even the animal within him can be humanlike, or so the narrator comically suggests. In this instant, the prince's perspective on civility begins to shift: from isolating, solipsistic authenticity he gradually, almost imperceptibly, progresses to intersubjective and sociable sincerity.

Yet just as Marcassin's demetamorphosis comes into view—just as he seems to dominate his violent impulses once and for all—d'Aulnoy's tale introduces an element of skepticism about the consequences of women's civilizing influence on men. At the crucial moment when Marthésie must choose whether or not to marry him, Marcassin, unlike either Straparola's or Murat's heroes, commits one final act of aggression. Reneging on his promise to allow her to choose freely, he holds her captive against her will. After protesting loudly, though, Marthésie inexplicably relents:

> Elle redoubla ses pleurs & ses prières, il n'en fut point touché, &, après avoir encore contesté longtemps, elle consentit à le recevoir pour époux & l'assura qu'elle l'aimerait aussi chèrement que s'il était le plus aimable prince du monde.[71]

> [She redoubled her tears and her prayers; he was unmoved. And, after protesting for a long time, she consented to receive him as her husband and assured him that she would love him as dearly as if he were the most handsome prince in the world.]

Represented with the incongruous conjunction *and,* Marthésie's change of heart in this scene is all the more jarring since, up until this point, she has proven to be a fiercely independent and distinctly unsubmissive heroine. What this incongruity suggests, I would argue, is a certain distance from the time-honored topos of women's civilizing influence. Men's violence may not be completely eliminated by contact with women, who may actually suffer when they take on the task of civilizing men.

This, however, is not d'Aulnoy's final word on the matter. During the improvised ceremony and, especially, the wedding bed scene, d'Aulnoy's tale seems to adopt the vision of the animal-groom tale-type formulated by Bettelheim. Once Marthésie consents to stay, Marcassin shows nothing but devoted affection for his bride-to-be. And, putting aside her misgivings, she returns the favor: after a pastoral wedding feast, she makes a bed of moss, grass, and flowers. As they lie down, "elle eut grand soin de lui demander s'il voulait avoir la tête haute ou basse, s'il avait assez de place, de quel côté il dormait le mieux" [she was very careful to ask him if he wanted his head higher or lower, if he had enough room, and which side he slept best on].[72] Erotically allusive, Marthésie's affection for her groom is one more instance in which she submits to Marcassin—even if the topos of women's civilizing influence would seem to suggest the contrary. In accordance with the classic structure of the animal-groom tale-type, though, Marthésie reaps the rewards for her submission. In the middle of the night, when she awakes, she finds not a boar, but a man.

And yet, all of these details do not make d'Aulnoy's *conte de fées* an unequivocal endorsement of female submission through the motif of the animal-groom. Rather, the *conteuse* gestures toward a certain reciprocity between the spouses, especially by emphasizing the bride's contentment. Thus, in contrast to Straparola's Meldine, who must endure her husband's stench and filth, Marthésie awakens on her wedding night to find that "son lit était meilleur que lorsqu'elle s'y était mise" [her bed was better than when she got into it].[73] Even before they fall asleep, though, the couple engage in pillow talk suggestive of mutual satisfaction:

> Le bon Marcassin…s'écriait de temps en temps: "Je ne changerais pas mon sort avec celuy des plus grands hommes; j'ai enfin trouvé ce que je cherchais, je suis aimé de celle que j'aime." Il lui dit cent jolies choses, dont elle ne fut point surprise, car il avait de l'esprit, mais elle ne laissa pas de se réjouir que la solitude où il vivait n'en eût rien diminué.[74]

> [The good Marcassin…exclaimed from time to time: "I would not trade my destiny with even the greatest of men; I've finally found what I was looking for: I'm loved by the woman I love." He told her a hundred little niceties, which did not surprise her at all since he had a gift for conversation; but she was nonetheless very pleased that the solitude in which he lived had not changed him.]

Beyond a description of reciprocal wedded bliss, this scene resolves the bride's and the groom's opposing conceptions of civility. Marthésie recognizes that the court is not the essential sine qua non for sociable pleasures. For his part, Marcassin seems finally to have acquired the art of pleasing women with his intuitive *esprit*. Marthésie has learned that refinement is not exclusively bound to space (the court), and Marcassin has demonstrated he possesses that quality so necessary to please others, notably at court. More precisely—and paradoxically—by relinquishing her attachment to the court, Marthésie lays the groundwork for the flowering of Marcassin's *esprit* and paves the way for his return to court. Together, then, the couple constructs an ideal of courtly masculinity that eschews flattery and self-deception and lays claim instead to the refinement of the natural and the authentic. They retreat to the pastoral idyl of the forest and the cave all the better to return to the court having reinvented royal masculinity.[75] But they do so, the tale is careful to point out, at considerable cost to Marthésie, who must endure six months of marriage to the royal boar, isolation in his cave, and separation from her mother.[76] Even in a fairy tale, women's civilizing influence is hardly magical. Instead, it exacts a toll on the very agents who exert it.

Adding one final twist to an already complicated plot, the end of this tale develops further still this ambivalence toward civility. Rather than clearly resolve the tensions between being and appearances, rather than definitively transform nature into culture and animal into human, d'Aulnoy's dénouement and final moral are at best inconclusive. Marcassin's final demetamorphosis is, in fact, more of a triumph for the fairies and their magic than for the hero. Absent during most of the tale, the prince's fairy godmothers reappear just before he marries Marthésie in order to explain that he will now be able to remove his pigskin at night, but that he must conceal this from her until further notice. When, six months after their wedding, Marthésie happens upon the pigskin in the middle of the night, he reveals the fairies' secret to her. He then attempts to don the pigskin, only to discover that it has shrunk so much that he can no longer wear it. As he despairs, six distaffs—three black and three white—come crashing through the ceiling of the cave.[77] A mysterious voice then tells the couple that they will be happy if they interpret correctly what the distaffs represent. Marcassin guesses, correctly, that the three white distaffs are the three fairies, and Marthésie that the three black ones are her two sisters and Corydon (the fiancé who committed suicide along with Ismène). At that very instant, the three white distaffs become the three fairies, and the three black ones transform into Ismène, Corydon, and Zélonide. When Marcassin expresses his surprise at this mass resurrection, the fairies explain that they were not dead at all and that:

> "…vos yeux ont été la dupe de nos soins. Tous les jours, ces sortes d'aventures arrivent. Tel croit sa femme au bal, quand elle est endormie dans son lit, tel croit avoir une belle maîtresse, qui n'a qu'une guenuche, & tel croit avoir tué son ennemi, qui se porte bien dans un autre pays."

> "Vous m'allez jeter dans d'étranges doutes," dit le prince Marcassin: "il semble à vous entendre qu'il ne faut pas même croire ce qu'on voit."

> "La règle n'est pas toujours générale," répliquèrent les fées, "mais il est indubitable que l'on doit suspendre son jugement sur bien des choses, & penser qu'il peut entrer quelque dose de féerie dans ce qui nous paraît de plus certain."[78]

> ["… your spellbound eyes have been duped by our efforts. These sorts of adventures occur every day. One man thinks his wife is at the ball when she is asleep in her bed. Another man thinks he has a beautiful mistress when he only has an ugly hag. Still another thinks he has killed his enemy who is actually alive and well in another country."]

"You're going to make me have strange doubts," said Prince Marcassin. "Listening to you it seems that we should not even believe what we see."

"The rule is not always true," replied the fairies, "but it is certainly true that people must suspend their judgment about many things and realize that a small dose of fairy magic can enter into even the things that appear to us to be absolutely certain."]

The advice the fairies give in this dénouement is, if anything, ambiguous. Ostensibly demonstrating that the six distaffs, not unlike the prince's former likeness as a boar, were but deceptive appearances, their "rule" can also be applied to Marcassin's newly found human form. Neither the animal nor the human are all they seem at face value, and the prince himself recognizes this long before the end of the tale. When he uncovers his second wife's plot to kill him, for instance, he despairs:

"Est-il possible…qu'une personne si jeune & si belle soit si méchante?… Je suis homme sous la figure d'une bête, combien y a-t-il de bêtes sous la figure d'un homme? Cette Zélonide que je trouvais si charmante, n'est-elle pas elle-même une tigresse & une lionne? Ah! que l'on doit peu se fier aux apparences!"[79]

["Is it possible…that someone so young and beautiful can be so nasty?… I am a man in the form of a beast, how many beasts are there in the form of a man? Isn't the Zélonide I found so charming actually a tigress and a lioness? Ah! how untrustworthy appearances are!"]

Marcassin, too, recognizes the unreliability of appearances—as well he should, we might say. But the fairies go beyond his observation to advocate an exegesis of implausibility, an interpretive outlook based not on the plausible, the real, and the human, but their opposites, a perspective that admits the "dose de féerie" in even the most "certain" of things. To illustrate their point, the fairies cite examples of men deceived by appearances. What husbands, lovers, and soldiers think they know about their wives, mistresses, and enemies may in fact be false. Without the aid of the transcendent feminine power of fairy magic, so the tale jokingly tells us, masculine knowledge—particularly about women (wives and mistresses)—stands on shaky epistemological ground. Ultimately, the fairies seem to invite us to ask whether Marcassin is one of these men and whether what we think we know about him is indeed the case.

What is implicit in the fairies' pronouncement is made explicit in the final moral:

Le plus grand effort de courage,	[The most courageous effort,
Lorsque l'on est bien amoureux,	When one is really in love,
Est de pouvoir cacher à l'objet de ses vœux	Is to be able to hide from the object of one's desires
Ce qu'à dissimuler le devoir nous engage:	What duty requires us to conceal:

Marcassin sut par là mériter l'avantage	Marcassin was able in that way to deserve the privilege
De rentrer triomphant dans une auguste cour.	Of returning triumphant to an august court.
Qu'on blâme, j'y consens, sa trop faible tendresse,	One might, I concede, blame his insufficient tenderness,
Il vaut mieux manquer à l'amour,	It is better to commit a fault against love,
Que de manquer à la sagesse.[80]	Than to commit a fault against wisdom.]

What at first sight is a gesture to generalize from Marcassin's example—a movement away from his particularity—is simultaneously a return to and an interrogation of it. The beginning of the moral announces an abstract lesson about the traditional dichotomy of love versus duty and lauds the hero's supposed courage. It transforms the prince into a self-sufficient hero and obscures the fairies', his mother's, and his wife's role in his demetamorphosis. Yet the moral also invites a critical reflection on this ostensible lesson. The reference to the prince's dissimulation has comical erotic overtones: although he hides his pigskin from Marthésie, he certainly does not hide his human form from her at night in bed! An allusion to courage and duty appears to be even more off the mark when the moral admits that Marcassin's "tendresse" was "trop faible." To describe his violent treatment of the first two sisters as "tenderness" is, of course, blatantly ironic. Using a term from the courtly amorous lexicon only encourages readers to reconsider the prince's uncourtly conduct all the more. By respecting the *bienséances* and thus distancing itself from the hero's physical reality, the moral, paradoxically, accentuates his monstrous animality.

In the end, the moral only reinforces the skepticism of the entire tale toward the civilizing process. The prospects for masculine acculturation remain uncertain at best. D'Aulnoy counters Murat's utopian vision of feminine power and influence with a dystopic humor that undercuts civility's faith in appearances and, even further, the late-seventeenth-century valorization of sincerity for individuals and groups alike. Since d'Aulnoy's *conte de fées* implies that Marcassin's superlative human state can never be verified, it even invites readers to question the exemplarity of royal masculinity and, if only implicitly, nobles' purported advantage in the civilizing process. The intervention of fairies, the queen, and Marthésie notwithstanding, the pig coexists with the prince, and nothing, seemingly, will ever be able to suppress it completely.

🐖 🐖 🐖

"Men are pigs." In contemporary usage, this aphorism assumes a finality that Straparola, Murat, and d'Aulnoy would certainly reject. By imagining that a man could literally be a pig, they attempt to show how he can become a man. To be sure, the three writers diverge considerably in their descriptions of that process. Straparola insinuates that his hero is always already a man waiting for a woman to assume her rightful submissive place beneath him so that he can assert his dominance. By contrast, both Murat and d'Aulnoy confront, head on, the civilizing process and its impact on royal masculinity. Murat, of course, is considerably more sanguine than d'Aulnoy about the final outcome of the pig prince's acculturation. Where "Le Roy Porc" envisions a masculinity that is a collective, feminine effort but that eschews the stability of linear progress, d'Aulnoy questions the very possibility of a civilized masculinity. Nonetheless, for all their differences, both *conteuses* reveal uncertainties within the masculine civilizing process. Both highlight the epistemological difficulty of ascertaining its final product—Murat by having the hero's subjects nickname him "Roy Porc" and d'Aulnoy by having the fairies insist on the deceptiveness of appearances. Both also attempt to revise the *topos* of women's civilizing influence. If d'Aulnoy's skepticism about this influence is blatant, Murat's hyperbolically celebratory treatment suggests a compensatory move on her part. Women's refining impact on men is not nearly as straightforward as civility treatises would have it, or so they both seem to suggest. At a time when the sacrality of royal authority was waning, when this authority was increasingly decentered and competing with other poles of cultural power, and when the French courtier ideal was evolving toward a "flat" hierarchy (without a Christian or Platonic "beyond"), Murat and d'Aulnoy bear witness to the need to reconceive masculine subjectivity.[81] Making the prince a pig, stripping the prince of his outward humanity, is itself a reflection on how all men, in late-seventeenth-century France but also at the beginning of a new millennium, might go about assuming for themselves the dictates of culture and the civilizing process. Pig or prince? The answer for us today is obviously neither. But the question is still part of the search for an alternative that neither Murat nor d'Aulnoy offers.[82]

Notes

1. "What a monster is the great lord who has no civility," from Antoine de Courtin, *Nouveau traité de la civilité qui se pratique en France parmi les honnêtes gens,* (n.p., 1702).
2. Although there is considerable theoretical overlap between them, the "Christian moralist" strain, especially as defined by Erasmus's *De civilitate morum puerilium,* was addressed to a much broader audience than the courtly civility in the tradition of Castiglione's *Il Libro del Cortegiano.* For over-views of the reception of civility in early modern France, see Maurice Magendie, *La Politesse mon-daine et les théories de l'honnêteté en France au XVIIe siècle, de 1600 à 1660,* 2 vols. (Paris: Félix Alcan, 1925); Pauline M. Smith, *The Anti-Courtier Trend in Sixteenth-Century French Literature* (Geneva: Droz, 1966); Roger Chartier, "Distinction et divulgation: La civilité et ses livres," in *Lectu-res et lecteurs dans la France d'Ancien Régime* (Paris: Seuil, 1987), 45–86; Jacques Revel, "The Uses of Civility," in *A History of Private Life: Passions of the Renaissance,* ed. Georges Duby and Philippe Ariès, trans. Arthur Goldhammer (Cambridge: Harvard University Press, 1989), 167–205; and Emmanuel Bury, *Littérature et politesse: L'invention de l'honnête homme, 1580–1750* (Paris: Presses universitaires de France, 1996).
3. See esp. Magendie, *La Politesse mondaine,* and Bury, *Littérature et politesse.* See also Rolf Rei-chardt, "Der Honnête homme zwischen höfischer und bürgerlicher Gesellschaft: Seriell-begriffsge-schichtliche Untersuchungen von Honnêteté-Traktaten des 17. und 18. Jahrhunderts," *Archiv für Kulturgeschichte* 69 (1987): 341–70.
4. Norbert Elias's influential account of the "civilizing process" describes the gradual suppression, from the Middle Ages through the nineteenth century, of outward manifestations of interpersonal aggression. In Elias's theory, these manifestations are controlled/repressed by increasingly powerful internal constraints; see Norbert Elias, *The Civilizing Process: The History of Manners and State For-mation and Civilization,* trans. Edmund Jephcott (Cambridge: Blackwell, 1994).
5. See esp. Carolyn C. Lougee, *Le Paradis des femmes: Women, Salons, and Social Stratification in Sev-enteenth-Century France* (Princeton: Princeton University Press, 1976); Ian Maclean, *Woman Trium-phant: Feminism in French Literature, 1610–1652* (Oxford: Clarendon Press, 1977); and Linda Timmermans, *L'Accès des femmes à la culture (1598–1715): Un débat d'idées de Saint François de Sales à la Marquise de Lambert* (Paris: Champion, 1993).
6. This disparity should not surprise us if we recall that public space was unequivocally gendered mas-culine. It was men above all who needed advice on how to succeed professionally and socially, even if women were not excluded from public.
7. Although originally published in 1671, Courtin's treatise was substantially augmented in successive editions (1672, 1679, and 1702). The chapter "De la bienséance que doivent garder les personnes supérieures à l'égard des inférieures" (to which I refer here) originally appeared in 1672. See Marie-Claire Grassi, introduction, in Antoine de Courtin, *Nouveau traité de la civilité qui se pratique en France parmi les honnêtes gens,* ed. Marie-Claire Grassi (1671–1702; reprint, Saint-Etienne: Publica-tions de l'Université de Saint-Etienne, 1998), 23.
8. Courtin, *Nouveau traité de la civilité,* 191.
9. See Orest Ranum, "Courtesy, Absolutism, and the Rise of the French State, 1630–1660," *Journal of Modern History* 52 (1980): 426–51, and Robert Muchembled, *La Société policée: Politique et poli-tesse du XVIe au XXe siècle* (Paris: Seuil, 1998), 132, 136.
10. Of course, seventeenth-century kings sometimes fell short of the ideal they themselves were pre-sumed to uphold. For instance, the coarseness of Henri IV and his court is traditionally cited as an important impetus to the creation of the salons (and particularly of Mme de Rambouillet's *chambre bleue*); and his son, Louis XIII, was known to be of anything but a sociable nature. However, official propaganda prevented such shortcomings from tainting the collective imagery. By the time of the Sun King, when the royal propaganda machine was functioning at its well-oiled best, the king him-self was by most accounts the exemplar and enforcer of social grace, decorum, and the *préséances.* If anything, it was his dogged attachment to these codes—and not breaches of them—that was draw-ing criticism, especially as his reign wore on.

11. Well over one hundred literary fairy tales (*contes de fées*) by sixteen different authors were published in France between 1690 and 1715. Studies of this vogue include: Mary Elizabeth Storer, *Un Episode littéraire de la fin du XVIIe siècle: La Mode des contes de fées (1685–1700)* (Geneva: Slatkine Reprints, 1972); Jacques Barchilon, *Le Conte merveilleux français de 1690 à 1790: Cent ans de féerie et de poésie ignorées de l'histoire littéraire* (Paris: Champion, 1975); Raymonde Robert, *Le Conte de fées littéraire en France de la fin du XVIIe siècle à la fin du XVIIIe siècle* (Nancy: Presses universitaires de Nancy, 1982); Lewis C. Seifert, *Fairy Tales, Sexuality, and Gender in France, 1690–1715: Nostalgic Utopias*, Cambridge Studies in French, 55 (Cambridge: Cambridge University Press, 1996); and Patricia Hannon, *Fabulous Identities: Women's Fairy Tales in Seventeenth-Century France*, Faux Titre 151 (Atlanta: Rodopi, 1998).

12. Henriette-Julie de Castelnau, comtesse de Murat, "Le Roy Porc" in *Histoires sublimes et allégoriques par Mme la comtesse D***, dédiées aux fées modernes* (Paris: J. et P. Delaulme, 1699), 1-65.

13. Marie-Catherine Le Jumel de Barneville, baronne, "Le Prince Marcassin" in *Contes*, eds. Jacques Barchilon and Philippe Hourcade, 1697-1698, 2 vols. (Paris: Société des Textes Francais Modernes, 1997-98) 2:429-98

14. Scholars agree that Murat's and d'Aulnoy's tales rewrite Straparola's literary version rather than the corresponding folkloric tale-type AT433 (The Prince as Serpent), which is only rarely found in the French folkloric tradition. See Robert, *Le Conte de fées littéraire*, 132, and Paul Delarue and Marie-Louise Tenèze, *Le Conte populaire français: Un catalogue raisonné des versions de France et des pays de langue française et d'Outre-mer*, 4 vols. (Paris: Maisonneuve et Larose, 1976), 2:117–18. Since it was the version available to the *conteuses*, I refer to the 1585 French translation of Straparola's text by Jean Louveau and Pierre de Larivey (republished in Lyon, 1595, 1601, 1611, and 1615).

15. Reichardt, "Der Honnête homme," 366; Muchembled, *La Société policée*, 168.

16. See Jorge Arditi, *A Genealogy of Manners: Transformations of Social Relations in France and England from the Fourteenth to the Eighteenth Century* (Chicago: University of Chicago Press, 1998), 101–2.

17. Perhaps the most influential version of this topos is found in books 3 and 4 of Castiglione's *Cortegiano*.

18. See Betsy Gould Hearne, *Beauty and the Beast: Visions and Revisions of an Old Tale* (Chicago: University of Chicago Press, 1989).

19. Ovid's rendition of the Adonis myth recounts how the hero is killed by a boar, in spite of Venus's warning that he beware of wild beasts in the forest. La Fontaine wrote a well-known poem of this myth, *Adonis* (1668).

20. Straparola, *Le Piacevoli notte*, 92.

21. Straparola, *Le Piacevoli notte*, 99.

22. Straparola, *Le Piacevoli notte*, 101.

23. Straparola, *Le Piacevoli notte*, 93.

24. Straparola, *Le Piacevoli notte*, 93.

25. Straparola, *Le Piacevoli notte*, 91.

26. Straparola, *Le Piacevoli notte*, 99.

27. The terms "abject" and "abjection" are introduced and explained in "Approche de l'abjection," Julia Kristeva, *Les Pouvoirs de l'horreur* (Paris: Seuil, 1980), 9-39.

28. The queen's affection is obvious in Straparola, *Le Piacevoli notte*, 93:

> Ce petit enfant, estant nourry en toute diligence, venoit souvente-fois vers la mère, et se levant sur deux pattes, luy mettoit le petit groin en son giron, et les petites pattes sur ses genoux. Et la bonne mère ne laissoit pas de le caresser en luy mettant les mains sur sa peau pelue, et le baisoit et embrassoit tout ainsi qu'une creature humaine.
>
> [This little child, being raised so diligently, often came to his mother and raising himself on his two feet, put his snout in her bosom and his two front feet on her lap. And the good mother did not fail to caress him running her hands across his hairy skin, and hugged and kissed him just as if he were a human being.]

After the murder of his first wife, the prince implores his mother to allow him to marry the second sister. When the queen consults the king,

> il respondit qu'il vaudroit mieux le faire mourir, de peur qu'il n'advint pour son regard quelque grand inconvenient en la ville; mais la mère, qui luy portoit grande affection, ne pouvoit endurer d'estre privée de luy, nonobstant qu'il fust porc. (Straparola, *Le Piacevoli notte,* 96)
>
> [He answered that it would be better to have him killed for fear that some disadvantage might arise against him in the city. But the mother, who had a great affection for him, could not bear to be deprived of him, even if he was a pig.]

29. Straparola, *Le Piacevoli notte,* 94: "Un jour entre les autres, s'en venant au logis ord et sale comme de coustume, se mit ainsi sur les vestemens de sa mère...." [One day among others, coming into the house filthy dirty as usual, he jumped onto his mother's clothes...]; "Le cochon, estant de retour au logis, tout souillé, courut versa mère..." [The pig, having returned home, completely filthy, ran toward his mother....]

30. Straparola, *Le Piacevoli notte,* 98.
31. Straparola, *Le Piacevoli notte,* 99.
32. Straparola, *Le Piacevoli notte,* 93.
33. Bruno Bettelheim, *The Uses of Enchantment: The Meaning and Importance of Fairy Tales* (New York: Vintage Books, 1977), 286.
34. Straparola, *Le Piacevoli notte,* 101.
35. In the *Avertissement* to Murat's *Histoires sublimes et allégoriques,* she states: "Je suis bien aise d'avertir le Lecteur...que j'ai pris les idées de quelques-uns de ces Contes dans un Auteur ancien intitulé, *les Facecieuses nuits du Seigneur Straparole,* imprimé pour la seiziéme fois en 1615" (n.p.) [I am happy to inform the reader...that I took the idea for several of these tales from an ancient author entitled, *The Facetious Nights of Lord Straparola,* printed for the sixteenth time in 1615].
36. See Seifert, *Fairy Tales, Sexuality, and Gender,* 196–98. See also the stimulating discussion in Anne Defrance, *Les Contes de fées et les nouvelles de Madame d'Aulnoy (1690–1698): L'Imaginaire féminin à rebours de la tradition* (Geneva: Droz, 1998), 95–113.
37. Murat, "Le Roy Porc," 9–10.
38. Murat, "Le Roy Porc," 34.
39. Murat, "Le Roy Porc," 11.
40. See Alain Viala, "La Littérature galante: Histoire et problématique," in *Il Seicento francese oggi: Situazione e prospettive della ricerca,* Quaderni del Seicento Francese, 11 (Paris: Nizet, 1994), 101–13.
41. Murat, "Le Roy Porc," 43–44: "Le Prince luy fit aussi connoître la puissante protection de la Fée qui avoit toujours eu soin de luy depuis sa naissance, dont il ne luy parla qu'en bons termes, & sans luy reveler le secret de la peau de cochon" [The prince also told her about the powerful protection of the fairy who had always taken care of him since his birth, of whom he only spoke in good terms, and without revealing to her the secret of his pigskin].
42. The effeminate courtier was a prominent figure of anticourtier literature, beginning especially in the 1550s. See Smith, *The Anti-Courtier Trend,* 83–86, 99, 108–10, 121–23, 141, 188–90. On the "softening" of the masculine courtier ideal in the seventeenth and eighteenth centuries, see Muchembled, *La Société policée,* 154–68.
43. Murat, "Le Roy Porc," 54.
44. See Jean-Jacques Courtine and Claudine Haroche, *Histoire du visage: Exprimer et taire ses émotions, XVIe–début XIXe siècle* (Paris: Rivages, 1988).
45. Murat, "Le Roy Porc," 63.
46. Murat, "Le Roy Porc," 65.
47. Luce Irigaray, *Ce sexe qui n'en est pas un* (Paris: Editions de Minuit, 1977).
48. Fairy-tale characters are often described as being one-dimensional; see, for instance, Max Lüthi, *Once upon a Time: On the Nature of Fairy Tales,* trans. Lee Chadeayne and Paul Gottwald (Bloomington: Indiana University Press, 1976), 24, 51.

49. D'Aulnoy, "Le Prince Marcassin," 433.

50. D'Aulnoy, "Le Prince Marcassin," 435.

51. D'Aulnoy, "Le Prince Marcassin," 435. Amy Vanderlyn DeGraff also notes Marcassin's ambivalence and self-hate. Unlike my own reading, she applies Bettelheim's model to discern what she considers to be the hero's progression from narcissism to "instinctual domination." See Amy Vanderlyn DeGraff, *The Tower and the Well: A Psychological Interpretation of the Fairy Tales of Madame d'Aulnoy* (Birmingham, Ala.: Summa Publications, 1984), 33–45.

52. The words "cochon" and "porc" are used almost exclusively for domesticated pigs. According to seventeenth-century dictionaries, they were also used figuratively in expressions designating unrefined appearances and behavior: "Il meine une vie de cochon...c'est un gros cochon" (Furetière, "Cochon") [He leads a pig's life...he's a big pig] "Il rotte comme un porc; il ronfle comme un porc; il suë comme un porc; il est gras comme un porc" (Furetière, "Porc") [He burps like a pig; he snores like a pig; he sweats like a pig; he is as fat as a pig]. Significantly, neither the Académie Française nor the Furetière dictionaries list figurative uses of "marcassin" or "sanglier" applied to humans. On the attribution of anthropomorphic traits to domesticated pigs, see Claudine Fabre-Vassas, *La Bête singulière: Les juifs, les chrétiens, et le cochon*, Bibliothèque des Sciences Humaines (Paris: Gallimard, 1994).

53. D'Aulnoy, "Le Prince Marcassin," 434.

54. D'Aulnoy, "Le Prince Marcassin," 463.

55. Unlike her counterpart in both Straparola's and Murat's tales, the third (evil) fairy in "Le Prince Marcassin" does not clearly reveal her spell to the queen during the gifting scene (more precisely, her laughter renders it incomprehensible). It is only just before Marcassin's demetamorphosis that it is revealed. On two occasions, one of the two good fairies appears to the queen to reassure her that all will end well, but her promises never indicate how this happy ending will transpire.

56. D'Aulnoy, "Le Prince Marcassin," 439–40.

57. D'Aulnoy, "Le Prince Marcassin," 445.

58. D'Aulnoy, "Le Prince Marcassin," 448.

59. D'Aulnoy, "Le Prince Marcassin," 449.

60. D'Aulnoy, "Le Prince Marcassin," 450.

61. D'Aulnoy, "Le Prince Marcassin," 450.

62. On the valorization of sincerity and authenticity among theorists of sociability in late-seventeenth-century France, see Elizabeth Goldsmith, *Exclusive Conversations: The Art of Interaction in Seventeenth-Century France* (Philadelphia: University of Pennsylvania Press, 1988), 17–40. On the notion of "honnête dissimulation," see Bury, *Littérature et Politesse*, 117.

63. He tells the queen: "Je n'ignore point mes disgrâces, j'y suis peut-être plus sensible qu'un autre, mais je ne suis point le maître de me faire ni plus grand ni plus droit, de quitter ma hure de sanglier pour prendre une tête d'homme, ornée de longs cheveux" (d'Aulnoy, "Le Prince Marcassin," 450) [I am hardly unaware of my misfortunes; I am perhaps even more sensitive to them than anyone. But I am unable to make myself either taller or straighter, to leave my boar's head and to take on the head of a man adorned with long hair].

64. See especially the "De la cour" section of Jean de La Bruyère, *Les Caractères de Théophraste traduits du grec avec les Caractères ou les moeurs de ce siècle*, ed. Robert Pignarre, 1688–1694, (Paris: Garnier-Flammarion, 1965). "Le reproche en un sens le plus honorable que l'on puisse faire à un homme, c'est de lui dire qu'il ne sait pas la cour: il n'y a sorte de vertus qu'on ne rassemble en lui par ce seul mot" ("De la cour," 1:202) [In a sense, the most honorable reproach that can be made of a man is to tell him that he does not know the court: there are hardly any virtues that are not instilled in him by this single phrase].

65. D'Aulnoy, "Le Prince Marcassin," 456.

66. D'Aulnoy, "Le Prince Marcassin," 458.

67. D'Aulnoy, "Le Prince Marcassin," 458.

68. D'Aulnoy, "Le Prince Marcassin," 460.

69. D'Aulnoy, "Le Prince Marcassin," 461.

70. D'Aulnoy, "Le Prince Marcassin," 461.

71. D'Aulnoy, "Le Prince Marcassin," 463.

72. D'Aulnoy, "Le Prince Marcassin," 464.

73. D'Aulnoy, "Le Prince Marcassin," 464.

74. D'Aulnoy, "Le Prince Marcassin," 464.

75. My assessment of the pastoral motif in this tale diverges from that of Hannon, who emphasizes the satirical jibes throughout the narrative; see Hannon, *Fabulous Identities*, 87–94. While humor is an important feature of this tale (and many others) by d'Aulnoy, it is used, in my view, as a means of creating a space of reflective distance instead of outright rejection of the pastoral retreat and the court.

76. D'Aulnoy, "Le Prince Marcassin," 465–66: "Six mois s'écoulèrent avec peu de plaisirs de la part de Marthésie, car elle ne sortait pas de la caverne, de peur d'être rencontrée par sa mère ou par ses domestiques. Depuis que cette pauvre mère avait perdu sa fille, elle ne cessait point de gémir, elle faisait retentir les bois de ses plaintes & du nom de Marthésie. A ces accents qui frappaient presque tous les jours ses oreilles, elle soupirait en secret de causer tant de douleur à sa mère & de n'être pas maîtresse de la soulager. Mais Marcassin l'avait fortement menacée & elle le craignait autant qu'elle l'aimait" [Six months passed with few pleasures on the part of Marthésie for she did not leave the cave for fear of meeting her mother or her servants. Since this poor mother had lost her daughter, she moaned incessantly and filled the woods with her laments and the name of Marthésie. At these sounds, which struck her ears every day, she sighed to herself for causing so much grief for her mother and for not being in a position to comfort her. But Marcassin had threatened her in no uncertain terms and she feared him as much as she loved him].

77. For an illuminating discussion of distaffs in the *contes de fées*, see Geneviève Patard, "De la quenouille au fil de la plume: Histoire d'un féminisme à travers les contes du XVIIe siècle en France," in *Tricentenaire Charles Perrault: Les grands contes du XVIIe siècle et leur fortune littéraire*, ed. Jean Perrot, Collection Lectures d'enfance (Paris: In-Press, 1998), 235–43.

78. D'Aulnoy, "Le Prince Marcassin," 470.

79. D'Aulnoy, "Le Prince Marcassin," 454.

80. D'Aulnoy, "Le Prince Marcassin," 471.

81. For a discussion on the decline of royal authority, see Emmanuel Le Roy Ladurie, *Saint-Simon ou le système de la cour* (Paris: Fayard, 1997), 101–42; for competing claims to cultural power, see Arditi, *A Genealogy of Manners*, 141–54; see Daniel Gordon, *Citizens without Sovereignty: Equality and Sociability in French Thought, 1670–1789* (Princeton: Princeton University Press, 1994), 119, for the evolution of the courtier ideal.

82. I am grateful to Kathleen P. Long and Catherine Velay-Vallantin for their invaluable comments on earlier versions of this essay.

Masculinity, Monarchy, and Metaphysics
A Crisis of Authority in Early Modern France

Catharine Randall

Figuring Masculinity Metaphysically

In the film *Tous les matins du monde*, the musical genius Monsieur de St. Colombe bitterly reprimands his protégé, Marin Marais, for his sexuality, lust for power, and disregard of true music. While ostensibly about the making of music, this film, and the novel on which it is based, explore a subtext: that of the relationship between spirituality and sexuality, the renunciation of the world and the quest for power.[1] The figures of the two men—in many ways antithetical constructs each of the other, yet in some ways twinned—mirror several of the forms available for the depiction of masculinity during the early modern period. As with virtually every cultural construct prior to the Enlightenment, their characterization and gender roles cannot be disassociated from religious and theological influences that structured the culture. M. de St. Colombe, a Jansenist, was a stern exemplar of a radical religious critique of autocracy and absolutism, his spare and unyielding portrait patterned on that limned by Racine in his sympathetic history of Port-Royal and Jansenism. He contrasts with sexually overeager, pudgy-fingered Marin Marais, lured by the glitter of royalty and the sheen of monarchy, who symbolizes Catholicism construed as orthodox.[2]

Jansenism was perceived to threaten both the Catholic Church and Louis XIV. Like M. de St. Colombe who chose to live out his reclusive, music-saturated existence in his isolated château deep in the country (*les champs*) away from court, Jansenism sought to rectify abuses that might be found in the church but which were primarily attributable to abuses of autocracy. In the scene in the novel between M. de St. Colombe and a prelate sent by the king to try to pressure the realm's most golden-fingered violist to come to play at court, the prelate portrays the antithesis of "true" religion: rolling in fat like a eunuch, pandering to his earthly master's will, he embodies pseudoreligiosity and hypocrisy. The stern, monosyllabic M. de St. Colombe with his ascetic lifestyle looms as a reproachful contrast with those who no longer heed their divine master—the only authority, ultimately, that Jansenists recognized. In contrast to the effeminate, bejewelled abbot, M. de St. Colombe's spartan figure, unadorned hands, and lack of wig, portray him as man in the state of nature, an Adam-like figure in a rural paradise. Yet however heroic M. de St. Colombe's depiction of metaphysical purity and focus, M. de St. Colombe, it must not be forgotten, is also a gendered being, rather than the ethereal "saint" of Jansenist aspiration. And in *Tous les matins du monde,* masculinity, in no matter what guise, wreaks great havoc and harm. Ultimately, both theological systems are indicted thereby. Shortly after coming to ask M. de St. Colombe to take him on as a pupil (with all the wrong motives: so that his glory may soar), Marin Marais ruthlessly debauches both of the Jansenist widower's daughters, themselves accomplished musicians. This deflowering demonstrates Marais's voracious desire to cannibalize any of the sources of, or contacts with, the coveted compositions of M. de St. Colombe.[3]

M. de St. Colombe, whose name means holy spirit, whose music is ethereal and otherworldly, does not escape the worldly blight of gendered masculinity. Only by coldly silencing his young daughters' prattle, relentlessly bending them to serve his will, does he attain the pinnacle of musical perfection that the world that he rejects so admires. Only upon the death of his wife does he begin to compose great works. And it is only through a eucharistic transubstantiation in which—alone in his cabin in the woods, through an alchemy of music, *gaufrettes,* and wine, in a symbolic sacrifice of her dead body—that her ghost returns to him. He uses this spectral interlocutor to create his greatest, most inspired music, the *Tombeau des regrets.* Women lie trampled underfoot by male ambition—whether that ambition be aesthetic and spiritualized or materialist and power hungry—in *Tous les matins du monde.* Both men incarnate different versions of power. Marais represents slavish devotion to earthly power and the lust for renown, while M. de St. Colombe displays how the heresy of Jansenism—so deemed by the Catholic Church for its emphasis on man's utter depravity; so reckoned by the king for its refusal to accept his absolute authority—can annihilate that which is properly "human" in us. Ultimately, M. de St. Colombe's music may be of an unearthly beauty, but it remains inaccessible, a tool for the critique of corruption and of absolutism that, in fact, is the consequence of considerable compulsion and autocratic behavior on the part of its performer.

Because of its Augustinian doctrine of predestination, Jansenism was construed by Jesuits as a lurking form of Calvinism at the very moment that Louis XIV's *dragonnades* were effectively eradicating the Huguenot heresy in the Cévennes. Like Calvinism, Jansenism viewed itself as deriving from, and perpetuating in its purest form, the Early Christian Church, identifying with the tribulations of ancient Israel: "Il y en a qui conservent … le même amour que les anciens Juifs conservaient, dans leur captivité, pour les ruines de Jérusalem."[4] Prominent Jansenist leaders, such as Jansénius and Antoine Arnauld, were persistently likened by contemporary Catholic detractors to Calvinists.[5] There were other, more legitimate affiliations drawn, such as the Calvinist and Jansenist emphasis on grace over works, the primacy they both gave to the writings of Saint Paul, their stern moral code, and their belief in predestination. Both Calvinists and Jansenists viewed themselves as a people apart, standing separate from the corruption of court and the blandishments of a misguided world. Necessarily, then, their conceptions of agency in the world, perceived in the early modern social and political domain as preeminently masculine, differed from those of Catholics and the sophisticated, *mondain* Jesuits. The Protestant patriarch, as will be discussed later in this essay, sought to offer a normative moral model for the entire realm, one that earned its legitimacy from conformity to biblical teachings and a determined, intentional self-scrutiny and self-shaping along the lines offered by biblical exemplars. The paradigm of the Jansenist elect was a sober and austere reader of his Bible whose stance was radically dissimilar to that of his worldly contemporaries. In the popular mind, and to arch-Catholics, Jansenism thus constituted the remnants of the Calvinist heresy still resisting the Sun King's unmitigated radiance and unchecked power. Jesuits leagued against Jansenists to extirpate the latter from Louis XIV's France.[6]

A variety of ways in which Catholic and Protestant thought and theology treated considerations of masculinity and of metaphysics existed in the sixteenth and seventeenth centuries. In her study *The Renaissance Bible,* Debora Shuger makes the point that late medieval, hagiographic representations of the crucified Christ portray him as beatific, beautiful in his impervious manhood, while Reformation writings on the Crucifixion focus on the battered, bleeding Christ, impotent and emasculated by torture and pain. She contends that Reformation thought created a conflicted self,[7] and that such internal division particularly displayed itself in representations of masculinity undone, which she attributes to growing anxiety as traditional roles for men, such as knighthood, were obviated by the different demands of newly urbanized existence.[8] She clearly perceives a strong ideological difference between Catholic and Protestant models of maleness, and uses such representations as emblematic of larger cultural issues:

> The catastrophic representations of male identity in the Calvinist passion narratives do not seem to be anomalous. Rather, one may view them as mythic versions of a larger crisis of manhood that leaves its traces throughout the characteristic discourses of the period. Perhaps crisis is the wrong word for something more like a convulsive shudder running through a culture, a conceptual disturbance that never achieves direct articulation but is obliquely apprehended through the distortions effected in a society's symbolic forms [which display] a diffuse anxiety about maleness.[9]

A parallel way of theorizing the Protestant difference also obtains in Julia Kristeva's compelling discussion of the divergent views of Christ's agony as painted by the Lutheran Holbein and the Catholic Mantegna, where masculinity as the cipher for metaphysical perspective.[10] Kristeva interprets Holbein's dead Christ as radically Protestant in that the relentless masculinity of the decomposing body stretched in rigor mortis shows a metaphysical doctrine: that of the necessity for incarnation—God made flesh—so that salvation may occur. She reads the Catholic Mantegna, on the other hand, as using gendered masculinity for purely pictorial purposes, beautifying the dead Christ with musculature and lovely lineaments, remaining rooted in the terrestrial, missing the theological point so crucial to Holbein as a Protestant.[11]

This essay proposes to survey textual representations of masculinity and their contextualization in cultural, theological, and political discourse from the late Middle Ages, through mainline Catholicism, to the similarities of Calvinism and Jansenism. Such ideological representations of masculinity, monarchy, and metaphysics finally culminate in the ultimate desexing, or ungendering of masculinity, the most threatening form of early modern spirituality, effected by the female-authored mystic discourse of quietism. Masculinity in this light is seen to be not merely a question of gender, but also a cipher in which to dramatize cultural critique.

Anxious Masculinity: 1530-1620

Salic law decreed that the person on the throne of France must be male in gender. Such was the custom, the expectation, and the law. Catholicism and a gendered expectation regarding the monarch necessarily went hand in hand. Yet during the French Wars of Religion, the world seemed turned upside down, a topos common throughout Europe during the early modern period, due to a variety of factors, most of them religious and/or political.[12] The iconography most frequently employed to symbolize disorder and lawlessness was that of a woman usurping some manifestation of male-encoded authority: folly and rage personified, as with Brueghel's images of Mad Meg; John Knox's trumpet blast against Elizabeth I's acceding to the throne of England; or a wife spanking her husband, forcing him to ply the distaff. Lyndal Roper identifies another image—especially emblematic of the concerns of the present essay in that it unites male authority with kingship in the symbolic lion, whose power and royalty are questioned and undermined by a gaggle of women—that is, the German woodblock, *The Taming of the Lion*.[13] While many writers during this period describe feelings of chaos, senselessness, and brutality, most common are laments over the loss of a sure and stable authority. In her study of emblems of death, a striking number of which contain engravings of castrated or emasculated corpses, Gisèle Mathieu-Castellani observes that this anxiety over the crux of gendered maleness contemplates a signifying void: that which is not represented, that which is no longer there, points to a crisis of meaning and galvanizes a search for alternative sources of authority.[14] The former locus of meaning had been rooted in the phallus, the male power to engender; these castrated corpses, rather, mime the deracinating of the traditional site of authority. Assault on the male body equates with assault on authority.

The King's One Body, Authority, and the Missing Phallus

For French Catholics, and in the past, for the French in general, authority found its seat in the person of the king. Consequently, we can observe an anxiety about masculinity, concerning its nature, function, and credibility, during this time of questioning the divine right of kings, of refusals to heed the king's mandates, and of assassinations of monarchs. Regicide represented the strongest assault possible upon a male embodiment of authority. In addition, particularly during the period of the Wars of Religion, since Henri III had no heirs, considerable anxiety prevailed concerning a specific gender absence: that of a male descendant to whom the throne—and authority—could legitimately pass.[15]

One of the first signs of a general cultural malaise centering around authority and its coded representation as hypermasculinity is the obsessive need to catalogue the essential definitive differences between men and women, so as to keep both in their place. In Béroalde de Verville's *Le moyen de parvenir,* for instance, an enormous number of the anecdotes concern such taxonomies:

> Or ne me faictes point de discours sur ce qu'ils ont de femmes ou non, je vous dis et déclare que qui n'aime point l'animal de société, qui ne fait point cas des femmes, est sot, meschant, ou sodomite. Fi, laissons ces loups-garoux, instruments de toute souillure; un homme qui honnestement ayme une douce femme est…gratieux; mais cettuy-là qui les rejette est ennemy de Dieu et des hommes; et qu'il s'aille faire couper le bout.[16]

> [Now don't go talking to me about whether they have women or not; I tell you and firmly state that he who does not like the social animal, who is not interested in women, is stupid and evil, or a sodomite. Who cares, let's leave those werewolves alone, those instruments of all dirtiness; a man who honestly loves a sweet woman is gracious; but he who rejects such (women) is an enemy of God and of men; and he should go have his penis cut off.]

Béroalde's insistence on castrating the unnatural man (*qu'il s'aille faire couper le bout*) demonstrates how deeply invested the culture is in maintaining the strongly defined masculine role as that which ensures order. This text is interesting, too, in that Béroalde was a humanist Catholic who later went over to the Reformation. This text, in parts critical of the Calvinist perspective, appears to have been written prior to his conversion, and does epitomize the more Catholic approach to masculinity as essentialist rather than attributive.[17] Another large percentage of the stories which Béroalde recounts deal with the apparently arbitrary and uncurbed exercising of power by men over women. The tale of Marciole and the cherries is a particularly egregious example. A nobleman orders the daughter of a peasant who has come to him bearing a gift of a basket of cherries to strip and bestrew the cherries over four large sheets that he has caused to be laid on the ground. As the naked girl bends and stoops, the company of noblemen amuse themselves by commenting on her body parts. The voyeuristic feast places special emphasis on trying to discern the site of the girl's virginity, her cherry, thus enacting a visual deflowering of the maiden. Maleness is thus associated with *droit du seigneur,* scopic violence, arbitrary demands, and the expectation of unprotesting acquiescence. Significantly, her would-be avenger menaces the noblemen with castration: their power has been unjustly used, therefore they deserve emasculation. He maintains: "Vous payerez chacun ce que vous avez dit…si mieux que vous n'aymez avoir…les vits coupez." [Each of you will pay for what he has said…so much so that you would prefer to have…your penis cut off.][18]

The proliferation of Baroque poetry and prose in which not eccentricity but downright acentricity prevails illustrates the related male anxiety about attacks on power and authority in the gendered male body. Théophile de Viau's celebrated "Ode" circles neurotically around an empty space smack at the center of the poem, or, in more anthropomorphic terms, its groin. Nothing is there; a poetics of emasculation displays the hole where the phallic authority once was rooted. The ode's structure mimes this lack of center: two stanzas are drastically divided by a gap on the page (present between the verse, "Je vois le centre de la terre," and the following line, "Un ruisseau remonte en sa source"), and where de Viau claims to see a center, none can be found. Only Charon, avatar of death and nothingness, can be heard (but not seen):

Un corbeau devant moi croasse,	[A crow caws before me,
Une ombre offusque mes regards…	A shadow clouds my gazes…
Les pieds faillent à mon cheval,	My horse's feet falter,
Mon laquais tombe du haut mal,	My lackey falls down in an epileptic fit,
J'entends craqueter le tonnerre,	I hear thunder crack,
Un esprit se présente à moi,	A shade presents itself to me,
J'ois Charon qui m'appelle à soi,	I hear Charon who calls me to him,
Je vois le centre de la terre.	I see the center of the earth.
Un ruisseau remonte en sa source,	A brook returns to its source,
Un boeuf gravit sur un clocher,	An ox climbs into the bell tower,
Le sang coule de ce rocher…	Blood flows from that rock…
Le soleil est devenu noir,	The sun has become black,
Je vois la lune qui va choir,	I see the moon about to fall,
Cet arbre est sorti de sa place. [19]	That tree just moved from its place.]

The *constatation* of a-centricity and spatial and experiential "scrambling" (all is "sorti de sa place") announces a frenzied series of *monde à l'envers* images displaying the male "je" as chaotic nonsense. Similarly, Montaigne expresses his intention to include, within the body of his *Essais,* the body of the text of his friend Etienne de La Boétie. But in the end they construct a frame that gapes empty; Montaigne never does print within the body of his text the heralded text of his friend. La Boétie's textual authority is discussed, but not displayed; it provides no *auctoritas.* [20] By announcing that he will fill a gap in his text with the corpus—and corpse—of his friend, Montaigne deliberately scars his own text, and represents his own impotence to reproduce the voice of the other. He undermines his own authority in a form of autoemasculation reminiscent of the emblems of death discussed by Mathieu-Castellani.

A Protestant Difference

If mutilated bodies and emasculated men provided images of the seething inner anxiety experienced by Catholics during the Wars of Religion, Protestant contemporaries responded to the "troubles" in a somewhat different way. A split, both phenomenological and theological, existed between contemporary Catholic and Protestant perceptions of the disruption of authority that we have been discussing. If Catholics looked to the throne to dispense authority, Protestants quickly ceased to do so. Agrippa d'Aubigné sums up the argument in his *Debvoir des Roys et des subjects,* stating that "le Prince qui rompt la foy à son peuple rompt celle de son peuple" [the prince who breaks faith with his people breaks the faith of his people].[21] And if, as Neil Hertz, Lynn Hunt, Lewis Seifert, and others have shown, "in specific moments of revolt or revolution the questioning of social or political hierarchies is expressed in terms of sexual disorder [while]…the threat of social or political instability is sometimes given a decidedly sexual turn," this turn is taken with a very distinctive twist on the part of Protestants.[22] The "people of the book," as Protestants were known, sought scriptural justification and warrant for their behavior. God's concern, in the Protestant view, was not with the human as gendered, but rather with the human creature in right relationship with God. Theirs was not an essentialist view of authority, but rather an attributive understanding, and that attribution occurred always through scriptural mandate. The Protestant understanding and use of gender, while it may first focus on the gendered person, generally seeks to move beyond that, toward an un- or degendered status where the focus is scriptural: on the human creature in right relationship to God. Such an approach contrasts with Catholic differentiation between male and female; "while [Calvin] may have thought of woman as the weaker vessel, in spiritual matters he treated her as if she were equal to man."[23] Such equality, however, does not seem to have been a gender-to-gender equality, but rather a worshipful person's equality with another Christian. Gender gets undone, as is fully illustrated in Théodore de Bèze's *Abraham sacrifiant,* where Abraham really is an everyman cipher for all Christians, male or female. He exists to do God's will, not to experience on his own or to possess a distinct personality or gendered being. Similarly, Sarah is not really effectively delineated as a woman, but simply as fulfilling her most important role: that of effective and faithful witness:

Et qu'ainsi soit, maint loyal personnage	[And therefore may it be so that many a loyal person
En donnera bien tost bon tesmoignage:	Will soon give faithful testimony to it:
Bien tost verrez Abraham et Sara,	Soon you will see Abraham and Sara,
Et tost apres Isaac sortira.	And soon after Isaac will appear.
Ne sont-ils point tesmoins tresveritables	Are they not trustworthy witnesses
…qui de Dieu tasche accomplir sans feinte,	…he who tries to do the bidding, without fault,
Comme Abraham, la parole tressaincte,	Like Abraham, of the holy word,
Qui nonobstant toutes raisons contraires,	Who, disregarding any contrary reason,
Remet en Dieu et soy et ses affaires,	Puts himself and his affairs in God's hands,

Il en aura pour certaine une issue
Meilleure....[24]

[He will for sure have
A much better fate....]

To similar effect, the Calvinist writer Agrippa d'Aubigné, even as he excoriated Henri III in *Les tragiques* for being sexually deviant and for cross-dressing, was more concerned that religion was being travestied. He saw Henri III as the embodiment of the worst extremes of Catholic abuse: believing in holy water was bad enough, but using it as an ingredient in a hemorrhoid preparation was much more reprehensible. D'Aubigné was not anxious over the perversion of male authority or any perceived diminishment in power gendered as male, but about the ignorance or downright flouting of scriptural authority:

Quand j'oy qu'un Roy transi, effrayé du tonnerre,[25]

[When I see that a king is transfixed, afraid of thunder,

Se couvre d'une voute et se cache sous terre,

And covers himself in a vault and hides himself beneath the ground,

S'embusque de lauriers, fait les cloches sonner,

Decks himself with laurels, causes the bells to ring,

Son péché poursuivi poursuit de l'estonner,

The sin he has insisted on now pursues him and terrifies him,

Il use d'eau lustrale, il la boit, la consomme

He uses holy water, he drinks and consumes it

En clysteres infects, il fait venir de Rome

In filthy anointing; he causes to be sent from Rome

Les cierges, les agnus que le Pape fournit,

Tapers, beads blessed by the pope,

Bouche tous ses conduicts d'un charmé grain-benit;

And sticks these and charmed rosary beads into every hole in his body,

Quand je voy composer une messe complete

When I see an entire mass said

Pour repousser le ciel, inutile amulette,

To fend off the heavens, a useless amulet,

Quand la peur n'a cessé par les signes de croix...

When signs of the cross cannot dispel fear,

Le peché de Sodome et le sanglant inceste

Sodom's sin and bloody incest

Sont reproches joyeux de nos impures cours.[26]

Are the joyful reproaches of our impure courts.]

Significantly, Henri III ritualistically obsesses about filling in gaps and plugging up holes (*il bouche tous ses conduits*), as though desperately trying to grasp at the missing phallus which he so craves and needs, as it is emblematic of authority. D'Aubigné's reference to him as a sodomite is a representational strategy designed to indict a heretical, rather than a sexual, deviance; Randle Cotgrave's *A Dictionarie of the French and English Tongues* indicates that *bougre, pédéraste,* and *sodomite* "connoted debauchery in a general sense and were often classified alongside [that is, expressly associated with] heresy and sorcery as 'great evils.'"[27]

It is therefore significant that d'Aubigné's Protestant take on Henri III's homosexuality does not decry his gender transgression as merely symptomatic of degenerative government, but rather, by equating homosexuality with heresy, the king's corrupt body represents him as damned—a metaphysical perspective on masculinity. Another somewhat later symbol of such a metaphysical interpretation of a sexual deviance is Cardinal Mazarin's penis, portrayed in the *Mazarinades* as the tool by which the devil destroys the world: "Engin qui tous nos biens nous couste, / Engin instrument du Demon."[28] Protestants take aim at what should be the human person but what has now degenerated into a gendered being.[29] What matters is not really sexual deviance, but rather the significant swerve out of alignment with God. Just so, d'Aubigné launches his Calvinist screed against Jesuits, whom he portrays as demonstrating a misbegotten and exaggerated form of papocracy/masculinity. Verbal potency runs riot in the following quotation, as abusive power rapes feminine France, and Christ's message is forgotten and distorted in the Jesuits' deviant maleness (*vostre evangile... le nom menti de Jesus*), as opposed to genderless Calvinist personhood:

Voilà vostre evangile, ô vermine espagnolle,	[There is your spawn, O Spanish vermin,
Je dis vostre evangile, engeance de Loyole,	I say your gospel, spawn of Loyola,
Qui ne portez la paix sous le double manteau	Who does not bring peace under a turncoat
Mais qui empoisonnez l'homicide cousteau.	But rather poisons the homicidal knife.
C'est vostre instruction d'establir la puissance	It's your mission to establish the power
De Rome, sous couleur de points de conscience,	Of Rome, as though obeying a case of conscience,
Et, sous le nom menti de Jesus, esgorger...	And, using the slandered name of Jesus, to slit throats
...Allez, preschez, courez, vollez,...semez....[30]	...Go, preach, run about, fly...sow (discord).]

It is clear that Huguenots experienced differently from Catholics the crisis of masculinity as related to authority.[31] This is not to say that Calvinists ignore deviance, or never portray metaphysical disorder without resorting to images of sexual impropriety. In several unpublished polemical pamphlets, d'Aubigné uses anatomical images, gendered references, and explicitly homosexual slurs to connote Catholic corruption not only on a sexual/physical plane, but also, and perhaps especially, on a spiritual level. In *La responce de Michau l'aveugle,* d'Aubigné links the themes of abusive authority and sexual deviance, creating an equation as well between errant theology and pederasty:[32]

> Ceux qui se révoltent de la raison, vont ordinairement cacher leur honte sous la robe de l'authorité. Et sur toutes les authoritez les plus faciles à corrompre sont les plus propres à cacher les corruptions. C'est la cause pourquoi les Papistes ont etabli sur eux, & deffendent si courageusement la monarchie Papale.... De là s'eschaufe aujourd'hui la dispute de la souveraineté du Pape, detestee & niee par ceux, qui ont cherché la liberté en Christ; approuvee & deffenduë par les estafiers de l'Antechirst; sur tout par les Jésuites, qui sont aujourd'hui mignons de ce cabinet.... Et en advient aux Royaumes comme de la dissipation des bourdeaux, qui font en detail presques autant de mal, comme ils faisoyent en gros.[33]

> [Those who rebel against reason, generally go about hiding their shame beneath the cloak of authority. And that authority easiest to corrupt is the kind of authority most likely to hide corruption. That is why the papists have dominion and have defended the papal monarchy so vigorously.... That is also why today the dispute over papal authority has heated up, a sovereignty detested and denied by those who seek liberty in Christ; a sovereignty approved and upheld by the standard-bearers of the Antichrist; a sovereignty especially espoused by the Jesuits, who are currently the darlings of the papal cabinet...and it is coming to pass in kingdoms as affairs are in a brothel, where small things do as much evil as do large.]

Here, d'Aubigné skillfully draws an adversarial portrait of Protestants and Catholics; antithetical parallelism opposes "those who seek liberty in Christ" to "the standard-bearers of the Antichrist." D'Aubigné talks about erroneous authorities, which are used as a deceptive veil cast over the truth. The pope is the avatar of such deceit, as "the easiest authorities to corrupt are those most likely to hide their corruption." The site on and through which abuses of authority operate is corporeal: the Jesuits are "darlings of this cabinet." They pullulate in low and evil places, "like the dissipation of brothels." A body out of order is a country deranged, while authority, meant to mirror metaphysics, is debased and vile.

Calvinists may not have traced the same etiology linking problems in the monarchy with a crisis in masculinity as did the Catholics because of the peculiar way in which Calvinists understood kingship to be, at origin, contractual. Because of their notion of the contract, they regarded the personhood and certainly the masculinity (or lack thereof) of the king as relatively unimportant; what mattered was the abstract entity of the state or nation with whom the people had contracted for good governance.[34] Preeminent symbolically was not the body of the king, but rather the body of the people—God's people.[35] Further, the Bible abounded in examples of Israel's rejection of bad kings.[36] The Protestant move, then, was not as conservative as the Catholics, who fretted over masculinity and monarchy because they did not envision working outside of the system. Rather, the Protestants swerved away from the nation into their own private scriptural space from which, simultaneously marginalized yet omnipotent in their critical capacity, they could construct an alternative subculture.[37] Ultimately, as the space for the exercise of authority closed in on itself for Protestants, they shifted from a public to a predominantly private sphere, existing as cells of dissension, often persecuted but occasionally tolerated within the realm of France. Within this private sphere, authority did come to be vested in the patriarch of the household, but only inasmuch as he was the instrument for the transmission of God's word through reading and praying.[38] Protestant women retained, in that private space, the important responsibility of educating children in the faith, and were seen as partners in the scriptural enterprise. The household economy, a unit of scripturally ordained roles and interrelationships, while appearing gender-based in its allocation of tasks (for example, men were to lead family prayers; women were to teach the children biblical literacy), in fact functioned as a seamless, gender-neutral unit in which the highest task of every person was to glorify God as his creature, in his creation. When men, women, and people in general are "considered from the perspective of the *cogito dei* (that is, from the perspective or the knowledge which God has), woman is seen to be the equal of man."[39] The companionate marriage, praised by Calvin as the ideal, deemphasized biological gender; no longer was the focus placed exclusively on woman as womb to produce offspring.[40] Such an essentially organic division of labor in a common enterprise, when contrasted with the rigorous Catholic separation of the sexes, as in monasteries/nunneries, would seem to attest to considerably less anxiety about specific gender issues among Protestants. Lyndal Roper has argued along these lines, and makes the case that greater liberty was obtained for Protestant women in Reformation Augsburg than for their Catholic counterparts because of this Protestant model, precisely because they were perceived as fellow believers rather than solely as women.[41]

The patriarchal model that Protestants upheld was eloquently portrayed in many texts, and constituted a focal point of their thought equivalent to the emphasis placed by the culture at large on the crisis of masculinity. Olivier de Serres, the Calvinist architect, having personally experienced persecution at the hands of Catholics and kings' men during the religious conflicts, wrote movingly in *Le théâtre d'agriculture* (1600), ostensibly a tract about raising crops and tilling fields, but in reality about being a good steward of God's creation in all venues, including political, of the right order, peace, and harmony that prevail in the household of the patriarch.[42] He begins by describing a scene of menace and threat. His family cowers within their ancestral home, fearing assault by marauding troops. De Serres decides to purchase and raise peacocks, known for their guard-dog vigilance and loud cries of alarm. De Serres's scenario stresses the threatened household and the need to preserve it, for it seems the last bastion of obedience and righteousness in an insane world:

Mon inclination et l'estat de mes affaires m'ont retenu aux champs en ma maison, et fait passer une bonne partie de mes meilleurs ans, durant les guerres civiles de ce Royaume cultivant la terre par mes serviteurs, comme le temps l'a peu porter. En quoy Dieu m'a tellement beny par sa saincte grace, que m'ayant conservez parmi tant de calamitez, dont j'ay senty ma bonne part, je me suis tellement comporté parmy les divers humeurs de ma Patrie, que ma maison, ayant esté plus logis de paix que de guerre, quand les occasions s'en sont présentées, j'ay rapporté ce tesmoignage de mes voisins, qu'en me conservant avec eux, je me suis principalement addonné chez moy, à faire mon mesnage.[43]

[My temperament and the state of my affairs having kept me in my fields, and caused me to spend a good part of my best years during the civil wars in the kingdom cultivating the earth with the help of my servants as best we were able; in which God blessed me greatly by his holy grace, that having been preserved from so many calamities, of which I nonetheless felt my share of the effects, I steered such a course through the various moods of our country that, my house having been a dwelling more of peace than of war, I received such witness from my neighbors that, safeguarding them with myself, I occupied myself with the affairs of my household (rather than those of state).]

Faire mon mesnage becomes almost a formula for right governance, as de Serres, the archetypal Protestant patriarch, does a far better job of regulating and preserving his kingdom than any king (including Henri IV, to whom he addresses his preface), sounding a cautionary note about the possible "péril d'issue, semblable aux excés des guerres civiles, tirans en ruine le vainqueur avec le vaincu" [the possible negative outcome, similar to the excesses of the civil wars, causing the winner to be vanquished with the defeated].[44] If there is any body under discussion here, it is not a specifically male body, or even the king's body, but the notion of the one body (of the church, intended to be organically united in Christ): if Catholics persecute Protestants, ultimately they damage themselves. De Serres intentionally recalls the gospel in his treatment of the patriarch and his discussion of the body. Rom. 12:4–10 provides this corporate and corporeal, ungendered (and a-hierarchical) pattern:

Just as there are many parts to our bodies, so it is with Christ's body. We are all parts of it, and it takes every one of us to make it complete, for we each have different work to do.... Love one another.

De Serres provides a recipe for the Protestant patriarch (who, we hear him thinking, would make an awfully good king):

Le Père-de-famille aimera aussi ses subjects, s'il en a, les chérissant comme ses enfans, pour en leur besoin les soulager...mesmes en cas de nécessité, du passage des gens de guerre…les gardant de foules et sur-charges, d'exactions indeuës, et semblables violences.[45]

[The father of the family will also love his subjects, if he has any, cherishing them as if they were his children, and, if need be, comforting them…even, if necessary, protecting them from passing soldiers…protecting them from searches and excessive taxation and similar violence.]

This well-ordered household space is paradigmatic and pedagogical: "de là nous apprendrons de policer nostre maison."[46] De Serres never goes so far as to suggest that the king should emulate the patriarch; that would be dangerously overtly critical, but the hope is implicit. The epigraph to his text—a poem—uses this telling simile:

Sur ce vers dit le Poëte:	[Concerning these verses, the poet says:
Que son vers chante l'heur du bien aisé rustique	That his poetry sings the happiness of a comfortable peasant
Dont l'honneste maison semble une Republique….[47]	Whose house seems to him his own republic….]

Clearly, de Serres's concern with the person of the king is not with any threat to masculinity or unquestioned authority, but rather with the need for royalty, as an institution, to submit itself to scriptural mandates—to become ungendered and obedient to God: "nostre Père-de-famille sera averti de s'estudier à se rendre digne de sa charge; afin que sçachant bien commander ceux qu'il a sous soy en puisse tirer l'obeissance necessaire (ce qui est l'abrégé du Mesnage)."[48]

Protestants ask different sorts of questions, and have different, more specifically metaphysical concerns from contemporary Catholics: they do not remain as firmly embodied in their understanding of humanity as do the former. Catholics retain a medieval emphasis on embodiment. The radical embodiment that Catholics believe occurs at the elevation of the wafer—the doctrine of transubstantiation—is another example of the insistence on the enfleshing and containment of the divine in a substance, while the Protestant *extra Calvinisticum,* asserting that Christ is present both in the wafer and simultaneously in heaven, already reveals a move away from the confines of terrestrial experience, toward a more elastic, mutable perception of the body.[49] Catholics eventually also looked elsewhere for the locus of authority; they found it through a strategy of signifying voids: they would evacuate the self (whence the significance of the term *retraitants,* in that they retreat from themselves, abandoning any authority that they might formerly have wielded as male persons), the specifically male person, to focus on Christ's body as a visual scripture. For this reason, Ignatius begins the *Spiritual Exercises* with a prayer featuring genderless (and nonauthoritarian) corporeal images.[50] But this is a later, Catholic response to the Protestant Reformation, and not the initial Catholic reading of gender during the period of the Wars of Religion.

Protestants ask how patriarchal authority can be reasserted if gender is no longer a sufficient, adequate, or appropriate container (if it ever were) for authority. If we could characterize a Jesuit understanding of the body, for instance, as performative, wherein one does certain acts, meditations, a planned sequence of retreats to become like Christ, we could call the Calvinist understanding predestined, in the sense of a theological overriding of gendering: we are saved or damned, all is preordained in our creatureliness as God perceives it, and gender is a very minor and inconsequential component of that. The Protestant concern lies elsewhere than with an anxiety over masculinity. But Protestants eventually learn to turn a cultural crisis concerning masculinity to their own purposes.

What Happens to Male Bodies: To 1715

While differences in intensity and in kind concerning Catholic and Protestant understandings of masculinity exist, it is undeniable that political and theological dramas did get played out in the theater of the body in the early modern period. Perhaps most interesting is not a specific crisis of masculinity, but rather its consequences: the transmutation of gendered maleness from its use as a cipher for authority to a rampant femaleness meant to convey lubriciousness and the disruption of (male) order. If the religious wars prepare this sort of metamorphosis and problematizing of masculinity in France, the reign of the lustful but often impotent Louis XIV is their culmination. In him we find crystallized those images of transvestism that typified Henri III, but now the king's body is rendered not as if feminine, but rather as dominated by that which is female.[51] The majority of such libelous tracts, published anonymously abroad but circulated within the kingdom of France, were penned by Protestants, exiled for their faith.[52] Through the salacious depiction of a king deprived of power and potency (progressively feminized, the kingdom in disorder), these satirists hold up as a mirror to Catholics and against the power hierarchy the very images of anxiety concerning masculinity that the Catholics used, a scant century earlier, to express their dismay at political disruption (caused, some would add, by Protestant dissension). The male body here is not mimetic merely of anxiety over maleness; it is doubly mimetic, both of that anxiety and (inasmuch as it perceived itself to be) of the embodied cause of its own neurosis.

The female body now assumes center stage as the archetypal form of social and theological disorder. She is no longer the presumptuous power-usurper, however. Instead, with the mystic discourse of Madame Guyon, the woman's body claims to be the new, privileged conduit for God's will on earth. She stands, however intentionally, directly over and against the king, and is perceived as challenging his divine right. A mystical metaphysics passes through the medium of the woman to undo the power of the man, as the female body—in its fullness and self-proclaimed plenitude, its pregnancy with the divine Word, its phenomenological experience of splitting in twain with the force and superabundance of grace—bypasses traditional religious channels of mediation and political frameworks of power hierarchies:

Vous [Dieu] me montrâtes à moi-même sous la figure de cette femme de
l'Apocalypse: vous me montrâtes ce mystère, vous me fîtes comprendre cette
lune; mon âme au-dessus des vicissitudes et inconstances...le soleil de Justice
l'environnait, et toutes les vertus divines...faisaient comme une couronne
autour de [ma] tête....J'étais grosse d'un fruit; c'est de cet esprit, Seigneur...le
démon jette un fleuve contre moi: c'est la calomnie: la terre l'engloutirait,
elle tomberait peu à peu: j'aurais des millions d'enfants....[53]

[You showed me to myself in the form of that woman of the Apocalypse: you
showed me this mystery, you caused me to understand [the meaning of] that
moon; my soul above vicissitudes and change...the sun of justice surrounding it, and every divine virtue...made as it were a crown about my head...I
was pregnant with a fruit: of the spirit, Lord...the devil threw a river against
me: it was calumny: the earth swallowed it up, the river receded bit by bit: I
shall have thousands of children....]

This is a wholly new phenomenon, a paradigm shift of considerable magnitude and
consequence. If Catholics retained and applied in various ways gendered masculinity,
while Protestants bypassed it to reach a sort of gender-neutral human creature aligned
with God's will, here Guyon asserts femininity as the privileged form for spiritual
experience. Madame Guyon's quietism threatens Louis XIV's absolutism more than the
Jansenists ever did, because, unlike the Jansenists, firmly locatable at Port-Royal, her
person knows no place or bounds; her language, unlike the rarefied, excruciatingly
correct logic of the Jansenists, acknowledges no social constraint or ordering: she cannot be found to be confronted; one cannot reason with her voice. Her prophetic vision
portrays her as the woman of the apocalypse, with justice surrounding her like the sun,
a crown of virtues upon her head. What more specific symbolic challenge could an
image pose to the crown of the Sun King?

Guyon's writings and theology enjoyed enormous popularity and were surprisingly resistant to attempts to eradicate them and to silence her. Indeed, her theology
persists today both in Europe and in America in tributary forms such as Quakerism and
Methodism. One of the primary reasons that Jesuits, Louis XIV, and especially the
king's polemicist Bossuet found Guyon so threatening was her relentless situating of the
site of authority in the female body, as well as her unvarying portrayal and metaphoriz-
ing of the recommended religious state as being female: plenitude like pregnancy, abandonment as a form of female ecstasy, and reception of the Word as a birthing process.
Bossuet inveighed against Guyon as an hysterical female, a temptress, a promiscuous
slattern, although no evidence supported his claims. With Guyon, the metaphysical
use-value of masculinity comes to an end: the masculine body is now extraneous,
defunct, barred from any power role, be it metaphysical or political. With the female
figure now ensconced as the channel through which divine inspiration flowed, masculinity, monarchy, and metaphysics clearly can no longer conjoin.[54]

Notes

1. Pascal Quignard, *Tous les matins du monde* (Paris: Gallimard, 1991); ibid.: film (New York: October Films, 1992).
2. Racine, *Abrégé de l'histoire de Port-Royal, Œuvres complètes*, ed. Raymond Picard (Paris: Gallimard, 1952), 56: "Tout ce qu'on en voyait au dehors inspirait de la piété. On admirait la manière grave et touchante dont les louanges de Dieu y étaient chantées, la simplicité et en même temps, la propreté de leur église, la modestie de domestiques, la solitude...le peu d'empressement...en un mot, une entière indifférence pour ce qui ne regardait point Dieu...du parfait désintéressement" [Everything one saw there inspired piety. One admired the grave and touching manner in which the promises of God were sung, the simplicity and, at the same time, the cleanliness of their church, the modesty of the servants, the solitude, the lack of hurriedness...in a word, complete indifference for that which did not concern God...a perfect altruism].
3. Eventually, the youngest daughter kills herself, making a rather obscure, but traceable, Jansenist comment as she dies. The comment at first strikes the reader as bizarre: she recalls Marais's childhood, which he had rejected, as the son of a cobbler. She hangs herself with the laces of a pair of shoes Marais had given her upon the birth of their illegitimate child. This shoe imagery appears gratuitous, until we read Racine's remark in *Abrégé de l'Histoire de Port-Royal* that anyone, even a shoemaker, can be elect in God's eyes, if the occupation is not construed as an end in itself.

   > Je vous dirai en même temps qu'il y a des choses qui ne sont pas saintes, et qui sont pourtant innocentes. Je vous demanderai si...le plaisir de faire des sabots...[est] fort propr[e] à faire mourir le vieil homme... (*Œuvres complètes de Racine*, 29)

   > [I will say to you at the same time that there are things which are not sacred, and yet which remain innocent. I will ask you if...the pleasure of crafting shoes...might be sufficient to kill the old Adam in us.] (All translations are mine.)

   Such an occupation as shoemaker is acceptable in God's sight, even commendable, as are others, if they are not made into idols—as Marais does with music, venerating its potential to bring him social advancement. Marais's rejection of his father's craft thus stands as a willful repudiation of his hope for salvation in the Lord, his relentless search for earthly power and pleasure, and the direct undoing of M. de St. Colombe's daughter.
4. Racine, *Port-Royal*, 59: "There are those who retain...the same love as that which the ancient Jews kept, during their captivity, for the ruins of Jerusalem."
5. Racine, *Port-Royal*, 59: "Antoine Arnauld...quoiqu'il eût toujours été très bon catholique...leurs écrivains n'ont pas laissé de le traiter de huguenot, descendu de huguenots" [Antoine Arnauld...although he was a very good Catholic...their writers continued to depict him as a Huguenot, descended from Huguenots] and 67: "Jansénius, qu'ils traitaient de calviniste et d'hérétique, comme ils traitaient ordinairement tous leurs adversaires..." [Jansénius, whom they depict as a calvinist and a heretic, as they depict all of their adversaries].
6. See Racine, *Port-Royal*, 68–71.
7. Deborah Kuller Shuger, *The Renaissance Bible: Scholarship, Sacrifice, and Subjectivity* (Berkeley: University of California Press, 1992), 113: "This complex and conflictual Christian subjectivity differs profoundly from prior conceptualizations of ideal selfhood.... Calvin largely abandoned the [Catholic and Erasmian] model.
8. Shuger, *Renaissance Bible*, 120: "It is not difficult to hypothesize that the total or partial loss of the ancient ideal images of masculine identity—of idealized social roles based on the renunciation or mystification of violence—produced, for a time, a sort of shuddering uncertainty about 'man's work.'..." and "[Protestant] texts' dark fascination with urban catastrophe lends support to Bouwsma's claim that the shift from an agrarian to an urban society lies behind the pervasive and unfocused anxieties darkening the interior landscape of the Renaissance" (124).
9. Shuger, *Renaissance Bible*, 116.
10. Julia Kristeva, "Holbein's Dead Christ," in *Fragments for a History of the Human Body*, ed. Michael Feher (New York: Zone Press, 1989), pt. 1, pp. 238–69. "Did the Reformation influence such a

concept of death, and more specifically, such an emphasis on Christ's death at the expense of any allusion to the Redemption and Resurrection? Catholicism is well known for its tendency to stress the 'beatific vision' in Christ's death without dwelling on the torments of the passion, understanding that Jesus always had the knowledge of his own resurrection. Calvin, on the other hand, insists on the *formidabilis abysis* into which Jesus had been thrust at the hour of his death, descending to the depths of sin and hell..." (252); "Holbein's chromatic asceticism renders this composition between form and death..." (254); "Man is...provided with a powerful symbolic device that allows him to experience death and resurrection even in his physical body, thanks to the strength of the imaginary identification...with the absolute Subject (Christ)" (262).

11. Authority being vested without precedent in a woman, for instance, was to them—at least in theory—not problematic, as long as that woman was acting in conformance with God's will. In Du Bartas's play *La Judit*, for example, no one, either within the play or in its audience response, was horrified that Judith hewed off Holofernes's head, acting in a self-determining and authoritative way, because they knew that her action was inspired by the Holy Spirit. Guillaume Salluste Du Bartas, *La Judit*, ed. André Baïche (Toulouse: Faculté des Lettres, 1970). See treatment of this play by Michio Hagiwara, *French Epic Poetry in the Sixteenth Century* (The Hague: Mouton, 1972).

12. Natalie Zemon Davis, Barbara Babcock, and Richard Kuntzle have explored the imagery associated with the "world turned upside down" motif. See, for instance, Natalie Zemon Davis, "Women on Top," in *Society and Culture in Early Modern France* (Stanford: Stanford University Press, 1965), 124–51. When Cornwallis's troops laid down their arms during the colonies' War of Independence in America, for example, their fifes accompanied the troops' surrender by the air of "The World Turned Upside Down."

13. Lyndal Roper, *The Holy Household: Women and Morals in Reformation Augsburg* (Oxford: Clarendon Press, 1989), 187. The woodblock is Geisburg no. 1431, Kupferstichkabinett SMPK, Berlin, and is attributed to the German school.

14. See Gisèle Mathieu-Castellani, *Emblèmes de la mort: Le dialogue de l'image et du texte* (Paris: Nizet, 1988),137:

> Ce corps ouvert sous le regard s'offre comme un 'charnier de signes,' se donne comme une tombe de maux ensevelis. Le modèle médical de la dissection est contaminé par le modèle religieux de la prédication, l'ouverture d'un tombeau devant un public...l'ouverture du corps provoque. Ce que l'on voit attire l'attention sur ce que l'on ne voit pas: 'Mais considère aussi ce que tu ne vois point,' les signes appellent d'autres signes, le vertige sémiologique gagne l'observateur.

> [This opened body offers itself to the gaze as a "charnel-house of signs," offers itself as a tomb of buried wrongdoings. The medical model of dissection is contaminated by the religious model of preaching and opening a tomb in front of the public...the opening of the body provokes. That which one sees draws the attention to that which one does not see. "But consider also that which you do not see," signs call up other signs, and semiotic vertigo overtakes the observer.]

15. Jean Delumeau, *La peur en Occident: XIVe–XVIIIe siècles* (Paris: Fayard, 1978), 206, notes that

> les guerres de religion en France [coïncidèrent] avec la vacance quasi permanente du pouvoir qui commença avec le décès inattendu d'Henri II et culmina avec l'assassinat d'Henri III. L'inquiétude durant le règne de celui-ci fut continuellement entretenu par son absence de descendance.

> [(T)he Wars of Religion in France (coincided) with the near-permanent vacuum of power which begins after the sudden death of Henri II and ends with the assassination of Henri III. Anxiety during the latter's reign was continually sustained due to his lack of an heir.]

16. Béroalde de Verville, *Le moyen de parvenir*, ed. I. Zinguer (Nice: Université de Nice, 1985), 13–15.

17. See his anecdote against overliteral Calvinist interpretation of the Bible in "Palinodie," *Moyen*, 226.

18. Béroalde, *Moyen*, 13:

...tant les regards tiroient au but où chacun eust voulu donner, tous n'ayant intention qu'au precieux coin où se tient le registre des mysteres amoureux.

[... so much so that all eyes were drawn to the goal at which all wished to arrive, all (the spectators) having no aim other than to end up in that precious corner (hole) where is kept the register of all of love's mysteries.]

19. Théophile de Viau, *Ode* in *La poésie baroque et précieuse (1550-1650)*, ed. André Blanchard (Paris: Seghers, 1969), 158-59.
20. "Montaigne attributes this [problem in authority]...to the depravity of his age and to the disarray of France itself.... Montaigne's attempt to work out a type of posthumanist notion of exemplarity may be seen as the necessary ethical response to the absence of such models as La Boétie.... This fracturing of ancient authority is described...[through] bodies that are somehow marked, scarred, or...deformed." Timothy Hampton, "Montaigne: Writing against History," in *Writing from History: The Rhetoric of Exemplarity of Renaissance Literature* (Ithaca: Cornell University Press, 1990), 136-97.
21. Agrippa d'Aubigné, "Debvoir de Roys et des Subjects," in *Œuvres complètes*, ed. H. Weber (Paris: Gallimard, 1969), 487.
22. Lewis Seifert, "Eroticizing the Fronde: Sexual Deviance and Political Disorder in the Mazarinades," *Esprit créateur* 35.2 (summer 1995): 22-36.
23. John Thompson, citing Charmarie Blaisdell, in "Calvin's Letters," *Sixteenth Century Journal* 13.3 (1982): 67-84.
24. Théodore de Bèze, *Abraham le sacrifiant*, in *Four Renaissance Tragedies*, ed. Donald Stone (Cambridge: Harvard University, 1966), p. 13, vv. 40-44, and p. 52, vv. 90-93.
25. I find it striking that in two of the examples I've used here thunder is a dominant motif. Thunder epitomizes fear, nature in wrathful disorder, and punishment for sin. Thunder may also recall the sound of battle. There is a similar, phenomenological basis for anxiety between Catholics and Protestants; they focus on different issues, however.
26. D'Aubigné, *Les tragiques*, "Princes" in *Œuvres*, pp. 78-79, vv. 1043-57.
27. Lewis Seifert, "Eroticizing the Fronde," 24.
28. "Mechanism that deprives us of all that we cherish, / Mechanism instrumental in furthering the Devil's ends." Anonymous, *Satyre ou imprécation contre l'engin du surnommé Mazarin*, 3-4, cited by Seifert, "Eroticizing the Fronde," 29.
29. Greek: *persona*: a full character, with all its attributes in active proportion, rather than determination merely through sexuality.
30. D'Aubigné, "Misères," *Tragiques, Œuvres complètes*, 50, vv. 1245-51.
31. There are, of course, notable exceptions to the Protestant paradigm I am positing, if one expands the sphere of inquiry to include non-Huguenots. A particularly strident example is John Knox, *First Blast of the Trumpet against the Monstruous Regiment of Women* (Edinburgh, 1571). See also Brendan Scott, "La valorisation du corps dans les *Exercices spirituels* d'Ignace de Loyole," in *Le corps au XVIIe siècle*, Actes du premier colloque conjointement organisé par la North American Society for Seventeenth-Century French Literature et le Centre International de Rencontres sur le XVIIe siècle, University of California, Santa Barbara (17-19 mars 1994), ed. Ronald Tobin (Paris: Papers on Seventeenth-Century French Literature, Biblio 17, 1995), 102-8.
32. Recently attributed to d'Aubigné by its editor, Jean-Raymond Fanlo, *La responce de Michau l'aveugle* (Paris: Champion, 1996).
33. D'Aubigné, *La responce*, 10.
34. "Beza and the author of the Vindiciae groped...towards a unified conception of authority that was distinguishable [from representative/monarchical]...law was linked to 'sovereignty' in a relation that implied the presence of the state as an abstract entity...to maintain the laws of a polity was to maintain the 'public benefit' and the 'state of the kingdom.' In that case the state was identifiable with those laws.... Sovereignty was the contract itself. The king was [merely] its administrator." Howell A. Lloyd, *The State, France, and the Sixteenth Century* (London: Allen and Unwin, 1983), 154.
35. "You will say, it may be that the towns appertain to the prince. And I answer, that the towns consist not of a heap of stones, but of that which we call people, that the people is the people of God, to

whom they are first bound by oath and, secondly, to the king…. God in truth is the only Lord proprietor of all things, and it is of Him that the king holds his royalties, and the people their patrimony"; Languet, *Vindicae* (Cambridge: Cambridge University Press, 1994), 2:104–5. "The whole body of the people is above the king"; Languet, *Vindicae*, 3:124. "Huguenot theory relied far less upon precise judicial considerations of property than upon historical examples and broad principles of natural law. From the former it was evident that kings were originally elected by the body of the people…. The relation between king and kingdom could thereby be described in contractual terms"; Lloyd, *State*, 154.

36. For most of the Protestants, however, such rejection did not extend to regicide. The tyrannomach Calvinist political theorists, however, like Hotman and DuPlessis-Mornay, found apparent permission for such extremism even in Calvin's predominantly cautionary language: "We are not even permitted to inspect the prince's claim to be entitled to hold his office: 'We are subject…to the authority of all who…have got control of affairs…'; 'All one may do is pray for deliverance, petition, and remonstrate, or take flight. At best, there may be magistrates who happen to be appointed to restrain wicked rulers; ephors, tribunes, and perhaps, as things now stand, such power as the three estates exercise in every realm when they hold their chief assemblies,' [Calvin stated]. This exception, pregnant with momentous possibilities for later Calvinism, was all that Calvin would allow." Harro Höpfl, *The Christian Polity of John Calvin* (Cambridge: Cambridge University Press, 1982), 49.

37. One example is, of course, Calvin, who set up his anti-Rome, but with no pope.

38. "Without controversy, Sarah was the minister of a great and tremendous judgment…. But even if she sustained a higher character than that of a private woman, she does not seize her husband's authority but makes him a lawful director of the ejection"; John Calvin, *Commentary on Genesis 21:12*, cited in John Thompson, *John Calvin and the Daughters of Sara* (Geneva: Droz, 1992), i.

39. Thompson, *Calvin and the Daughters of Sara*, 21.

40. "Calvin…emphasizes that a wife is to be more than merely the bearer of a man's children and his remedy against fornication…. Calvin…encouraged friendship between husband and wife…. From his own estimate…his wife was 'the best companion of my life'"; Thompson, *John Calvin and the Daughters of Sara*, 12, quoting Calvin's letter to Pierre Viret dated 7 April 1549.

41. Lyndal Roper, *The Holy Household*, chap. 6, "The Reformation of Convents," 205–51.

42. De Serres, *Théâtre*, preface, 8:

> Ainsi par degrés appert, que quelque chemin qu'on tienne en ce monde, on vient finalement à l'Agriculture: la plus commune occupation d'entre les Hommes, la plus saincte et plus naturelle…ce n'est donques aux habitants des champs que nostre Agriculture est particuliere: ceux des villes y ont leur part.

> [Thus, little by little it becomes clear that, no matter what path one may choose in this world, all end up in agriculture: the most common occupation of all men, the most holy and most natural…it's not, therefore, limited to our fields: people in towns have their own form of agriculture.]

43. De Serres, *Théâtre*, preface, 1–2.

44. De Serres, *Théâtre*, 16.

45. De Serres, *Théâtre*, 13.

46. De Serres, *Théâtre*, 13, risks a little sermonizing:

> Mais digne de louange est l'homme, qui se voyant possesseur legitime d'un si beau domaine, passant plus outre, s'esvertue, non-seulement à luy faire produire ces fruicts à l'accoustume, ains…contraint…sa terre…à luy rapporter plus que de l'ordinaire.

> [But that man is worthy of praise who, seeing himself the lawful possessor of such a beautiful domain, will strive even more not only to produce as formerly, but…causing…his land to produce even more than usual.]

47. De Serres, *Théâtre*, ii.

48. [Our father of the family will be alert to learn how to be worthy of his charge; so that, knowing well how to command those beneath him, he will obtain their necessary obedience (this is the summary of a household)], De Serres, *Théâtre*, 9.

49. We find a similar sort of disembodiment, or abstraction of the body, in seventeenth-century legal treatment of it: "Car le corps est avant tout un texte, un montage abstrait qui permet d'édifier d'autres corps: le corps social de la magistrature, le corps des lois, le *corpus juris*, le sujet et la personne...c'est donc sur la notion de la personne juridique remplaçant abstraitement le corps...le corps n'est plus, dès lors, un corps qui héberge une âme...mais un remplacement de l'âme et du corps sur la scène juridique" [For the body is above all a text, an abstract montage which allows the building of other bodies: the social body of the magistrature, the body of laws, the legal body, the subject and the person...it is thus on the notion of a juridical person replacing abstractly the body; the body is no longer a body housing a soul...but a replacemtnt for body and soul on the legal stage]; Christian Biet, "Le corps dans le droit: Enquête sur la personne et le personnage au VIIe siècle," in *Le corps au XVII siècle*, ed. W. Tobin, 343. To the extent that the Protestant disregard of gender, or reference to it only to move beyond it, treats the body as a component in a larger, metaphysical mise-en-scène, it prefigures the legal understanding of person found here; only, in this later text, the authority is no longer metaphysical, but rather juridical.

50. Ignatius of Loyola, *The Spiritual Exercises of St. Ignatius*, trans. A. Mottola (New York: Doubleday, 1964), 36. "Soul of Christ, sanctify me. Body of Christ, save me. Blood of Christ, inebriate me. Water from the side of Christ, wash me. Passion of Christ, strengthen me. O good Jesu, hear me; Within thy wounds hide me; Suffer me not to be separated from Thee...." Jesuits seek to read themselves into, and imagine themselves a part of, Christ's passion. This is Ignatius of Loyola's response to the Protestants: a kind of militant *kenosis*, or self-emptying.

51. Kathryn A. Hoffmann, "Le phallus du Roi défaillant et dévoilé," in *Le corps au XVIIe siècle*, ed. Ronald Tobin, 336:

> Les histoires secrètes n'ont conservé l'image de la guerre que pour la réduire à la banalité comique de la titillation érotique. Elles ont remplacé l'exposition des exploits masculins par des scènes du désir féminin jamais assouvi... Louis XIV... était un roi constamment amoureux et fréquemment impuissant.... Les histoires érotiques secrètes ont écrit un monde de révélations indiscrètes de faiblesse et d'impuissance royales, un monde privé vicié dont les échecs contaminaient la puissance et la gloire de la monarchie absolue.

> [The secret histories reduce the image of war to a comical and banal evocation of erotic titillation. They replaced the discussion of male exploits with scenes of insatiable female desire. Louis XIV...was a constantly amorous monarch who was also frequently impotent.... The secret erotic histories penned a wealth of indiscreet revelations concerning royal weakness and impotence, a private world whose failures sullied the power and glory of an absolute monarchy.]

52. Hoffmann, "Le Phallus du Roi," 339–40:

> Ces membres retranchés du corps métaphorique monarchique, des protestants exilés...ont utilisé le genre de l'histoire secrète pour démembrer le spectacle du pouvoir officiel, pour briser donc le corps métaphorique.... Le roi est devenu objet/phallus défaillant/victime du voyeurisme.

> [Those members lopped off from the metaphorical monarchic body, were those of the exiled Protestants...[they] used the genre of the secret history to dismember the spectacle of official power, to break the metaphoric body.... The king became the flaccid object/phallus, victim of voyeurism.]

53. Madame Guyon's *Vie*, quoted in Bossuet's *Relations sur le quiétisme* in *Œuvres* (Paris: Gallimard, 1961), 1109.

54. Elizabeth Goldsmith, "Mothering Mysticism: Mme Guyon and Her Public," in *Women Writers in Pre-Revolutionary France: Strategies of Emancipation*, ed. Colette Winn and Donna Kuizinga (New

York: Garland, 1997), 127–39: "At the heart of Madame Guyon's notion of her relationship to her readers is the concept of spiritual motherhood.... The metaphor of the mystic as mother was not new to religious writing at the time Guyon was proselytizing, although the image of the spiritual bride was...much more commo[n].... But Jeanne's extensive use of bodily metaphors of mothering was striking...and it contributed to her being labeled...'dangerous'"; 128–30.

Contributors

Tom Conley, professor of Romance languages and linguistics at Harvard University, is author of *The Self-Made Map: Cartographic Writing in Early Modern France* (Minnesota, 1996), and of *L'inconscient graphique: Essai sur la lettre et l'écriture à la Renaissance* (Presses de l'Université de Paris–VIII, 2000). Current projects include work on space and subjectivity in sixteenth-century French writing.

Mitchell Greenberg is professor of French and comparative literature at Cornell University, and author of *Detours of Desire: Readings in the French Baroque* (Ohio State, 1984); *Corneille, Classicism, and the Ruses of Symmetry* (Cambridge, 1990); *Subjectivity and Subjugation in Seventeenth-Century Drama and Prose: The Family Romance of French Classicism* (Cambridge, 1992); *Canonical States, Canonical Stages: Oedipus, Othering, and Seventeenth-Century Drama* (Minnesota, 1994), winner of the MLA Jean and Aldo Scaglione Prize in Comparative Literature. His most recent work is *Baroque Bodies: Cultural Resistance in the Age of Absolutism* (Cornell, 2000).

Kathleen Perry Long is associate professor of French at Cornell University, and has published articles on the figure of the hermaphrodite in Renaissance France in *L'Esprit Créateur* and in various anthologies (*Wonder, Marvels, and Monsters in Early Modern Culture,* ed. Peter Platt; and *Monster Theory: Reading Culture,* ed. Jeffrey Cohen). Her book, *Another Reality: Metamorphosis and the Imagination in the Poetry of Ovid, Petrarch, and Ronsard,* appeared in 1990.

Virginia M. Marino received her Ph.D. from Yale University and is now an independent scholar and vice president of TradeWeb LLC in New York. She has published articles on Diderot, Voltaire, and dreams in eighteenth-century literature.

Stephen Murphy received his Ph.D. in comparative literature from the University of North Carolina at Chapel Hill, and is currently associate professor of French at Wake Forest University. He has published a study of humanist poetics, *The Gift of Immortality,* and articles on Petrarch, d'Aubigné, Ronsard, and others. His current interests include parody and cento.

Jeffery Persels is associate professor of French at the University of South Carolina. He has published articles on Rabelais, Marguerite de Navarre, and French religious polemic. He is currently completing an edition of Jean Dagoneau's *Guerre des masles contre les femelles* (1588), editing a volume on the use of scatological rhetoric in sixteenth-century European literature, and preparing a book-length study on rhetorical strategies in sixteenth-century French Calvinist and Catholic writing.

Catharine Randall is professor of French and chair of the department of modern languages and literatures at Fordham University. She is the author of five books, the most recent being *Building Codes: The Calvinist Aesthetics of Early Modern Europe* (University of Pennsylvania Press, 1999). She is currently working on a book-length manuscript on material culture, decorative art objects, and the role of objects in the narrative of Marguerite de Navarre, with the provisional title of *Earthly Treasures: Materiality and Metaphysics in the* Heptaméron.

Kirk D. Read is associate professor of French languages and literature at Bates College. He received his Ph.D. from Princeton University specializing in women's writing of the sixteenth century. His scholarship over the past seven years has concentrated on the portrayal of gender and sexuality in both men and women writers of the Renaissance and early seventeenth century, most specifically on the ways these writers transgress traditional gender roles in the service of their literary production. Most recently, he has been investigating the impact of changing attitudes towards anatomy and medical practice as evidenced in the works of midwives and surgeons.

Lewis C. Seifert is associate professor of French studies at Brown University. A specialist in seventeenth-century French literature, he is the author of *Fairy Tales, Sexuality, and Gender in France, 1690–1715: Nostalgic Utopias*, 1996. His current book project concerns masculinity and civility in Early Modern France.

Amy Staples holds a doctorate from Cornell University and is currently an assistant professor at Wells College. Her dissertation follows the trajectory of the "orientalist" movement in late-seventeenth- and eighteenth-century French literature, and centers on the portrayal of women in French "oriental" novels, more specifically on the staging and evolution of women's speech as a metonymy for their desire.

Cathy Yandell is the W. I. and Hulda F. Daniell Professor of French Literature, Language, and Culture at Carleton College. Author of the recent *Carpe Corpus: Time and Gender in Early Modern France* (University of Delaware Press, 2000), she also edited Pontus de Tyard's *Solitaire second, ou prose de la musique*. She has contributed essays to *Montaigne: A Collection of Essays: Language and Meaning,* ed. Dikka Berven (Garland, 1995); *Renaissance Women Writers: French Texts / American Contexts,* ed. Anne Larsen and Colette Winn (Wayne State University Press, 1994); and *The Dialogue in Early Modern France: Art and Argument,* ed. Colette Winn (Catholic University Press, 1993). In addition, she has published articles on Nicole Estienne, Pernette du Guillet, Montaigne, Catherine des Roches, Ronsard, Jacques Tahureau, Pontus de Tyard, and the *blasons anatomiques du corps féminin*. Her current research focuses on pedagogical discourse, rhetoric, and authority in Early Modern French texts.

Index

continued